PARAS

VOICES OF THE BRITISH AIRBORNE FORCES IN THE SECOND WORLD WAR

ROGER PAYNE OAM

AMBERLEY

First published 2014
This edition published 2016
Amberley Publishing
The Hill, Stroud
Gloucestershire, GL5 4EP

www.amberley-books.com

British Library Cataloguing in Publication Data.
A catalogue record for this book is available from the British Library.

ISBN 978 1 4456 5529 1 (print)
ISBN 978 1 4456 3841 6 (ebook)

Typesetting and Origination by Amberley Publishing.
Printed in the UK.

CONTENTS

Preface

This book is full of untold short stories of men who created a legend, the legend of the British airborne forces during the Second World War. Their stories start when the Airborne was first formed in 1941. The government, especially Winston Churchill, had learned a hard lesson from the Germans. He realised the potential of troops who could parachute behind enemy lines and take and hold or destroy key objectives while ground troops advanced toward them. By the end of the war Britain had two divisions, well over 20,000 men, from every corps and regiment, both parachute and glider-borne.

Although many joined for the challenge it offered, others had more down-to-earth reasons: the extra money – the two shillings per day if you were a parachutist, and six pence a day for the glider-borne soldier. The military had a unique method of selecting which units should fly in gliders: they simply informed the commanding officer. Both he and all the officers were 'expected' to remain with the unit, whereas the other ranks couldn't be compelled for obvious reasons. Some devious COs, fearing they would lose a large number of their men, asked them to try a flight in a glider to see if they would like it. Unbeknown to the men, the factor deciding if they would remain with the unit was that first flight. If they went on that flight then it became a court martial offence to refuse to continue doing it.

I have deliberately not included certain stories of well-known individuals in both the 1st and 6th airborne divisions during this period as they have been thoroughly documented already. The stories have been grouped loosely into chapters covering the training period at Hardwick Hall and Ringway and the various campaigns fought by the Airborne during the war.

Acknowledgements

I would like to thank Glen Scally, Bill Dunstan, Rod Brady and 'Bobby' Mayne for their help when I needed it most, my wife Ann for her invaluable knowledge and wise decisions, and my children for simply putting up with me. I would also like to acknowledge all those men whose stories are in the book, for without their incredible exploits and the extraordinary things they achieved I wouldn't have carried on when it would have been easier to give up.

1

The British Airborne Forms

Forming up – Roger Payne

The order to form a parachute force came from Winston Churchill in 1940 and not long afterwards Number 2 Commando was redesignated airborne and began intensive parachute training at Ringway airport near Manchester in June of that year. The unit was posted to Knutsford in Cheshire and on 31 August 1941 became part of the new 1st Parachute Brigade under Brigadier Richard Gale. The selection and training for all future members of the airborne forces was to be located at Hardwick Hall, near Chesterfield in Derbyshire. Number 2 Commando never did the selection course as they had already completed the equally tough Commando Course in Scotland. The unit was originally 500 strong, but this was reduced to twenty-one officers and 321 other ranks by September 1940. Although there were a few serious injuries, almost all the failures occurred because men refused to parachute. The RAF, and their own officers, believed that the large number of refusals was due to a combination of inexperience and a fear that their parachutes would not open. In fact, almost all of them deliberately failed because they simply didn't want to become Airborne when they already considered themselves to be Commandos, and so they were returned to other Commando units. In another identity crisis, throughout the war a large number of guardsmen also entered the airborne forces; they too still considered themselves to be guardsmen after they qualified, and not privates.

Thereafter, with few exceptions, every parachutist, regar of rank, had to pass the pre-parachute selection cou

Hardwick Hall. It was a brutal introduction to the airborne forces that saw at least 60 per cent fail. Although it had proper single-storey buildings constructed to accommodate the administration and permanent training staff, course members had to live in bell tents. Initially, a parachute jump tower and trapeze swing training structures were also constructed. In addition there was an extensive assault course that ran across what had once been two ornamental lakes, a fitness area with logs and rudimentary fitness equipment, ropes and chin-up bars, plus a firing range. When course members successfully completed the two-week selection course, they were required to march the 50 miles to the parachute school at RAF Ringway near Manchester. They would be dressed in full marching order, including ammunition. While at Ringway they were also required to march 5 miles back to Ringway from the Tatton Park drop zone each time they jumped. Late in 1942 the tower and trapeze were moved to Ringway and all pre-parachute training ceased at Hardwick Hall; at the same time the famous maroon beret was introduced for all qualified parachutists, although they did not receive the parachute wings until they had completed two balloon jumps and at least five descents from an aircraft. Initially, members of the Parachute Regiment wore the Army Air Corps cap badge. In May 1943, the famed winged cap badge was introduced.

The First Parachute Battalion – Raymond Shadwell

Lying underneath the balloons, I watched the lads exit and descend, fast and straight down, and then, as their parachutes opened, drifting with the wind to clear the balloon cable. It seemed so idyllic and carefree until suddenly there were only four of us left and we ascended in the balloon. Sitting alone, perched on the edge of the aperture, I waited for the command to 'Go!', then after a free fall lasting only brief seconds, my parachute opened and I contemplated the scenery below as I descended gently downwards. WHAM! Suddenly my canopy collapsed and my speed of descent increased. Fortunately it quickly stabilised and I hit the ground and rolled. As I had disappeared through the aperture in the floor, the RAF sergeant instructor had quickly followed me and landed on top of my parachute. I amused him no end; naturally, I wasn't so thrilled! After a series of night and day jumps, seven in all, we were presented with our coveted parachute wings and pronounced fit to take our place in the unit, 11 Special Air Service Battalion, which was then split into two separate bodies, each accommodated in civvy billets, one at Congleton and the other, to which I was assigned, at Knutsford. I could not, however, but admire the man who, despite an overwhelming fear of heights, had forced himself to complete the whole sequence of jumps, five to be precise, before requesting to be 'Returned to Unit'. He was a Commando so he didn't have to prove himself to anyone; he simply wanted to be back in the Commandos with his mates. It was about this time that Guardsman 'Frankie' Garlick, having exited from the belly of a Whitley in the prescribed manner, found himself suspended beneath the aircraft and was reluctantly compelled to survey the panorama below. He had a bird's-eye view of the landscape near Edinburgh, in Scotland. The Whitley continued its journey back to Manchester, with its unscheduled passenger still dangling beneath the fuselage. The plane landed slowly on the grass next to the runway with the tail lifted higher than normal, and Frankie survived, almost free of injury, to continue his participation in the affairs of the battalion. The RAF safety officer asked him 'why he couldn't simply exit the aircraft in the prescribed manner like everyone else?'

Besides the Commandos that had been forced into the Regiment, almost every other member of the unit seemed to be a guardsman; in truth, most regiments of the British Army were also represented. General Browning was from the Guards and he seemed set on getting as many guardsmen into the new regiment as possible. But as we grew, and new battalions were formed, it consisted of the most cosmopolitan collection of individuals it was possible to imagine. There were Irish, both northern and southern, Scots, Welsh, a Spaniard, Jews and a Pole in my company. One was a committed Communist who had seen action in the Spanish Civil War, and another professed admiration for the Fascist philosophy, elements which would normally create ethnic and political tensions, but overriding all this was the overwhelming common bond, a fierce pride in the unit, which we designated 'The Battalion', and a common fear of failing to measure up to the high standards required, with the resultant ultimate punishment of return to parent unit, which was a mortal shame. Although we were highly trained, we were not uniformly attired, for we continued to wear the headdress and cap badges of our original regiments, but with the addition of a parachute badge worn on our right arm; this created many an exploitable situation in the local pub while relaxing in remote areas. The eventual deeds performed by the battalion were as nothing, especially compared to the vivid exploits recounted over many a free glass of brown ale while a young lady became engrossed with our tales. The threat of invasion was now no longer imminent, but still a possibility, so from time to time large or small groups would be missing from the normal activities. They would be dropped in some vulnerable area of England with a specific target, which would be defended by troops stationed in that area. The exercise could be a brief encounter lasting a few hours or a more complex affair spread over a number of days.

These schemes served to keep morale high and also gave attackers and defenders much-needed practice in deployment and tactics. The downside of the coin was the inevitable list of casualties and the expense involved. We were dropped with only meagre food supplies and instructions to fend for ourselves, just as we would in actual combat, and any vehicle that was considered a source of danger was to be immobilised by removing the distributor. This distributor was to be placed in a bag, suitably identified, and handed in at the conclusion of the exercise. The bags, however, were frequently lost in the heat of the moment, which was inevitably a source of some embarrassment to the unit. All aspects of parachute operations were at this stage subject to experiment and frequent changes of direction. This applied particularly to the aircraft. The hole in the floor exit of our main carrier, the Whitley, was a cumbersome method of disgorging troops; it meant they were spread too far apart on the dropping zone. It was obvious that a better means of exit was needed, such as through an open door in the side of the aircraft, as all troop transport aircraft had these doors already. The evolution of the various methods of dropping weapons and the changes in fighting apparel are well documented. Another most welcome innovation was a light, but very warm, sleeping bag, which made cold nights spent in the open a much more endurable experience. Life at this time had a touch of the bizarre. It was inconceivable, given an invasion force poised in France to attack us, and with our shipping carrying vital supplies of food and materials being sunk at an alarming rate, our cities and centres of production being devastated, and with Britain alone in a position to resist the seemingly inevitable subjugation of Europe, that the reason for continuing the conflict, the eventual defeat of the Axis forces, could be seriously considered. Yet here we were, training to be dropped into enemy territory!

Suddenly, almost overnight, the whole war situation changed. On 22 June 1941, Germany embarked on a campaign, code-named Barbarossa, against the Soviet Union. Hitler had made his first blunder. This switched the German priorities, both in manpower and resources, to the confrontation on the Eastern Front. It now meant that Britain could actually speculate about a victorious outcome. Winning the war was no longer an idle concept and the psychological effect of this turn of events lifted the spirits of everyone. So 11 SAS, originally 2 Commando, once again changed its identity to become 1st Battalion the Parachute Regiment and moved to Hardwick in September 1941 under the command of our new CO, a martinet by the name of Lieutenant-Colonel Down, who told all of us on the first parade that our days of 'ballet dancing' were over and he was universally booed in response, which made him laugh. He was a ruthless sod, and he rarely showed any sympathy toward anyone, officers, senior NCOs or us peasants. We soon named him 'Dracula' because he always demanded blood. He would turn up anywhere and whatever we were doing, he would join in. And to see him jogging up and down the ranks on a 20-mile route march was enough to make you sick. He was hated at first, but then he became a sort of mascot; a 'we had him and none of the others could have him' sort of thing. But he was still a bastard if you didn't match up to his standards. It was then that the persistent rumours we'd been hearing of newly formed airborne units became a confirmed fact. However we, as long-established pioneers, regarded ourselves as somewhat superior to these other 'Johnny-come-latelys' so it came as an immense shock to our self-image, and was the cause of much inter-battalion friction, when C Company of the 2nd Battalion was chosen to make what resulted in an archetypal Airborne assault on a German radar installation at Bruneval, on the coast of France, in January 1942.

The Unusual CO – Adam Wesley

When the regiment was first formed, our CO had some unique ideas as to how things should work. The first was to inform us that anyone who completed fifteen descents could wear wings on both arms. Naturally, the notion was enthusiastically accepted by all, and within a day someone had 'acquired' a balloon and Tidworth parade ground saw dozens of men flinging themselves from the sky as fast as they could go up and down. Needless to say that upon finding out about it, the brigadier quickly put a stop to the idea and the balloons soon disappeared. The CO also had a thing about the most common 'Anglo Saxon' terms and issued an order that said that any man caught using such language was to be placed under close arrest. Within a few hours the guardroom was overflowing and the RSM had to introduce a staggered confinement system, with men on the outside waiting to go into a holding pen of barbed wire; others in the holding pen slept under the stars while waiting to rotate with those in the cells. It was a rare case of the men in jail being envied by the men not in jail, especially when it rained. It took three days before the order was countermanded because so many men were awaiting confinement that in one case a platoon was down to four men: two corporals, the sergeant and their officer.

'Winnie the Pooh' – Ian Tailstock

I remember when Winston Churchill, the prime minister, was loved by the man in the street because of his careful motivational catchphrases, ever-present cigars, and 'V' for Victory sign. One day he was making a flying visit to the 1st Airborne Division, a unit he had ordered formed in 1941. In typical style when an important visitor comes, he met the senior officers, watched a battalion drop from Whitley bombers, then as a division we all eventually had a chance to see the man and listen to him speak when he stood up on a dais for several minutes and spoke to us. I was at the back of the crowd and all I could see was the man's beret in front of me. Anyway, if I could have seen where he was, he was so far away I would have needed a pair of binoculars. After he drove away individual RSMs were told to take control and march us away to our lines. As we were moving off, one of the lads who clearly hadn't been close enough to see the great man asked, 'Was that actually Winnie?'

Sid, the platoon smart aleck, replied, 'Na, it wasn't 'im. I seen 'im before. Tha' wus a fat little sod posing as 'im. We wouldnta known would we, not where we wus standin? They dressed tha little bugger up in fick coat, one of those bloody poncy cravat fings, an' a bloody bowler 'at, stuck a dirty big cigar in 'is gob and told 'im to give a couple o' 'undred 'v' signs.'

'But we heard him talk?'

'Christ, don't yus know anyfing? They used bits of string to move is mouf and probably used Morse code ta make 'im talk!'

'Bloody hell!' the first man said and we all laughed and got a rebuke from the CSM.

2

Hardwick Hall:
The Selection Process Begins

Unforeseen Problems – Stan Howden

When the Parachute Regiment was in the embryo stage and Hardwick Hall was running its first courses, there were an exceptionally high number of volunteers who failed the selection process in under a week, some in only two or three days. The signal and poster that had gone out to all units of the Army simply said volunteers required for a new parachute unit – there was no explanation of the pre-selection requirements. As a result, a large number of volunteers who arrived for the course thought that parachuting would be 'fun' – it never occurred to them that a tough selection process would take place before they got to parachute school. On top of this, two unforeseen things cropped up, both involving unit commanding officers. Firstly, many refused to let some men go because they were the best they had. Secondly, they 'volunteered' other men who didn't want to go. This second group were made up of the troublemakers who were disciplinary problems, so what better way of getting rid of them than sending them to another unit? The posting orders these men got were often vague, simply stating they were to report to Hardwick Hall in Derbyshire, and that was it; the course could have been for anything. Many of these troublemakers weren't physically weak, they simply didn't accept military discipline, and rebelled against it, and the only way the system had of disciplining them was to lock them up, but often even that didn't work. Many of them had been brought up in the back streets of the sprawling British cities, where surviving from day to day was a constant struggle. The average worker after the 1914–18 war, right up until the early 1940s, was malnourished and often treated like an indentured serf, so locking him up and feeding him three reasonable meals a day was an unheard-of luxury for many of them. But sending them on a physically arduous course didn't solve the problem, and although a few took to this new life like a duck to water, the majority had to be returned to their parent units because they simply couldn't adjust to the role of the paratrooper. It took some time before COs stopped sending these men, but the problem still remained that units were doing all in their power to stop men going on the course, as they were too good to lose.

The Selection Process – Bernard Bandsdale

Hardwick Camp was built on a slope, which meant you were either running uphill or down, and run you did, everywhere, even to meals, the toilet and ablutions. Walking was a severely punishable offence. There were two huge ornamental ponds that were connected by underground culverts, and five smaller ponds that drained the higher ground. Across these there was an assault course designed by a sadistic megalomaniac. It ended up at a quarry-face that you abseiled down, and then you were on the 100-yard rifle range. In two weeks, the aim was to push you to your physical limits as you were expected to be a fully trained soldier when you arrived, therefore you didn't need to be taught any military skills. Besides speed marching, the greatest test you had was the assault course. You did it for the first week dressed in denims. That was bad enough, but with a helmet, pack, rifle, webbing and ammunition, it was an absolute nightmare.

It began with a 20-foot-high obstacle that consisted of scaffold poles lashed together to form 4-foot squares. You had to scramble over these before dropping into the first of the lakes, where enthusiastic and merciless instructors pelted you with thunderflashes and slabs of gun cotton. Deafened, you then had to squeeze into a long culvert that went from the first lake into the second. Going though this culvert was like being a cork in a champagne bottle ready to explode, especially as you had to keep moving because everyone was 'nose to tail'. If you suffered from claustrophobia you had major problems because the man behind just kept pushing until you literally popped out of the culvert and dropped several feet into the second pond. Trying to keep your rifle dry in this situation was nigh on impossible, yet if you didn't you were thoroughly abused by the instructors.

This abuse continued all along the course as you could never seem to do anything right. As you waded across the second pond there were more thunderflashes and slabs of gun cotton exploding around you. You clambered up the far bank, ran down a slope and were confronted by tripwires and a 10-foot wall. The first man in your section then had to lean against the wall, place both hands, one on top of the other, on one knee and allow the remainder to step onto his hands and he would assist them to the top of the wall. When everyone was over the wall, the last man stayed on the top and pulled the first man up by means of his rifle. By now everyone was on a mad charge down the hill until you reached the small muddy ponds where 4-inch-wide rails were mounted on top of posts. It required a great deal of agility and confidence to run along these rails as you were coated in dripping filth and your boots were muddy. Anyone who on a slipped a rail either went head first into the muddy water or ended up astride the rails, and that definitely was an unpleasant experience nobody would ever forget as the pain was excruciating. After the rails there were trip wires and other obstacles, including a 10-foot-wide ditch filled with coiled barbed wire. Still running downhill, you arrived at two cables, one above the other, that hung over another small pond. It only took one man to wobble the cables and he and several others were flung into the filthy water below. Once you got over that obstacle, you scrambled out onto so-called 'dry land', which by now was one long mud patch. You now had to negotiate a wire mesh fence and abseil down a 40-foot cliff face. You were now effectively on the rifle range and you were forced to crawl across it while a machine gun on fixed lines filled the air with a constant stream of bullets no more than a foot and a half above your head. Once you cleared that you had to double to the firing point, where an armourer used a rod and pull-though to ensure your rifle barrel was clean, then issued you with five rounds, which had to be fired as quickly as possible from the lying prone position, and woe betide you if you didn't hit the target 100. It was a minor miracle if you had the energy to aim let alone hit the target. Once you finished firing, you cleaned yourself up, were given fresh clothing and doubled to the shower block to shower, change into dry clothes, wash your dirty clothes and hang them in the drying room. You were not allowed to walk anywhere on the course, even to meals. If like me you were on 'jankers', you just had time to eat your meal, then report to the cookhouse for punishment duty.

The two-week course was non-stop fitness, all day long. There were log exercises, ropes, chin-ups and other callisthenic-type activities, as well as speed marches. It was all designed to prepare us for the now infamous 'Bash', a 10-mile march and run in full battle order, including rifle, ammunition and helmet, which had to be completed in two hours regardless of the weather conditions. The route took us through the peaks of Derbyshire and before that final march we had done others over the same route, but although they were extremely hard, nothing prepared us for this as they increased the tempo considerably. Webbing, water bottles, rifle slings, chin straps, helmets, and rifles rubbed you raw, and the blisters that appeared on the heels, soles and toes played havoc with your mind. In many cases, if it hadn't been for the instructor swearing at them a lot of men would have failed; as it was, there were huge numbers that did. The roadway was littered with heaving bodies, none of who got a bit of sympathy. That last mile felt like 5 miles – every step was agony. By now a lot of our mates had been sent back to their units for a number of reasons, some simply because the psychiatrist said they weren't suited. On the big day, I ended up carrying a mate's rifle, someone else his webbing, another his pack, but we weren't going to leave him behind after all we had gone through to get here.

We stopped just short of the camp to 'sort ourselves out', then marched in as a section with rifles at the slope, well what was left of our section anyway! All the other sections were in the same boat. Once we had been formed up inside the camp and inspected by the CO we had to double to our tents, stack our rifles and webbing, and run to the showers, then run back. On our backs and hips there were huge raw rub marks where our equipment had cut us, but our feet looked like someone had taken to them with a razor blade because there was so much raw skin and blood, but we'd passed when many others had failed, and it felt so good. I still had 'jankers' that night and after our meal I had to stay behind and be humiliated by the amused cooks, all of who had done the course, so I couldn't complain. But the following morning it was all over and those of us that had been successful now lined up for a 50-mile march to the parachute school at Ringway in twenty-four hours. Our backs hadn't healed; neither had our feet, but we were finally free of Hardwick Hall.

Passing the 'Bash' – Peter Faggetter

Having established myself in the Parachute Regiment, I now had the good fortune to part with the regulation gas mask in favour of a smaller box type. This type, however, had its drawback for instead of your shoulder, it was clamped to your web belt, smack in the small of your back. Unfortunately, it was the ideal position to make more misery by gouging huge strips of flesh from your back as it bounced around on long marches or when you were charging over the obstacle course. By its very nature, parachutists' equipment needed to be lighter and more compact to allow greater mobility, but it was this smaller mask that saw me enduring my second dose of gas poisoning. If I thought that getting gassed was rated as some of the worst minutes of my army training, it was soon overtaken by the 'Bash' at Hardwick Hall in Cheshire. Everyone on the selection course had to endure the pounding to gain their 'wings' and all agreed that it nearly killed them.

The 'Bash' consisted of a 10-mile run and forced march wearing full kit and carrying your rifle, and it had to be completed in less than two hours. Known universally as the '10-mile bash', it could literally be a killer. It followed an intensive two-week physical training course designed to motivate all limbs to the extremes of fitness, and left no room for half-wits or weaklings. Our course 'Bash' began at 10 a.m. on what was already proving to be a warm and sultry July day. This was exactly what we didn't need for this final test before going on to

Ringway for parachute training. Failure to complete this two-hour slog on time meant a rejection ticket, no second chance and return to your old unit immediately. For weeks we'd been training for the privilege of joining the elite Regiment and all that that entailed – the aeroplanes, parachutes, balloons, and perhaps gliders. My flying ambitions were but a 'slog' away.

Of the 300 or so men and teenagers ranged in platoons, my group of thirty-two set off in the seventh slot. At long last, the expected sweating agony had begun. We knew from experience that many would fall by the way, and by the second mile the odd man was already squatting at the roadside verge, bringing up his breakfast. Sweat was already irritating maddeningly as it exuded from every pore, while the first blister points – the heels and soles – were making themselves known yet again. Other sore points such as where the full water bottle bounced against your hip, the galling, never used gas mask chafed the small of one's back, and the full ammo pouches niggled the ribs, were already indicating the pain to come. Then there was the shoulder, where the rifle sling constantly re-dug its customary, never-ending groove. By the end of the third mile some men had already called it a day. Perhaps they knew they'd never finish the 10 miles and the first signs of blisters made the decision for them. Maybe they were beyond their peak of fitness, too tired before they even started out. You easily recognised them, for they lay resting on a comfortable grassy bank or sitting on a convenient kerbstone. Those who were genuinely unwell lay flat out, while those suddenly taken short with the runs were over the hedge – some were caught short before they got to a hedge and were within laughable sight.

All of us felt the blisters burst before or during the fourth mile, a testing time for many of us. Sweat had turned to slush in your socks, and your shirt clung wetly to every stinking part of you not covered by sticking khaki denim trousers. More sweat stung your eyes and dripped off ears and nose, while your thumping head and heart threatened to burst. Your chest heaved and sank rapidly as it searched for bigger demands of oxygen, and again you asked, 'Is all this worthwhile?' For an extra shilling a day, definitely 'No'! But for the extra money and the chance to fly, the answer was a clear-cut 'Yes!' I had waited too long and struggled too much to allow anything to stand in my way now. Towards the end of the fifth mile, the trailing 'blood wagon' was picking up casualties and damaged men – those who had collapsed and hurt themselves on the unyielding road. Others were merely rolled aside to recover their senses, in which case they could either lay there moaning or, according to their frame of mind, clamber with left-over strength onto a following pick-up lorry. These chaps would have probably failed the test unless some mitigating factor of health prevented a better performance. Even a common cold could prove too big a handicap. Others might look despondently tearful, and some, utterly clapped-out, wouldn't care less – they were beyond caring. The two prior weeks' hardships were already too much – they'd had enough: it would mean going into a different regiment where such stringent fitness wasn't needed or necessary.

The sixth mile saw several of my platoon either pull up or pass out as they ran. Crash! – down they would go, sprawling onto the roadway, rifle clattering as it hit the ground, and there they would stay. Some would wobble sideways first, check themselves, then stagger as they desperately tried in their driving desire to continue on before buckling into a grazing skid, their helmets banging against the road. My chest felt like a sledgehammer was banging against my ribs, for there was little worthwhile air about and I had really to work my lungs to find the vital oxygen. On the run stages it became a continuous process of gasp, blow, gasp, blow that lasted for ten minutes, before the short marching periods gave respite. Then the heart pounding and blood-bursting run of gasping for air had to be tolerated all over again. It was a cruel and torturous abuse of organs already at the end of their tether. Some Hardwick bashes had taken place in rain! In wintertime! How I envied them on that humid, awful, hot and airless day.

Of those who'd fallen out, deliberately or through fainting, some cast dull glances at us tougher types as we pounded past them at a run, or when we were marching gave us the customary paired fingers in defiance of our rude remarks about their useless or gutless weaknesses. Some were strong lads I had known for the past three months. A few I had boxed; now here they were, defeated, creased up, grovelling in grit, unconscious, or holding their heads between grazed fingers and hands. I could see them wondering why the tiny and weedy boys like me could keep going. What was driving us, when they thought their stronger, bigger and solidly meatier bodies would outlast us anytime? I was the youngest of the bunch at just eighteen years and compared to them it was a beanpole. By the finish of mile seven all the platoons had sadly depleted numbers. Ten or so of our thirty-two had bitten the dust, including a couple of my regular mates. The roadside was beginning to look like a battlefield as others suddenly weakened and allowed themselves to give way. I was determined not to and with another two mates for company we kept up the bantering aimed at the weaklings and plodded on. By now my feet were a mess of blisters, while my back was a mass of torn skin. I alternately swopped my rifle from one shoulder to the other and cursed it twice every minute. In fact I cursed everything, including myself. As for my bloody hard black boots, designed in the Boer War, what I wouldn't do to the blasted man who invented them. But it was this raging 'blind' mentality that kept many of us going: a fierce resentment; bloody defiant defiance; sheer willpower to out-smart and prove something – a 'win even if it kills me' approach to what was obviously an extraordinary 'Bash' and the test of our lives. Even officers training with us had collapsed, to say nothing of some of the training instructors joining the roadside dropouts. This heat was a friend to no one, especially as you weren't allowed to drink from your water bottle.

My body was mechanical rubber when the eighth mile was behind us. By now, medics were already lining the route ahead of us in anticipation as we slogged past them. My mind registered that yet more of our chaps were going down, and tears crept down my cheeks to mingle with dried salty sweat. We were virtually dried out; and even my shirt didn't stick disgustingly to every part of my upper body. And like the others still loudly cursing the bouncing water bottles, I was very tempted to guzzle the contents regardless. But I'd have to fall down first – and then get permission, as the Army rules regarding drinking were stupidly strict. There was little doubt the hot and humid weather was responsible for this high drop-out rate and casualties, for we'd had many training sessions with far less. The stifling atmosphere was causing much difficulty when I breathed. Gasping was hardly the word for it. And through my boggled mind the possibility of self-destruction from exertion was now giving me dreadful thoughts; yet others seemed to be gliding through the whole thing. The finish was less than 2 miles off and I was determined not to give in, even if it killed me. 'Press on regardless' was an Army coined phrase long before I showed up, but it applied equally well to us. How I managed to put the ninth mile behind me I'll never know. We few who were still moving had given up all talk and banter a couple of miles back. There was nothing funny anymore. To smile wasn't possible. We were stupid rubber automatons, sick and worn out at that. Within yards of the point where the ninth became the tenth and last mile, the tall chap in front of me suddenly went down heavily in complete collapse. Unable to slow my running legs, I went sprawling full length over his inert body, banging my knuckles and rifle onto the ground.

Already crying, I was content to stay down, but my mates Len and David wouldn't hear of it and dragged me upwards and onwards. How they found enough strength to lift me I can't imagine, for my sagging heap couldn't have been any help. Every bone now ached, made worse by the unhelpful fall. The few moments of inactivity had given me a taste of bliss. But it didn't pay to stop; not even for a moment. The last mile was a tearful stagger home – what I remember of it. Twelve of us arrived, deadbeat and stinking of dirty sweat. Other platoons had less in numbers; what a marathon! After a drink, I lay down on my bunk and sort of slept. The only thing was I'd left my eyes open! Thirty minutes later, a gathering knot of worried chums had collected around me, wondering what to do because I looked dead but was breathing! I didn't see them, or answer when they spoke to me. Finally, a good shake brought a response. It was time for dinner. By evening it had become apparent our casualty figure was very serious; exactly how bad we didn't then know. Death was talked of, but nothing was mentioned directly to us.

The following morning saw us packing our kit and preparing to move to Ringway for the parachute course. More news became known and the trail of collapsed bodies had overloaded the hospitals and put three in the mortuary; I could believe it. Heart and arteries bursting accounted for the deaths, while the strain on organs and hearts for the remainder of us would be unmeasurable. What was somewhat galling about our 'Bash', though, was the fact that those chaps who'd fallen out in the last few miles passed the test too! Not that I minded that in itself; I was glad for them. But I could have done the same thing; I could have remained stretched out on that spotty-faced chap and still departed for Ringway! I needn't have run that grizzling last mile! My writhing corpse could have done it on a stretcher. I'll know next time.

Unfit For Airborne Forces – Tommy Blackburn

There were a dozen ways to be returned to your unit as unfit for the airborne forces. Some were sent packing because they were psychologically unsuited; we never found out what the causes were – they were just sent. The majority left because the daily pressure was too much for them. Some lasted a day, some two days; some even got as far as the last day then gave up. All of us must have thought about giving up a hundred times, but something deep down inside made you keep on going. They never played favourites, they swore at all of us, and threatened to send each of us home at some point. They were just trying to get under your skin, to see how far they could push you before you broke. They were experts at it, and what was worse, you knew they had been where you were and had taken the same constant abuse, but had withstood it. I saw some very strong men give up, and two of them swing punches at the instructor. They were gone within the hour. But the really hard part was when you'd finished each day, you still had to run everywhere, even to meals. Now that was one time you really wanted to walk, but you always knew someone was watching you.

3

Ringway:
The Parachute School

The Parachute School – Harold Wynn

When we arrived at the parachute school outside Manchester, there were all kinds of rumours floating around about balloon jumps from an old barrage balloon and jumps from Whitley bombers. It seems that the RAF instructors were literally learning on the job and we were going to be among their first guinea pigs, even though two courses had already gone through. It appears the instructors had attempted jumping from the rear of the old converted Whitley with the rear gun turret removed. They'd stand facing outwards and throw their canopy into the slipstream, where it was supposed to inflate and drag them off the aircraft. To say it was perilous was an understatement as it caused them to somersault and do all kinds of fancy gyrations before the parachute opened. According to rumours the parachutes often didn't open properly and some of them were nearly killed because of it.

As luck would have it, the senior officer in charge told us they had stopped doing it before the first course started, but the stories persisted even though we would be doing aperture jumps from the Whitleys. But he didn't tell us that the so-called 'Whitley Hole' had its disadvantages as well. It was a tube about 3 feet deep and unless you got a perfect exit out of it you would strike your face on the edge of the hole and get what became known as 'ringing the bell', which often resulted in a pugilist's nose. We all assumed that the RAF would be training us, yet in those first few years there were a lot of Army instructors as well, and they were all as good as one another. We started by doing what was known as ground training: rolling on the mats and jumping from ramps and fuselages until we could automatically land safely from a 12-foot ramp, which duplicated the speed you would land when in a parachute. We were among the first to jump from a barrage balloon. This was again an aperture jump, where you sat on the edge of a hole in the floor and pushed yourself off.

During the opening briefing before we began training, one of the lads asked the obvious question, 'Sir, what happens if our parachute doesn't open?' With everyone literally straining their ears for an answer, the officer smiled and answered, 'So far Private, all of them have opened, although a few have had malfunctions, all of which were caused by the parachutist not doing the correct drills. Contrary to the mis-informed rumours, nobody has yet been killed. Trained packers now pack every parachute and they are required to parachute on a regular basis. But should yours fail, then please bring it back and we will be happy to give you a new one!' The whole room broke up laughing. I must admit, going up in a balloon was terrifying the first time, not that I liked it much afterward. The instructors talked all the way up and they told you the most dreadful stories about how men had smashed into the ground when their parachutes failed to open – we only had one parachute. They would then tell us how they had to scoop their remains up with a spade and put them in a chaff bag. In fact, it was all a ruse to test you and see if you would refuse to jump, and a couple did too. But most of us were determined to go, especially after suffering hell at Hardwick Hall. The day I got presented with my wings was a very special day in my life that I will never forget. All the pain and agony I had gone through to get them was well worth it.

Ground Technique – Mathew Broderick

I had just been commissioned as a second lieutenant and had managed to scrape through the training at Hardwick Hall when many fell by the wayside and now I was doing ground training at the parachute school near Manchester. My instructor was a colourful character to say the least. He was a flight sergeant in the RAF and his descriptive abilities and lyrical tone would match the famous poet William Wordsworth.

Unfortunately, at the time I had two left legs, and no matter what the flight sergeant told me to do my landings looked like I'd got no bones in my body. I think he thought I was doing it deliberately, but I wasn't. He was extremely patient considering all the things I was doing wrong, but in the end it got to him and I still hear him screaming, 'SIR, YOU'RE A BLOODY USELESS BAG 'O' SHIT. YOU'D BE BETTER OFF IF YOU GOT A PERMANENT ERECTION, THEN AT LEAST THE KNOB-END WOULD STOP YOU FALLING FLAT ON YOUR FACE WHEN YOU LAND!'

New Boys – Dale Smith

One group of men had done all their ground training and had just completed their final exit drill from an aircraft fuselage into a sandpit and were formed up in front of the RAF instructor. He stood there for a few second then said, 'Right yous lot, tomorrow yous'll do your first jump from a balloon at 500 feet, any questions?' No sooner did he say those words than a voice from the rear: 'We are using parachutes, aren't we Sarge?' The sergeant looked long and hard at the young soldier and replied 'NO! You bloody idiot, we expect you to flap your arms until we're confident you can use the parachute properly without damaging it!'

How it Works – Frank Wilson

In the old days, when parachutists only wore one parachute, I had just passed the horrendous selection course for entry into the Parachute Regiment and all I had to do now was complete eight parachute descents from an aircraft. After a welcome briefing to the Parachute School, and an explanation of what they would be doing by the officer in charge, we were shown how a parachute deploys. A flight sergeant wearing the 28-foot X-type parachute walked down the centre of the room while another sergeant held onto the parachute static line that would normally be fixed inside the aircraft. As each part popped onto the floor, the officer explained what was happening. When the final section of the parachute large canopy lay there for everyone to see, the officer finished by saying, 'Are there any questions?'

Nobody wanted to be branded as 'chicken', so they shut up and didn't say what must have been on their minds. But being naive, I decided that I wanted to know and up went my hand and I asked, 'Sir, do we only have one parachute?'

'Yes, that's all that is required!'

To me it was logical to ask, 'But what happens if doesn't open?'

With a completely straight face, the officer said, 'We have an excellent safety record, and you will be trained to deal with every eventuality if something does go wrong. But in the unlikely event that your parachute doesn't open, please bring it back and we'll give you a new one!'

'Red On! Green On! GO!' – Peter Bishop

On the parachute course at Ringway you had to do eight jumps in order to claim the very coveted parachute wings and the 2s a day extra parachute pay. The long hard path of fitness training – the awful 'Bash' routines so well known to everyone who went through Hardwick Hall – was now all behind me, and before me were three ubiquitous balloons sitting tethered to mobile lorry winches; those huge silver-grey wind-bags with their great lop-ears were ready to carry everyone aloft within a soft-topped wicker style cage dangling on cotton-thin threads below their blimpish, bulging underbellies. Having watched the first groups fall about 100 feet before the snap of a parachute opening, then heard the relieved calls from happy mates, it was all too soon time for me to go and I figuratively swallowed my Adam's apple yet again.

'Five men jumping, 700 feet,' yelled the RAF sergeant dispatcher to the waiting winch man, and five more of us went drifting upwards for the first time. All the way up I wished the instructor would shut up as he was telling us all the things that could go wrong in the sky. By the time the balloon stopped moving I was terrified and wished I'd failed Hardwick Hall – nobody could convince me any different! Straight down from an unsteady little floor hovering at 700 feet that looked closer to a mile, while the big grey belly just above appeared ridiculously flimsy, and even a bit bloated, and it actually flapped a little, making 'snapping' sounds. Going through my mind every ten seconds: 'Was this the one knocked about by a Messerschmitt at Dover and damaged, or shot up by a Heinkel bomber over London? Have they pumped it up enough? Is it leaking gas? Will it 'pop' with a sudden burst and zoom all over the sky dragging us with it, or break away to search the upper clouds for an everlasting life of freedom?' And I really wanted to go to the toilet!

All such possibilities and other insecurities about the parachute on my back crossed and re-crossed a precariously balanced numbed brain about to commit its body to such a foolhardy act as jumping from that flimsy cage. Inwardly, I said to myself, 'This nail biting must stop.' Suddenly there's the order to, 'Stand next to the aperture number three!' Believe it or not the dreaded moment in time had come; surely I could put it off for a few more seconds? But no – the sergeant wouldn't like that one little bit, he'd got dozens more to throw out in the blue sky today. At the door a whole world appeared spread beneath my knee-shaking body. What had I done – why had I volunteered? The sergeant's voice yelled out: 'RED ON!' followed by a long pause. Then out came 'GREEN ON – GO!' And suddenly I felt the strong slap of a hand on my shoulder propelling me forward and into the big hole. At that stage in life I had to go regardless; discipline ensures it; a big sergeant had ordered me – the fear of cowardice and what the others would think of me should I refuse, and the promise made to myself about 'even if it kills me' – all the heart-bursting training would be wasted; and yes – that extra 2s a day 'danger' money. I was now committed to a long sickening drop, then there's a slight jerk at my shoulders followed by feet bouncing upward as the parachute opened with an unexpectedly loud 'snap', and I'm still alive! I'D DONE IT! There's nothing to it, and I remember I swallowed my wretched heart for nothing. Casting a few glances around the countryside I saw the world in all its beauty. THIS IS EASY!

It was then I heard a voice on a megaphone yelling for me to keep my feet together and to pull down on my back lift webs; a few seconds later I gently landed on Mother Earth so softly that I could have gone to sleep afterwards. Pretending not to feel a sharp ankle twinge because I didn't have my legs together, I freed myself from the parachute harness, folded the parachute up and carried it off the DZ. Afterwards, I joined the others making for the tea wagon and a puff of cigarette; I definitely needed that cigarette even if I was full of pretend bravado. I could barely walk without a limp, but I couldn't do without that cigarette. Whatever was wrong with my ankle would have to wait until I could secretly inspect the damage. Regulations clearly stated that one must report injuries; it was mandatory. But I didn't, and although some days it gave me hell I gritted my teeth. Later on I found out I'd suffered a stress fracture in my right ankle, but by then I'd completed the required number of jumps without further damage, and avoided all the DZ observers' watching eyes. With only the final night jump from an aircraft to cope with, I kept my fingers crossed for the long, dark drop. At least no one would see my final shielding of ankle sprawl in the dewy grass. I had successfully cheated the system – and death? Later, I made Dakota jumps on Salisbury Plain and more jumps from the Halifax. Then balloon jumps caught up with me again. I bloody hated balloon jumps. I could jump out of an aircraft any number of times without any problems, but that bloody balloon always scared the hell out of me.

Bessie One, Two, Three and Four – Roger Phillips

Initially, the parachute course saw potential parachute soldiers jump out of converted Whitley or Halifax bombers. It was a slow method of getting men on to a drop zone at Tatton Park because they had to exit out the rear end of the aircraft using a tube cut in the floor. It was then that someone had the bright idea of using barrage balloons with a special wicker cage slung underneath, similar to the ones used by artillery spotters during the First World War. A balloon could take up three times the number of men in one hour that an aircraft could. From then on it was mass production; two to three jumps from a balloon, followed by a further four or five from an aircraft to finally qualify. In the early days you qualified for your wings after the third jump, but you didn't get your extra 2s a day parachute pay until you'd completed seven.

The four barrage balloons were eventually given the names Bessie One, Two, Three, and Four. Curiously, Bessie One seemed to have a mind of her own and was typically female with a very 'unruly' temperament. On two occasions she broke her moorings with five men and an instructor on board; on the first occasion she headed for Manchester after everyone did a very fast exit; on the second occasion she got as far as Coventry; and each time it happened the lads were out the aperture in the floor faster than a speeding bullet, followed by the instructor. On the third bolt for freedom they had devised a set 'escape drill' for Bessie and her sisters. The students would go out the aperture in the floor in quick succession followed by the RAF instructor, whose last task was to pull a cord attached to the underside of the balloon. This cord ripped a large patch off the underside of the balloon and began the deflation process and all the ground crew had to do was follow the slowly deflating balloon as it made an erratic journey across the sky, much to the amusement of all the staff and students. Thereafter Bessie One was tamed and behaved herself.

Even with the greatest of intentions, some men were reluctant to jump. In the early days it was rare to go up in a balloon and come back down in the cage having refused. Quite a few actually stepped into the aperture and then made a grab for the lip, hanging there for all they were worth. They were never hauled back in, for once they took the plunge the RAF instructors tended to step on their fingers before offering them any other form of assistance and once you arrived on the ground, as long as you got up from the landing and didn't appear to be hurt, nobody seemed to mind how you did it. On one famous occasion, a major came down in front of his commanding officer. His landing was unconventional to say the least, but he finally got to his feet without any problems. As he began taking off his parachute, his commanding officer called out to him, 'John, are you playing a round of golf this afternoon?'

'No Colonel!' was the reply.

'Thank God, your clubs would have been bloody ruined after that landing!' The major took the hint and did his very best to improve next time. What made it even more memorable was a captain followed the major down and did an equally terrible landing. As he got up the colonel rebuked him with: 'Captain Horrocks, do you bloody play golf?'

'No Colonel!'

'Good. After that landing at least you have one thing in your favour!'

His Parachute Didn't Open – Frank Dorsey

Big Frank, as my best mate was called, was an ex-Grenadier Guardsman. His career in the Regiment is remembered by many of its original members because at Ringway, during his parachute training, he had the misfortune of having his parachute caught up in the rear of the Whitley after he exited from the aperture. He was just hanging there outside the aircraft on the end of the strap, spinning around and around while the pilot circled a few times in an effort to shake him free, but to no avail. Eventually, it was decided to land with Frank still attached to the Whitley. The pilot made an incredible landing on the long grass next to the runway and kept the tail of the aircraft up as long as he could. As luck would have it, Frank was able to stop spinning and actually landed on his back and the parachute absorbed the shock, even though it was almost torn to shreds. Luckily he was not seriously hurt, but suffered a nasty shake-up, with severe shock and a few bruises that needed attention. While he was lying there, still shaking, the RAF safety officer arrived in his vehicle and walked over to see if Frank was seriously injured. When he wasn't, he said, 'In future, Private, we would prefer if you landed by parachute when it's NOT attached to the aircraft!'

Evidently Frank wasn't amused by the attempted humour and informed the officer that he was not a private, he was a guardsman!

No Extra Money – John Ross

My dad was born in 1914 and was called up for the Second World War. He originally joined the infantry, but he volunteered for the gliders when it was announced he'd get an extra 6*d* per day for Mum. When they came around looking for volunteers to learn to parachute and he heard they would get 2*s* a day, he again volunteered and went to Ringway Airport for training. After ground training, he said he was made to jump from a huge tower where you were in a parachute and they dropped you from about 200 feet to get you used to floating down in a parachute and landing. Having done all this, they were lined up and asked by an officer if they were prepared to jump out of an aircraft.

My father asked, 'Do I get the extra one and sixpence if I do?'

The officer replied that as he was already in the Airborne and was getting an extra sixpence a day for being in an Air-Landing Regiment, he wouldn't get the extra one and sixpence, so my father declined and did not become a parachutist, although he did remain in the 6th Airborne Division and landed at Normandy and over the Rhine, which he never talked about. He told me after the war that it was extremely dangerous jumping out of aircraft, as he'd seen a man die when his parachute didn't open because of the buffeting he got in the slipstream, and he saw lots of men getting seriously injured when they landed. I said that it must have been dangerous flying and landing in a glider as once you were in the air there was no way of escaping.

He said, 'Oh it was, but you weren't looking out the windows when you were coming in to land so it didn't matter.'

I said, 'But what about the anti-aircraft guns?'

He replied, 'By that time you were too scared to worry!'

And this was a man whose glider crashed on landing at Normandy and was riddled with bullets landing at the Rhine Crossing.

What Religion? – Mike Pearce

Many European Jews enlisted in the British Army during the Second World War, and quite a few entered the airborne forces. All of them were advised to change their names and put another religion on their ID tags, just in case they were captured by the Germans. So they enlisted as a Catholic, Atheist, Protestant or numerous other religions, anything except Jewish. Throughout its development in the war, the 21st Independent Parachute Company included at least twenty-six Austrian, German, Polish and Czech anti-Nazi Jewish refugees, who initially volunteered from the Pioneer Corps, where Jews were put upon enlistment. For some unknown reason they used mostly Irish and Scottish names on their enlistment papers. One man by the name of Angus McGregor had the strongest German accent I'd ever heard. One amusing incident at Ringway occurred when we were on church parade and were lined up in our different groups, ready to be marched away. There were three men left, two Welsh Guardsmen who were Methodists, and a Polish signalman, a Jew. Evidently the RSM made some flippant comment about Methodists not being real Christians, after which he asked the signalman which religion he was. The reply he got took him by surprise: 'Whichever one does the best Bat Mitzvah, Sir!'

4

The Glider Pilot Regiment

Glider Training – Harry Cole

Walter Cronkite, the world-famous American radio presenter, once wrote, 'I'll tell you straight out: if you've got to go into combat, don't go by glider. Walk, crawl, parachute, swim, float – anything, but don't go by glider. Riding in one of those things was like attending a rock concert while locked in the bass drum. When I did, the landing the field was scattered with gliders on their noses, on their sides, on their backs. It was a scene from hell, yet everyone seemed pleased that it was a successful glider operation.'

The basic British workhorse was the Horsa Mark I. It had a wingspan of 88 feet (27 m) and a length of 67 feet (20 m), and when fully loaded weighed 15,250 pounds (6,920 kg). It was considered sturdy and very manoeuvrable for a glider, and like all military gliders was basically a flying box with the aerodynamic qualities of a brick. Its design was based on a high-wing cantilever monoplane, with wooden wings and a wooden supported framework. It was intended to carry thirty troops or the equivalent amount of freight.

On operational flights the main tricycle landing gear could be jettisoned and landing was then made on the nose wheel and a sprung skid under the fuselage. The wings, like all British gliders, carried large 'barn door' flaps which, when lowered, made a steep, high rate-of-descent landing possible, allowing the pilots to land in constricted spaces and to get quickly below any flak being fired at them. Unfortunately, the pilot had only one chance to lower the flaps as the gas in the cylinder that controlled the flaps could only be used once. The pilot's compartment had two side-by-side seats and dual controls. Aft of the pilot's compartment was the freight-loading door on the port side. There was also the Hamilcar, the largest of the gliders, designed to carry heavy equipment such as the Tetrarch light tank; then there was the Hotspur, which was used to train pilots. A fourth glider, a replica of the American WACO, renamed the Hadrian, was also used because it was easier to build, although very few pilots liked it because it was very basic in its design and didn't have the guidance system that British gliders had. The other drawback with flying a glider was there wasn't a method of escaping should it be badly damaged. The pilots and those inside literally had to pray they were not hit by incoming fire in flight.

Glider pilots were not only required to fly gliders; they had to become infantrymen once they were on the ground. The RAF taught them to fly and the Army taught them to become infantrymen. There were two distinct pilots. The first were staff sergeants and above, who flew the gliders, and the second were sergeants who acted as back-up pilots as every glider needed two men to fly it, especially on long flights. Staff sergeants and above spent twenty weeks learning glider principles in various gliders; sergeants spent only eight weeks. Staff sergeants wore a badge on the chest comprising a lion surmounting a crown between two blue wings, while the sergeants wore one comprising the letter 'G' between two blue wings.

Crash Landing – Ernie Green

During my first night flight in a Hotspur glider we had just lifted off the ground when the Miles aircraft towing us suddenly plunged earthward. It happened so quickly that we had no time to disengage the towrope. The Miles hit the ground and exploded, creating a huge ball of fire that blinded us. I remember flying through black smoke and flames, and then the Hotspur nose-dived into the heath beyond the wire. I can recall coming around in a contorted position in the long grass, unable to move. There was an eerie red glow all around me, and then I blacked out. When I woke up in hospital they told me I'd landed over 40 feet from the cockpit and I was the only one to survive from either aircraft.

How to Fly a Glider – Douglas Smithson

I had passed the selection process for the Glider Pilot
Regiment and was on my first flight in a fixed wing aircraft,
and I completely blew it. So much so that when we landed
and got out, the RAF instructor said to me quite seriously,
'Corporal, when you were selected for the Glider Pilot
Regiment did anyone point out to you that should His
Majesty ever allow you to fly one of his gliders, you had better
understand that it doesn't have an engine, it isn't made of
toilet paper and balsa wood, and it certainly won't fly on just
a wing and a prayer with a pilot who has no idea what he's
doing?'

Obviously I improved as I passed that part of the course.
Everybody trained on the Hotspur glider, an ideal training
aircraft and very stable in the air. The crew sat one behind
the other, with the second pilot slightly higher than the first.
Both pilots had to wear helmets as on rough landings your
head often did a wonderful 'machine-gun action' against
the top of the cockpit. Mind you, because landings could be
'hard' it wasn't unknown for the first pilot's harness to break
and his feet would penetrate the thin wooden nose of the
glider, ending up sticking outside the nose like a crude set of
booted brakes, which always caused a great deal of hilarity
and embarrassment.

Given the chance, pilots and tow crews often did 'chicken
runs', crazy antics that got them a boot in the backside if they
were caught. One of the best chicken runs happened one night
when an unmitigated maniac was towed at about 15 feet above
the ground along the long, tree-lined drive of Blenheim Palace,
the birthplace of Winston Churchill, frightening the deer and
swans on the ornamental lake and convincing the Staff that
the Germans' Fallschirmjäger (paratroopers) had come for
Churchill. As the glider cleared the main building, they bombed
the place with several dozen toilet rolls and several boxes
of condoms. The hue and cry afterwards reverberated from
Downing Street right down through the chain of command.
Nobody knows who did it as well over two dozen gliders were
in the sky at the time.

Unusual Flying Skills – Ken Bailey

It was 1942. I had just completed my first flight at the controls of a Hotspur glider, an eight-seater glider used only for training. The RAF instructor never said a thing as I came in for the landing. Admittedly, it was a bit steep and the glider did do several wonderful bounces before I managed to bring it under control and stop it. Even when we both got out, the Flying Officer said nothing. It was only when we were walking back to the hanger that he said, 'Before you came to us Corporal, you didn't happen to be in charge of one of those huge helter-skelter contraptions on the foreshore at Blackpool where people paid money to get frightened, did you?'

Instant Darkness – Harry Archer

I was now flying the Hamilcar, which was capable of carrying a light tank. I had just got a new co-pilot, Johnny Wilson, and the pair of us had been towed up to 4,000 feet for night flying. We had flown around the base behind the tow aircraft for half an hour when we were informed we should cast off. A minute or so later, I released the towing rope and we began to circle several times in readiness for landing. Suddenly all the lights on the airfield went off and immediately I thought there must be German night fighters in the vicinity. I turned to tell John, only to find he'd his Webley pistol in his hand and was aiming it out of the side window. He was going to take on a German fighter with a pistol! I couldn't help but laugh out loud and comment about how close the night fighter would need to come if he wanted to hit it with his pistol, and that I thought the fighter would have a slight advantage in firepower. After that he looked at me and put it away. From then on we had to do everything by rule of thumb even though we had an altimeter. We dared not dive too fast because we couldn't make out the lie of the land, as there were lots of small woods and slight hills around the airfield. Everything that night was pitch black and overcast and although we had a fair idea where the airfield was by using the compass, it was still very much a touch and go thing as to where to land, especially as there were other gliders in the air at the time. As we dropped lower and lower, the pair of us tried to see something we recognised.

I circled three or four times, but I couldn't apply the flaps as you only had one go at them because the gas tanks that supplied the gas to move them was quickly used up. At the last minute I saw something really dark stand out; it had to be a building by its shape and from what I remembered a building of that size was near the landing strip, so I made the decision to apply full flaps. I didn't have much choice as I had nowhere else to go. I lifted the nose slightly and kept the flaps on and as soon as I felt the thud of the glider hitting Mother Earth, I yelled to John to release the drogue parachute in the tail. We bounced and skidded along the ground with full flaps on, the drogue parachute helping slow us down. It was released when we'd decelerated to a reasonable speed. Not long afterward there was a heavy jolt and the whole tail end lifted, settled, then we stopped. Poor John, who was on his first night flight in a Hamilcar, gave out a loud excitable yell, undid his harness, and headed out of the cockpit to the side door. He dragged it open, stepped out and promptly fell 8 feet into the centre of the base sewerage plant and nearly drowned. For a second time that night, I couldn't stop laughing. So I simply lit up a cigarette and stayed where I was until the recovery crew came about an hour or so later, after John had walked to the tower and told them where we were. Evidently they understood his predicament but they still wouldn't let him in the door, so he had to shout up to the tower crew, who were all crowded on the platform above. To make matters worse, the driver of the jeep sent to pick me up made him sit in the back on several large sheets of open newspapers, and he drove like the wind both ways so that he couldn't smell the stench. Poor John never lived it down.

Fitting Parachutes – Bernard Black

It came as a big shock to be told we'd only wear a parachute during initial pilot training; after that you wore your underpants tied very tightly at the bottom of each leg. Logically, if you got shot down you'd never be able to get out anyway. When the big day arrived for us to begin actually flying training, we were required to fit a parachute. It was a new experience in humiliation and hilarity. At the time, RAF females were responsible for packing all parachutes, and they were also responsible for showing us how to fit these parachutes over the bulky clothing we wore doing initial flying training. The parachutes sat on one's backside and were wrenched open by pulling a red handle on the side. Putting them on the first time was a test of ingenuity and hilarity, and each pilot had a female helping him. In an age when sex wasn't openly discussed there were so many sexual innuendoes that someone would crack up laughing every two minutes. The girls were used to it and played it up. The men weren't, even though we tried hard to hide the fact. When the fitting was finished, we were asked to walk in a circle round the fitting room. We looked ridiculous and were like waddling pregnant ducks, and it was totally unnecessary, but it gave the girls a giggle to see us struggling to walk. The next thing was to explain how the parachute worked. After counting to ten, you simply pulled the red handle. One particularly attractive and well-endowed female corporal had already embarrassed her charge several times. Now she was making minor adjustments to a leg strap near his crotch while talking about how you pulled the handle. She bent forward and deliberately brushed her breasts against the back of the poor man's hand. Unfortunately, he was holding the red handle and was so shocked to feel the softness of her breasts that he pulled his hand away. Regrettably, he pulled the red handle as he did so, causing the parachute to explode outward, lifting him, and her, off the floor, and filling the room with the canopy, which slowly descended upon everyone like a death shroud. It took twenty minutes before the laughing stopped and everything was back to normal.

Just a Piece of Rope – Bob Howell

While watching the 60th Anniversary of D-Day on TV and seeing the airborne landings, I wondered if anyone ever thought anything about that piece of rope connecting the tug to the glider. I recalled the hours I spent servicing them and endlessly changing the fittings, and thought it might be of interest to pass on a few details of what it was all about. When I heard I was being posted from a very cold Netheravon, on Salisbury Plain, I was at first very pleased, but on learning I was detailed to the Rope Section, my heart sank. The Rope Section comprised a small workshop in the corner of a hangar filled with hundreds of ropes, all stacked neatly, each with different labels attached, but as I got interested I found it was much better than I anticipated.

There were in fact two types of rope. The smaller was 350 feet long, by 3.5 inches in circumference. (A rope is measured in circumference not diameter.) These were used to 'tug' Horsa, Waco and Hadrian gliders. The larger ropes, still 350 feet long but 4.5 inches in circumference, were used to tug our biggest glider, the Hamilcar. Each rope had a log book recording its serviceability and number of 'tugs'. Each rope had a number, and when it was new ten pieces of tape threaded between its strands. After each 'tug', one tape was removed, the rope inspected, splices checked and details entered in its logbook. Later on, all ropes had a radio cable threaded through the middle to allow the tug and glider pilots to communicate.

The greatest amount of work we had to do was on the 'connecting' fittings spliced to each end of the rope. The English and American couplings were different (what's new?) – the American was basically a big hook and eye but the English had what was called 'Lobel' fittings. The easiest way I can describe them is: clench one hand into a fist and then clasp it with the other hand. To release was, of course, to open the second hand. Both tug and glider were able to make the 'release', but other than in an emergency, it was always the glider pilot that made the release. However, I did hear that over Sicily American pilots released their tows miles out to sea and a lot of our lads drowned because of it. It was a constant job changing these fittings. We (British) had four types of tug: Whitley, Halifax, Stirling and Albemarle, having, of course, standard 'E' type fittings. The Hadrian had 'A' type fittings and the Horsa 'E'. Of course, the American tugs differed, for instance the Dakota having an 'A' type to the Hadrian's 'A', and the Horsa's 'E'. There seemed to be endless combinations, but the easiest pair to connect was the Halifax, the most powerful tug, to the Hamilcar, because both fittings were always the same.

Another change came when the Mk 2 Horsa came into service, this having a 'straight' rope pull from the tail of the tug to the nose of the glider. (The Mk 1 Horsa had a 'Y' pull from the tail of the tug to the glider's main planes, 'wings'.) Of course, questions were always asked following rope breaks, but the answer was never due to lack of maintenance. They usually occurred when the tug and glider were not in line, mostly caused when the glider pilot lost sight of the tug in cloud. The glider had an instrument in the cockpit to show the angle of 'tug to glider' but this was not very good if the angles changed very quickly. Another reason for breaks was when the glider changed from 'high tug' to 'low tug'. When the glider flew through the tug's slipstream, a 'push-pull' effect occurred and this would cause the rope to break. So weather was really the problem, in particular cloud or crosswind. An interesting trial we carried out was to simulate 'snatching' a glider from the ground. This was done by placing two poles 12 feet high 20 feet apart, over which we draped a 2-inch nylon rope 220 foot long, forming a big loop. The tug flew very low over the rope, collecting the loop on the hook. The cable unwound from the winch until the weight of the glider was reached and slowly took off. When airborne, the winch wound in the cable until the 2-inch nylon rope reached the tail of the tug. The first 'tries' were with the Whitley tug and a Hotspur training glider, but for intended operations, a Dakota was used snatching a Hadrian glider. In the Far East we were told that it proved very successful in jungle clearings, where they were able to 'grab' gliders full of wounded and get them back to hospital in hours rather than in days if they were carried by hand.

Operation Bunghole – Supporting Yugoslavian Partisans – Cornelius Turner

In early 1944 a group of senior Russian officers had to be taken to meet with the partisan leader, Tito, at his mountain enclave 100 miles inside Yugoslavia and well behind the German lines. The flight had to be done in daylight, so it was fraught with danger. This was the first daylight glider landing of the war and was given the code name Operation Bunghole. At the end of January there were whispers of an operation where they might need Horsa gliders. Unfortunately, they had none, but we'd heard of three that were left on an airstrip in Tunisia after the Sicily job, and so I was sent to have a look at them. The night before I'd been to see Bill Needle, the American executive officer on the airbase, and within a couple of hours he had three crews laid on. Bill simply asked for a pencil ring on the map to give him an idea where the gliders were. He said he'd even come over himself for the ride. That was the difference between the American way and the British way. The RAF would have taken ten days, with every possible snag thrown in our way. It was an attitude I came across many times over the years; the English disease is a very real thing.

Well, we found them, looking very lonesome and forlorn on a salt flat. An RAF detachment had come up from Algiers and the sergeant fitter thought they'd be OK once we shovelled them clear of sand. Nothing seemed to be hanging loose, so we plugged in the towropes and took off on a wing and a prayer and flew them across the Mediterranean to Sicily. Back at Comiso we did some more testing and set out, fully loaded, to fly to Bari, where I heard I was to lead a flight of three gliders and some Russian General Staff into Yugoslavia. There was no way we could expect to get any of those Horsas to a height of 7,000 feet and cross the Dinaric Alps into the interior, so in the end we used new American Wacos. The brief was to deliver thirty-six Russian officers under a Marshal Korneyev to a point on a mountainside called Medenapolu, some 2 miles north-west of the town of Basan Petrovac, 100 miles inland of the Yugoslav port of Split. It was to be in broad daylight, a first for gliders, and we would have twenty-four Spitfires for outward escort over the sea, with twenty-four Mustangs taking over on the other side up to the LZ. My tow-ship pilot, Wendell Little of Indianapolis, wished us the best of luck just before take-off. 'You'll need it,' he said. 'It's all over town this secret of yours; I hope they don't jump us.'

At the airfield the Russians were done up in heavy-duty field coats, which for the humid weather conditions here was a bit much, but I didn't argue as the Russians wouldn't have taken a blind bit of notice anyway. They also had a huge metal box with them that they guarded jealously. And so Operation Bunghole took off at noon on 19 February 1944, course approximately true north – visibility unlimited. As we neared landfall, scattered white islands in a black sea, we could already see the towering saw-tooth horizon of the mountains some 60 miles away. There was the town and harbour that could only be Split, so we were dead on course. 'Droop' Newman, my co-pilot, hardly said a word. He was doing most of the flying while I checked on our course. The Russian marshal sat behind us, the muzzle of his PPSh-41 machine pistol nestling about six inches from the back of our necks. I hoped the safety catch was on as I'd seen the damage one of those things could do as they only fired on automatic.

As we approached the peaks, 'Droop' had all his work cut out to hold the bucking glider on course. I was certain we were drifting east of track by several miles as we staggered over the divide. By now both the tow ships and gliders were leaping all over the sky like wild horses. We tumbled over the icy teeth of the ridge with a mere 100 feet to spare. The interior opened up before us in a great white valley, timbered on the high slopes, and beyond the forests gentle hills losing themselves into the northern mists. Our dead reckoning time was up and there, coming up below, was the first town we had seen, not easy to pick out in the dazzling carpet of snow, but 2 miles to our left instead of to the right. We were east of track as I had thought, and flying straight on. Dare I say pull off? I was certain I was right, but there's no going back once you're off tow. I'd checked the map every mile of the way. No! This was not going to be another Mount Etna in Sicily. We were at 3,000 feet and could reach the LZ easily. So I said, 'I'll take her Droop! Hit the tit! We're going down.' He held up his hands then hit the release lever without a word. Up came the nose to get the speed down to 70, swinging to port as the rest of them flew straight on below.

Yes, this must be Petrovac, there's the LZ 4 or 5 miles away dead ahead. 'They're coming round,' Droop shouted. The train had gone straight on for a couple of miles but were swinging round and well above me, and overtaking fast. There was a wide white shelf on the hillside and a fire. Yes, a big fire, two fires, little black dots against the snow. We were there! Then flashing past them at 50 feet were the Mustangs doing a mock beat-up, then they were up and gone. The others were now following them down into the deep snow, three perfect landings. Once we stopped, everybody embraced everybody else; the Partisans – Drugs (Droogs) they called themselves – were armed to the teeth, rifles, crossed bandoleers, knives and grenades hung everywhere. They certainly looked the part, although later on I found out that looks could be extremely deceiving as they tended to prey more on their own people than the Germans.

Almost all of them were bearded and stunk to high heaven, and they swarmed all over us, laughing and calling out to each other. They weighed the gliders down with fallen timber, and everyone then climbed on to waiting sleds and set off for town with the precious box the Russians had brought with them balanced precariously on one sledge, guarded by a poor Russian lieutenant sitting on top of it. He looked ridiculous. The unfortunate pony towing it was having a hell of time pulling the thing through the snow, it was so heavy. No sooner did we arrive than the first thing off was the box, then the Russians took off their coats and underneath they were dressed in their Sunday best, medals by the dozen. They immediately opened the box and it was full of Russian vodka, caviar and numerous other delicacies that they handed out to the Yugoslav leaders. They were clearly buttering up their hosts, something we never did. And to be truthful, I am not sure the Yugoslavs were bothered that much. Afterwards it was a heavy night in the little town hall, as from six to near midnight we all sat and drank toasts to the whole free world.

'My government will not forget you and your pilots,' someone who was translating said. 'Tomorrow we meet our honoured leader Tito – he will regret he was not here this day.' And so we continued to drink until everyone fell into a deep inebriated sleep. The next morning I woke up with a hangover to beat all hangovers. Eventually I did meet Tito and he was a very intelligent, insightful man too.

Operation Voodoo – Fredrick Stephenson

On 23 June 1943 a Hadrian glider nicknamed *Voodoo* took off from Royal Canadian Airforce Base Dorval and set a course for Goose Bay, Labrador, towed by an RCAF C-47, a distance of 809 miles (1,301 kilometres). The purpose of this mission was to fly the glider, loaded with 3,360 pounds of special medical supplies, engine and radio parts, in three legs from Canada to Scotland. Also on board were flotation bags to keep the glider afloat in case of a ditching, so the supplies could be recovered. Both aircraft had no form of defence. Three days after landing in Goose Bay, it began its voyage over the Atlantic, landing in Iceland after a flight of 7 hours and 15 minutes. To get there they had flown 1,542 miles (2,482 kilometres) non-stop from Goose Bay, a world record still not beaten. The following day they took off on the final leg. They arrived in Prestwick, Scotland, after twenty-eight hours of flying time against strong buffeting winds the whole way, a distance of 833 miles (1,341 kilometres). When they came to a stop, the pilots were met by the CO of the airfield, who said with a smile, 'Congratulations, you're late. You should have been here two hours ago!'

The reply he got made him laugh. 'We're sorry, but we fell off the map at Iceland and turned left instead of right!' They'd flown a total of 3,184 miles (4,774 kilometres).

Pilots Lost at Arnhem – Ken Cooper

Before the battle of Arnhem the Glider Pilot Regiment had a total of around 2,000 pilots, and after the battle approximately 200 came back. So with future glider operations in jeopardy, the planners had no option but to ask the RAF for the 'loan' of 2,000 of their pilots to transfer to the Army, and I was one of them. Loan wasn't really the right word as many of us were simply transferred without so much as a please or thank you, a somewhat worrisome concept considering none of us had ever fired a rifle, there were no parachutes, no armour plate under your seat, and no satisfying drone of four large engines on the wings. And what was worse, you were expected to land in German-occupied territory in the dark without landing lights.

5

Tunisia, Sicily and Italy

A Letter From North Africa – Alistair Robinson

Tom,

You asked in your last letter for a few 'tips on the fighting' over here, so here they are. As a platoon commander in North Africa you have to be constantly on your toes. I was still a second lieutenant when we arrived. We were all fit, well trained and eager to get to grips with the Boche. One of the first things we found, when you attack, you nearly always had [sic] several miles to cover, usually in the dark, before you reach the place from which it starts, and the condition in which your men reach that assembly area is going to make a whole lot of difference to their performance when the big moment comes. If the march has been a scramble, and they are rushed into the attack on arrival, their enthusiasm to come to grips with the Boche will not be as high as if the march has been orderly, with plenty of time to check up on everything and rest the men at the assembly area, after which they will inevitably be full of confidence and will usually do a top-notch job. In attack, our initial tendency, and it wasn't altogether the platoon commander's fault, was to rush in without a thorough reconnaissance, and without going over with the NCOs every bit of information we had about the Boche positions. Once you're committed, it's hell's own game trying to see where the bullets are coming from unless you have a fair idea where the swine ought to be. Even then, it's not so easy. We have lost a lot of men and officers through platoon

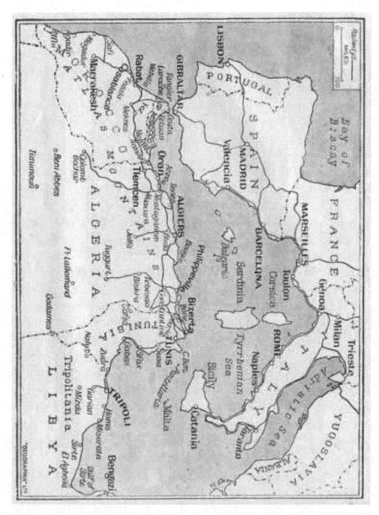

The Mediterranean and North Africa.

commanders being too eager and moving right up with their leading sections. You can fight your platoon a darned sight better by staying in a position from which you can manoeuvre your reserve sections when you have seen what fire the lead sections draw. Practise lots of frontal attacks. Boche positions are invariably mutually supported so platoon-flanking attacks are damned hard, especially as he will have MG34 machine guns firing from around 2,000 yards at around 900 rounds per minute. They are the Devil to overcome.

Defence took rather a back seat at home as we were supposed to be 'aggressive assault troops', but, assault troops or not, most of our time is spent in defence, because whenever you are not actually attacking you have to be ready to defend yourself. And whatever area you have to defend you must have a mobile reserve in the rear of your position, because the Boche don't always stick to the tactics book when they attack, so you have to use a lot of common sense when placing your men. Whenever possible, we position ourselves on a reverse slope as any movement on a forward slope is guaranteed to bring the artillery or mortars down on you, and it is not easy to stay still and hidden all day. If we are forced to take up a forward slope position, we put out OPs; the rest of the men remain undercover until you are attacked. It is then that your fire control comes in. The first time we were attacked almost everyone but the old sweats blazed off as soon as the Boche appeared, giving all of our positions away. These days it is much more satisfying to let them come up a bit, and then catch them wholesale on some open stretch. If by chance they knock out one of our OPs and start getting in among us, you can thank God for the men you have in reserve so you can counterattack straight away, preferably with well rehearsed supporting fire, then you get stuck into them almost as soon as they arrive in your position, or, better still, get them in a flank as they advance. At night, sentries should always man the Bren gun in the same trench with the section commander, as he has a Tommy gun, a couple of grenades, and a Very pistol with plenty of cartridges, and is ready for anything. If a Boche patrol attacks, they will let off lashings of automatic fire at random, to draw ours so he can see where we are, and when they retire, it will be under cover of mortars. The answer is simple; we stay still and hold our fire until we can pick out a target. Not long after we arrived we were attacked by a patrol some fifteen strong. They fired literally thousands of rounds without causing a single casualty. We fired about twenty rounds, and killed an officer and two men. I don't think it's worth chasing a retiring patrol, as they want you to leave your trenches, so as to catch you with their mortars or machine guns. Instead, you try and guess their line of retreat and chase them with mortar fire and machine guns.

The best patrolling troops we have come across are the Moroccan Goums, whose success as compared with any other unit is phenomenal. Even against the best the Boche have, they never fail. Why are they better than we are you may asked? First, because they are wild hill men and have been trained as warriors from birth. Second, because the preparation of their patrols is done with such detailed thoroughness. No fighting patrol is sent out until its leaders have spent at least a day watching the actual post they are after, and reconnoitring exact routes and so forth. If the leaders are not satisfied at the end of the day, they will postpone sending out the patrol, and will devote another day to the preliminaries. Initially, our men were a little too inclined to think about doing a patrol late in the afternoon, then send it out that same night. To be worth a damn, a fighting patrol must start off with an odds-on chance of two-to-one, not six-to-four or even money, but a good two-to-one bet. To do this, information on the Boche has to be really good and up to date. As regards the composition of fighting patrols, there is a wide divergence of opinion. In my battalion we go on the principle of maximum firepower with minimum manpower. This means the patrol consists of an officer, three grenade throwers, three with Tommy Guns, and a support group of a corporal and three with Bren guns. The reconnaissance patrol is different. The best result is one composed of an officer or sergeant, and two men, who go out at night, remain awake and observe all the next day, returning during the second night. We learned early on that the dimensions of a slit trench are vitally important, especially after being dive-bombed and machine-gunned from the air. This attack went on intermittently all the following week, plus more than enough shelling. Since then, everyone digs slit trenches automatically, even if they arrive somewhere soaking wet at three in the morning. Their trenches are always 5 feet deep. Anyone will tell you tales of miraculous escapes due to slit trenches; shells landing a couple of feet away without hurting the bloke inside, and so on. I don't think you could ever shell our battalion out of a position, if only because we are safe in our slit trenches.

Incidentally, machine-gunning from the air is perfectly bloody, worse than bombing or shelling. The accuracy of it is something I never imagined. An unopposed fighter can guarantee that he'll hit a solitary motorcycle. But, on the other hand, if you have dug good slit trenches, you don't suffer casualties from this type of attack, and you find that, after all, the noise was the worst part of it. The Boche also does much more air reconnaissance than we do. Every morning, 'Gert and Daisy' take a look at us, and if the camouflage is bad he'll attack you with aircraft, or artillery. All the hours we put in perfecting our camouflage has paid off, while other units near us get pounded regularly, we rarely do. All our men carry Hawkins antitank grenades. Our PIATs will knock out a tank, but a Hawkins will disable one and make him a prime target for the PIAT, especially if you get it near the tracks. Several of them will also knock out a tank. Somebody once said, 'Warfare consists of boredom punctuated by occasional moments of excitement.' This is absolute rot! When the weather is shocking, with nothing but a gas cape over your head and with thirty men expecting you to okay their letters for censorship, dish out NAAFI stuff, make the best of the rations, and get them new equipment, there's too much to do to get bored. You, in turn, always insist that they are ready to fight, that they are in good heart, that they are clean and healthy, and that the NCOs are doing their job; you may get fed up, but never bored.

Discipline is the hardest and most important thing to keep going. Airborne units are highly motivated, but even they become bored when they sit around a lot, and when that happens discipline becomes lax, so you have to keep on top of it. I'm not talking about mindless Guards discipline, but the discipline that keeps a fighting unit at its best. I find that the best way is to keep a strict routine, however rotten the conditions. That is, I stipulate a definite timetable for everything which must be done daily. If you insist on this routine you've always got them under control when the trouble starts. Finally, 'There is no such thing as bad troops, but there is such a thing as bad leaders.' It is horribly true, as I have seen out here. I have also seen second rate fighting units fighting magnificently, simply because they were under first-rate officers and NCOs. It makes you realise the vital importance of you doing your job, and doing it properly. Having said all this, expect lots of casualties however good you are; we have suffered enormously because the Boche rarely give up without a good fight, and it's hard getting sufficient replacements because we are an airborne battalion and all of our men have to be parachute trained.

Our Glider Sank – Clive Osborne

On the invasion of Sicily from Tunisia, we took off in our Waco glider towed by a Yank Dakota whose pilot had a touch of the 'chicken in him'. Because of the flak as we reached the coast, he released us too early and so we crash-landed in the sea in the dark. As we hit the water, I was literally thrown through the top of the glider like a cork out of a champagne bottle. I was lucky I wasn't seriously hurt. When I sorted myself out I reached back inside and grabbed Tom Arkwright and pulled him out onto the wing, then I helped a couple more. Others got out by themselves; regrettably some didn't make it. It was not long before the glider started to break up and the only thing keeping the wrecked parts from drifting away was the wire attached to them. Because there was a risk that our body weight might sink the wreckage, we ditched almost everything we were wearing. I just had my shirt on and in the pocket I had my wallet with personal photographs, as I wasn't going to get rid of them. During the night the searchlights from the shore were probing the sea for gliders; when one was found other searchlights joined in and we could see and hear the machine guns open fire on the unfortunate lads in the water. The gunners were Italians, the bastards. The next day, when they saw the fleet, they put up their hands and gave up. I would have given them 'give up'. I'd have turned their own machine guns on them for shooting defenceless men. We were lucky we were so far away from land. Mind you, I would have also turned the machine guns on the bloody Yanks that put us here in the first place. Never have liked them ever since. I lay on the wing of the glider and held on as best I could as I had no lifebelt, nor could I swim. When daylight started to appear, we saw a ship in the far distant and I persuaded Tom Arkwright to take off the only thing he had on, a white vest. He stood up and waved it for all he was worth while two of us held his legs, but I guess no one saw it.

A while later we saw lots of landing craft heading towards us. They were bringing in the seaborne troops. I remember one seaman shouting to us, 'Sorry lads can't stop!' Although I understood the reason, I didn't like the idea of being left to die. Not long after that, a naval gunboat came towards us; as it did, the underwater tow of its propellers sucked the wreckage down and I fell off and started to sink. It was then that I saw a strip that I now know was glider canvas being torn off the wing and thrown to me; I grabbed it and pulled myself to the surface. When my head came out of the water Dave Mumford, who'd thrown it, helped me back onto the wing. The gunboat had lowered a rowing boat to pick us up. We shouted and told them to get one of the seriously injured lads, who was floating away. Without any hesitation this very large rating with a blue pullover and woolly hat dived in to rescue him; he seemed to go through the water like a torpedo. He reached him and held him out of the water until the boat reached them. After 10 long hours in the freezing cold water, we'd been rescued. I was so angry because four of the lads didn't make it; they drowned when we first hit the water – those bloody Yanks have got a lot to answer for. We were given a hot drink with rum in it while we stood shivering on deck. It was the best rum I have ever had in my life. If the truth were known I was bloody glad I had survived, as I was certain that I was going to drown a few times during the night. I still think about the lads that never made it. They were all around eighteen years of age and if they were going to die it should have been in combat, not because some bloody pilot wanted to save his own skin!

Captured At Sicily – Bill Halliwell

We were towed by an American tug to Sicily, but when we came under anti-aircraft fire were cast off by the Americans and ditched about 2 miles from the coastal fishing town of Avola. Although the pilots did a textbook landing, the glider flipped and only two of us survived. Dave Crossman was trapped inside the glider after we hit the water and his thigh had been split open. I cut open the fabric with my knife and pulled him out and then I applied a tourniquet and wrapped my shell dressing around it. Part of the wing broke off and the two of us used it to propel ourselves toward land and the salt water helped to congeal the blood flow. Some hours later, we managed to reach the shore in an exhausted state. Waiting for us were Italian troops, and as we got out of the water we were physically beaten. I received a rifle butt to my head that caused me to fall back into the water. With my head throbbing and bleeding, I was unable to help myself and would probably have drowned but for an Italian who pulled me out. A couple of them then hauled and carried me up the cliff face and dumped me unceremoniously onto the ground. I tried to get up to help Dave Crossman, earning myself another bashing from an Italian officer. An English-speaking Italian corporal informed me that my friend would be cared for, so I asked that he get him to a doctor, but shortly after an Italian lieutenant ordered me to help Dave to his feet and for both of us to start walking, even though they had taken away our boots.

Dave simply couldn't walk so I ended up carrying him across my shoulders for around 3 miles, as he was delirious. My back was hurting and my feet were terribly sore and bleeding. I stopped to rest from fatigue, but the Italian lieutenant struck me twice and poked his pistol in my face, threatening to shoot me if I didn't continue walking. Dave still hadn't received any treatment for his wounds and I was sure that he was going to die on my shoulders there was so much blood dripping from the wound. Our destination was a barracks. On arrival we were stripped of our clothes and personal possessions. Naked, I was forced to stand for about two hours while being brutally interrogated by the Italian lieutenant. When I repeatedly protested that his questions and my treatment were against the rules of the Geneva Convention, I was hit in the ribcage with a rifle butt, and ended up so covered with lumps and bruises that I was unable to stand. Apparently my treatment was reported to a colonel, his commanding officer, who angrily dismissed the lieutenant and ordered the guards to help me to an empty room with a bed and blankets, and a young corporal came in and gave me a drink of water, some lemon squash, and a cigarette. He also went and gave Dave the same, although I don't think Dave was in any shape to appreciate it. Although Dave didn't get to see a doctor, an Italian soldier with rudimentary medical skills took off the tourniquet and my shell dressing and rewrapped the wound with a large pad and some bandages. It may have been crude but it probably saved Dave's life.

Despite the attention of a multitude of mosquitoes I was quickly asleep, only to be awakened after a brief interval by with an urgent order to accompany the guards to the colonel, who was standing in lookout tower. He pointed out to sea, and in the pre-dawn mist I could make out the shadowy silhouettes of an Allied invasion fleet. He asked me, 'What are those ships?'

I replied something to the effect that it was 'not likely to be Admiral Nelson parading the ships for his benefit'. I think the joke was wasted upon him though. Suddenly, from one of the ships, there was a huge flash. Moments later, with a tremendous roar, an enormous shell landed about 200 yards from our position and shook the whole camp from top to bottom. This was followed in rapid succession by a host of further projectiles. Hastily, we all retreated downstairs into a 70-foot-deep bunker. With each burst the ground heaved and cracks appeared in the walls, and then two soldiers came in carrying a stretcher, on which lay a wounded soldier. It was the young corporal who had, the night before, given me a drink of water, a cigarette and had shared his lemon squash with Dave Crossman and myself. He was unconscious and dying and all I could do for him was to mop his brow. When he did die I felt very sad, as he'd been the one man who had gone out of his way to help us.

Once the bombardment finished I was summoned once again by the colonel, who was ready to surrender, but two other officers persuaded him to carry on with the fight. The initial attempt to land been repelled because of the forbidding outcrop of rocks on the coast, but a further attempt to the south of these features proved successful. During these events I was left free to roam around their headquarters and so I made my way back to rejoin Dave Crossman, who, although he was seriously hurt, was uncomplaining. From a vantage point I watched the 2nd Battalion of the Hampshire Regiment mount a precise battalion attack that brought them into close proximity to the barracks. The colonel now requested me to approach the attackers, while waving a white flag, and to convey his willingness to surrender. At first I refused, but when he pointed his pistol at me, I protested but in the end naturally accepted his proposal. Taking the white piece of rag they handed me, I approached the Hampshire position, crawling the last fifty yards to a low wall, on my belly, naked. As the noise of battle abated, I called out as loud as possible that I was British, not daring to project my arm in case they opened fire. An answering voice called out, 'Who are you?' I answered, 'I'm English, taken prisoner by the Italians, who now wish to surrender!' After what seemed like an eternity, a voice demanded that I stand up with my hands on my head. Unable, with my hands in this position, to cover myself, I stood naked, half expecting roars of laughter. Confronted by a seemingly empty expanse of barbed wire, as I stood there, six or seven British soldiers slowly rose up into view. They cut through the barbed wire and identified me by means of my identity discs. The Italian colonel and his officers duly surrendered, all except the pig of a lieutenant who had tortured me – he was not among them. The colonel ordered all ranks to join him in captivity and as they filed past, I stood there with a blanket wrapped around me and closely inspected them. Suddenly, two of the enemy soldiers seized one of their own and brought him to me. It was the bastard who had so viciously interrogated me and denied Dave Crossman medical aid. He was now dressed as a rank and file soldier. The sergeant major of the Hampshires had lost two men through the treachery of the Italians in North Africa, and when I informed him of the methods used to interrogate me, he said, 'Leave him to me!' He had him escorted to the back of the building and I heard a burst of fire from a Sten gun. The sergeant major, on returning, said, 'He tried to escape.' I thought at the time that he deserved it. The sergeant major then left to organise transport for Dave Crossman. The last time I saw my friend he was being carried by stretcher into an ambulance to be taken away.

At the battalion HQ, a lieutenant-colonel equipped me with some oversize, old clothes, a jumper and slippers and some emergency rations, which were gratefully accepted. I was then taken to 231 Brigade HQ and after being questioned by the brigade major, I was taken in turn to the commander, Brigadier R. E. Urquhart, who was later to command the 1st Airborne Division at Arnhem. Suffering from a lack of sleep since the start of this operation, I was tightly secured in a Sherman tank, with a blanket to cover me. Despite the noise and smell of the engine, I slept as the tank moved slowly to its destination. When I awoke it was daylight and the tank captain, a member of the 6th Armoured Brigade, explained that my unit was at Syracuse, which was about 50 miles away, and that I should be leaving soon to rejoin them. Before I left, he gave me a letter addressed to any British or American officer, identifying me and explaining my circumstances, which he signed personally. I then set off on foot and had covered about a mile when I came across a corporal from the Military Police. Suddenly, our meeting was disrupted by a large group of armed Italians who emerged from the trees nearby. Nervously, the corporal, who fortunately could speak a smattering of Italian, demanded that they surrender, which thankfully they did. The officer in charge delivered up his pistol and ordered his troops to lay down their arms and to accompany us to the Military Police base at

Avola, a coastal fishing village. After reporting to the military authorities I was supplied with a meal consisting of fresh fried fish and black bread, and lashings of tea, with saccharine and goat's milk. It was just what the doctor ordered.

Interviewed at leisure by the divisional intelligence officer, I told him of my disastrous arrival by glider and of the subsequent events. He already knew of my landing in the sea and informed me that the glider hadn't sunk after all, but was floating just below the surface; the Navy eventually rammed it as it constituted a dangerous hazard to the incoming landing craft. I still think of all the lads still inside it. Some time later, and after a welcome rest, I informed my rescuers that I was anxious to rejoin my unit. They said that unfortunately they were unable to provide me with transport to my destination, still some 30 or 40 miles away. So off I set again, this time with a Sten gun and several magazines in case of trouble. After I had covered about 3 miles, with a rag around my head and neck to guard against the oppressive heat of the Sicilian sun, quite suddenly an armoured scout car belonging to the 6th Armoured Brigade overtook me. The officer in command, a lieutenant-colonel of the Grenadier Guards, was unimpressed by my apparel and curious as to my status. After reading the letter I was carrying he acknowledged that, coincidentally, he had been made aware of my fate and so welcomed me aboard. He informed me that he would be crossing over our original target, the Ponte Grande Bridge, en route to Augusta. He informed me of the terrible losses sustained by the Air Landing Brigade and the South Staffs in particular, who lost all but thirty men. Proceeding on our way, we were strafed by a lone Messerschmitt 109. Missing us at the first attempt, it circled for a further attack but was beaten off by the small arms fire of nearby British troops. They dropped me off at the bridge, which has been renamed Pegasus Bridge, in honour of the 300 men of the 2nd Battalion, South Staffordshire Regiment who gave their lives to capture it.

As to the battle, the South Staffs and the Border Regiment attacked the bridge in an action that continued all through the night. Once captured, a meagre force of eighty-five men remaining, under the leadership of the deputy brigade commander, Colonel Jones, held on grimly until around 5 p.m.; down now to only thirty men, mostly wounded, out of ammunition, and exhausted after a succession of hand-to-hand encounters, they were forced to surrender. The relieving force, 5th Corps of the 8th Army, was hours late, having been held up by a spirited defence made up mostly of Germans. The Italians, however, were unable to destroy the bridge because of the success of our engineers, who had dismantled all the wiring and charges, dropping them into the river. So angry were the Italians they hanged two glider pilots and were preparing to hang a Roman Catholic chaplain when No. 3 Commando, in a determined assault, recaptured the position and killed the would-be executioners. Searching again for my unit, I came across one of those who'd survived, who guided me to their position, and I was greeted like a long-lost friend. After a welcome meal and the opportunity to wash, shave and change my clothes, I went to pay my respects to my dead comrades in a building set aside for their bodies. There were about 200 of them, but none of my anti-tank comrades, and I unashamedly shed tears at the sight of all these dead comrades.

Cast Adrift – Barry Webber

After about two and a half hours' flying, we sighted the Sicilian coast and saw the searchlights, flak and machine-gun tracers. From a distance it looked like a fireworks display. We were still a few miles from the coast when suddenly we felt the towrope released by the tug; they weren't supposed to do that – it was the glider pilot's job to do it. The next thing I heard was our Scottish pilot shouting to us that we were coming down in the sea. After that, it seemed like no time at all before the glider was in the water and sinking. To this day I wonder how the pilot landed that glider as he did. It was entirely due to him that we survived as there was a gale blowing, and with the roughness of the waves it was a miraculous feat. When the glider hit the sea the water came pouring in and in no time at all was lapping round our knees. I used my rifle butt and smashed through the fuselage, emerging under the wing of the glider. As my movements were considerably hampered by the weight of my kit, I decided to get rid of it, and I finished up wearing only my underpants. Fortunately, the wings and front of the glider remained afloat, so I scrambled onto the wings and I found five others already there. The body of the glider containing the jeep and trailer had broken off and must have gone straight down. The remaining four men must have drowned and went down with it as I never saw them again. We were expecting a dingy to be dropped from the tug, as that is what they were supposed to do in case of emergencies. Well, the sod didn't do that either; he just scarpered, the bloody gutless bastard. The coward must have said, 'I'm alright Jack, those buggers can die.' After collecting ourselves together, we found we were about 2 miles from the coast and roughly in the middle of the bay. The sea was rough and the waves were considerable, and with each successive wave the nose of the glider was lifted up and then crashed down again. During the night we imagined we were drifting in towards the coast, but in actual fact we were going the other way. I was cold, wet and uncomfortable. One consolation – the glider was standing up well to the buffeting it was getting, and it seemed to be keeping its buoyancy. The hours passed slowly until dawn came. It was a fantastic sight that greeted us at first light. During the night the invasion force had gathered, and there was a huge fleet of ships anchored in the bay. In the misty light we could see a line of assault boats approaching with a gunboat leading them. It was evident that they were heading for the beach and we thought they wouldn't bother with us, but the last assault boat pulled alongside and we were hailed by megaphone: 'Who are you?'

Quick as a flash, our officer shouted, 'We're bloody British – who did you expect, Noah and his Ark?' and to our great relief they stopped and took us aboard.

Overseas – Ray Goldie

November 1942 saw the 1st Brigade, as part of a huge escorted convoy, on a long and tortuous voyage heading for the port of Algiers as a component part of Operation Torch, tasked to seize and occupy northern Tunisia to cut off Rommel's escape route to occupied Europe. The three battalions of the Brigade were each given a specific objective, to deny the enemy vital airfields in the vicinity of Tunis. The 1st Battalion dropped unopposed on an airfield at Souk-el-Arba, leaving the airfield in the hands of the friendly French garrison while we proceeded in commandeered French vehicles to Beja, a primary objective situated at a vital road junction. It was a requirement to persuade the French garrison to support the Allies. To convince them that we were a considerable force, we marched through the town twice, at intervals, each time dressed differently, once with steel helmets on and again with red berets, well spread out and in different formations on both occasions – it worked. The weather over the next two months deteriorated rapidly. It became freezing cold with incessant rain, so the battalion was reluctantly forced to adopt a defensive role, occasionally moving to a fresh area, the monotony relieved only by the numerous fighting patrols sent out to reconnoitre the enemy positions. Several such patrols became legendary, unfortunately resulting in many casualties, depriving the battalion of the services of outstanding soldiers. One such casualty was the CO, Lieutenant-Colonel Hill; command of the battalion was then taken over by Major Alastair Pearson, who was to become one of the most famous battalion legends of them all. It was during this period that I acquired my only war souvenir, a German cutthroat razor, the expert use of which I mastered, very slowly and very bloodily. Sometime in early January, we were withdrawn from the front line and returned to our base in Algiers.

On arrival I reported sick and was despatched to the hospital. On the original voyage from England, I contracted an ear infection that, having been untreated for two months, got progressively worse. It was diagnosed at that stage as quite serious and possibly contagious, so I was confined there for the duration of the campaign. It was here that I found that having the red beret does not automatically find favour with the hospital nurses. Having passed the horrors of Hardwick, I failed to overcome the sturdy but equally horrendous defences of nurse Wendy C., a veritable Venus de Milo, something I regretted for many months afterwards. After a period of convalescence I returned to the battalion to find, to my horror, that it had virtually ceased to exist as I remembered it. Familiar faces were very few and far between. I had missed a long period of intense training and my physical fitness would obviously have been suspect, so I was assigned to a platoon commander, one of the new, yet to be blooded replacements, as his batman, a career move to which I was singularly unsuited.

The evening of 13 July 1943 saw us winging our way across the Mediterranean, en route for Sicily, to capture a vital bridge at Primosole in Catania. The journey was uneventful until the pilot took evasive action to counter an attack by a German plane, then as we approached the coast of Sicily the Allied invasion fleet fired on us because we had strayed into a forbidden zone. The pilot again took violent evasive action, pitching us forward to the floor of the aircraft, an ominous sign for the course of the coming battle. As we crossed the coast, we stood up and hooked on and checked the static line of the man in front. I was jumping number two after the lieutenant and so had a perfect view through the doorway. Although it was around 2200 hours and would normally be dark, the landscape seemed ablaze with what seemed like burning undergrowth and haystacks, and I could clearly hear the noise of anti-aircraft gunfire above the roar of the engines. When the green light came we charged as fast as we could out into the night sky. I descended quite rapidly, although all of us seemed to be drifting apart. I hit the deck in regulation fashion, but quite hard, and as I looked up I could see the telltale trail of tracer bullets, curving upwards toward the remainder of the stick, who were still suspended in the air.

As I gathered in my parachute, I realised that two of my rigging lines had been severed, presumably by these selfsame tracer bullets. It shocked me, and for the first time in my life I realised someone was trying to kill me. Standing up, I looked for my lieutenant, but in vain, and I never saw him again. Together with the remainder of the platoon, and under the leadership of our sergeant, we set a course for our objective. On the way we encountered a number of Italian troops, some with suitcases and all eager to surrender. Leaving them protesting bitterly, we proceeded on our bearing, with the sounds of battle growing every more acute as we neared the bridge. Our strength, once we assembled ready for the assault on the bridge, was well under what we needed; consequently the composition of our forces was urgently revised and as such I found myself in the group assigned to the assault and seizure of the bridge.

We proceeded in single file and I was in the rear. We moved along an embankment that sloped down from the road. The other side of the road was a long row of high factory buildings that we understood would be occupied by our own men. Suddenly, a speeding vehicle passed us. Before we could do anything it exploded and burst into flames, accompanied by screams of agony as the occupants perished; they'd run over a mine in the road. Standing in the glow of the flames on the embankment was an Italian soldier with a rifle. He'd been totally ignored by those in front of me. My instinctive reaction was that it would be dangerous to leave him behind us, with him knowing the strength of our force and our direction of advance, so I climbed the embankment and motioned him to come with me. Without warning, a grenade landed between us and exploded, killing him and blowing me over. When I staggered to my feet, the blood from my facial wounds had saturated my smock. As I stood there in shock a figure in a smock approached me and asked, 'Where's S Company, mate?'

'Sod the stupid 'S' Company, I'm bloody bleeding to death! Where's the bloody MO?' I yelled. When I eventually got to the MO, he bandaged my wounds and gave me a shot of morphine and I was directed to join the growing band of wounded some distance along the riverbank, amid tall reeds. We remained there the rest of that night, all the next day and the following night, constantly tormented by the ceaseless bites of mosquitoes, interspersed with frequent sounds of fighting, sometimes nearby, sometimes in the near distance. It was clear that someone was determined to get the bridge back. We received word that the relieving force of British troops was close at hand. By now, the sounds of battle were constant and shelling, mortar fire and the distinct chatter of German machine guns could be heard. It was a pitched battle, with neither side willing to give an inch. At one point we heard German tanks being used. None of us risked moving as we would of little help to our side, the state we were in, and most of us didn't have any weapons anyway. Just then, on the opposite bank, there emerged the welcome sight of a British tank and some light armoured cars, followed up by infantry.

We wounded were collected by ambulance and put on board a Red Cross ship bound for Alexandria. One of the badly wounded soldiers was informed that a blood transfusion was imperative if he was to live. He was German SS, and that the blood he was to receive was British was unacceptable to him, so he rejected it out of hand, and consequently he became the only burial at sea that I have witnessed – serves the bugger right! The ward to which I was assigned in the hospital at Alexandria was totally American, except for myself, so when General Eisenhower toured the hospital, handing out Purple Hearts, it is not surprising that I was included as a recipient. The mistake, however, was quickly noticed and in a very short time the buggers took mine back, even though I complained bitterly that I was wounded too. It's nice to know our allies are as tight as a fish's arse when giving out medals for bleeding to death! Because the battalion was again under strength and destined to play a leading role in the invasion of Italy, my stay at the hospital ended very abruptly; happily recovered from a serious bout of malaria, resulting from the mosquito bites sustained in Sicily, but before any major surgery could take place, I rejoined the battalion in good time to play my part.

Just Made It – Jim Wallwork

On the day of the invasion of Sicily, I flew a Waco with a lieutenant, ten riflemen, and a hand-trailer full of ammunition. The tug pilots were Americans, flying Dakotas, which to be fair to them had no self-sealing tanks and no armoured plate. Their orders were to avoid flak at all costs. When they approached the coastline and flak began to appear, most of them cast off their gliders and turned back to sea. As a consequence of being let go too far out, twenty of the twenty-four gliders never made it to shore, and many of the men were drowned. In my case, I kept telling the tug pilot, 'Get In – Get In!'

But instead, the pilot turned away to sea, made a second run, and called to me to 'Drop Off!'

I refused point blank, seeing that the coast was too far away, and I again yelled out, 'Get In – Get In!'

The pilot tried a third time, but still I refused to release. I had the distinct feeling he was going to cast me off, but to be fair to him, he didn't. On the fourth pass, the pilot said calmly but firmly, 'James, I'm going now. You've got to let go.'

So I let go, thinking I could just make it. And I did, skidding in just over the beach, on a little rough field, fairly close to an Italian machine-gun nest. The Italians opened fire and we were all forced to jump out really quickly as the glider was getting chopped to bits. I turned my Sten gun on them, thinking, 'Right, this will do you buggers.' But when I pulled the trigger nothing happened. The Sten had misfired, but the platoon Bren-gunner knocked the post out and made a right mess of them. The section then began to unload the glider and while that was happening the lieutenant asked me, 'Well, where in the hell are we? Do you know where we are?'

I replied, 'As a matter of fact, Sir, I think you should be congratulated. You are probably the first Allied officer to attack the soft underbelly of Europe through the toe of Italy.' I don't think he was too pleased!

Beaten by a Shower Bath – Bernard Howarth

After the debacle that was the assault on Sicily, where quite a few American pilots cast gliders off over the sea and headed for home because of the intense anti-aircraft fire from the coastal gun batteries, one of the gliders had my mate Barry and twenty-seven others on board, all of whom were expecting to land on Sicily. At one point they felt the glider do a long sweeping turn and didn't think much of. But an hour later some of them were beginning to wonder when they would be cast off. Even so, the pilots appeared to be happy so nobody said a thing. In the end they were finally cast off in broad daylight and landed on a long sandy beach. The pilots had not said a word so they charged out of the glider and did all round protection, but far from encountering German troops, or even Italians, they were amazed to find that their whole invasion force had apparently been beaten to Sicily by a RASC Mobile Bath Unit that passed by on a road about 300 yards to their front. Then the truth dawned on them. They were not in Sicily at all; they had landed back on the mainland. The glider pilots flying the aircraft had no choice but to follow the American tow aircraft as it turned because they were still well out over the sea and dare not risk casting off. Having flown back to the mainland, the American pilot then cast them adrift near the beach rather than risk their wrath if they landed back at the airfield. In the end seven gliders were towed back to North Africa, including Barry's; one even ended up in Malta. None of the American pilots were punished, as the Allied high command didn't want to cause a political rift between the two forces. It was left to members of the 1st Airborne Division to seek justice for themselves, which in a number of cases they did.

You're Bloody Late – Phillip Saunders
Of the gliders carrying the 1st Airlanding Brigade that reached Sicily for the attack on the Primosole Bridge, most were scattered all across the south-east corner of the island, and many of us spent the day trying to find our units. Countless groups linked up with other groups as they went along. Our platoon from the 2nd Battalion was an extreme case. Our Waco glider, having been cast off in the wrong place, landed miles to the west of our LZ so it wasn't until the early evening some two days later that we finally rejoined the battalion, having suffered no casualties despite numerous brushes with the Italians, who seemed to be everywhere. Luckily, most of them seemed to want to surrender, although not all, but one look at us and the majority were quite willing to let us go without any problems. We managed to bring all of our equipment with us, including a handcart full of ammunition that one of the lads wanted to throw down the nearest hole, but as our platoon commander said, 'If you do, both the platoon sergeant and I will throw you down after it.'

When we arrived and mixed with the rest of the lads, someone was heard to say, 'Typical, yus wankers would bloody miss the time 'o' day if it wasn't on yus lieutenant's watch!'

The lieutenant, who was standing nearby, answered for the rest of us, 'That can't be true as I lost my watch on landing.' The lads all burst out laughing.

Sicily Bound – George Pratt

We got keyed up for a hot reception from enemy flak. Well, they didn't disappoint us. It was truly terrifying as it exploded in the sky all around us. It was then that our aircraft was hit in the port side engine; it choked up, burst into flame and suddenly stopped. From then on the pilots had one hell of a job keeping us in the air. We were tossed from one side of the plane to the other, waiting to get the order for 'Action Stations'. We knew that any second it would be time for us to jump. On came the red light and the dispatcher yelled 'Action Stations! – Red On!' and we all moved towards the door, with the lieutenant standing right in front of it. The green came on instantly; there was no need for the dispatcher to say anything, we just went. It was just like jumping into an inferno; the countryside for miles was ablaze with tracer bullets and flak. What was worse, the aircraft had lost height and we'd jumped from about 250 feet. As my parachute opened I saw it glide in a flaming ball toward the ground then explode on impact – only the dispatcher got out. In no time at all I hit the ground; I'd hardly had time to lower my kitbag. It was such a shock that I lay there for several seconds before getting up, and it took me several seconds to pull myself together as I had a rough landing, but when I got up I had an even bigger shock. I found that something had severed the rope attaching my kitbag to me. All I had was 6 feet of rope. There was nothing else for it but to head for the bridge, our target. I wasn't sure of my exact position, but I went forward about 200 yards and took a look round but couldn't see anything, but I could hear enemy voices – you can't mistake German accents. I didn't fancy that at all, as I had no proper weapons, just two hand grenades and a fighting knife, so I scrambled through the bushes under cover of darkness.

It was then that I saw another parachute hanging over some telegraph wires. I stopped and a quivering, uncertain whispered voice came from a bush: 'Who's that?'

For the life of me, fancy asking, 'Who's that?' I could have been a German for all he knew. Anyway, I quickly gave the password. The poor devil couldn't have been more than eighteen years of age, and he was scared stiff as this was his first time in combat. Just like me, all he had was hand grenades and he was ready to throw one at me if I had been the enemy. We had another look round and we could still hear enemy voices, even nearer than before, and more of them; then I said, 'Let's go, it's dangerous hanging around near parachutes,' so we went and looked for anyone else, and we found another of the lads not far away, but he was slightly hurt from a bad landing. We still had to get to our containers for our weapons as we had nothing but the grenades to defend ourselves. We eventually found one – what a sight! Then my heart went down into my boots as the parachute of the container had failed to open and it crashed to the ground; the weapons were smashed beyond repair, absolutely unserviceable.

While this went on bullets had begun to fly all over the place, so you can guess what we felt like. From the time we jumped until now couldn't have been more than fifteen minutes. At least we now had some idea where we were by the lie of the land and the firing that was going on. So we decided to head for our objective, the bridge about 1,000 yards away. On our way we stumbled across a container with weapons in it; I could have jumped for joy. So we armed ourselves with a Bren gun and two rifles and stocked up on ammunition. This cheered us up because we could at least defend ourselves. The attack on the bridge was now in full swing so we joined it and let fly with all we had. We finally took the bridge after half an hour of really vicious fighting as there were two concrete bunkers with machine guns, one either side of the road, that were mutually supporting, so we took a lot of casualties. Once we put them out of action the rest of the Italian defenders took to their heels. We now had to dig in and wait for a counter-attack that would probably be coming from both the Italians and the Germans.

There were bodies all over the place, both theirs and ours. The biggest problem was holding the bridge once we got it. What we didn't know at the time was that the Germans had dropped paratroopers near the bridge with the idea of giving us a surprise attack at dawn. Fortunately, those two bunkers on the bridge now provided them with a headache. And the positions we'd dug around them gave us good cover from the mortars they began using. Initially, we managed to give them a good fight for their money. Yet this was not the end by a long chalk: Jerry wouldn't give up that easily and he had the numbers, whereas every man we lost we couldn't replace. As the day wore on, we had more and more casualties. Anyone who could still fire a weapon stayed where he was. The Fallschirmjägers were combat-hardened and single-minded, determined to take the bridge. They leapfrogged forward in small groups, covering each other the whole way, making it hard to pin them down, and they used their mortars very effectively.

My Bren gun hardly stopped firing the whole time. Then, one the lads next to me was shot in the face; his head literally exploded and sent bits of tissue and bone all over me. Like an automaton, he staggered backwards before colliding with the back wall, and slid down it, leaving a big blood smear where the back of his head had contacted the wall. Not five minutes later, the young lad who'd landed with me got killed; he was flung onto his back having been shot in the chest, blood pouring out of the wound. How I didn't get killed I don't know as enough bullets were coming through the slit to kill a dozen of us. Jerry was only 80 yards away by then. At that range it was difficult not to hit someone, and I can honestly say I shot quite a few, but the ammo was still my main worry and I had to be very frugal when I fired to make it last. I only had two men left in my section and they were both wounded. One was giving me fresh magazines while the other one loaded new ones for me.

The final blow was the shoulder-fired Panzerfaust anti-tank rocket. The Fallschirmjäger began using them once they were within range, about 60 yards. First they took out the bunker on my left, and then it was my turn.

I got one of them as he was about to fire. I must have hit him with ten rounds I was so determined that he wasn't going to fire at me. By now one of the other lads with me had been killed giving me a new magazine and just as I thought, 'This is it – I'd better move or get killed,' I got the order that I had to hold on and give the wounded men cover as they withdrew over the bridge. I was praying they would get a move on so that I could get the hell out of there before the bunker got flattened. When I heard the whistle I knew it was time to move, and none too soon, as the moment I skedaddled out that door there was a huge explosion and I was thrown to the ground. I got up and sprinted across the bridge, expecting at any moment to be shot. Within 10 minutes they had overrun us; we simply couldn't stop them and we had to surrender or get annihilated, but they'd lost a lot of men in the process, and so had we.

Singing Opera – Desmond Haggerty

Me and Ernie landed in Sicily, miles from anywhere, and we were heading to where the battalion was supposed to be when we spotted about 120 or so Italians near a cave. Just as we saw them, they saw us. We thought we were certain to be captured, as we had no hope of fighting them. The next thing we know, their officer waved a white flag and walked over to us. Using sign language, he explained they wanted to surrender to us. We thought it was some kind of a joke, but it wasn't. They were all armed and could have killed or captured us without any problems at all, but the funny thing was they were carrying suitcases. It was if they were going to Clacton-by-the-Sea for a holiday and were going to do a bit of grouse shooting along the way. They'd clearly made their preparations to surrender some time in advance and we just happened to be there. We didn't want to look after so many of them in case the Germans came along, so we told them to throw their weapons into a pile and walk toward the advancing 8th Army, and they were quite happy about that and off they went toward the coast, singing as they walked. I'd been in the desert with Wavell when we captured thousands of them, but I'd never heard them sing something like 'O Solo Mia' at the top of their voices. As they left, Ernie turned to me and said, 'Brum, how come the Italians get suitcases and we only get kitbags?'

Jokingly, I told him, 'You can't carry those fancy opera records in kitbags mate, they'd break!'

He said, 'That opera singing is like bloody tomcats howling with their nuts cut off!'

I had to smile. 'I'm told the Yank gangsters like Al Capone liked it as well!'

He didn't seem too impressed by that and said, 'That explains a lot about the Yank gangsters then!' And we carried on walking.

A Picture of Tunisia – Tom Ashley

One night, my company was to carry out a night raid on an Italian encampment that was about 10 miles away, on the other side of an adjoining valley. We followed a winding trail alongside a narrow-gauge railway which first meant going very quietly through some sparsely populated and uninteresting piece of ground. Our object was to surprise the Italians when the majority of them would be asleep. As we quietly moved through the valley on a beautiful moonlit night, the stillness of the air was broken only by the distant chorus of giant bullfrogs croaking somewhere to our flank, which grew progressively louder as we approached, rising to a crescendo and then fading away again in the distance as we plodded quietly on. We expected to be challenged at any time from someone stationed in the villages, but we weren't. For every mile of the journey, my 3-inch mortar equipment seemed to double in weight. Each bomb-carrier had six bombs weighing ten pounds each that fitted into a type of harness that went across the shoulders like a waistcoat, while the mortar crew carried two bombs and a part of the mortar each. When we got within a quarter of a mile or so of the Italian camp, we left the path alongside the railway line and laboriously worked our way up the steep slope onto the hillside. When we got there we moved quietly forward to a vantage point overlooking the camp. The perimeter was lit up like Blackpool Illuminations so we had a perfect marker to aim at. We lost no time in getting organised. Soon, every man was in his position with all the mortars set up, mounted for action and ready for the attack. A red flare zoomed into the night sky and for a brief moment seemed to hang in mid-air, bathing the camp below in a crimson glow. This was the moment we'd been waiting for. The company 2IC's whistle blew for us to 'Fire!' and mortar shells rained down on the huts that housed the unsuspecting sleeping Italian troops. Bill, my mate, shouted across, 'I don't like this idea, Nev. It bloody well seems like taking an unfair advantage!'

I've never got involved in any arguments about 'All's fair in love and war' as I'd seen too many of our own lads killed over the past months, but thought it helped considerably in easing Bill's conscience and my tension that had built up waiting for the fireworks to start. Pandemonium had now broken out down below as the cries and screams of terror rent the sky. Men ran here and there half-dressed, some only in their underwear. And as they came out of the huts they ran straight into the stream of Bren gun and rifle fire, which had been lined up for this very purpose. More flares added light to the subject, the strange glow giving a theatrical effect to the whole scene of confusion. Those in the gallery positions high on the hill were comparatively unmoved emotionally by the look of unrealism about it all. The Italians helped unwittingly in their own destruction by switching on lights in many of the huts. Then fires broke out, leaving the camp a blazing inferno. Some of the Italians, after getting over the initial shock, let blast in the general direction of the hillside positions, but this was mostly ineffective and of no great concentration at all. We had just received orders to dismantle the 3-inch mortars and prepare to withdraw when a tumultuous explosion occurred to the right of our positions, giving off a blinding flash and sending lumps of earth, branches and fragments of rock whistling through the air above our heads. We learned later that a detonator had been accidentally ignited, setting off a stack of mines, killing a dozen or so members of a small detachment of Royal Engineers who were carrying them, wounding a number of others by flying shrapnel from the terrible blast.

The accident marred what would otherwise have been a completely successful operation. We quickly clambered down the rocky slopes, carrying some of the more seriously wounded to the railway track in the valley below where we commandeered a small, manually operated truck used by the railway workers for maintenance work along the line. This proved ideal as an ambulance for taking the badly wounded back to our positions. After a couple of hours of the long, weary trudge back, the first sight of daylight came, giving rise to a warm grumbling wind which seemed to be urging us to hurry along. The faces of the wounded lads were pale and drawn in the light of the early morning sky, emphasised by the triangle of yellow coloured silk material which we wore around our throats as a means of identifying ourselves to any Allied aircraft that might swoop down upon us. We would do this by holding out the loose ends in front so that the aircraft above could spot the coloured material. Suddenly, from over the hills, as if crystallised in the early morning light, there appeared two black-crossed fighter planes, sweeping their way along the railway track. Their cannon blazed away, spitting out hot lead as we raced for our lives to the shelter of a dip in the side of the track. The deafening roar of the aircraft gradually faded as they disappeared over the hills, allowing us to breathe freely again. We figured that they probably had a more important assignment than us to deal with that morning. By some miracle, the wounded had not suffered any further injury. The German pilots were probably more interested in us, the moving targets, diving for cover in the ditches.

By the beginning of January 1943, the brigade was taken back to rest at Boufarik, a village near Algiers. The battalion put up at the farm of Saint Charles. It was situated in a beautiful setting of tangerine groves, with lovely blossoms giving splashes of bright colour and the outline of a range of purple hills fading away in the background. At the farm there were huge vats where the wines were fermented and it was not unusual to see one of the boys, after coming home the worse for drink late at night, with his mouth stuck under the tap at the base of one of the vats. Myself, Joe and Bill used to go down to Algiers and explore the dimly lit cafés and bars. Sampling the various wines, which could be bought cheaply, we would sit sheltering in the shade of the palms in the big squares adjoining the boulevards, which were lined with colourful orange trees. Beneath these trees, Arabs sold glasses of iced lemonade, their cries of 'Cool Johnnie, Cool!' sounding above the tinkling of ice cubes as the vendor shook his jug at the appearance of another prospective customer. It was difficult not to notice the varying shades of sun tan on the bodies of service personnel and others who had come to Algiers for a rest period as they stretched out cross-shaped like victims on the beaches in the noonday sun.

The shoeshine boy in these places was certainly a person of some importance, with a really professional touch to his work. His kit box consisted of a choice of brushes and polishing cloths, the polish being mixed with gasoline to bring up a glossy surface from deep within the leather. The importance attached to having one's shoes shined seemed to be an obsession with so many people, especially the officers. In the sophisticated 'joints', half-naked Arab girls could be seen dancing to the sensuous rhythm of weird, almost barbaric, tunes from wailing instruments, accompanied by the jingling of coin bracelets which adorned their dusky arms and ankles as they moved and swayed around, leaving behind them the mingled scent of flowers and sweaty flesh.

There were a huge number of brothels in Algiers, usually kept by some 'Madame Something-or-Other' who paid the girls who worked for her on a commission basis by the number of clients they 'entertained' in their 'labour of love'. These places were kept under close scrutiny by the Military Police and other authorities and raided from time to time. Another place of great interest was the Casbah, the notorious Arab quarter of the city that was a refuge for thieves, tricksters and many other shady characters wanting to escape the long arm of the law. It was a maze of narrow, foul-smelling streets and intricate patterns of alleyways with their little arched doorways leading into a labyrinth of passages and tiled courtyards which often led again into seemingly endless alleys not much wider than the full span of a man's arms. It was rumoured that a Coldstream Guardsman had been found castrated with his testicles stuffed into his mouth but how true this was, we never did find out.

Troops were advised never to go unaccompanied through these parts, as many Arabs were believed to be pro-German.

During this period of respite at the farm, the lads often sat around talking in their so-called bunker, a stone cellar that housed the huge fermenting vats. Among the topics of conversation that arose was the question of religion and whether one believed in God and if so, what was one's conception of God? Little Taff Williams, a dark, quiet and serious chap, argued that man's purpose on Earth, if carried out as it was meant to be, was to express God in his own way of life, and the reason why all this killing was allowed to go on between peoples and nations was because God has given men the freedom of choice to choose between good and evil, and if there was any divine intervention in any way by a supreme power, whenever it was thought necessary by an action brought about by man's folly, man would be reduced to an automaton or robot. However, we were soon to be awakened from our reveries as we heard the orders that the brigade was to go back to Tunisia to reinforce the line where the enemy had broken through. This time they were to go by sea as far as Bone. It was a pleasant little cruise in the Commando ship, HMS *Beatrix*. From there, trucks then took us to our positions in the line, where we were to spend the next few months as infantry. By this time, the brigade was getting back nearly to full strength again as we had been joined by reinforcements from home and many of the less seriously wounded had recovered and rejoined, fit and ready for action. The more serious casualties had been operated on in the field by the doctors and orderlies of the 6th Parachute Field Ambulance, who parachuted in with the fighting troops and thoroughly distinguished themselves as men of skill and courage, surpassed by none. Lieutenant Robb, the surgeon, having injured his knee on the parachute drop at Souk-el-Arba, managed to conceal the fact and carried on his work leading his surgical team, performing 162 operations in the field with only one patient dying in their hands.

On one occasion, when they were holding positions in the hills in the Medjez-el-Bab section of the line, I was acting as lookout from the roof of an old farmhouse, which the company was using as its HQ. As I watched, a group of about six unescorted Blenheim bombers returning from a bombing raid on Bizerta flew overhead. Suddenly, a pack of Messerschmitts appeared from out of the clouds and attacked the low-flying bombers from above. What a sense of dismay and helplessness I felt as the fighters opened up and flashes came from behind the Blenheims. Flames and black smoke spewed out from their engines as they were mercilessly shot down, each of them in turn leaving a trail of smoke as they crashed into the surrounding hills and exploded. One rear gunner continued firing as his aircraft ploughed into the mountain, his incendiary shells clearly visible in the sky. There was no hope of surviving the flaming holocaust, which left nothing but a mass of debris. Another farm which many of the lads of the battalion will remember was 'Coxon's Farm', so called because the attack on it was made by A Company, led by Major Coxon, a large, bald-headed, broad-shouldered man who seemed to revel in the skirmishes they were having, leading from the front and loving every minute of it.

It appears that after capturing the farm, which was held previously by the Germans, some of the lads killed and ate a pig. Their horror can only be imagined when they noticed later that the pigs were fattening themselves up on the corpses of the dead Jerries that lay about the yard. Many others had been dead for days in a huge water storage tank, floating on the surface, their bodies grotesquely bloated, blown up like balloons and almost comical in a macabre sort of way. On countless nights while standing shivering on guard duty against the stone walls of the farm outhouses, our only companions were the fat and repulsive rats, silhouetted in the clear night sky as they crawled along the rough walls; I gave a shudder as a slight feeling of nausea passed over me. I would feel thankful for the sight of Bill, who invariably did guard duty at the same time as me, standing at the far end of the yard, just a dark shadow with no visible personality, like me wishing away the hours, envious of our mates inside the barns and stretched out luxuriously on the rough stone floors with the warmth of a blanket.

That Sinking Feeling – Bill (Bilbo) Aldcroft

In December 1942 some 200 of us new paratroopers were bound
for North Africa on the SS *Strathallen*, an ex-passenger liner,
probably luxurious but a different kettle of fish when carrying
5,000 troops. Soon we slipped down the Clyde to take up a
station in what was a very large convoy of ships. We took a wide
sweep around Ireland in order to avoid U-boats. We met very
heavy seas in the Bay of Biscay and it was something of a relief
to enter the Mediterranean, and quite a novelty to see towns full
of lights on both Moroccan and Spanish shores. The weather
was vastly different to that which we had left in Glasgow. We
actually started to enjoy the voyage, then a few days later at
around 0100 hours there was a terrific roaring crash that shook
the ship from stem to stern – the poor *Strathallen* seemed to
be shivering and shaking for what seemed like minutes. We
realised that we had been torpedoed, pitch darkness of course,
but emergency lights were quickly taken from their glass cases
and lit. I don't remember any panic; in fact I am sure the
transition from living deck to boat stations was very orderly
by all units who were aboard. Nevertheless, I was happy to see
the sky when we emerged on to our boat deck, very high on the
ship. By the time we got to our boat station all the lifeboats were
away; only those on one side of the ship could be used anyway
as by now the *Strathallen* was listing badly. In any case, I don't
think there were enough lifeboats for 5,000 people.

Naturally there was a certain amount of confusion on deck
but the ship's captain quickly sorted it out, and by the tone
of his voice he was certainly Anglo-Saxon. It was: 'Get those
fucking lifeboats away from my ship, get those people out of
the water, who fucking ordered them in anyway, and the rest
of you shut your fucking row, you are making enough noise
to wake fucking Davy Jones!'

My first realisation on our boat station was that we were
completely alone; the rest of the convoy had gone. It was convoy
rules; you never stopped for a sinking ship. Next thought then
was, 'What do I do if I have to go in the drink?' At the time I
didn't think much of those kapok Mae West life jackets, nor of
the sea itself, though it looked calm enough. I eventually espied

wooden dining chairs in one adjacent saloon; I thought one of those would do, and then I saw a large lifebelt hanging on the rail and thought, that's better, so I commandeered it and agreed to share it with the man next to me. There were others who saw the funny side of this and I wasn't allowed to forget the incident for months afterwards; me, I think they were just jealous and would have liked the lifebelt for themselves. Nothing much happened during the rest of the night-time hours; the silence was eerie, broken only once in a while by the captain yelling at someone or other for stuffing up. He called for volunteers from the Engineer unit, especially those who had knowledge of ships' engines, but by now the engine room was almost underwater. When dawn came we were joined by an ocean-going tug and a couple of destroyers; they got lines aboard, which broke very easily with the tension on them.

An RAF Catalina flying boat passed low; one of the aircrew was trying to give us comfort by giving the 'V' sign but someone should have told him the 'V' sign required the palm of the hand to be outwards, not inwards. By now all the lifeboats had disappeared and in the morning we heard that one of these, with Army nurses on board, had been overturned by panic-stricken lascars, causing loss of life. The crew of the *Strathallen* was predominantly lascar and apparently their contracts gave them prior use of lifeboats in situations like this. Only five or six were left were on board in the morning, and I remember one was very good. He did his best to get us food by taking small groups from each boat station down to the galley to bring food back. By now more destroyers were arriving and each started to take people off, beginning with the lower boat stations. Around 1400 hours it was our turn and we were more or less the last off. The first lad off did a side right parachute landing onto the destroyer's deck and that made everyone laugh, so the rest of us did the same – the matelots all thought we were mad.

We arrived in the port of Oran just after darkness and gave three rousing cheers as the *Pathfinder* slipped away into the night. I remember thinking, 'Blow that for a life.' Very soon we were put aboard SS *Duchess of Bedford*, a real cold tub this one. Soon we were off on the final leg to Algiers, then to a tented camp at

Maison Carrée about 5 or 6 miles down the coast, where we were kitted out, having lost all but what we stood in on the *Strathallen*. While we were there, Admiral Darlan was assassinated; he was Vichy Commander North Africa, but must have turned over to the Allies, as he was buried with full military honours. We spent Christmas Day at Maison Carrée – no turkey or plum duff though. A couple of days later we went by train up through Algeria to join 2nd Battalion in Tunisia; although the journey was only 1,000 miles or so, it would take days, making frequent stops to gather wood to fire the engine's boiler. Eventually we arrived at Beja, and in a school we met members of the original battalion. You could tell by their looks what they were thinking, something like 'Gawd, look what they've sent us', in typical old soldier style. We told them of our ordeal and said, 'Aren't we entitled to Survivors' Leave?' Do you know, they completely ignored us and talked only of a place called Depienne; however, it doesn't take Paras long to get friendly. I always remember the battles for Corkwood, savage, bloody battles where we and the Germans lost a lot of men over a piece of ground that was left behind once it was over. It may have been left behind but the ground was saturated in blood and there were a lot of good men on both sides who still remain in graves we dug before leaving.

Tunisia – The War in the Heat – Tom Davies

As the 1st Battalion moved into Souk el-Arba, a French Army commander met us with some of his men, who were obviously impressed and much heartened by our appearance, and they offered to join us. The assistance of a French intelligence officer who could speak Arabic and acted as an interpreter when Arabs were brought in for questioning proved invaluable in gaining information on the whereabouts and movements of the German forces in the area. As we entered the village of Souk el-Arba, a lone German bomber flew low over us, its black crosses clearly visible, probably returning safely to base from a bombing mission. Life in these remote parts, where even the wheel is not frequently used on the sparse mountainsides, is certainly no bed of roses. The locals' very meagre existence amounted to keeping a few chickens, possibly a goat, and the benefit of the little food they could grow from the hard earth. On one occasion, an Arab was suspected of indicating the position of one of our companies to the enemy by marking the shape of an arrow pointing to the hillside we'd occupied by ploughing, or I should say scratching the ground with a primitive implement. From the air a German reconnaissance plane would be able to see the arrow of freshly tilled earth clearly pointing the way. We were soon to lose the services of Lieutenant-Colonel Hill, who was badly wounded when he, together with Captain Whitelock and two men, attacked a couple of German tanks. After disposing of the first one with a Gammon bomb, the commander of the second tank raised his hands in surrender, but a few seconds later his machine-gunner opened fire, wounding both officers.

The anger this action caused ensured the tank was destroyed and none of the crew was allowed to surrender. Major Pearson, previously a company commander, took over the command of the battalion. He was a heavily built, dark-featured man who hailed from Glasgow, a dour Scot, very curt and abrupt in speech and manner. He was a 'go getter' soldier who had the habit of dropping his head forward when he walked as if pondering over some problem. He was soon to earn great distinction in the field as a lieutenant-colonel, gaining the DSO and the MC in a matter of a few weeks. A mate of mine, Bill Wilson, related with amusement how, when on guard duty one night, a figure appeared out of the gloom and was challenged by Bill: 'Who goes there?'

It was answered with: 'Your bloody CO! Who do you think it is?'

The nights on the hillsides of Tunisia were bitterly cold in contrast to the blazing sun of the day. Huddling together for warmth among the rocky slopes under the starry sky, awakening to the first light of day, always gave us a great sense of communion that was a life apart from the peace and security we had experienced prior to the outbreak of war. This true spirit of comradeship, forged by unnatural conditions of constant danger which were our life, made each of us lose a little of himself, whatever he had done in peacetime, and moulded each of us into the fighting soldier equipped to brave the stark elements of the fiercely hot days and the bitter nights among those hills, fighting for survival against the German army. All we carried with us were our arms, ammunition and emergency rations.

Our objective was to move on to the heights overlooking the Tunis plain and establish positions around the area of Medjez-el-Bab until the main forces of the 1st Army joined up with us with supplies. The problem with this was that the Germans had the same idea and sent an airborne force, the elite Fallschirmjägers, possibly from Sicily, with the same purpose in mind. So, in the early days, a state of guerrilla warfare ensued with a series of bloody skirmishes going on all the time. Often, both sides would close with each other and ferocious confrontations took place. Battles were so close that often you didn't have time to reload your weapon, or risk firing it for fear of hitting your own side, so you used rifle butts, bayonets and anything else you got your hands on. Splashes of sweat and blood from our enemy often sprinkled us as we fought, and death this near is a terrible thing and is something I will never forget. We lost many a good man in these battles, as did the Germans.

We slept in old disused locals' houses among the rocks and hedgerows, anywhere that offered cover of some kind. It was only to be expected that we did not smell too sweetly, caked with dust and stained with sweat, a few weeks' growth of beard on our faces, as washing facilities were pretty hard to come by. When we did come across the occasional stream or brook, we went wild with delight, stripping off, and after a thoroughly good wash, meticulously going through the seams of our clothes in search of lice, as many of us were plagued by the discomfort of 'crabs' and other skin pests. Bill Wilson and I, always on the look-out for something to supplement our rations, picked and ate what resembled corn cobs from an allotment kept by the local Arabs, which gave us both a violent bout of dysentery, leaving us feeling very weak and washed out. This was a lesson we learned the hard way and thereafter took great care with what we ate and drank, ensuring that we boiled every drop of water, often after having scooped tiny newts and minute insects out of the mess tin before making our tea, the water perhaps having been taken from a nearby stream. Without fail, the tea tasted like wine to us. I now know the meaning of 'Nectar of the Gods' and I can assure you it wasn't alcoholic.

One Day At Corkwood – Henry Bagley

Corkwood in Tunisia was a butcher's shop for the German Fallschirmjägers, and us. During one of the many battles they threw everything had at us, including the kitchen sink and all of the cooking utensils. You had to give them their due; they were determined to take the bit of ground we were occupying, come what may. It was almost suicidal, the way they pushed on, as we were well dug in and the last 50 or so yards they had to attack over open ground. I remember taking aim at one particular Jerry who was about 30 yards or so away – his chest just filled my sights, I couldn't miss him. When I fired, he just flung up his arms, dropped his rifle and tumbled over backwards as if I'd struck him in the chest with a sledgehammer. I quickly cocked my rifle and lined up the next one. I fired and he went down as well. I'd forgotten all about the first one when, out of the corner of my eye, I saw him move. He slowly rolled over onto his stomach, pushed himself onto his knees, turned his head, gradually reached out for his rifle, took hold of the sling and then began to crawl straight toward our lines, dragging the thing behind him. I stopped firing as I couldn't believe my eyes; he was knowingly crawling toward his own death, pulling a rifle he couldn't possibly use. Behind him, his life's blood was a thick sandy red trail on the ground. How he was still alive I don't know.

By now the attack had petered out and the rest of them had withdrawn, leaving behind a lot of dead and wounded, yet here was a man fighting his own little war on his hands and knees, determined to continue the attack. Deep down he must have known he was dying with each move he made. I'd seen many men die in this war, but watching a man's lifeblood ooze out of him like that in front of your eyes, even if he is your enemy, is soul destroying. Every so often he would slowly lower his head as if exhaustion had finally got to him, then, after several seconds he would raise it, orientate himself then continue moving forward as if he was in a dream. What little I could see of his face under his helmet was etched with grey and his eyes appeared to be sunk into his skull, but somehow he was still struggling on, forcing his body by sheer willpower to move. I can remember thinking, 'Why is he doing this? He must know that it is a futile gesture.' Twice more I lifted my rifle to shoot him, and twice I lowered it. I just couldn't pull the trigger.

No matter how much I thought about it I simply didn't have the heart to finish him off, even though I knew he was literally dying in agonising pain before my eyes. He just dragged his rifle behind him and crawled like an automaton, first one hand, then a knee, then the other hand, and opposite knee, an inch at a time. He'd covered no more than a mere five or six yards when the rifle became too much, so he let it go. Yet it didn't stop him and he carried on crawling. Suddenly, two medical orderlies ran out to him and gathered him up and put him on a stretcher. He was simply too weak to stop them. It was only then that I realised that everyone on both sides had stopped firing – we were all completely mesmerised. On the stretcher he was lying on his side as they passed me and I could clearly see where my round had hit him in the centre of the chest; it was the perfect killing shot. I followed them with my eyes as they turned and went down the gradient behind me and I could see where the round had come out. The hole in his back was the size of my fist. How he was still alive I don't know. Evidently the MO took one look at him, shook his head, and let him die peacefully about fifteen minutes later after a dose of morphine had been administered. One of the medical orderlies told me that nobody could believe that he had lasted so long – it must have been sheer willpower that kept him going. Later that night, he was buried alongside our lads that hadn't made it. I asked to go and be beside his grave when they covered him up. There were no crosses to go on his grave, so we stuck his rifle into the ground, barrel facing downward, where a cross would normally would go; this was his last resting place – he deserved that at least.

North Africa Holiday – Thomas Davies
I recall the prominent hills and mountains of North Africa as if it was yesterday. The locals called them Djebels. One

such mountain was Djebel Mansour and it stands out in my mind like a molten burning fire. It was here that some of the bitterest fighting we experienced took place. It was in the hands of the German Fallschirmjäger, elite paratroopers, who were well dug-in when the battalion attacked. After many hours of attack and counter-attack, we eventually forced our way up the mountain, in the process crawling and scrambling up different paths under murderous fire. The rounds from the German machine guns, rifles and mortar bombs burst on the rocks all around us and threw up vicious fountains of earth and sharp stones. The deadly rat-tat of MG34 machine guns and the counter fire from our Bren guns along with rifle shot reports from every direction sounded like a continuous whiplash. My breath was rasping as I took in great painful gulps of air when we finally reached the summit. From there, we drove the Germans down the slopes at the far end of the mountain and into the valley below. We may have got the top but none of us had any illusions that they would leave it at that. It was just a matter of time before they would put in an attack. We lost no time in trying to establish a firm base while attending as best we could to the huge number of casualties we'd sustained.

The bodies of a large number of Germans who would take no further interest in the war lay strewn around, some caught in the oddest poses. One, probably a sniper, whose helmet had dropped off, revealing a shock of blonde hair, was wedged in the fork of a small tree, his eyes staring wild and unseeing into space. He was suspended like a huge rag doll whose seams had come apart, spewing mangled intestines through his parachute smock, most likely the result of the cruel blast from a three-inch mortar shell. Mind you, the battalion's dead were also strewn all over the side of the mountain like lifeless mannequins whose strings had been cut, leaving the body discarded. A few short hours later, we were on the receiving end of an attack by the deadly Stuka dive-bombers. I cannot imagine anything more terrifying to exhausted troops as there was no way of defending ourselves. There is nothing one can do but hold tight and watch them plunge down from above like huge birds screaming their way earthwards, able to pull out of their dive after they had jettisoned their bombs. The whole mountainside trembled with the impact of the explosions, as earth, stones and shrubs were thrown into the air, half-burying us as debris beat a tattoo on our helmets. After this 'softening up' process, the Fallschirmjäger started a counter-attack, throwing everything they had into the onslaught in a fight to regain the ground they'd lost. One Bren gunner, Jock Miller, a big Scottish lad, fell backwards into the mortar pit next to me, shot clean through the forehead. He died in my arms not able to say a word, just a faint rattle coming from his throat as his colour changed from a deep tan to a greyish-white in a matter of seconds.

We were taking a terrible hammering and getting desperately short of ammunition. Apparently the mules that were being used for transporting the ammunition up the mountain had stampeded in terror at the sight and sound of the shells landing close by. Their drivers, tall, lean Senegalese Africans who were serving with the French North African forces, were unable to check them – nobody could have. Our position now became hopeless, the Fallschirmjäger relentlessly fighting their way up the slopes regardless of cost, steadily closing in to gain a firm footing once again. The order to fix bayonets was passed around and we expected at any moment to hear the command to charge, which would start the shouts of 'Wahoo Mohammed!', the battle cry adopted by the 1st Airborne Division that was to strike terror and dismay into the hearts of the enemy long before the campaign was over. The idea for the call came from the lads imitating the Arabs, who used to shout 'Wahoo Mohammed' to their donkeys when urging their animals to move. It was amusing to think it started that way and now was used to give us the extra courage to fight harder when we needed to charge the enemy. However, instead of the order to charge being given, we were ordered to withdraw as we were simply taking too many casualties. It was terribly hard having to leave behind many of the more seriously wounded. The reasoning was they stood a better chance of survival if they were taken prisoner as they were in dire need of medical attention and they would get this from the Fallschirmjägers, who we knew were honourable soldiers and respected us, and who would certainly send them to Tunis for hospital treatment, which was only 30 or 40 miles away. As we withdrew we half-carried, half-dragged as many of the wounded as we could manage through the undergrowth, forcing our way into the thorny bushes as a thunderstorm of gunfire echoed throughout the hills.

We groped our way down rocky slopes, some of the wounded bleeding profusely and screaming out in pain when an arm or a leg would catch in undergrowth or on a rock. It was not easy to distinguish the wounded from the rest of us as we were all covered in blood, a gory sight, and stinking because of the sweat and dust of the past few days. We were given covering fire by a contingent of the French Foreign Legion, who set up a rear-guard action, enabling the remnants of the battalion to be guided through a wide gully at the foot of the mountain. We shouldered our way through this ravine to the accompaniment of falling mortar bombs and eventually arrived with a shambling gait at a large olive grove, exhausted, dazed and glad it was all over. After a while we ceased to hear even the remotest echo of the battle. Licking our wounds, we took a count of the casualties, which were considerable, about three-quarters of the battalion having been either killed or wounded.

Around us, the Foreign Legion certainly did not cut the romantic figures I had imagined them to be. There was nothing uniform in their appearance – they seemed to be wearing anything they could pick up – but they fought courageously and with reckless abandon. They appeared to have practically every nationality under the sun in their ranks, including Germans. I suspected that one would have quite a different picture of them under the severe disciplinary conditions at their headquarters in Sid-el-Abbes in Algeria. After this General Flavell, commanding the 1st Airborne in North Africa, urged GHQ to withdraw the 1st Parachute Brigade from the front so that it could be could be brought up to strength with reinforcements and retrained as an airborne force of specialised troops. However, such was the general situation in Tunisia that we were moved about, plugging up the gaps in the line to help in the struggle to restore positions where and when it was necessary.

One such position was between Djebel Abiod and Sedjenane, in which Lieutenant-Colonel Jock Pearson, commanding the 1st Battalion, rallied his men, including the cooks, clerks, batmen and everyone else who was capable of holding a rifle. As they charged the German positions, the dark valley reverberated to the cries of 'Wahoo Mohammed!' mingled with the reports of machine-gun, rifle and mortar fire, until finally they gained their objective. Each side lost a lot of men, both in killed and wounded, but then all the battles ended like that because you inevitably wound up fighting at close quarters with bayonets, rifle butts and anything else you could get your hands on. I strangled a German in one battle because both of us had lost our weapons.

It all took place about the time that Hitler spat out his abusive threats of hate and vengeance, referring to the Airborne as the scum of society, branding them as a military unit formed of ex-jailbirds, guttersnipes, Jews and homosexuals. He called us 'Red Devils' because of the red berets everyone wore, many finding them more comfortable than helmets in the hot North African climate. He ordered that none of us were be to taken prisoner, but would shot immediately after capture. This proved to be just another of his idle threats. Because fighting soldiers on both sides had a common bond, except for a few in the SS they refused to shoot prisoners, regardless of his orders.

In contrast, these remote hillsides held some of the pleasantest memories of the whole campaign for me, such as the times we sang around the campfire. Bill Windows, a heftily-built lad from Wembley, who saw to the food rations for our section, usually struck up a note while the tinned rations were being warmed. With his eyes half-closed against the wisps of smoke curling up from the fire, he would say, 'C'mon Taff, how about a song?'

Soon, he would have everyone harmonising to the popular tunes of the day like 'Sierra Sue,' 'Chapel in the Moonlight' and many others. It was therapeutic, relieving the gut wrenching tension that had been building up in our systems, especially after the action at Djebel Mansour. At the time I felt as though my whole inside had turned to stone, completely insensitive to any feelings and incapable of appreciating anything funny. There was nothing but numbness throughout my whole body.

Luckily, there was a very strong sense of camaraderie among the lads, each of us depending on the others for his existence and understanding how the other felt. We ate, slept, shared the washing water when we were fortunate enough to obtain it, and did practically everything one could imagine in each other's company to the extent that our very souls revealed to each other intimate details we would never tell anyone else, even our families or wives.

One day, while searching among the bushes in the area of Tamara, Bill and I were met with an appalling stench of death. The warm breezes always carried the stink of corpses. It is an indescribable smell one can never forget. In this case, it guided us to a body that had been overlooked. It was decomposing very quickly in the warm climate of North Africa. The smell of the decaying flesh as we searched bodies for means of identification was nauseating. Bill said, 'Go on Llew, have a cigarette.'

Being a non-smoker, I realised, as did Bill, that it would have helped considerably in the circumstances, but I eventually pushed away the packet that was held out. I just didn't want to start again, having gone so long without it. We would occasionally find a photograph among the papers in the clothing of a body, a snap of a smiling, good-looking youngster with a mop of curly hair. It was difficult to associate the lad with the pitiful, squelching heap we were burying. Death under these circumstances is a terrible thing, regardless of who it is – German, Italian or British. Sometimes we'd find a body half eaten away by maggots, stripped of shirt and jacket by some local thief who would leave a trail of letters or pages from the soldier's pay-book strewn about the place. These had to be collected, along with the brown vulcanised-fibre discs which were stamped with the bearer's name, number and letters denoting the religion to which they belonged, and passed on to the adjutant, whose unpleasant duty it was to notify the unfortunate wife, sweetheart or mother. One day I remarked to Bill on the way back to our position how I kept seeing the smiling faces on the photographs of the lads we had buried. 'Aye,' said Bill. 'Just think, it's possible that a wife or mother is at this very moment reading a letter just received from them full of good news and the joys of life; or they might still hear from them in a week or two what with the speed of the post.'

Much of the battalion movements when filling the role of a 'stop gap' in different parts of the line were made in trucks. We had nightmare experiences when attacked by German fighters that 'hedge-hopped' along the hillsides, swooping on the convoy as they rolled along the dusty roads. Their cannon blazed away as the vehicles screeched to a halt and everyone poured over the sides from under the tarpaulin, scattering in all directions, desperately seeking some means of cover as the fighters peppered the ground, throwing up spurts of earth that chased along after us. I watched with some measure of relief when the Messerschmitts turned and made off over the nearby hills. On one occasion, when we returned to the trucks nearly half the occupants of one of them had been killed, not having had time to vacate it, the flimsy tarpaulin sheet being no protection at all from the heavy cannon shells that ripped mercilessly through the men as they'd frantically tried to get out. We pulled around the truck while the bloodied victims of the attack were being laid out in a row along the sandy verge until arrangements could be made for suitable burial. As we sat looking at each other in a kind of stunned silence, I could not help but think of the tragic lesson we'd just learned about the urgency of abandoning the trucks with all possible speed whenever the need arose.

Needless to say, after that nobody required to be reminded to keep a sharp lookout for enemy aircraft. Every pair of eyes scanned the skies from underneath the tarpaulin, which we rolled up as high as possible. What I found particularly nerve-racking were the 'listening patrols' that would comprise an NCO and three men. The object of the patrol was to go out at night into the dead ground between our position and the Germans, lay 'doggo' at some vantage point, and give the alarm in the event of any movement of the enemy. This enabled the battalion to take full advantage of the night and snatch a few hours of much-needed rest. Two of the patrol could sleep while the other two kept watch. The mind would play amazing tricks as one stared into no man's land. In the moonlight, the rocks and undergrowth would come to life and take on whatever shapes the mind could conjure up. I often broke out in a cold sweat when I thought I saw a German patrol moving stealthily towards us that then turned out to be just a line of shrubs. It was always a great relief at the first sign of daybreak as, stiff with cold and thankful to get our circulation going again, we would make our way back to the company lines, where the company would be preparing to 'stand to' as the sun came up.

In some places, where the nature of the ground was suitable, we'd lay out a line of barbed wire in front of our position and often a surprise attack in the dark would be foiled as we heard the screams of pain and terror from an unsuspecting patrol who had got themselves entangled in the wire, leaving them at the mercy of raking machine-gun and rifle fire. Of course, this traffic was not all one-way and many of our patrols sent out to reconnoitre were never seen again. Relaxing one evening during a lull in activities, and after a meal of steak-and-kidney pudding, marvelling that such a grand feast could come out of a tin, we were looking across the little valley to the slopes beyond, where we presumed the Germans were also taking things easy. Joe, after a good stretch, raised himself into a comfortable position, nodded in the general direction of the enemy and remarked, 'I don't expect they wanted anymore to do with this business than we do.'

Bill looked at him and snorted, giving voice to thoughts that I was trying to frame: 'Och! A dozen or so of those bloody high-ranking German officials in some government building, drunk with power and their own importance, raised their hands in favour of something or other and the German nation is plunged into war!'

Big Frank raised his shaggy head and with Cockney good humour said, 'They ought to shove 'em all, British and German, into a big arena and let 'em shoot it out among themselves. They'd soon learn to settle things in a more civilised manner!'

Joe shook the dregs of a brew from his mess tin, which gave emphasis to his words: 'Those blokes over there are fighting for the very same reason that you and I are fighting, and that's defending their homes, parents, wives, brothers, sisters and everybody and everything they hold dear. It has nothing to do with their bloody Führer!' Everyone looked at one another because there was nothing they could add.

Walking in Circles – Stanley Tynan

I remember the 1st Battalion's first operation; it was a parachute assault into Souk el Arba, a small town deep behind German lines in Tunisia. The CO, Colonel Hill, had received orders to secure the area around the town, which was flat so it was ideal for use as an airfield. Once that was done, we had to march 40 miles north-east of the town to capture a vital rail link at Baja. This was done to encourage the Vichy French garrison there to join our cause. As the battalion approached the town, the CO had us don our helmets and march through the main street, then circle around and then half of us replaced our helmets with our berets and did the same thing again. It worked; the French thought there were twice as many of us as there really was and they came over to our side without a shot being fired. As we marched through a second time, I jokingly said to my mate, 'Harry, is it your turn to be B Company or mine?'

A tired Harry replied, 'How would I bloody well know? I think I'm A Company and Trevor's B Company; maybe you're BHQ?'

'Bugger,' I replied, 'I hate being BHQ, they never have any fun!' Some of the lads around us laughed.

The CSM told us to 'bloody well shut up or we'd be on a fizzer'.

The Lord's Domain – Ray Sheriff

I was in North Africa in 1943, where the fighting was very heavy and many casualties occurred. My sergeant was Allen Watson and he would often ask me to accompany him on patrols; these were extremely dangerous and I would not have been with anyone else. Later, when I was positioned about 200 feet up on the side of Green Hill, the Germans had launched their usual dawn attack, causing many wounded, and I received a chest wound. The medical orderlies were unable to evacuate the wounded quickly as the ground was so precarious when hauling stretchers. The company commander therefore ordered all walking wounded to make their own way to a gully below, where they would be collected and taken to headquarters, situated about a quarter of a mile away. I was bleeding rather badly so, holding a field dressing to my chest, I decided to make my way down to the gully. I rolled and staggered to the bottom of the hill, and then after a pause to readjust the dressing and check direction, went on my way.

My progress was rather a stoop – stagger and rest. Moving towards the headquarters, I had not been mobile for long when I was abruptly halted by a roar: 'Corporal Sheriff, if you can't walk in a soldierly manner, lay down!' Naturally, I quickly obliged and I saw the now famous RSM J. C. Lord standing over me. As he was carrying a Sten gun in his right hand, I thought he might just shoot me. 'What's your trouble, Corporal?' he asked. I replied that I had a chest wound, hoping vainly for some show of sympathy. John Lord glanced me up and down for a brief moment then said, 'You haven't shaved this morning Corporal.'

'No Sir,' I admitted, 'I didn't have time as the Germans attacked at dawn.'

There was a pause as 'J. C.' growled that this was no excuse, but he then softened, suddenly stooped and made me comfortable and handed me a cigarette. He then went away to find a couple of men to carry me in, and still affected by the confrontation, I was lying in a position of attention and smoking by numbers when he returned. As we waited he spoke of the days gone by and of the many men of the battalion who were now missing. There was a chink in his armour after all.

The Battle of Tamera – Robert Brown

During September 1942, the 1st Brigade was sent to Tunisia for its first serious battle. Each of the three battalions went on individual operations behind enemy lines, and these ranged from the highly successful to complete disasters. In December the brigade was reunited and deployed in an infantry role, eventually ending up at Bou Arada in January 1943. In February we were transferred to the 19th French Corps and charged with the task of relieving French units on the front line that were to withdraw and re-equip. On the night of 2 February, the 1st Battalion were ordered to attack two hillsides. One of our patrols had already managed to mark a safe path through a minefield and also took out several machine-gun positions in the process; however, S Company became lost and ran into mined ground and enemy heavy machine-gun fire, and at 800 to 900 rounds a minute they did a lot of damage. Nevertheless, we eventually made our way up the hill before dawn and, after encountering a determined opposition, controlled it before first light, but at one hell of a cost. An attempt was made to take the second hill and we held it for a while before the Germans forced us to withdraw. Casualties were so heavy that the CO requested that a Grenadier Guards battalion take the other hill instead. They did so on 4 February, but they too were soon driven off by heavy counter attacks. These attacks then turned on us and although weak in numbers and now low on ammunition, we held our ground for about twenty-four hours before the hill was declared indefensible and we were forced to abandon it. The 2nd and 3rd Battalions joined us at an aptly known place called the 'Happy Valley'. Whoever named it must have been joking as on 26 February a mixed force of Germans, Austrians and Italians launched an all-out attack, of which the 3rd Battalion bore the brunt. They almost overwhelmed the battalion and the fighting ended up within touching distance of one another. Rifle butts were swung like clubs, men used their fighting knives, shovels were used as axes, and picks became ancient maces; at one point, men had to stop firing their weapons for fear of hitting their own side.

In the end, sheer desperation won the day and the enemy broke and were forced to withdraw and seek shelter in a close-by dry, rocky, riverbed where they were exposed to machine-gun and mortar fire. The CO didn't hesitate and ordered the area cleared and within half an hour about 1,000 mortar bombs fell among the enemy while the battalion's machine-gun platoon poured a murderous fire upon them. The enemy lost over 400 killed and 200 captured. Somehow, a miracle happened and the battalion only lost fourteen men and had forty wounded. Having failed to destroy the 3rd Battalion, the Germans made a move moved against the 2nd, but couldn't make them budge.

They then attempted to infiltrate between the flanking positions of the battalion, but the well-sited machine-gun and mortar platoons once again held them at bay. Meanwhile, our battalion broke up an attack on our positions by catching the Germans in a series of awkwardly positioned barbed wire entanglements that led them directly into a lethal crossfire at close range. Vickers machine guns may only fire 500 rounds a minute but they can do it all day long, and add to that Bren guns, which with a good team can fire 520 rounds a minute, and you have a deadly combination. Finally, the German Parachute Engineers, the 10th Panzer Grenadiers and other Fallschirmjäger units were so badly mauled they ceased to be effective fighting units. Our battalion followed up these attacks and captured over 400 Italians in a single engagement and by 29 March, the brigade had achieved its objectives and consolidated its positions. We remained there until 14 April, but there was little enemy activity and we were moved into reserve. And so the Battle of Tamera ended. In five months the brigade suffered 1,700 casualties, some 800 killed, but had inflicted over 5,000 on the enemy, of which some 2,100 had been killed, and had been responsible for the capture of a further 3,500.

Trading Shots – Arthur Speers

The war in Sicily was a vicious, no-holds-barred conflict with horrendous casualties on both sides. The battalions were often alongside the French Foreign Legion, who were definitely the scruffiest dressed soldiers in the war. They all wore uniforms begged and borrowed from everyone, yet their fighting skills were second to none. Mind you the lads looked like Fred Carno's army as well. There was nothing guardsman-like about the way they dressed. They were fighting men, not drill soldiers. The units we were up against were mostly Jerry airborne, the famous Fallschirmjäger, formidable fighting soldiers.

After one vicious battle there was a lull in the fighting, except for the occasional sniping and a bit of mortaring. On the second day I noticed that in the forward Jerry trenches, some 400 yards away as the crow flies, on the side of a hill, there was a stick with a white card fixed to it being waved up and down. I called out to Frank, our platoon sergeant, to look at it through his binoculars, and he yelled back that it was a target with several circles drawn on it. So I nudged Isaac, my mate, who was a marksman, and told him to take a shot at it. He took aim and fired; a moment later a stick came up on the Jerries' side and pointed to where Isaac had hit the target. The next minute Frank threw down his notepad and told us to do the same. Some ten minutes later we had a target fixed to a stick, and were waving it back and forth. Sure enough there was a single shot and a hole appeared near the middle of the card I was waving. I held up the card and, using another stick, pointed to where the Jerries had hit it. I was half expecting a sniper to line one of us up, but no, it seems this shooting match had taken priority on both sides; even the OC crawled forward to Frank's trench to watch the outcome. We went through three sheets of paper before both sides called it quits, and according to Frank the scores were about equal. It had been a quiet three hours except for the two shooting. It couldn't last, and it didn't.

Taranto, Italy – John Potts

My first impression of Taranto, Italy, was the appalling smell of a cinema that had been bombed with a full house inside, and not dealt with. Unfortunately, that wasn't our job; we had to go about getting ready for battle. Once the battalion had landed, our priority was to commandeer transport, as there wasn't any for us to use straight away. So we went on a big 'scrounge'. The Honourable Piers Saint Aubyn and 4 and 5 Platoons acquired an ancient bus and followed the Recce Squadron up the road to Motola. Next was our doctor, John Buck, on a large, ancient motorcycle with an equally large sidecar that had a huge medical box perilously balanced on the back and a large number of stretchers jammed inside it, with one of his medical orderlies grimly holding on for dear life. There was no doubt that in a different life he could have been a roving buccaneer on the high seas. Before he left, I persuaded him to take our signaller with his heavy set. The poor man was precariously balanced behind John's sergeant and definitely didn't look at all happy with his lot. In fact, if the truth were told there wasn't enough room on the whole contraption to push a knife between anyone, yet John roared away without a care in the world. Even the CO laughed when he saw them. Having finished my HQ 'O' group, we followed everyone on our requisitioned bicycles. One of the signallers had a woman's bicycle that had two flat tyres. How he managed to keep it moving, I don't know, as it had his huge radio set on his back. I can honestly say he literally wobbled his way to the forming-up point. The rest rode on an assortment of rickety bicycles as best as they could. There was even one tricycle among them, as well as a donkey and cart filled with mortars and part of the mortar platoon. I still wonder how the soldier driving it acquired the thing, although he seemed to know how to gee up the donkey.

In a typical flamboyant style, the adjutant came past in an ancient car whose engine rattled like a tin full of shaken nuts and bolts. We needn't have worried about finding our way as the engine left behind a trail of black smoke you could see for a mile. It was driven by his orderly and in the back were the RSM, trying to look regimentally dignified, the quartermaster and the RQMS, both of whom tried to ignore our grins. Every inch of the car was piled high with weapons and the other paraphernalia that a battalion HQ needed. As we all streamed out along the dusty road, we came across a wrecked Reconnaissance Squadron jeep on its side with a covered body alongside it – an unforgettable reminder of the cost of our advance. As for the rest of us, perhaps the enemy thought it was simply an unusual Sunday school outing coming up the road, as 4 and 5 Platoons were able to get to the debussing area without hindrance, and as we arrived on their heels we all shook out, glad our little trip was over with. I often wondered what the locals though about all of these bicycles and odd modes of transport simply left lying there.

The colonel called his 'O' Group as soon as he got there, and as I got up to go a mortar bomb landed at my feet, but it must have been faulty as it just split into two bits, neither of which detonated. Mind you, it did make everyone else scatter, which was most amusing from where I stood. Motola looked formidable on the top of its hill, but we had some useful smoke from the mortars, and the enemy seemed ready to go anyway. As we reached the village, the whole population flooded into the streets, cheering and bringing jugs of rough wine. I had avoided drinking with my own soldiers up to that day but my orderly, Rotherham, came up with a jug. 'Come on, Sir, this will do you good,' he said, and it certainly did – I slept like a log that night. Our next battle was centred on a farm called Castellanita. On this occasion, the colonel's 'O' Group worked its way forward through vineyards to get a better view, when suddenly we met a German patrol. Fortunately they were not keen to do battle, but we all took up fire positions, ready to use our revolvers as recently taught by Grant Taylor, the veteran of the American Mafia, who had been employed by our brigadier, 'Shan' Hackett, to teach his officers to use the revolver effectively. As the colonel gave his orders we all guzzled grapes, and 'any questions' were punctuated by pip spitting.

The CO wanted A Company to do the initial assault while Support Company and the Vickers machine guns and Bren guns of B and C Companies gave covering fire. It went according to plan, and as we left the vineyards to go down the forward slope, everything opened up. I just said 'Father', and experienced a deep peace inside, and the ability to get on with the job. Crossing the deep gully at the bottom and climbing up towards the farm, I realised that we had suffered a number of casualties, and that too many of their comrades were risking their lives in the open to help them, instead of leaving it to the stretcher-bearers. As 4 Platoon moved through a little wood on our left, they had quite an intense scrap, but as the rest of the company reached the farm, several young Germans from a Parachute unit seemed keen to give themselves up. We consolidated as night closed in and after checking our sentries I went back with a few men to clear the battlefield. We found two dead, which considering the amount of fire put down on us we were lucky to get away with. It was late and dark when I got back to the farm, and Rotherham met me with, 'Here you are, sir, just the place for you,' as he shone a torch on a pile of straw, where I slept warmly till dawn came. The strengthening light revealed the source of my central heating – two huge oxen towering on either side of me, really magnificent beasts with wide-spreading horns.

Not so long after that, we were digging trenches in a very rocky area when we heard that 'no planes – no planes at all' (Major General Hopkinson, the divisional commander) had been shot through his beret by a machine gun after being warned not to look over a wall. Months later, when we were back in England, Field Marshal Montgomery visited us just before D-Day to give us a pep talk. The whole brigade was formed up in a hollow square at Oakham. Instead of his usual black beret and half a dozen silly badges, he was wearing a maroon one that was too big for him, and a single Parachute Regiment cap badge. He began his talk by saying how proud he was to wear the beret of our late divisional commander, still pierced by the hole where the bullet had killed him in action. It was in extremely bad taste to say the least. And what is worse, he didn't even seem to know it, and neither did any of the 'yes men' that surrounded him. I doubt if any of us remembered much of what he said, we were so shocked he would do it – it was unthinkable.

On promotion, Major General 'Ernie' Down succeeded Major General Hopkinson after his untimely death. Down was a great soldier who gave me an imperial rocket for ineffective digging in a rocky position. Soon afterwards, he gave a thrilling talk to all officers on how he intended fighting the Airborne battle with close air support to make up for lack of artillery. 'I know,' he said, 'I know what needs to be done.' What a contrast to poor George Hopkinson. Had Ernie Down still been with us at Arnhem, I am sure the result would have been very different; but sadly he was soon posted to the Far East – such a waste of an excellent officer. I've often wondered why he was removed when it was obvious he was the ideal commander for the division. Anyway, as the Allies swept on beyond Bari, we got rather left behind, but A Company did get involved in one other little operation.

We were asked to provide a boarding party for a Royal Navy destroyer that was ordered to capture a German supply vessel working for their troops along the Dalmatian coast. It was great fun and most impressive to see and hear the Senior Service in action; but what I most remember was the agility of Rotherham, as he leapt aboard like a pirate and was up on the bridge of our quarry in seconds. Inevitably, I soon needed another orderly on his promotion, but he deserved it and went on to be a very good sergeant. I have few memories of our voyage home, except that our engine drivers from the battalion drove our train down to Taranto. I don't think they knew the meaning of brakes. We flew like a fighter plane the whole way. Compared to that, our journey by train from Liverpool to our billets in Uppingham was wonderful, not only for the joy of being home again for Christmas for the first time since the day war was declared, but also for the positively blooming good health of all the people we saw on the way, especially the children. Rationing and the discipline of wartime must have done us quite a lot of good!

Reinforcements – Anthony 'Ginger' Davenport

I brought reinforcements to the battalion, not anywhere near enough for what they needed, but then we never did get enough until we went back to England. I handed over the men and was then given control over two Vickers machine guns. No sooner had I settled in than the Germans attacked in force. They were Fallschirmjäger, the best troops the Germans had, and they didn't give ground easily, but in the end they were beaten off and lost three armoured cars in the process. As they withdrew, the CO decided it was the right time for us to put in an attack and catch them off guard. The Germans, although they had suffered a lot of casualties, still held their line in strength, and it was a day of bitter fighting with both sides taking a lot of casualties in dead and wounded. The machine guns were in action all day and succeeded in 'killing' an 88mm anti-tank gun that had stopped four tanks supporting us. Night fell and there was still no real winner. The lads fought like tigers, but the Germans had tactical advantage, and to be truthful they fought as well as we did. As night finally fell the call went out to cease fire, as it was now so close that it had become vicious hand-to-hand fighting.

In the darkness, it was difficult to tell friend from foe as each were just dancing shadows in a backdrop caused by the moon. Individuals literally stalked each other, firing at gun flashes. Some of the Germans appeared to be drunk or on hallucinating drugs, I don't know which. In fact, they were trying to make the lads react and open fire, thus giving each other away. They were shouting 'Jager-Jager!' They also called out to the lads in English: 'Hello, who's there?' and 'Come on boys get your ice cream.' It was surreal, but it didn't work – the lads were too good to fall for it. During the night word came down to withdraw 500 yards while our artillery moved forward. The fighting had been so bitter the Germans didn't even send out patrols to find out why things had gone quiet and with the dawn the guns opened fire and caught them by surprise. Their accuracy was incredible, and with the Forward Observation Officers calling in the targets, they pounded the German lines, blasting huge swathes of ground to smithereens. Even the famous Fallschirmjägers couldn't take a pounding like this. When they ceased, we literally walked up the hillside and took their positions. There were bodies everywhere in the most grotesque positions, with limbs missing and torsos torn into dozens of bits. It was so bad it was difficult to recognise many of them as human.

How anyone survived was a miracle, but they did. When one of the lads brought in twenty or so forlorn looking prisoners and walked them past us, he called out: 'This fucking lot wanted some ice cream. I told 'em to fuck off as it'd all melted – but they could 'ave corned beef an' hard tack!' We all laughed.

It was decided that the battalion would advance on Oudna from a drop zone somewhere around Depienne. Luckily, a suitable area was found and the daylight drop was unopposed, but a German patrol saw us, and they immediately reported it in. Local Arabs, who were determined to pilfer the contents of the supply canisters even when fired upon, had also seen us but once a few rounds had been sent their way they desisted. Those who'd been injured on the drop were taken care of by the French inhabitants of Depienne, and as ordered by brigade HQ, a platoon was left behind to retrieve all the parachutes and opened canisters; why, nobody knew, but orders were orders and had to be obeyed. Anyway, the battalion was able to set off on its long march to Oudna before midnight. We were heavily laden with equipment, but kept moving across hilly terrain and through the biting cold until we arrived within sight of the airfield by late morning.

But for a lone aircraft wreck, the area appeared to be deserted. Nevertheless, A Company began to make its way forward, while C and HQ Companies moved around their left. Once they were close enough, German machine-gun and mortar fire opened up from the airfield and caused a number of casualties. A Company managed to reach the airstrip, but as they did so German tanks appeared, together with a number of Messerschmitt fighters that strafed the battalion and this was followed up by attacks from Stuka dive-bombers. However, we all hid ourselves among the rocks and no serious casualties were sustained by the attacks from the air, and the tanks were beaten off. One of them sustained a hit from a PIAT. Unfortunately, it was still able to move, but there was smoke pouring from it as it did so, which made everyone happy. As dusk fell we withdrew to some nearby high ground that was better suited for defence. In the morning we were bombarded by artillery and indirect machine-gun fire. Our mortars returned the favour and eventually forced the enemy to withdraw, though occasional shots were still exchanged throughout the day.

The battalion's radios had so far been unable to contact the British 1st Army, but when they finally established a link they received information that shocked us all. The drive to relieve us had been postponed, and so the battalion was entirely alone and deep inside enemy territory and would not get any support, not even air support. Talk about being left out on a limb, the useless buggers. The Germans sent a captured man to Colonel Frost to inform him that he was surrounded and that it would be futile for any action other than surrender. He was never a man to give in that easily and as dusk fell we sneaked away to fresh positions on a hill a mile or so to the south. The Germans soon found where we were and throughout the following day they gave us hell with artillery, tank and machine-gun fire and we sustained even more casualties, including the OC of C Company, Major Cleaver. The Germans must have fired the equivalent of a 25-pounder on an almost flat trajectory and he stopped it all by himself. One moment he was there, the next there was nothing of him but a few hundred bits. His orderly, who was right next to him when it happened, was flung onto his back and rolled over and over down the hill with the sheer pressure caused by the shell. He eventually got up and was all right apart from being dazed and shocked from what had happened. The shell kept on going and detonated a couple of hundred yards away. We were now very low on ammunition, medical supplies and water, and our casualties were mounting all the time.

That night we did it again, sneaking away once more; however, we had to leave behind many of the wounded as it was impossible to carry them with us. We also left behind a platoon from B Company to search the area for wounded that we'd missed. C Company had all but ceased to exist, but luckily the Germans were not keen to fight at night so they made no attempt to challenge us during the darkness; as dawn came it was obvious that some sort of defence would be needed or we could get annihilated if caught out in the open. A reconnaissance patrol was sent out and returned with news that the El Fedja Farm lay ahead and the Arab owner was keen to provide us with fresh food and water at a price – typical Arab. But the Germans soon caught up again and began to encircle us and not long afterwards the attack began. By mid-afternoon mortar bombs started to land on us, and machine guns swept the area. Luckily, in preparation for the inevitable attack, we'd been told to dig deeper than normal and very little damage was done. A Company was attacked twice in the evening, but both attacks were completely broken up by accurate fire, causing a large number of casualties to the Germans. The main attack came at dusk, but this too was dealt with and the respite that followed enabled us to sneak away yet again.

By now, all of us were exhausted and perilously low on ammunition. The CO now headed to Medjez-el-Bab, 20 miles away, as it was the only place that we were sure Allied troops would be. On the way it became obvious we were being tracked and during the morning an armoured patrol came very close, but luckily they did not find us. We half expected an airborne attack but it didn't materialise. We were very lucky as we were out in the open most of the time. On the afternoon of 3 December we finally arrived at Medjez. It was a miracle, and everyone's spirits immediately lifted; we had beaten the odds. The CO ordered us to line up in three ranks, shoulder our weapons and march into the place like a 'Guards battalion'; well, some of us thought that was a bit much, but we still marched with our backs straight and heads upright past the shocked Frenchies, as they never knew there were any British units in the area. The whole operation had been a nightmare, all because someone didn't plan it correctly and didn't have the proper intelligence on the intended targets. Another operation much later in the war, Market Garden, suffered the same problem. It was only due to our skill and pure good fortune that so many of us managed to evade capture. However, sixteen officers and 250 other ranks were lost, and B and C Companies were decimated. Two hundred reinforcements eventually arrived to replenish the lost numbers, but many of them had previously been gunners and so had no infantry experience, but within weeks they had been trained to the standard the battalion required and made damn good infantry soldiers afterwards.

Lili Marleen – Dean Casey

When the battalion was in Tunisia, the days were scorching hot and the nights were bloody freezing cold. At one point we had a Fallschirmjäger regiment facing us, and they were damn good soldiers too. Both sides fought hard but fair, and it wasn't uncommon for there to be a short cease-fire while each side collected their dead and wounded. At the time, along with Vera Lynn, Marlene Dietrich was everyone's favourite. Both had voices that were reminders of what was at home waiting for you. The difference being, Marlene Dietrich had a song out called 'Lili Marlene', and when she sang it she had a husky, sensuous, nostalgic, honeyed voice that seemed to reach out to you on a personal basis and it was a Forces favourite on both sides. At 2155 hours every night, the German broadcasting service signed off with 'Lili Marlene', and if we were near a radio set the lads would tune in so we could listen to it. At one point old Jerry broadcast it so loud that both sides could hear it over the valley where we faced each other. It was almost as if the war had stopped as we took up the tune and sang it in English, and they sang it German. You just don't forget moments like that.

Empty Airfields to POW – Henry Blackwood

The 2nd Battalion were supposed to attack some airfields in Tunisia and destroy the aircraft on them but some idiot higher up who sent us there hadn't done his job and none of them had any aircraft on them. Instead, we ran into a whole swarm of German tanks and armoured cars and got chased all over the place by them. And when our CO, Colonel Frost, asked for help he was told he was on his own and would have to do the best he could; they wouldn't even give us aircraft support. There we were, hundreds of miles from our lines, and the big wigs had written us off, 600 men, and the generals didn't care if we lived or died. But the CO wasn't going to give up, so he told us that we would fight our way out come what may, and he wasn't joking either. Jerry surrounded us on three occasions and gave us one hell of a pasting but on each one we sneaked out during the night. My platoon copped one hell of a battering. We got mortared and lost about half the platoon from a mortar bomb landing right in the middle of us. Our platoon sergeant, Sergeant Holmes, tried to attack a tracked Hanomag armoured car with a Gammon bomb and got his leg shot off. He was screaming out at the top of his voice from the pain, and there was absolutely nothing we could do for him except make him comfortable, shoot some morphine into him, give him a water bottle and leave him. He knew he was dying just as did we. I never want to do that to anyone again. What was left of the platoon eventually rejoined the battalion and we all headed into the hills and dug in once more. It wasn't long before Jerry spotted us and brought up tanks, machine guns, mortars and artillery and tried their hardest to blow us off the top of the place. We were short on ammunition, medical supplies and water. The only thing we weren't short of was wounded and dead. One of my friends, Len Hoy from London, was just taking aim with his rifle when a bullet hit his finger and smashed it; naturally, he started shouting and bawling. I wasn't sure if it was from pain or anger but he was using some choice words anyway. The officers were running from place to place, encouraging everyone. One of them was about 30 yards from my trench when an artillery shell fired on an almost level trajectory hit him. Well, it didn't hit him; it just took him apart and carried on for a further 300 yards or so before detonating. One moment he was there, the next there was nothing of him but a few hundred bits. A corporal, who was about 5 yards away, was flung 10 or 12 feet onto his back and rolled over and over down the hill from the sheer pressure caused by the shell. We thought he was dead but he surprised us all by eventually getting up and was OK apart from being dazed, deaf and shocked from what had happened.

By now Jerry machine guns were playing havoc; you couldn't lift your head without getting shot at. One of the lads got so fed up with it he crept down the hill, sneaked up on one of them and then threw a Mills bomb at it and got away because the Jerries weren't expecting someone to attack them. He came back and everything was all right for about 30 minutes, then they got it working again. So off he went a second time and completely destroyed it. It must have given them one hell of a shock the second time. When he went to go after another one, we told him he was pushing his luck a bit so he stayed put. A mortar bomb killed him about half an hour later. At nightfall we were told we were going to creep out once more. We knew that Jerry wasn't happy about fighting in the dark although he'd still be on his toes. By this time we were all shattered by lack of sleep and very little food and water. In small groups we followed Colonel Frost off the hill. All that was left of our platoon, four of us, thought we were going in the right direction. Daylight came and we were lost and desperate for something to drink when we came across a lone farm. The occupants took one look and said they didn't want anything to do with us, or our war. We said that all we wanted was water. At first, they thought we were Jerries, but when we said we were English, that did it. Now, they definitely didn't want anything to do with us. So we said that if they didn't give us some water we were going to shoot 'em all, so they brought us some jugs of water and filled our water bottles and told us to piss off quickly before they called old Jerry. Then they slammed the door in our faces. We drank some of the water and then set off across an open field in what we hoped was the right direction.

It was then I saw a big cloud of dust coming toward us, so I said to our platoon corporal, 'There's some tanks coming.' Then I saw them and added, 'It's three tanks.'

He took a look and said, 'Oh don't you worry, they'll be ours, we'll be alright.'

I thought, 'Wait a minute, they can't be ours as the battalion is 50 miles behind Jerry lines!' Sure enough, as they got nearer and nearer I saw the shape of them and they didn't look like Shermans. Then I saw the big black cross on the front one and I said, 'Eyup, corporal, it's Jerry, those bastards at the farm must have told them about us. What are we gonna do?' Well, I'd a Sten gun, George, my mate, had a rifle, the other one had a rifle and the corporal also had a Sten gun, and apart from a Gammon bomb apiece, that was all we'd got. So we all agreed that we couldn't fight tanks with what we'd got. So the corporal said, 'We'll give ourselves up, are you all in favour?'

By that time they were getting close, so I said, 'Right, we'll give ourselves up.' I dropped my Sten gun on the ground and put my hands up; so did George. The corporal and the other lad held their weapons in one hand and put the other up to surrender. All of a sudden the lead tank opened fire with its machine gun. The corporal stopped a full burst in his guts that literally cut him in half, killing him outright. The other lad stopped just one round above his private parts. Once they'd shot those two, the tanks stopped and so did the machine gun. George and I simply threw ourselves on the ground and didn't move. A Jerry officer got down from the lead tank holding a Luger. He pointed it at us and said in perfect English, 'Up Englander, on your feet, get up! For you the war is over.' Because we didn't move fast enough, he yelled, 'I said get up!' When me and George were standing with our hands in the air, I said, 'Can I help the wounded man?' So we were allowed to look at the lad with the wound next to his private parts. We bandaged him as best we could and gave him some morphine and carried him to the tank and put him on it where the officer pointed. Then I asked if we could bury the corporal; the officer said, 'You and your friend there – dig a grave.' So we started digging and only got it a foot or so deep when the officer said, 'Leave it, come with us – now!'

There were a lot of the locals around, so the officer said, 'They'll bury him.'

I thought, 'Yes, I know what they'll do. They'll strip him and take all his clothes and anything else they can find but they certainly won't bury him.' But we had no option – we had to leave him. It's amazing how out in the middle of nowhere Arabs appear as if by magic, especially if there's something in it for them. Once we'd left the grave the officer walked us out into the middle of the field. At first I thought he might shoot us, but he said, 'There are some of your friends around here, I want you to go to them and ask them to surrender.'

'What if they won't?' I asked.

He told me, 'Well, if they don't we'll just kill them.'

'What about me?' I asked.

'Well my friend, if you're with them,' and he left it at that.

I shouted, 'Hang on a minute!'

He said, 'Do as I tell you.'

Those tanks were bloody big and one of them had his machine gun pointed right at me; so George and I marched ahead of them straight towards a thick clump of cactus-like bushes. When I was about 30 yards from the bushes the Jerries started firing into them. George and me flung ourselves onto the ground once again. The officer up in the cupola yelled, 'Up, get up and do your job!'

I was scared stiff, I can tell you. I set off walking again with my beret in my hand, waving it back and forth. Then all of a sudden, there were yellow dusters waving on a rifle, so the Germans held their fire. Nine men and a sergeant came out, but one man didn't want to give up; not that I knew at the time. He didn't want to be taken prisoner. They only had six rounds between the lot of them and he took them and disappeared. They searched all of us and the first thing they went for was the killing knife – they prized the things. The officer said, 'Put your berets on.' Then he made us get on top of the tanks, which were red-hot. They eventually took us through into Tunis, where there were quite a lot of the lads that had been taken as prisoners. We were all locked up in a huge ramshackle building while we waited to be taken to a POW camp. And that was the end of the war for me.

The 10th Battalion, North Africa – John Myles Henry

With a single, burnished pip on my shoulder, I was placed in command of a Bren gun carrier platoon, part of the 2nd Royal Sussex, a lorried infantry battalion that formed part of a brigade in the 44th Division. After strenuous training we embarked in May 1942 for service with the 8th Army in North Africa. I soon saw plenty of action, being involved in the battles of Alam Haifa and Ruwesat Ridge at the end of August, and in October the eleven-day battle for El Alamein, which finished Field Marshal Erwin Rommel's overstretched advance toward Egypt. Few people know that Monty was actually going to withdraw because of the casualties and loss of tanks he was suffering. He was certain he was losing the battle, but intelligence intercepts in England learned that Rommel was almost out of fuel and had suffered so many casualties that he was forced to withdraw, so Monty kept pushing and won a very uncertain victory. It wasn't his generalship that won the battle; it was the man on the ground with the bayonet that won it for him, just like all of the battles that followed. And the country wanted a hero so Churchill gave them one, Montgomery. Unfortunately, a few weeks later I was laid low with a rare virus, resulting in me being put in hospital for several months. When I recovered, I rejoined the battalion in March 1943, in time to move with them through Iraq and Jordan to take up their new station in Palestine with 'PAI Force'. As early as January 1943, the 2nd Royal Sussex was scheduled for conversion into a parachute battalion.

This was initially to be known as S Battalion, but later that same month, the War Office changed its mind and ruled that 2nd Royal Sussex was not to be transferred en bloc to the Army Air Corps as previously directed. As a consequence of the new ruling, the battalion was to remain and be strengthened by personnel from the previously disbanded 4th and 5th Battalions. Luckily, the 200 officers and men who had volunteered had already participated in parachute training. As such, we formed the nucleus of the newly formed 10th Battalion, then undergoing training at Kabrit. This new battalion was to be commanded by Lieutenant-Colonel K. Smyth and was to form part of the new 4th Brigade. In July 1943, Benito Mussolini, the fascist dictator of Italy, resigned, but the Germans had no intention of surrendering Italy without a fight.

So in September 1943, after intensive training at Kabrit and Ramat David near Nazareth, the 10th Battalion was mobilised for their first taste of action as an airborne fighting unit – destination Taranto, Italy. Much to its chagrin, however, the fledgling battalion, after many months of arduous training, found that in the absence of sufficient transport aircraft, it was to be utilised instead as a seaborne element of the brigade, and as such embarked aboard various Royal Navy cruisers at the port of Bizerta. We in B Company travelled separately from the main body aboard a converted cross-Channel packet, the *Prince Albert*. At that time I was B Company 2IC and Myles Henry, Mike Bellow and Nick Hammer were the platoon commanders. Meanwhile, Major General Hopkinson, commanding the 1st Airborne Division, was ordered to occupy the port of Taranto and hold it against all attacks. The 4th Brigade's immediate task was to form a bridgehead against any possible German attack while the remainder of the division was put ashore. After the 1st Brigade had established a defensive perimeter around Taranto, the 2nd and 4th Brigades were despatched in a relentless pursuit of the retreating Germans. The immediate enemy was the elite German Fallschirmjäger from the 1st Parachute Division, who had previously fought so grimly against the 1st Brigade in North Africa. The German division had suffered a large number of casualties in the battle for Sicily and as yet had not been brought up to full strength. Nevertheless, it was capable of putting up a dogged rear guard defence even though they lacked artillery support.

The Germans fought like cornered tigers in the ensuing battle for Castellaneta, which finally fell on 12 September. Our next objective for the brigade was the capture of Gioia del Colle and its airfield, the importance of which was fast increasing, as it was urgently required as a fighter base to cover the Salerno landings. The brigadier ordered a fighting patrol from our battalion to push forward and determine the strength of the German positions at

Gioia del Colle. B Company was selected and at 1930 hours on 15 September we left the battalion area to drive to Gioia, a point 3 miles to the east. After a compass march in pitch darkness, we moved into position on the outskirts of Gioia del Colle at dawn, taking the German sentries completely by surprise. But the surprise was short-lived and there then ensued a fierce five-hour pitched battle with the now alerted Fallschirmjägers. Outnumbered and taking heavy casualties, I ordered the men to withdraw. Having successfully extricated ourselves from a very hot situation, we made our way back to the battalion by midday on the 16th. Before we withdrew we did inflict numerous casualties on the enemy and gained much useful information.

But the cost had been extremely high; the total casualties sustained by the patrol were five killed and five wounded – I was one of them. Regrettably, two officers and seven other ranks were reported missing. The Germans decided to withdraw on the night of 16/17 September. On the 18th the front line offensive was taken over by the 1st Air-Landing Brigade and 4th Brigade withdrew to Taranto for a brief respite. On 29 October it was decided that the division should be withdrawn from Italy and on 24 November the battalion embarked aboard HMS *Staffordshire*, bound for England. Following much training and large-scale exercises, the battalion was held in readiness to support the planned landings in Normandy. Regrettably, we were not called upon to participate.

I'll Be Back – Andrew Walton

The fighting in North Africa was so bitter that we often took ground only to lose it the next day, and then retook it a day later. Often you had no time to collect your belongings; you simply withdrew with only your weapon and basic equipment. The battalion had been fighting as normal infantry ever since we landed and our losses had mounted until some companies were less than three-quarters their normal strength, even after receiving reinforcements. I was always an avid reader and had just received a book in the mail from my mother. It was an old classic, *Lorna Doon* by Richard Blackmore, and every chance I got I read a few more pages. Then one afternoon we became the focus of a renewed attack by the Fallschirmjäger, our old enemy. First there was a concentrated mortar and artillery barrage then they attacked, supported by tanks. We held them for a short while, but in the end the order to do a fighting withdrawal was given and I was forced to leave my pack and my precious book behind. A day later it was our turn and we put in a counter attack with artillery and tank support and retook the position. When the firing had died down I walked over to my old trench and found everything was as I left it; even my pack was untouched, and there on top of it was my precious book, only it had a bit of folded paper stuck in between the front cover and the first page. I picked the book up and removed the piece of paper and opened it. There, in a neat old German script, but in English, was a quickly written note from a German Fallschirmjäger oberleutnant. It read: 'An exceptional read. I only got as far as page 43 before you attacked. We will be back. Please leave the book so I can finish it off.'

The Germans at Sicily – A Letter Home – Herman Kuster
Dear Family:

23 July 1943
I want to send you a report about these past few days, so that in case I never come home, you will know what we are putting up with down here in Sicily. British Fallschirmjägers landed and we fought a battle to hold an important bridge across the Simeto River. They fought like tigers and eventually took it with terrible losses. The fighting was horrific with men milling around and shooting and bayoneting each other they were so close together. I have never seen men fight one another the way both sides did in the battle. There was no quarter given by both sides. Even the Italians fought well. Some hours later we took it back after they ran out of ammunition and we captured those still alive. But it was too late and the British who'd landed on the coast retook it before the Italians could blow it up, and we were forced to retreat, leaving the prisoners behind. The Italians fought well at the bridge, but elsewhere they are giving up in their hundreds. We simply don't trust them anymore and

have to take precautions every time one of their units is in the line with us. The Americans and British have gained so much ground, and succeeded in bringing so many troops, that it is impossible to anticipate a battle with equal forces. On 14 July we missed being captured by just one hour. We took up a new position, which the British promptly covered with artillery fire. From this position we retreated again – toward the flank – and took up still another position. This move nearly sealed our fate. I am supposed to keep my vehicle near the commander, and serve as a communication trouble-shooter. Whenever the telephone line is damaged, the order is, 'Get out and repair.' (We are fighting in the central sector, and are opposing crack Canadian and British troops.) Such an order came at 2100 on 20 July, three nights ago. Right after we had left our position, a terrific barrage started and an infantry sergeant swore he had never experienced anything like it, even in Russia. Many of our men were killed. I was right in the thick of it. It is impossible to describe the terror of that experience. We pressed our faces to the ground and waited for a direct hit.

Meanwhile, people back home in Germany were vacationing, going to cafés and movies, and enjoying themselves. I asked myself, 'Where is the justice in that?' At 0400 we got back to our position. At least we were still alive. We could hear machine-gun and rifle fire. We eventually got some sleep even though our commander had already departed. Half an hour later, I was awakened suddenly. There were orders for me. The Canadians were in the immediate vicinity, and all lines had to be disconnected. Ten of us men had a large personnel carrier and a small one. It was necessary to go slowly on the dirt roads, but on the highway we travelled as fast as we could go. It seemed impossible to take the vehicles any distance across country, because of the nature of the ground, but we made it. Then it happened. We rounded a curve and ran into heavy rifle and machine-gun fire. I felt as if God had suddenly put a wall of flying steel in front of me! At this moment I thought of all of you.

I had to get the car through, and somehow or other I succeeded. Afterward, the man in the seat beside me looked at me and I looked at him. We were white as chalk. But we had survived. A short distance away my friends were waiting for us. They had observed everything through field glasses. When we reported that the other car could hardly be expected to come through, our young lieutenant, who was already there, gave us a tongue lashing. He said that he had expected more of us to get through, and that we should be ashamed to say such things. I had to hold myself back in order not to leap at his throat. He didn't know the whole story inasmuch as he had left the position an hour earlier. However, some of the missing men eventually got through. We shelled a town occupied by Canadians. In return, the Canadian artillery fired on our positions, costing us a number of wounded and dead, forcing us to retreat once again. We had already retreated 30 kilometres and had had only a single day of rest. But here 'rest' means air attacks! Enemy air reconnaissance discovered us, and the next day the Canadians placed artillery barrages on our new position. It became a miserable hell, and we had to abandon it. We haven't seen one of our own aircraft in days. It's always British ones.

As a rule, we travel only at night – in pitch dark, without lights, and seldom on roads. You can imagine what this means – especially when we are forever under fire. At noon, I was ordered to take out a detail and look for our motorcycle runner, who was missing. We searched for him until it was nearly dark without success. We returned, hoping to get some sleep after the misery of the past two days, but found that everyone had moved again. They had simply left us. We had a corporal with us who said he knew the route, but he didn't, and at daylight we were still moving. A hundred times we had to drop to the ground because of hostile planes. Planes are always around – nothing but American and British ones. We rode through a town, but had to stop 500 yards beyond it, inasmuch as we didn't know whether this road was still in our hands. Here we experienced another bombing attack. We were terribly frightened, but we had to get through. Luckily we did, but we lost one truck and several of our friends. We had already been posted as missing and our lieutenant himself had gone out to look for us. Miraculously, our motorcycle runner had returned safely, too! Today our infantry has repulsed two heavy attacks, but I doubt they will be able to do it again. As a result we lost our light truck, which was blown up. While we were moving British planes appeared overhead. A moment later a nearby explosion threw my assistant driver and myself out of the car. I happened to land in the soft earth of a bomb crater, and wasn't badly hurt. But my assistant driver was thrown on to the hard surface of the road and was still lying there when I found him. I took him to a field hospital. He had suffered terrible head and face injuries. I feel very close to this fellow, since he and I have been through so many sad hours together. I hope he will soon be with us again, but I doubt it. We are always being pursued. Half the time we don't know what day or date it is. As you can probably guess, I have been writing this letter piecemeal from time to time.

28 July 1943
Yesterday things were fairly quiet in our new position, although occasionally we could hear artillery. A tremendous number of bombers passed overhead. Our flak guns are constantly being fired, yet I have never seen a plane shot down. Our Luftwaffe must be employed elsewhere, because I still haven't seen any of our planes to speak of. Tonight there is a terrific thunderstorm going on, and our comrades who are further up front must be wretchedly uncomfortable. I can hardly stand listening to the noise any longer. The lightning – coupled with everything that has happened – shatters my nerves. I find it impossible to sleep after a storm like this. All I can manage are little naps, in which I have bad nightmares. Oh, if I could only have a roof over my head again! We're always sleeping on the ground, and in a different place every night. The Canadians and Americans are attacking again and our infantry are trying desperately to stop them. It is futile as they have overwhelming firepower so all we can do is try and hold them up while as many units as can retreat to the next position. If we keep this up we'll be in the sea soon.

I will send you another letter when I can.

Love
Your Son Herman

Spoils of War – Dicky Hull

During the battles in Italy some units became adept at sending raiding parties behind enemy lines to capture prisoners and bring them back for interrogation. My company was filled with a bunch of reprobates who took to 'finding' booty like a duck takes to water when they searched their prisoners; so much so that there were complaints made by both the Germans and Italians that they were being relieved of their personal items, which under the Geneva Convention wasn't allowed. We didn't care as all around us we saw officers as high as the rank of general acquiring the so-called 'spoils of war' and nobody ever questioned them about it. There was no doubt it was happening and the finger was squarely pointed at my company in particular. We weren't the only ones doing it; it was just that we appeared to be better at it than most of the others. In the end high command issued an order forbidding it and made a rule that any item taken off a prisoner must be signed for in the shape of a receipt signed by the individual who removed the item. Thereafter, receipts began turning up with the names 'Jerry Hitler', 'Fred Mussolini,' 'Pudding Churchill' and 'Captain Montgomery'. GHQ got so angry they ordered the MPs to raid suspected units when they were pulled out of the line. No sooner did we get off the trucks·than the buggers grabbed everyone and made us tip up our kitbags. The stupid buggers never found a thing and weren't they pissed off. All the big stuff was already on its way to the rear, hidden in the stores truck with the CQMS and a cook sergeant as an escort. They would flog it off and split the money with the rest of us when they got back. Stuff that we wanted to keep was sewn into the bottom of our kitbags and when we were forced to upend the bag everything else would fall out but 'our acquired valuables'. The MPs were livid, especially as some of the lads burst out laughing. They never did find out where we hid the stuff.

Normandy:
6 June 1944

'Esprit de Corps' – Eddie Simonds

Esprit de Corps – the loyalty and devotion to each other that united members of the British airborne forces – had seen men do feats of outstanding valour during battles in North Africa, Tunisia, Italy and Sicily, but this great spirit could be equally demonstrated in non-battle situations in England. Those American and British soldiers who were stationed in many camps across barren Salisbury Plain managed to get a good deal of practice in the art of street fighting and unarmed hand-to-hand combat, although the method employed will not be found in any military manual, nor did it have the approval of the mayor, aldermen, councillors or citizens of the City of Salisbury, where most of the battles occurred on Friday, Saturday and Sunday nights; that was assuming that the airborne soldiers' meagre pay had not run out, or the taverns of the city had not been drunk dry. In those days it was not unusual for the public houses to have sold their quotas of beer by Friday night, in which case the long-suffering people of Salisbury enjoyed a comparatively peaceful weekend.

The worst trouble usually began when a group of our lads entered a pub and met up with some black American soldiers. They were really friendly lads and we always seemed to get on well with them. The only form of entertainment at the time was usually a battered old piano, but the black lads were very musical and there was usually one among them who could knock out a few tunes, so we would soon be enjoying a singsong. All would be enjoyable until some white Americans came in.

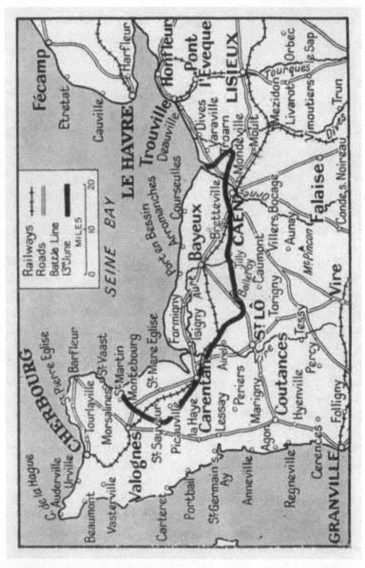

Normandy, showing the front line on 13 June 1944, one week after D-Day.

The black lads would then tell us that they had to drink up and go. When this first happened, we could not believe our ears. We were all in this bloody war together, and would all be dying for the same cause when the time came – the right to individual freedom – so what the hell gave the white Yanks the right to expect their coloured countrymen to leave any pub that the whites chose to enter?

After experiencing this inequality a few times, we got mad and told the black lads, 'You stay put – you were here first and if they don't like drinking in the same pub as you they can push off and find another one.' This was easier said than done, for when a pub ran dry it was a case of touring round the city centre to find another one which was still open. When the colour problem arose, the whites would stand just inside the door glaring at the coloured lads, and us, until we told them in no uncertain terms to 'Push Off!' They would then withdraw with shouted threats as they left and when we eventually emerged it was not unusual to find a large mob of them waiting for us. If we were outnumbered, we would immediately yell out our battle cry that had been originated by the 1st Airborne Division in North Africa and adopted by all Airborne men thereafter. Up would go the cry 'Wahoo Mohammed!' The effect of that cry was truly amazing. Within minutes, and from all directions, Red Berets would appear and a pitched battle would commence. Our unwritten airborne law was clearly understood by every Red Devil – at least amongst the lower ranks – and regardless of which airborne unit they served in: if an Airborne man was in trouble and called out our battle cry, it didn't matter what you were doing, you immediately responded to the call. Many a lass, out walking with an Airborne lad, would be dumbfounded as her escort, on hearing the battle cry, would say, 'Sorry – I've got to go!' and he would rush off to join in the fight. If it dragged on, it often meant a long walk back to camp with a black eye, a bleeding nose, or a thick lip because the last lorry would have left in order to return the troops before midnight.

The long walk also meant that we would not arrive back in camp until well after midnight, which forced us to find a way of getting inside without entering the guarded entrance gate. But we always succeeded, usually with the help of the patrolling guard. What always amazed me, and still does, was that the white Yanks never cottoned on to our system and adopted their own. Time and again they started fights in which they greatly outnumbered us, but invariably, when our battle cry was yelled, within minutes they were overwhelmed beneath a sea of Red Devils. It was all good and brutal fun and, when the chips were really down, we all managed to achieve a degree of togetherness that enabled us to beat the real enemy and win the war. And, who knows, perhaps our frequent battles around Salisbury helped to give us the courage to fight hard when it was really needed when the odds were stacked against us and when no amount of 'Wahoo Mohammed' would bring us reinforcements!

Thunder And Lightning – Martin White

As our Dakota neared the French coastline on the evening of 6 June 1944 the dispatcher moved to the rear of the aircraft and looked out of the open door as we crossed the coast. At the same time the German anti-aircraft units began to switch on their searchlights, and their anti-aircraft guns began to pour fire into the night sky. I was standing just behind the dispatcher and had something of an angled view outside the aircraft. At eighteen years of age I was overexcited at the momentous occasion I was about to become involved in and yelled into the dispatcher's ear, 'Jesus, all we need is that bloody thunder and lightning to jump into!'

I was somewhat taken aback when the dispatcher yelled back at me, 'What the hell are you looking at, you idiot? That's not thunder and lightning – that's bloody flak!'

Adrenaline Rush – Humphrey Booth

Our platoon was in the back of a Horsa glider over the Channel and everyone was chatting away, some were smoking and a few were singing. Then the German searchlights flashed on and the anti-aircraft fire began to shake the glider. Suddenly there was a loud bang and the whole framework shook and everything became deathly silent as we all realised this was it, no more playing soldiers, we were in the real thing and if we got a direct hit then it was absolute curtains for all of us and more than a few wished they'd gone and done the parachute course. Then, out of nowhere, someone yelled above the noise of the droning engines, 'OK lads, now the CSM has got your attention he's going to read us all a bedtime story beginning with "Once upon a time in a far-off land over the sea"!' The whole glider suddenly broke up laughing.

Airborne Humour – Ellis Blackmore
Early in the morning of 5 June the 6th Airborne Division began landing north-east of Caen, France, to secure the left flank of the invasion force by controlling bridges over the Caen Canal. Gliders were landing all over the place. Ours had come down next to a river and was balanced precariously on the very edge of the bank. While he dragged the co-pilot out of the cockpit the pilot yelled, 'Cut holes in the side – we're going to slide into the river any moment!'

Seconds later, everyone was hacking at the side of the fuselage. It didn't take much before there were huge holes in it and everyone scrambled out. As the last of the lads emerged the Horsa slid from view as the river grabbed it and dragged it away. With that, the platoon commander asked had everyone escaped and had they all got their weapons and packs? The young Toddy answered, 'No Sir, the PIAT went down when the glider sank.'

Angrily, the platoon commander said, 'Why the hell didn't you get it you fool?'

Dumbfounded, Toddy looked at him as if he was mad and replied, 'You yelled get out quick Sir, and it was a choice between it or me, and when I asked it, it said to save myself!'

His First Kill – Alan Salter
About twenty of us glider pilots had collected together under our OC after we landed. The LZ was reasonably quiet with only the occasional burst of machine-gun fire and a few mortar rounds landing among the gliders. Considering the number

of gliders that had landed, very few had been destroyed. But now we were down, we were required to do fighting patrols. The OC didn't want us going off half-cocked and annoying the Germans too much as we didn't have anything to stop armoured vehicles of any sort except some Gammon bombs and they were a bigger danger to us. Anyway, he just wanted to find out where they were. So we formed small patrols and began to search the edges of the LZ. Only two of us in our patrol had seen action before – both of us were in the desert against the Africa Corps – the rest of them were complete novices, but we'd done enough infantry training to be able to hold our own if we came across any Germans.

Led by the staff sergeant, Terry Hay, we moved off. Around us the battle was beginning to hot up as the Germans finally realised this was the start of the big battle they had anticipated. We'd been going for about an hour when we spotted a farm. Coming from one corner of the yard were bursts of heavy machine-gun fire aimed into the sky. They were obviously targeting parachutists or gliders. It seemed incredible that only a mile or two away there was the biggest air armada the world had ever seen. From all over the area the same thing was happening. Long lines of tracer arced upwards as aircraft passed overhead. And at 500 feet an MG 34 or 42 can do a lot of damage, as both can fire around 900 rounds a minute out to a range of 1,800 metres. After a quick 'O' Group it was decided we would take out the gun and the farmhouse, as there had to be more Germans inside the building. Three of us got the farmhouse while the other three crept around to the machine-gun post. I was amazed that we were able to get so close to the main building without getting spotted. There was a war on and there appeared to be no guards posted. It couldn't last, and it didn't. A door suddenly opened just as we crept up to the building and light from inside spilled out on to where we were. There in the doorway stood a German obviously coming out to check the area. Right alongside me was a young sergeant with a Sten gun.

The German and him had literally come face to face. Luckily the sergeant was the quicker of the two and emptied a magazine from his Sten gun into the German from no more than 3 feet away. Hit with over thirty rounds, the German was dead on his feet only his body didn't know it, so he was physically pushed backwards into the farmhouse by the sheer impact of the rounds hitting him. Luckily, I had a hand grenade ready, and it went in after him. The other sergeant threw one in as well, and then we then took to our heels. As we ran we heard a couple of other explosions coming from the farmyard; these were followed by bursts of Sten gun fire. The others had managed to take out the machine-gun post. When we got back and told the OC what had happened, I made mention that the sergeant had fired a whole magazine into the German to kill him. I wasn't angry over the waste of ammunition; I was simply making a comment that a short burst would have been sufficient. The OC looked at me and said, 'When one makes one's first kill, even from 3 feet, it is far better to overdo it, than under do it, as you never know, you might miss!'

A 'Cynic' in the Airborne – William Holding

I was mates with Ozzie and Harry, both of whom had been in North Africa, where Montgomery had insisted on having an advantage of 3 to 1 in men, 5 to 1 in tanks and artillery, and 100 to 1 in aircraft before he'd attack the Germans in Egypt. It seemed to us squaddies that it didn't take a military genius to achieve 'a glorious victory' when the odds were so heavily weighted in your favour. Even then, the Germans gave us a bloody nose before they finally gave up. Compared with Stalingrad and Kursk, Alamein had been but a 'petty skirmish', and all the while the bulk of the British Army, including the 6th Airborne, was in England champing at the bit to get at the Germans in Normandy. The hero of Alamein, the so-called mightiest general since Alexander, came home to tunes of glory and accolades beyond belief, then one fine day he was brought, all conquering, into the wilds of Wiltshire, where he would rouse his airborne division to his own level of bloodlust. We brave paratroopers, many of whom hadn't yet fired a shot in anger, had been stood for hours in carefully prearranged 'spontaneous' welcoming formations overlooking a sort of platform while we waited for the great military genius to arrive. When he did, he was in the middle of a flurry of flunkies who eventually hoisted him aloft on the podium. We simply couldn't believe our eyes; the unremarkable-looking little fellow who was pushed in front of the rest of the red-tabs couldn't possibly be anyone but a warm-up comedian, but to our astonishment he was introduced as General Montgomery, the hero of Alamein. Around me there was a great deal of sniggering from within the ranks – this was the 'modest' hero, the genius that would lead us to victory?

From this bank-clerkish figure there issued forth a clerk's voice; a piping, snooty squeak in which we were informed that we were the world's finest soldiers and that we were led by the world's finest officers. If that was true, then how did we get kicked out of France, Greece, Crete, and pushed back by Rommel in the desert? How did we lose Malaya and Singapore? And if God was on our side why then why were the Germans claiming he was on theirs? One of us must be wrong, mustn't he? As he addressed us, Montgomery, mighty conqueror of Rommel's invincible army, was looking for an ocean he could push the 'Narzis into'. For a battle cry, it was hardly *Henry V*, but then Montgomery wasn't Olivier – he was more like Stan Laurel. The jokes and laughter at his expense when he left he certainly wouldn't have been happy about.

My platoon was to drop close beside a little bridge that spanned the River Orne near the Normandy town of Troarn. Our job was to seize the bridge and hold it until glider-borne sappers, together with their explosives and a good number of infantrymen, landed close by. We were then to give the sappers a hand to blow the bridge, after which we'd settle down for twenty-four hours and wait for the seaborne troops to relieve us as they dashed like hares towards Paris. It was a simple plan; by denying the Wehrmacht use of the Troarn bridge, fewer of them would be able to get to the beaches to carve up our soldiers landing on them. It looked foolproof and, to make us feel even better about it, we were shown photographs of our bridge and then trained on a scale model of it. We grew so fond of it that in the end we didn't really want to blow it up. Our scepticism turned out to be well founded.

We asked ourselves whether or not this was going to be just a safe little curtain-raiser to the main event, and were we really going to put the Wehrmacht through the mincer and end the war in the blink of an eye? On top of which, would our seaborne comrades relieve us within twenty-four hours as our generals had promised, and would we really capture the city of Caen, as Field Marshal Montgomery had personally sworn we would, within the first few days? And after Caen would the roads to Paris and Berlin be wide open? Hadn't he sworn it would be all over after a few short weeks? But then, he hadn't told the Germans that, had he? On the evening of 5 June 1944, together with two-thirds of my platoon, I was squeezed into a DC3 at an airport near Burford. I use the word 'squeezed' because we were encumbered by monstrously heavy loads. Besides a parachute and the usual battle gear, each of us carried either a 2-inch mortar tube or its base plate, or two of its bombs. We also had bandoleers of extra ammo for the Vickers machine gun and extra rations, so in the end we had to be pushed up the landing steps by loaders as if we'd been cattle off to the slaughter. Some of the relief and the excitement we'd felt about at last going to war evaporated very quickly and it didn't help to be told that our Canadian pilot had never dropped parachutists before.

Welcome aboard a one-way trip to nowhere! To add to our misgivings, once aloft we circled for what seemed like hours while history's largest air armada got into formation. Finally, buffeted by the slipstreams of hundreds of aircraft all around ours, we literally bounced our way across to France. I wasn't the only one to be airsick; I hoped we'd be shot down and so have done with it. I was so happy when we got the order to stand up and get the green light on to go. I waddled like an overweight duck to the doorway and fell through it, turned left and like a ton of bricks dropped into the dark French sky. It was midnight and was an unusual mode of immigration, I suppose, but there I was, overseas at last. Knees locked together, I rolled over nicely to settle comfortably onto the French grass. I banged the 'box' on my chest to break the lock mechanism that closed my parachute around me and stood up to look for my mates and, I hoped, for road signs reading 'Troarn That Way ½ kilometre'. Above all, I looked for a flashing purple light from a scout who had been dropped ahead of us and would beam a signal that we'd been told to aim for. Our platoon was to converge upon that light and, once formed up, be led by a French resistance fighter to our bridge. We'd also been told that there'd be no enemy soldiers about and that we'd be at our target within an hour of getting out of our parachute harnesses. What met my eyes instead was a dazzle of brightly coloured lights, several of which were purple, flashing from all directions. It was as if I'd landed on Blackpool Promenade at Illumination time. For another stomach-churning thing, the only other living creature I could see was a white horse I'd nearly landed on; what's more, judging by the sound of gunfire blazing away on all sides, there were plenty of angry soldiers about; a good many of them appeared to be German, having been told that God was definitely on their side.

Far from being on our bridge within an hour, I was still in the field I'd landed in. I had managed to rendezvous with five others, all of them privates. We weren't to know until much later that the fireworks, the lines of tracer-bullets we'd seen, and the din of small-arms fire we'd heard, weren't being directed against us or our missing mates; no, they came from enemy guns alright, but far from the Germans having been alerted to our arrival by filthy spies, they were engaged in a night exercise, blasting away at each other with blank ammunition. Not understanding this, we six forlorn creatures viewed our situation with alarm. Looking on the bright side, though, we worked it out that if we weren't far away from our bridge then we were near to our platoon mates, who might be about to blow the bridge. Ergo, wait for the big bang and make tracks in its direction. The bang never came. Another thing we didn't know was that the plane carrying the other half of our platoon, including our lieutenant, had been shot down; overall, the battalion already had some 210 men dead, wounded and missing before that battle had even started – nearly half the battalion! All right then, we still needed to know the way to Troarn. Never doubting that we'd soon come across a place

name, 'Troarn – Bienvenue!', we set out looking for a road –
any road.

Sure enough we soon came to one, and sure enough it had its
name-sign. Mystifyingly, however, instead of proclaiming the
village ahead to be Troarn, it said that it was Herouvillette, a
place we'd never heard of, and a place moreover that on closer
inspection appeared to be lifeless; not even a dog to bark. In no
mood for heroism, we six decided that the most sensible thing
to do was to hide in the outskirts of Herouvillette and wait
for daybreak. We chose to secrete ourselves about a quarter
of a mile from town, in a deep ditch beside the road. One
of us, the platoon signaller, was humping a thundering great
wireless set that he couldn't get a spark out of. He wouldn't
dump it, though, because come the morning light he might be
able to fix it and maybe find out what the hell was going on?
Poor sod, he became the first man I saw die. Unfortunately, he
wasn't the last. He perished, not by bullet or bomb or bayonet,
sinking in a split second into the mire at the bottom of the
ditch. He and his wireless disappeared with a sort of watery
whoosh – Roger and out, and we couldn't help him because
he'd simply disappeared below the surface before we realised
what had happened. We had no option but to abandon him
to his watery grave and the remaining five of us fled to higher
wooded ground, where dawn found us hugging the earth while
shells from our own ships out at sea screamed over our heads.

Our position an hour or so later was that while the shells
told us which way was north, we remained confused because
we'd still no idea where we were in relation to Troarn. There
were still no signs of soldiers, either friend or foe, and our
spirits were lowering by the minute. Then all of a sudden,
just as though he'd known we were there, into our hideout
walked a thirteen-year-old local youth who introduced himself
as Daniel. After telling us how he hated the 'Boche', he said
that we were a long way from Troarn but he knew where there
were lots of Britons who'd dropped from the sky during the
night and he could lead us easily and safely to them. True to his
word, on the night of 7 June Daniel guided us through woods
and dales until on the morning of the 8th he brought us into

a shambolic gathering of a couple of hundred stragglers from our own battalion where even some of the NCOs didn't know what to do. God knows what Daniel thought of his first sight of the cream of the British Army; we must have looked more like cut-throats on the run than liberators. When we'd all put our stories together, it turned out that the Canadian pilots had cast us out of their aircraft while flying too high, meaning that few of us had come to earth where we'd supposed to, and we'd been scattered so far apart that, for instance, those carrying the 2-inch mortar tubes had dropped not metres but miles away from those carrying the baseplates, and so on. Nobody knew exactly where we were, where the seaborne soldiers were, or what was best for us to do. Everybody was in the mood to lynch Montgomery, he of precise planning and overwhelming odds fame. What it boiled down to was that the airborne operation, which we'd been conned into believing would be flawless (and heaven knows the brass had had long enough to make it so), had in practice been a right old balls-up. (The next one – Arnhem – was to be an even bigger one). But maybe the church parades had paid off after all because in reality there had been few casualties (even the rest of my platoon had walked away from their crash-landing into captivity) and the sea-landings had proved to be a lot easier than had been feared.

But confusion was piled upon commotion; the dash for Paris ground into the Normandy soil, and to our chagrin we were told to dig in like poor bloody infantrymen and help secure the beachhead against possible counter-attack. What happened to Daniel? Since we were unable to take him safely back home to Herouvillette, he was sent to help in the field kitchens and a stray shell (possibly one of ours) landed on the cookhouse and killed him – *C'est la guerre*. Finally, we were all together after the battalion had been dropped over half of France. We now found ourselves fighting a private war on the south-east corner of the division area. The commanding officer had only 141 men turn up at the RV and in the end he trudged off to Bois de Bavent, where the rest of us eventually found him. Luckily, the Engineers didn't need our help – they blew the bridges anyway. After that, having never fired my Sten gun in anger before, I suddenly found that the Germans were determined to kill me come what may. As usual, Montgomery had lied; the Germans weren't going to lie down and let us walk all over them – they were determined to fight it out regardless.

The terrain made big attacks impossible, and so I not only had to shoot the Germans trying to shoot me from a very close range, less than 100 yards mostly, I also had to walk very carefully in case I trod on a mine. Mines are very indiscriminate; they kill anyone stupid enough to step on them, and I was determined not to allow one to do it to me. During those first few days we all learnt how to chop down trees really quick and use them to cover our trenches, as the Germans seemed to like shelling us. I must admit that from that standpoint I came to really hate them as quite a few of my friends were killed this way. We also had a commanding officer that was a go-getter; he didn't believe in sitting on his backside, and he certainly didn't believe in us sitting on ours either. We patrolled far and wide in the surrounding area, sometimes as far as Bures and Troarn, a place I came to know well. So we were constantly making a nuisance of ourselves by laying ambushes, mining roads, and raiding enemy positions. Life in the Bois de Bavent was far from pleasant because little sunlight could penetrate the canopy of trees, creating particularly damp conditions that attracted flies and mosquitoes and made it impossible for clothing to be dried. Luckily, we were withdrawn from the area on 16 June to allow us to have some rest. But all good things come to an end and we went back and played war once again. Next, they let us follow the Germans as they withdrew. Montgomery had got one thing right: the Germans would withdraw; they didn't have much option because they were taking heavy casualties. But we took them as well; he didn't tell us about that one. We ended up in the Dives valley doing a frontal assault on a village called Annebault. We eventually took it but somehow the military experts, most of whom had never fired a shot in anger, created the impression we got away lightly in the casualty count. Whoever said it obviously wasn't anywhere near the battle. If he was, he must have been down a very deep hole throughout it. Once again, I left a lot of good friends behind in that terrible place.

Next, we had to take another place by the name of Beuzeville. This time it took us all day to gain a foothold. We got a hell of a licking as the Germans were determined not to give it up. We were lucky that we had Cromwell tanks supporting us or it would have been outright butchery on a grand scale. In the end, the Germans decided enough was enough and let us have the place. Personally, I would have let them have it, as by the time we got it there wasn't much left except German bodies inside it and ours outside it. More of my friends were left behind when we began the chase once again. At this rate, it looked like I wouldn't have any friends left. And this was the army that Montgomery and his henchmen said would fold like a pack of cards. In every town that was still standing, happy, newly freed Normans paraded in front of us haunted-looking, shaven-headed females, demented creatures with the eyes of caged animals. They'd been tried by kangaroo courts and convicted of having 'fraternised with the enemy'. Their summary punishment was to have their heads shorn by thugs wielding blunt, old-fashioned cut-throat razors; then, bloodied and horribly disfigured, they were put on display before a jeering populace and us. Most of us felt sorry for them in a funny sort of way, as from then on they'd have the 'Mark of the Devil' hanging over them. As Gabriel José Marquez, the famous Columbian novelist, once wrote, 'The greatest victory in a battle is to be alive at the end of it.' They were extremely lucky compared to the male collaborators; their homes were wrecked, everything of value inside was stolen, and they were lined up against a wall and shot out of hand. Curiously, few of us felt any sympathy for them at all as they hadn't simply been given perfume and other trinkets; they'd often made substantial amounts of money out of, and turned traitor on, their fellow Frenchmen.

In the end we lost well over half the battalion in Normandy, some 300 men; so did all the other battalions and we were eventually sent on a nice rest to replenish our numbers so they could find another battle where we could lose the other half. Unfortunately, it proved impossible to replenish any battalion back to full strength, as there simply weren't enough men passing though Hardwick and Ringway to do so. One of the problems that arose was the influx of new officers. Because we couldn't get enough, many of them weren't parachute qualified and the lads, especially the older ones, didn't like that one little bit. Then in December the Germans, who by now were supposed to be cowed and defeated, pulled another bag of tricks out of their pocket and attacked through the forest of the Ardennes. Our friend Monty ordered the 6th Airborne to move to Belgium and form a defensive line along the River Meuse. Then, another sneaky trick, we were told we were going to attack the leading German formation in the Rochefort area. Once again, we were thrown in. It was another shooting gallery; we'd attack, they'd attack, and then we'd do it all over again. For people that were on their last legs, the Germans did a bloody good job of fooling us. Finally we got the better of them and they withdrew, leaving behind a lot of dead and wounded; mind you, once again so did we. By then the battalion had been brought back to life almost twice over. Montgomery and his little gang thoroughly enjoyed it though, and he ended up with more kudos and medals. Me, I ended up with several bits of shrapnel in my arm. I supposed I should be happy about it; I could have easily been dead.

Then, in September 1944, Monty threw in the 1st Airborne Division to capture an unwinnable bridge at Arnhem, and lost it because he and a few other generals didn't plan it properly. A 'Bridge Too Far' that the gallant men of the 1st Airborne couldn't hold because Montgomery hadn't thought it through and couldn't resupply them, and when he sent in the armour to get them out, the Germans chopped them to bits because they were forced to attack down a single road, more bad planning and preparation that even a private soldier could have told you was insane. After a couple of dozen tanks had been destroyed along with a couple of hundred infantry, killed by the very Germans Montgomery said were on their last legs, and the 2nd Army was finally sitting on the banks of the Rhine, a stone's throw from the 1st Airborne, Montgomery wouldn't risk sending them over, so he played the numbers game again. Napoleon Bonaparte got it right at Borodino in 1812 when he said, 'Go, Sir, gallop, and don't forget that the world was made in six days. You can ask me for anything you like, except time.' When it was all over he'd praise the 1st Airborne while he and his lapdog generals added more accolades to the ones they'd already got, while all the men who'd fought themselves to a standstill got was a parade in front of the king and queen at Buckingham Palace. As if that made up for all the mates they left behind in that appalling place?

In March 1945, after the Americans had already crossed the Rhine, Monty did his now famous numbers game yet again. He wasn't going to cross until he had at least a 4 to 1 advantage and overwhelming firepower. We had to clear the way for him so he devised a 'fantastic' plan that would fool the Germans into thinking we wouldn't be stupid enough to drop during daylight. So what did we do? We dropped in daylight. The Yanks and us took more casualties that day than we did at Normandy, but according to Monty it was a brilliant success, and all the while General Patton's 3rd Army was driving onward from where they'd already crossed the Rhine ahead of us. It really made Montgomery mad as he hated Patton; in fact Montgomery hated all the American generals, and they hated the egotistical pen-pusher back. Having landed on the far side of the Rhine, we promptly ran into some of the best troops the Germans had, the Fallschirmjäger, and they weren't going to give up without a big fight. In some places it was hand-to-hand fighting in the end. After we finished them off, we then had to assault a position that had 20 mm anti-aircraft guns firing on a level trajectory. They stopped us with a wall of metal, but once again we won the day for King and Country.

This time I was really lucky I only got shot in the leg. As I think back on it, in any other walk of life, errors of judgement on the Arnhem and Rhine scale would swiftly have led to the wholesale sacking of the principals responsible, but this being the walk of death, the generals weren't pressed to even say 'sorry'. They went instead into an orgy of backslapping, singing the praises of each other's deeds, and awarded themselves higher ranks, medallions, sashes, titles and more pay. They even let the Russians take Berlin because it was politically the right thing to do, although Monty wanted to get there first, but the 'King-Maker' Churchill stopped him. And while this was going on, Adolf Hitler escaped his people's wrath by poisoning himself. Now the war was over, the great cigar-smoker chose to go for an election which, to his astonishment, he lost by many a mile because people were fed up with a 'supremo'. But what they hadn't forgotten was that during the First World War he was another abysmal failure and was sent to Coventry politically because of the slaughter at Gallipoli, when over 37,000 Allied soldiers died putting into practice a 'brilliant' plan he'd devised which failed miserably and which the Australians and New Zealanders still hated us for.

But of course, election defeat or not, Churchill's class held on to its domination of the British establishment. Atlee's so-called socialist government made noises that provoked the bourgeoisie to lay charges of 'Bolshevism' and 'Red Dictatorship' against it, but it lacked the guts fundamentally to try to alter the class structure. It remained easier for a working man to be appointed Minister of War than for him to get a royal commission in one of the armed services. True, he set alarm bells ringing with talk of 'democratising' the services, but he was easily neutered by being kept so busy inspecting parades and taking salutes that he lacked the clout to even promote lance corporals, let alone generals. And all the while, the architect of much of this butchery, Montgomery, paraded around like a tin god and nobody pointed a finger at him or 'Boy' Browning for the Arnhem cock-up or the Rhine butchery; no, they took the accolades and didn't give a toss about the poor soldiers who died in droves trying to uphold the pride of the Airborne.

Taking the Orne River Bridge – James Rutledge

It was early in the morning of 6 June and the pilots did a great job in bringing the glider down in the dark, and although we hit the ground with an almighty thump and slithered to an abrupt halt, nobody was injured. I am still not sure which glider landed first, but always thought it was ours. The platoon commander, Lieutenant Fox, quickly got everyone together and led the way across the fields to our target, a bridge that crossed the River

Orne. Fortunately, it was very lightly defended; the big bit of excitement occurred when a phosphorous bomb was hurled at German defenders who were attempting to man a machine-gun position. The situation was quiet almost as quickly as it started; it was all over in approximately fifteen minutes. Guards were left at the bridge and the remainder of the platoon was redirected across fields to join Major Howard's team at what is now known as Pegasus Bridge. One of my most vivid memories on reaching the bridge was finding myself lying alongside Sergeant 'Wagger' Thornton, who was armed with a PIAT. On the road on the opposite side of the bridge was a junction and from this emerged three French tanks that had been commandeered by the Germans following the Dunkirk debacle. Anyway, 'Wagger' sighted the PIAT and fired, hitting the foremost tank broadside on. It must have been a direct hit on its magazine, for there was an almighty explosion and ammunition continued to explode for more than an hour afterwards. The two remaining tanks quickly returned from whence they came. Another of my memories was of a German motorcyclist who had been blown off his machine by a burst of fire from a Bren gun. Both his legs were in one hell of a state and he was screaming his head off. A German officer who was also at the scene had immediately surrendered to me, passing over his revolver, which was a great souvenir. He was most concerned about his wounded colleague and in very good English asked for medical assistance, saying, 'I don't think you would want to leave one of your friends in this condition, would you?' I had to agree as the poor man was in one hell of a state, so I used my morphine syrette on him and he quietened down. I knew it was a risk as I might need it later on, but at the time it seemed the right thing to do. I assured the officer that I would return to his comrade with medical assistance as soon as he had accompanied me to an officer, which he did. Afterwards I went back to the wounded German and two of us carried him on a stretcher to the medics.

The following morning I said to my mate, 'I thought I could hear bagpipes.' Confirmation came a few minutes later as the sounds of the pipes grew louder and the Green Berets of Lord

Lovat's force came into view, advancing towards Pegasus Bridge to a tune I later found out to be 'Blue Bonnets over the Border'. Regrettably, as they tried to march over the bridge with the pipes leading them, German snipers killed several and from then on the march turned into a wild disorganised run. When they got to our side, Major Howard approached Lord Lovat. Holding out his hand, he said: 'We are very pleased to see you, Old Boy.'

Lovat responded with, 'Yes, and I'm sorry we are two and a-half minutes late.' It was typical of officers, always doing that 'pip-pip tally-ho' thing.

Typical Humour – Peter Stevens

When the Pegasus Bridge was taken, a number of other men from the company were tasked with reinforcing them as quickly as possible as it was assumed that the Germans would throw everything they could to get the bridge back. On the night of the actual attack, one of the best-known conversations took place in the middle of the bridge, when a back-up platoon arrived. Lieutenant Sweeney raced up to Lieutenant Fox and said, 'Dennis, Dennis – how are you? Is everything alright?'

Fox looked him up and down and said, 'Yes, I think so Tod, but I'm damned if can find the bloody umpires!'

The umpire reference refers to the dozens of practices we did on a similar bridge in England when we had to wait for the umpires to tell us whether we took it successfully or not. Quite often we ended up fighting with the bridge defenders, the Poles, who appeared not to understand English and refused to let us capture the bridge. At one point there was some heated discussion between the umpires, Major Frost and the Polish major. At the time we were having a ding-dong battle around them with everyone using rifle butts, boots and fists. It ended up with a whole load of Poles and our lads getting thrown into the river, which caused one hell of a problem as most couldn't swim.

Landing in Normandy – Ray White

Slowly, the Halifax tow aircraft increased speed and off we went with fingers crossed. There was slight slipstream trouble as we lifted clear of the ground; otherwise everything was OK. Once we were airborne, we did the usual forming up before crossing the coast. At 0320 hours we were approaching the French coast. Gunfire observed and flak encountered, creating a few hairy moments as a few of them detonated quite close. Cloud and smoke encountered, which made it rather difficult to concentrate on where we are. A little while later, a flashing green signal observed. At 0328 hours we got the signal to pull off from tug skipper. Away we went, making for the LZ on the starboard side. Unfortunately, the visibility was poor, but green landing lights were discernible to the co-pilot, who advised on the direction of approach. I dropped the nose down to avoid incoming flak, much to the consternation of our passengers travelling in the back. I don't know why as we had done this dozens of times in training, but I suppose when it's the real thing everyone is on edge, fearing the worst. Not long afterwards, I lowered the big barn door flaps, pulled the nose up and we had rather a bumpy landing and managed to avoid obstructions. All was not well, though, as the front wheel collapsed at the end of the run, but otherwise everything was OK. We all tumbled out but were unable to run the 6-pounder gun and jeep out of the tail owing to the position of the glider. In the end, we unloaded the gun through the front ramp, then tried to detach the tail unit, which we couldn't do, so in the end we decided to blow the tail off. Nice loud bang.

After a struggle to get things sorted out, we eventually moved off. In the darkness it was easy to misjudge where we were, as all around there appeared to be dozens of shadowy gliders lying at all angles and figures moving in the same direction. It took us a while to link up with the other guns. When we did, we moved into position with extreme caution as we had already lost one man to enemy snipers and were lucky not to have lost a few others. Once we were in position, we immediately began digging in and camouflaging up, ready for action. It was 0830 hours before things began to hot up. Sergeant John Thomas was on look-out up a tree and observed enemy movement on our left flank. Our gun was well concealed but not very well sighted in this instance. With the tank were the inevitable infantry; they may have spotted John, we don't know, but we came under small arms fire just as he clambered down. He was forced to throw himself on the ground or he would have been hit. Sergeant Fred Easton was on the supporting Bren gun and opened fire on them. By this time a self-propelled gun was in range but the gun layer did not consider he could hit it. In the meantime I had loaded a round in the breech and had a look through the sights myself. By this time it had turned and was travelling almost parallel with us, not 200 yards away, and it needed to be stopped.

I told the gun layer to change with me and while Fred Easton and the rest kept the infantry occupied with small-arms fire, I laid the gun. The first round missed by a whisker, so we reloaded and this time I let the beast run into my line of sight. No sooner had it entered the sight aperture than it stopped and began to turn toward us. I was expecting them to open up on us any minute and so I quickly fired; this time it was a hit and the tank went up in flames. While all this happened, the gun on my left flank hit a tank, and another one that was almost unobserved from our position was put out of action by a gun on our right flank. So, two tanks and a self-propelled gun were seen to be burning, and ammo was exploding in each at varied intervals. The infantry who were escorting the tanks were then engaged for the remainder of the day by small-arms fire. Along our front we must have accounted for at least fifty German infantry killed and a substantial number wounded before they withdrew. At one point they requested permission to recover their wounded, which was granted. But it was noticed that the so-called medical orderlies were trying to pin point our positions, so we fired over their heads and drove them away. Once this happened the Germans began mortaring and shelling us, but they didn't seem to have registered where our guns were so it had little effect on us.

Later that evening, reinforcements arrived by air and the enemy opened up with small-arms fire, especially machine guns, while the LZ was peppered with mortar fire. Late that night there was an increasing amount of activity in front of us, about 1,000 yards away. We could hear armoured vehicles and by the sound of them they were tanks or self-propelled guns and they appeared to be heading straight toward us. We were suddenly ordered to withdraw the guns to battery HQ while infantry took over our positions. Why, we don't know, as we had the hitting power to stop any tank the Germans had. But it's all down to numbers. We can ill afford to lose a gun this early in the battle, so we were sited behind the infantry. Throughout the night all hell breaks loose as the Germans desperately try to break the line. Artillery was used to break them up and our lads gave a good account of themselves with PIATs and mortars while firing upon the accompanying German infantry. We were not needed, although I was certain that on a few occasions we could have been extremely useful. By early next morning the attack was driven off and several more tanks and armoured vehicles were burning in front of our positions. Mind you, we haven't got off scot-free either and there was a steady stream of wounded being brought to the rear. Just as first light was beginning to show itself the guns were moved to Ranville, ready for an attack, and all glider pilots were relieved by regular anti-tank crews and we headed for home.

6 June – Andy Andrews

The smoke got thicker and demanded extreme concentration on the part of the tug pilot, Paddy, and myself. We didn't fancy landing in the Channel at any time, especially tonight. Paddy was talking over the intercom and I tried to observe the lights on the wings of the tug. Just when everything was disappearing and I was preparing to go into the low-tow position, the smoke gradually began to clear until quite suddenly we were in comparatively good visibility. Almost at once the observer, speaking as calmly as if he was ordering another beer, said, 'Oh! There are the two houses – bang on time too.' This was a great relief. The flak was coming up lazily but didn't seem interested in us until just before the tracer burnt out. Almost unconsciously Paddy, who was flying now, skidded away slightly out of position, but he soon corrected and I concentrated on finding those lights.

Our normal practice was to let Paddy fly the glider until I was quite certain of my landmarks, then I would say goodbye to the tug and take over for the landing. Between us we had calculated that at the operational height and the time of crossing the coast, we should fly between two houses, then 90 seconds later, whether the lights were visible or not, we could fly straight ahead and land within reach of our rendezvous. Well, the best-made plans do seem to go astray. There were no lights! In a voice which sounded rather unreal, I could hear myself asking Major Joubert [the tug pilot] about it and him, in a very cheery manner, replying, 'Don't worry, hang on, we have bags of time, I'll go round again in a second or two.'

Having looked for and failed to locate the lights, Major Joubert reported that he could see some lights to his right. Within five seconds it was just the right spot, so I said goodbye, and someone wished us luck, and then there was the familiar jerk with the noise of the wind gradually receding into the background and the speed dropped off to a modest 80 mph. Paddy had handed over the controls and was intently watching an ack-ack battery on our right, whose tracer seemed a bit too near. He drew my attention to it and almost at once, as I put on half flap, the flak turned and seemed to have found another target. Then we saw the target and another Horsa, well below us, flying towards the flak. Just a second afterwards it switched its emergency lights on and illuminated a small row of trees between ourselves and the 'T' along which it was flying. Then we were coming in just right. A little bump, and then another, something like a ditch I thought. Then a wheel seemed to stick and started to swing the glider round. I applied full opposite rudder and my brake, and no sooner had we straightened up than we stopped. I immediately shot out of my seat; we were on the first light and not in our correct position, on the extreme left of the T. Having been forewarned by a training mishap that this might happen, we had arranged that Paddy would jump out and wave his torch to show the rear of the glider. This he did with feverish haste. I collected our personal kit and rifles and jumped out. The two 'bods', whom I had completely forgotten about, were on the ground before me. They took up positions on either side of the glider while I went round to Paddy.

We got ready to beat a hasty retreat if another glider was coming in on top of us, but there was not a sign of anything in the sky. You have no doubt been at an appointed place at the right time, waited for someone to arrive, and had to go away in disgust. We felt like that at first. Then a feeling of loneliness crept over us; even the Germans didn't greet us! Where were the independent parachutists who had put the T out? Not a soul, not a noise, nothing. I looked at Paddy and said, 'Let's get the tail off.' We went inside the glider and began to undo the nuts holding the tail on, removing them within a quarter of an hour, but couldn't get the tail to budge! Even when Paddy jumped on the top, it still wouldn't budge! We called the two drivers over and then began the oddest tug-of-war I ever competed in. One Horsa Mark I and four tired and sweating Airborne types. The glider won and while we sat back, exhausted, for a moment, it sat back contentedly as if it was back in England. We thought of using the charge to blow the tail off, but apart from the noise, and the fact that we were undisturbed, the type of equipment we were carrying decided us against it. Then, just as we picked up the handsaw, we heard the sound of approaching aircraft, and right above us the air seemed full of parachutes. It was a wonderful sight and we didn't feel lonely any more. For the next five minutes we were busy dodging kitbags that dangled from the feet of heavily loaded paratroopers. One man even landed on the tail, but nothing happened, and when we asked for help to get the tail off, he grinned and vanished. An Albemarle on our left suddenly lit up in flames, which brought us back to earth with a jolt.

There was nothing for it but to saw the tail off. My knuckles were already sore from the exertions inside the glider, and Paddy, who was as strong in the arms as anyone I knew, took first shift. We must have been sawing for about forty-five minutes when the driver looking out on the left gave us warning. Silhouetted against the skyline were ten armed men coming towards us. We crouched on the ground and debated whether they were Germans or paratroopers. They moved up to within touching distance and then we heard them speak. They were ours. Thank goodness! The password, 'Punch', and the answer, 'Judy', for the night were exchanged. But would they help us with our tail? Not a bit of it! They moved on to Ranville, not a bit interested in our problems. We had already decided that the only way to get the tail off was to get more manpower. There could be nothing holding the tail on now except sheer willpower! Then the comparative silence was disturbed by the hunting horn, which we had read had been used in the African campaigns, and the attack on Ranville began in earnest.

For fifteen minutes there was a great deal of small-arms fire and a house burst into flames about a mile away. The fact that we felt sure that we were on 'British' ground gave us confidence and we decided to make our way towards the village. We crossed the road, Paddy darting across and knocking the compass out of my hand. I had already taken a bearing and we didn't need it anymore, anyhow. We crossed a small orchard when, in our tracks, and with a very low trajectory, something which I judged to be an anti-tank gun fired twice. We decided that we had best make a detour and went back to the road. 'Punch!' came the challenge. 'Judy,' we breathed. It turned out to be two signallers, one of whom had injured his foot in a tree, together with a Canadian major from the Engineers who, screened by the hedge, was trying to pick up his bearings. He had already walked a long way, he said. It turned out he was one of the brigadier's party. I told him where I thought we were and it agreed with his guess. I then suggested that the best plan would be to make for the rendezvous we were supposed to be at for dawn, as we expected by then that Brigadier Hill would be there to set up his HQ. There were two possible routes. One towards the coast and turn right, or towards Ranville and turn left. We chose the latter, and learned later that it had been the right choice.

The glider hadn't been forgotten, and together our party of seven made our way towards the glider again. It was still standing in glorious dignity. Then the major went up to it and said 'Is this the tail?' and gave two little pushes and the thing fell off! The drivers undid the locking chains, adjusted the steering wheels and we were all ready to go. Once again, the drone of aircraft distracted our attention. This time it was Hamilcars and Horsas. One landed not too far away, the others went over the brow of a small rise towards Ranville. We walked over to the other glider pilots, who were having no trouble unloading. We exchanged names, just in case, then went back to our jeeps. It was here that we met up with Lieutenant Dodwell's party. We decided that while Taffy Lovett and I went ahead on either side of the road, the two jeeps were to follow behind, carrying the others at a safe distance. The orders to the drivers were to make for Ranville with the jeeps if we ran into any trouble, while we gave them covering fire. We came to the crossroads and, turning our backs to Ranville, headed east. After about fifteen minutes we came to a small hamlet. Taffy stayed on the outskirts with the jeeps drawn into the hedge about a hundred yards back, while I crept cautiously along the street. It was more difficult to walk quietly now, and I was relieved when I came out on the road again at the other side. In a few minutes the rest of the party were through and we continued along the road, which now seemed to rise slightly. About ten minutes later, as we approached another crossroads, which could now be seen as it was beginning to get light again, a sudden burst of firing came from a light automatic weapon immediately to our front and a little to our left. We halted, and then decided, as there was no further noise, to make for the trees. They turned out to be the entrance to the drive of a house that was our destination, the dawn rendezvous. The jeeps backed cautiously into the bushes at the side and we hastily dug a few holes as a small defensive position. It was quite light now, and round the bend of the drive came the middle-aged lady of the house. She showed no surprise at seeing us, and said that over the road there was an injured soldier to whom she was taking some wine. Two of us went with her and we brought back a young lad from the 13th Battalion, part of a group that had been dropped in the wrong place. Unable to take him with them, the others had left him there after making him comfortable.

With the holes finally dug, we decided to investigate the shooting, and a small patrol consisting of the major, Paddy and myself with one of the signallers cautiously approached the crossroads. On reaching them, we decided to turn left along what appeared to be the fence of the house that had been selected as the HQ. The right-hand bank was quite high, with a hedge bordering it, and on the left a similar bank, terminating in a wire fence, which made it impossible to climb quickly. Through force of habit we walked on the left, at about arm's-length intervals, and had proceeded about 75 yards down the road when a noise resembling the low note of a cow call attracted our attention on the other side of the road. We stopped, listened again, but there were no further noises. Then, after another two paces, I turned round to the major and said, 'I believe it's groaning.'

He said, 'Maybe. Challenge.'

I still had my head turned in the direction from which we had come when I said in a fairly normal tone, 'Punch.'

A voice replied, 'Wer ist das,' and followed it up, before we could have answered, even if we had wanted to, with a burst of automatic fire. The bullets went up the road behind us by about 10 yards and by the time the last one had bedded itself in the bank, we were all lying full-length in a ditch with a very strong gravelly bottom, about 18 inches wide and 18 inches deep, and facing in the wrong direction. To make matters worse, our rifles were useless and even if we could have seen where the fire came from, there didn't seem to be a target. I had a grenade in my pocket and seeing that the major had one arm free, I passed it back to him. He removed the pin, waited for what seemed like an eternity, and then threw it. The explosion took place where we judged the firing had come from. We waited for an answering burst but none came, and so very gingerly we turned round and began to retrace our steps towards the crossroads, one at a time, only this time crawling in the ditch. My hands and knees were sore for days afterwards, and when I stood up to run the last 10 yards, I fell over again with cramp, but we all got safely round the corner and back to our HQ.

We felt that next time we should make a pincer movement, one from either side of the road, but from the height of the bank. We had chosen another two men, but before we could start on this little war of our own, the lady of the house came back and we decided to question her as to the whereabouts of the Germans. She informed us that next door there was an HQ with about seventy-five Germans. That explained the sentry we must have disturbed, and it rather changed our plans. The major and one of the others went off to decide the best way to attack the house, while the rest of us decided to have a brew-up. Paddy started to prepare and I decided to go to the entrance of the drive and look down the road. I was observing from the cover of some bushes when along the road towards us came a party headed by two glider pilots, with what looked like their passengers. They hadn't seen me yet, and when they were almost opposite, they sat down on the side of the bank with their backs towards me. I could have touched them, but I said 'Hello' instead. Their look of surprise couldn't have been more complete! Nevertheless, we now had some more reinforcements and they came back to our hideout to rest. The next to arrive on the scene were the RAMC. They were in a party of about forty strong and had a Polish prisoner with them. He was a youngster and nearly died of fright a moment or two later when the pattern bombing of the beaches started. Even at the distance we were inland, the ground shook as though a miniature earthquake was in progress. The senior officers now took command and decided to send us, the glider pilots, back to Ranville. There we were to rejoin the glider pilot pool of reserves that had been formed.

We started out cautiously, walking parallel to the road. We passed a sentry, who only just recognised us in time, and later saw what we took to be our own paratroopers picking up supplies that had been dropped, only to find out later that they were probably Jerries after all, as we had no troops in the position. We made our way through the village, which was looking a bit sorry for itself, and passed a badly damaged glider that had hit a stone wall. We met a couple of newspaper reporters in the street and they directed us to the divisional HQ, which had been set up in the outhouses of a farm, the approaches of which were already under fire by snipers, which we found out after a near miss. Having made our report to the general, we found a small corner behind some bushes and had a really wonderful cup of tea, made from provisions taken from our forty-eight-hour ration pack. Then, much refreshed, we moved off to the glider pilot rendezvous, where there were twenty–thirty glider pilots. The main intention was that on arrival of the main lift at 2100 hours that evening, all pilots should be taken to England as quickly as possible to get ready for another trip. Meanwhile, all we had to do was wait. Paddy and I dug a hole and had some more to eat. There was spasmodic firing in the direction of Caen, and now and again patrols were sent out to contact the troops immediately to our front and flank, and so the day passed.

As the time for the main force grew near, the firing from the Germans and our side grew louder, and the perimeter appeared to be hard-pressed. I learned later that the gliders were late, and that they arrived at a very critical time. Eventually, above the noise of the firing, we heard the approach of many aircraft; the engines became a roar, and the firing seemed to cease. Even the Germans were struck dumb by what they saw. It was a magnificent sight, the air full of gliders sweeping in towards the German lines and then turning lazily and making a left hand circuit over our slit trenches. They seemed very low, and yet none of them appeared to be hit by the ground fire. Dakotas, and the rest of our lads parachuting down, followed them. After the perfect silence, an absolute inferno of noise broke out. Our position, which up to that time had not come under fire, was plastered with mortars as Jerry tried to get the range of the landing zone and at the same time fired at the gliders still in the sky. The sky above us was filled with a veritable stream of tracer rounds and exploding flak and this forced us to keep our heads down. Later, after the firing had died down, I crawled cautiously to the high ground overlooking the landing zones. The area was covered with gliders, a beautiful 'Balbo', which earned for it the name of the 'Milk Run'. Out of curiosity, I glanced over to my own landing position a little to the right of the main body. I was surprised to see that what I had thought to be my brake binding had in fact been the wing of the glider knocking over an anti-invasion pole. My luck must have been terrific, for the glider had only touched this one pole, and in doing so had set me on a course between the remaining poles without me knowing they were there. We eventually moved to GHQ and awaited our return to England to fly out more gliders if necessary. While we were there, the news came through to prepare for an attack by the elite German Fallschirmjägers. We had left by then, though.

Taking Pegasus Bridge – Robert Ballard

I found out later that the German commander of the garrison in the area of the Pegasus Bridge, Major Hans Schmidt, was supposed to have the bridge rigged with explosives, but because he feared the French Resistance attacking it and blowing it up, he'd refrained from placing the explosives. His orders were quite explicit. In the event of an Allied landing, he was to blow up the bridge to prevent it being captured, so he was in a quandary even though German Fallschirmjäger units had done a copycat attack when they landed directly on to the impregnable Fort Eben-Emael in Belgium in 1940. So on the night of 5 June, an attack seemed out of the question, as winds would prevent a parachute assault. It simply never occurred to him that the enemy would use gliders to land right on top of the bridges; it was inconceivable, even for them. Only two sentries were patrolling the bridge, with the rest of the men sleeping in their bunkers or dozing in the machine-gun pillbox. To the east of Pegasus Bridge, Colonel Hans von Luck, the commander of the 125th Panzer Division, was working on some personal reports at his headquarters. On the night, Major Schmidt evidently had other things on his mind; he was out with his French girlfriend. Colonel von Luck, his CO, noticed something that no one else had. At around 0010 hours, von Luck spotted half a dozen aircraft flying at around 500 feet and that could mean only one thing – they were dropping something by parachute, probably to the Resistance, so he ordered the area be searched and that any of the Resistance members encountered were to be arrested or shot. One other German, a senior NCO in charge at the bridge, Sergeant Heinz Hickman, also heard low-flying planes; himself a Fallschirmjäger who'd served in Crete and Sicily, he came to the same conclusion that the colonel did – something was definitely amiss. What he didn't know was that flying over the English Channel were two groups of three Halifax bombers. Each was towing a Horsa glider. The men on board the gliders, although worried about the mission ahead of them, were keeping their spirits high by singing and chain-smoking cigarettes.

A little after midnight, the lead Halifax cast off its glider as it crossed the coast. The invasion had begun, and D Company was on its way. As the glider cast off, the singers suddenly became quiet – the moment that all their training had prepared them for had arrived. While waiting to touch down, Major John Howard ran his orders though his mind: 'You are to seize intact the bridges over the River Orne and canal at Bénouville and Ranville, hold them until you are relieved regardless of the cost.' At about 0015 hours, the lead glider was down to 200 feet, its airspeed just below 100 mph. The glider pilots could see the river and the canal, and then the bridge loomed before them. The Horsa was right on target; it couldn't have possibly got any closer. It hit the ground and both wheels were ripped off. It bounced into the air and then came down on its skids and came to a shuddering halt. So quickly had it stopped that the pilot and co-pilot were catapulted though the glider's Perspex windows onto the ground outside. On the bridge Private Vern Bonck, a twenty-two-year-old Pole conscripted into the German army, clicked his heels sharply as he saluted Private Helmut Romer, a sixteen-year-old Berliner who had reported to relieve him. As Bonck went off duty, he met with his fellow sentry going off too, another Pole. They decided they were not sleepy and agreed to go to the local brothel, in the village of Bénouville, for a bit of fun. They strolled west along the bridge road, then turned south at the T junction on the road into Bénouville. By 0005 hours they were at the brothel, and within minutes they were knocking back cheap red wine with two French prostitutes. Beside the bridge, on the west bank, south of the road, Georges and Thérése Gondrée and their two daughters slept in their small café. Georges and Thérése were in separate rooms, not by choice but as a way to use every room and thus to keep the Germans from billeting soldiers with them. It was the 1,450th night of the German occupation.

So far as the Germans knew, the Gondrées were simple Norman peasants, people of no consequence who gave them no trouble. Indeed, Georges sold beer, coffee, food, and a concoction made by Madame of rotting melons and half-fermented sugar, to the grateful German troops stationed at the bridge. There were about fifty of them, the NCOs and officers all German, the enlisted men mostly conscripts from Eastern Europe. But the Gondrées were not as simple as they pretended to be. Madame came from Alsace and spoke German, a fact she successfully hid from the garrison. Georges, before acquiring the café, had spent twelve years as a clerk in Lloyd's Bank in Paris and spoke English. Both hated the Germans for what they had done to France, hated the life they led under the occupation, feared for the future of their eight-year-old daughter, and were consequently active in trying to bring German rule to an end. In their case, the most valuable thing they could do for the Allies was to provide information on conditions at the bridge. Thérése got information by listening to the chit-chat of the NCOs in the café; she passed what she heard along to Georges, who passed it to Madame Vion, director of the maternity hospital, who passed it along to the Resistance in Caen on her trips to obtain medical supplies. From Caen, the information was passed onto England via Lysander aeroplanes and small craft that could land in fields and get out in a hurry. Only a few days before, on 2 June, Georges had sent through a titbit Thérése had overheard – the button that would set off the explosives to blow the bridge was located in the machine-gun pillbox across the road from the anti-tank gun. He hoped that information had got through, if only because he would hate to see his bridge destroyed.

Private Romer must have heard the crash, but paid no attention to it; he probably thought that it was part of a damaged British bomber hitting the ground, so he simply kept on walking up and down the bridge with his rifle slung over his shoulder. The platoon in the lead glider had managed to achieve a miracle: it had landed right on target and nobody had challenged it. The glider pilots had done a remarkable job in setting down the glider exactly where it was supposed to be, crushing the barbed wire defences in the process. Along with the pilots, everyone in the glider had been knocked unconscious in the landing. This part of the invasion could have failed right there if the German sentries had noticed the glider and the men in the pillbox had woken up quickly. In that case, the platoon would probably have been wiped out inside their glider. Gradually the men came to their senses and the endless training paid off as they automatically unbuckled themselves from their seats and made ready. As Major Howard escaped the glider, he looked at the bridge in front of him and then at the crushed barbed wire beneath his feet; he couldn't believe his luck. Having sorted themselves out, the platoon moved speedily towards the bridge. At that moment the second glider group was exactly one minute behind the first and moved from their LZ to meet up with the first group. As the second platoon was moving into position, the third glider touched down. It was 0018 hours and three gliders had landed and so far they only had one casualty – a man had drowned in a pond.

Major Howard encouraged his men as they moved toward the bridge. As they charged forward, the guard on the bridge, Private Romer, saw a large group of men he knew weren't German coming towards him. With a sudden outbreak of common sense, he ran back towards the west end of the bridge, shouting 'Fallschirmjägers!' to the others manning the bridge's defences. Lieutenant Dan Brotheridge emptied a full magazine into Romer and the remaining sentry as grenades were tossed into the pillbox. Both sentries died, as did those in the pillbox. Sappers were already searching for explosives underneath the structure. German soldiers manning bunkers and machine-gun positions awoke at the sound of the gunshots. Brotheridge was probably killed when Sergeant Heinz Hickman, the senior NCO in charge of bridge defences, heard the first shots, saw dark figures running across the bridge, and immediately emptied his machine pistol in their direction. He realised the bridge had been taken so he ran off to find Major Schmidt to inform him the British had landed.

The Wrong Way – Alan Jacobs

About 2300 hours on 5 June the armada of gliders started to take off at thirty-second intervals. The towing aircraft circled until all of them were in the air and then made for the coast. Not long afterwards our glider was over the English Channel, heading for France, when for some inexplicable reason we had a disaster; the tow rope was released by the tow aircraft and wrapped around our wing, with the shackle striking the wing and ripping it wide open. We all heard and saw a huge crack appearing across the wing's surface and bits fly everywhere. I must admit it was the nearest I ever came to instantly evacuating my bowels. We prayed that we were near enough to the coast to get back over dry land before we were forced to ditch, or the wing broke off. The pilot did a magnificent job of slowly turning 180 degrees and crossed the coast, landing on a potato field. The wings even stayed on when we came to an abrupt halt. We all expected the glider to flip over or do something just as bad – thank God it didn't. There was a farmer standing right next to his tractor. He'd been watching the incredible air armada come over and he must have been shocked out of his skin when one glider broke away and landed smack dab in the middle of his field. When we all scrambled out, he drove over and stopped right next to us as we collected outside the glider, and quite calmly said, 'Weren't you supposed to be going the other way?'

Wounded – Benjamin Haddrell

The morning we were going to advance, I was company runner. We had started to advance when the OC said to me, 'Where is number 2 platoon?'

I replied, 'I think they're still sorting themselves out Sir.'

So I was sent back to where they were and told them what the OC said. All the time the Germans were laying down a barrage from mortars that fire six bombs in succession. We called them 'Moaning Minnies' because they made a screaming noise as they were fired. They were really frightening. It was then that one bomb dropped behind me and knocked me out, and when I regained consciousness I had been wounded in the back and was bleeding rather badly. The platoon had taken the full force of the blast and every one of them was dead. After some time the stretcher-bearers, who were very hard-pressed, picked me up and took me back to the medical post where they gave me emergency treatment for my wounds. While this was happening the mortar barrage continued, and at one stage the medical corporal covered me with his body to protect me from further injury. He was killed as he lay on top of me. Bert Hadley, who was lying on a stretcher right next to me, was saying a little prayer to himself: 'Please God, I don't mind dying, but please don't let me die in a foreign field.' When the next mortar hit the ground he reached out and put his tin hat over his face in order to protect himself. He died with the helmet still over his face. I was petrified that I'd be next. At the time I was so thirsty I stretched out with one hand and dragged a Jerry can toward me. I fiddled with the lid and got it open, then tilted it toward me and took two big mouthfuls. I nearly choked to death; it was Calvados, an apple brandy that is a speciality of that part of Normandy. Where someone got a whole Jerry can of it from I don't know, but I had a warm belly for about half an hour – I didn't need morphine.

Mum's the Word – David Staines

As we were on the final run into the DZ on D-Day my aircraft, a DC3, took a direct hit where the wing and the engine joined. Luckily we were already standing up and hooked on and the dispatcher didn't hesitate and got us all out the door straight away. It wasn't a pretty sight, in fact it was a chaotic exit with no thought of proper drills, but we all got out. What eventually happened to the aircraft and crew I never knew; although the wing was on fire, it turned and just headed straight for home. I eventually found myself on the ground and collected up all my equipment and tried to figure out where the hell I was. I knew I wasn't on the correct DZ, as the green light we had to look for hadn't come on. An hour later and after several near misses with German troops, I heard an English voice challenge me. I stopped and gave the correct password and found myself with my sister battalion, the 12th, miles from where I should be. They were digging in and preparing for yet another attack from the Germans. As luck would have it, my brother was in the 12th Battalion so I asked someone if they knew where he was. About an hour later, while I was helping the platoon I was with dig even deeper, my brother actually turned up. The first thing he said to me was, 'Don't tell me – Ma sent you to see if I was OK. Did she give you the cheese and chutney sandwiches she promised me last time I was 'ome?'

Sheer Luck – William Haggarty

I clearly remember the breakout from Normandy in 1944. I was with the Airborne Reconnaissance Regiment and in command of a three-man Tetrarch light tank that was equipped with a two-pounder main gun. Because of its speed and long range it was ideally suited as a reconnaissance vehicle, although you had to be careful not to bump into any German tanks, as they would make mincemeat of us. We were having a well-earned break in a deserted farm after charging around the day before. We had settled down for a night's rest and as the early morning sun came up I roused the other two and while they made breakfast, I stood on top of the farmyard wall with my binoculars and had a shufti around. In the distance the road disappeared over a hill. As I looked at it, there appeared a small Volkswagen Kübelwagen, which slowly drove over the brow. It was clearly part of an advanced party of something bigger. I leapt from the wall and hid as it came to a stop and the officer in the front seat stood up to survey the area in front of him. Having apparently satisfied himself that all was safe, he continued to slowly drive on; the Volkswagen was followed by a four-wheeled armoured car. Some distance further on, they both stopped again and once more the officer took a look through his binoculars. They clearly didn't see us with our camouflage netting over the tank so they moved off again. To my amazement, next came an eight-wheeled command vehicle with what appeared to be a 'bedstead' type aerial on the top; I thought, 'What a target!' It was at the maximum possible range of our main gun, probably more, but I thought 'what the hell' – at least we could give it a go. So I called the others to pack up and get into the tank with me. Danny, my gunner, took a look, and I said, 'How about it?'

He responded with, 'I doubt we'll hit it as it's a bloody long way off!'

Nevertheless, I wanted to have a shot, so I said, 'If it comes off they'd never know where it came from and by the time they figure it out we'll be gone.'

Danny gauged it to be 800 yards at least. We didn't start the engine just in case the sound carried. By now Danny was fiddling with the gun and the range, and put a HE round in the breech. We used High Explosive to give us maximum damage if we hit it. By now poor Danny was fudging everything as he wound the gun to its maximum elevation and moved the turret so it lined up with where the armoured car would probably stop. By the time we were ready, the eight-wheeler and escort had come to a halt again. They were certainly very cautious. Now, eight-wheelers by design and shape give the appearance of a large black triangle. Using the centre of the triangle as an aiming mark and crossing our fingers, Danny finally let rip. There was a great deal of tension as we waited. Much to our amazement, we actually hit the target dead centre – bits went flying everywhere as it literally disappeared in a cloud of smoke and debris. We quickly sent down two more, but they were well off to one side, although they certainly frightened the Jerries, then we took to our heels before they reacted. As we headed back to our lines we could see the smoke from the armoured car rising in the sky. Our biggest disappointment was that nobody else was there to see what we did.

What Happens when You Miss the LZ – Ron Bartley

I flew a Horsa glider into Normandy with Jock Bramah. In the back were two medical jeeps and a trailer and two medical personnel. We were on the track, but when we were some miles off the coast, we ran into flak and a patch of dense cloud or smoke and everything went haywire and I felt a twang as the towrope broke. This was bad! A second later we came out of the cloud but could see no sign of the land at all. I gave the order to prepare for ditching and Jock grabbed the controls in a jiffy. I was out of my seat and started to hack an escape hole through the roof of the fuselage. I shouted to the two passengers to do the same and hardly had the words left my mouth when the noise of their hacking came to my ears. Fear lent speed to our actions and the cutting was well under way when Jock shouted that he could see the coastline and also thought that we could make it. I returned to the cockpit just in time to see the coastline disappearing underneath us. I could distinguish the houses on the seafront and one or two bursts of tracer greeted us, passing through the starboard wing. I could now see nothing but woods underneath and it looked as if a crash-landing was inevitable. It was straight into an orchard at around 100 mph. I can't recollect the actual landing, though I'm sure I didn't lose consciousness, for when I began to take note, I was on the ground with the cockpit crushed into matchwood above me, still creaking as it settled.

I whispered 'JB' and got a grunt in reply. However, he was only stunned and the next second we were struggling to free ourselves. My back hurt like the devil! Jock passed out the rifles and ammo, which took some finding and extracting from the debris, and then we thought about our two passengers, 'Harpo and Marx'. We called them quietly and got no reply. Considering the state of the glider, with her tail, in which they had both been sitting, perched on top of a tree, we said that they must be dead. The next second they emerged from the darkness and both were immensely relieved to find us alive and kicking. They in turn presumed that we had gone for the usual Burton! We posted one as sentry and set about trying to extract a jeep. The time would now be about 1 a.m. Our own Dakotas and other tugs overhead were dropping bombs to disguise the airborne landings as a routine bombing raid. Unfortunately, as far as we were concerned it came all too close. This, however, was probably a good thing, as it covered the noise we were making ripping up the glider.

As dawn approached, our chances of even salvaging one jeep seemed remote. However, with the driver giving her full throttle and the rest of us pulling and levering, she suddenly shot herself free. The wheels were buckled to blazes, one of them almost horizontal, however she went! The orchard in which we had landed was situated in a tiny valley, which was ringed by sturdy trees. There was no way out for the vehicle. We searched every corner and eventually ran the jeep into some marshy ground, from which it was impossible to extricate her. There was nothing for it but to abandon the hope of saving anything and move out on foot without further delay. We had no idea where we were, although I later discovered that we were in the vicinity of Blonville, some 8 miles as the crow flies from our LZ. We moved off through the forest in the hope of contacting some more of our troops, all of us walking like cats on a hot tin roof, expecting a tripwire or other booby trap at every step. I remember telling myself to breathe normally or I'd choke, I was so keyed up. We'd picked up two stray parachutists soon after moving off and nearly blundered straight into a helmeted Jerry sentry right in the middle of the forest – couldn't see what he was guarding though! Somebody said 'Shoot him' but I didn't agree, as it would have given us away. We drew back and bypassed him on the right. Hell of a lot of noise coming from what we took to be the direction of the beach – probably the battleships softening things up before the main landing began. We just managed to dodge down while a Jerry platoon passed along a small path in front of us. We seemed to have landed bang in the middle of Jerry activity.

We then decided to follow our survival training and contact someone local and when we got to the edge of the forest we saw a house not far away. Jock knew some pidgin French and crept forward to make contact. He returned with the news that there was an injured Para officer hiding in the top of the barn and that we were all to join him and plan from there. I led, with the others spaced line astern, across a small field towards the barn. We were spread nicely across the field when machine guns opened up. I spun round like a top and hit the ground. Picking myself up, I raced to a corner of the barn and when I looked back, all the others were laying spreadeagled where they had fallen. A woman opened the back door of the house about 80 yards away, and calmly emptied a jug or pot on to the ground: a bloody trap and all with the help of the Frenchman. I hope he got his two pieces of silver and dies in hell, the bastard! I thought all the lads were dead and then decided to sprint though a hail of bullets, and dived into the forest and under a small bush. I couldn't run another yard as my lungs felt as if they were bursting. I tried to wrap myself round a tree, but couldn't hide the fucking rifle! There were Jerries in the wood, shouting and shooting at random. I lay there all day, my back hurting like hell. On checking my kit, I realised why I had spun on being hit. My two large ammunition pouches were in shreds, with segments of the grenades lying in the bottom. The grenades were primed. It was incredible that I was still alive.

As evening fell, I couldn't understand why it was so quiet. I must have been further from the beach than I imagined. My thoughts drifted to the fact that I should have been back in the UK by now, lapping up all the glory, and leaving this kind of lark for the poor bloody infantry. As I made my way carefully down the valley side, I saw a cave on the other side and spent the night in there. A French woman eventually found me and for the next few days kept me supplied with food. She then took me to Monsieur Paul Haricot of the French Resistance, who already had several men of the 6th Airborne Division in his care. On around 20 June, Jock Bramah arrived. Despite appearances in the aftermath of the ambush, he had not been killed but badly wounded in a lung. Coughing up blood and drifting into a coma, he was left where he lay by the Germans, who assumed that death was imminent. By the following morning, however, he had recovered sufficiently to drag himself a farm in the Chemin du Bois. He was temporarily hidden beneath a bridge until he was taken to the home of Monsieur Salesse, where his wound was dressed each day by a local nurse, Mademoiselle Marie-Louise Le Franc. His hiding place was betrayed by someone and on 16 June a party of Germans arrived. When they entered his bedroom, Jock killed two of them with his Sten gun then took cover beneath the bed when a grenade was thrown into the room. He then escaped the house by sliding down the stay cable of a telegraph pole before disappearing into the night as the Germans set fire to the house. They probably shot Monsieur Salesse and his family, as that was the punishment for helping any escaping soldiers. Because we didn't know who the informer was, we changed houses regularly. In fact, we spent eighty days this way before we met up with the advancing Americans.

Bréville – Stan Weaver

We jumped onto the DZ at 2.00 a.m. on D-Day but everyone ended up all over the place. I wandered around for quite a while, trying to get orientated. Eventually I found the quarry, guided by the flashing red light we'd been told to look for. Other battalions were guided to their RVs by a hunting horn, a whistle, or other coloured lights. By now the DZ was coming under intense fire, but most of us were clear of it by then. I was the CO's signaller and reported to him on arrival. By around 3.00 a.m. we were still only half-strength. Because of the confusion and intense anti-aircraft fire, lots of the lads were dropped in the wrong place, and in some cases it took a few days before they got to us. Anyway, the CO decided to move on to secure Le-Bas-de-Ranville. Initially resistance was fairly light, the Germans having withdrawn to a wood to the south. By 4.30 a.m. we were well dug in and things were remarkably quiet for a short time, and then we heard the naval barrage starting and knew that the seaborne landings were about to take place. At daybreak our forward positions came under very heavy fire and they reported enemy troop movement in our direction, supported by at least four self-propelled guns. In the forward trenches there was a naval officer and a rating who'd parachuted in with us, and they'd established a radio link with a cruiser off the coast. Unfortunately, they were both killed in the first assault, as was a mate of mine who was on the radio. I was listening in to him telling the CO what was happening when he was abruptly cut off. He and others had copped it when a mortar shell landed right in their trench. The forward position, consisting of an officer and twelve men, was under really immense fire and suffered heavy casualties, though the officer and three of the men did manage to escape and pull back to the company position.

Of the self-propelled guns, one was eventually destroyed by a six-pounder as they got near the forward positions, and another was knocked out by a PIAT; the other two withdrew. If they had gone any further we would have been in serious trouble. We were now also under heavy mortar and artillery fire. Once that attack was beaten back another section was sent out to reoccupy the forward position along the hedgerow. They told us later the place was a mess, bodies everywhere, both ours and theirs, along with the self-propelled guns. Later that day a further attack was launched. Heavy fighting continued into the night, and that evening we witnessed the remarkable sight of around 500 aircraft and gliders streaming in over the coast; the gliders landed astride the Orne River and canal. It looked like we were well and truly there to stay. By this time, after having come ashore at Sword Beach and suffering quite a few casualties, the Commandos arrived at our position. We'd secured all our objectives and were holding firm despite being under continuous fire, which, of course, meant even more casualties, but were still chosen to take the village of Bréville, which was heavily defended. A number of units had already tried and had received a severe bloody nose in the process. We had around eight officers and 350 men to do the job, almost half our original strength. It was no use grumbling as the job had to be done, so we proceeded to a place called Amfreville, where we trooped into the local church for our briefing. The Black Watch had tried to take the village earlier on that day and had suffered enormously in their attempt. By now the Commandos had taken up positions on the outskirts of Amfreville, facing towards Bréville, and we took up position for the attack on the road alongside them. At 9.45 p.m. the attack was preceded by a barrage and we would be supported by a few tanks. We would move off at around 10.00 p.m. Regrettably, that first salvo of artillery fell short and landed on the road in which we were assembled. Our CO and several HQ personnel were killed, and a number of others were wounded. Just as the first company moved off the Germans laid down a counter-barrage, and the poor devils were cut to pieces in the open ground approaching Bréville.

I went in with the second company and had to pass through the dead and wounded. It was a dreadful sight as some of them we'd been chatting to not long before, and we had close mates among them as well. Their OC, although lying severely wounded, yelled at us to keep going. The village was on fire from end to end when we reached the edge of it, and we got pinned down in a ditch. After taking our bearings we moved out to the crossroads, exchanging fire as we went. I still had the wireless set on my back but the aerial had been shot off. The smoke and fires raging in each building hampered the attack as you could hardly see anything until you were on top of it. One Jerry stepped out from behind a building with a machine pistol in his hands. He was just about to shoot me, but was half a second too slow and I emptied half a Sten gun magazine into him; I got a great deal of satisfaction from that. By now things were still uncertain to say least. At the crossroads we came under very heavy bombardment and again had to shelter in a ditch for what seemed like hours.

Now we had a foothold, we had to fight for every inch to get any further. The Germans were determined to hold on to the place. We threw grenades into every building we came to, even if it was on fire. Little groups of us fought our own personal battles as we advanced because we couldn't see anyone else. Sometimes two groups would come together and we'd sort out where each was going next, and then leapfrog one another, giving mutual support as we moved. Another time a German leapt out of a window in front of me, went to run into the smoke, saw me, dropped his weapon and put his hands up; by that time I was so on edge I wasn't going to give him a chance as I'd seen too many of my mates gunned down, so I shot him. Any of the lads that were wounded were quickly given morphine, propped up and left. There simply weren't enough of us to stay with them, not if we wanted to keep momentum up. Finally, it was over bar the mopping up. There was a bit of spasmodic small-arms fire, but we had secured our positions. Once that was done, we sent teams back to fetch the wounded; the dead would have to lie where they were until we had complete control of the place. We lay hidden all night expecting a counter-attack, but at dawn patrols sent out reported that no enemy was contacted – they'd withdrawn.

Bodies were everywhere, both theirs and ours, but Bréville had been taken, and our bridgehead was complete. The cost was astronomical, with all our officers killed or wounded; the RSM was also dead, as well as most of our NCOs. There were 168 dead from all companies, with about 100 of the original battalion left and only thirty-five men without wounds. The Devon and Dorsets had another thirty-six killed. The Germans had numbered 546 men before the assault; by the time the village had been captured there were only around 150 of them left, and most of them were wounded. The following day we buried the dead, theirs and ours. I left a lot of good friends in that terrible place.

Airborne Medic – John Tranter

On the evening of 6 June I was part of the 6th Airborne Division landing at Normandy. I travelled in a Horsa glider with twenty men, a jeep and a trailer full of medical supplies. Our orders were to set up an advanced dressing station and begin treating men immediately. When we landed, we'd already lost one private and a sergeant through anti-aircraft fire coming up through the floor. The glider hit the ground like a brick and we ended up lying side-on to a couple of trees and had lost a large part of both wings and a huge chunk of the tail. It was one of those times when you were glad you had your feet up and arms linked as we felt like we were trapped in a whirlpool before we stopped. Having done so many practice landings on flat fields, it was a big shock to say the least. We carried out the two bodies and covered them up and then got the jeep and trailer out and headed to Pegasus Bridge. It was here I saw a captured French tank the Germans were using that had been blown up near the road junction. God, it was in one hell of a mess and was still smouldering. We drove to the village of Ranville and set up a forward medical station. For a long time we were under constant fire from German mortar bombs and artillery as well as indirect machine-gun fire. There were a number of heavy attacks by the Germans as they wanted the village back and casualties on both sides were really heavy.

Two days after we got there, the Germans put in yet another big attack supported by several tanks and self-propelled guns. A tank came within 100 yards of us but on seeing the Red Cross flags on the building it turned away and was hit by a six-pounder anti-tank gun as it moved to attack another part of the village. During this time a young French woman was brought into the aid station and gave birth to a little boy. For once, it was nice to see someone coming into this world and not leaving it. Later, some of us were sent to another medical advance station and took part in the liberation of Honfleur. The casualties and dead during that battle were enormous on both sides. British tank crews suffered a great deal as the German 88s and Tiger tanks outranged them and could punch holes in them long before they knew the Germans were there. Why our side persisted in building tanks that were deathtraps like that, I don't know. I learned after the war that we and the Americans lost 4,000 tanks in the Normandy campaign alone. Anyway, that day we finally beat the buggers back and the division took part in the breakout.

The 12th Battalion – Fred White

I was with the 12th Battalion. We landed on 7 June 1944, the day after D-Day, and advanced around Ouistreham to Ranville, where the battalion took over the village from the 13th Battalion, who had fought their way there on D-Day against some stiff German resistance. We spent two fairly quiet days, occasionally interrupted by German bombers – curious that, as we were supposed to have complete command of the skies. Our battalion had set up an observation post on a hill half a mile south of our headquarters, which, on the afternoon of 9 June, was manned by privates Jack 'Sam' Koster and George Lavender. Jack Koster, nicknamed Sam after the comedian Sam Costa, was responsible for frequently telephoning HQ with their observations of enemy movement in the valley below. His last call that afternoon was an urgent request for tea rations as they had manned the OP since noon. I was ordered to take it up to them. So I set out alone along the track leading to the OP carrying my rifle and a can full of hot sweet tea. It was like taking a solitary walk on the South Downs in the Sussex countryside. Eventually I reached the OP on the brow of the hill, where I was enthusiastically welcomed by both of them. I handed them the tea and said that I was to stay to relieve one of them, who was to return to HQ. Within minutes of my arrival the OP was under heavy fire.

As there was no form of cover we all three dived as flat as possible and I felt a heavy blow on the side of my head. After a pause to make sure the firing had stopped, I congratulated everyone on that 'near miss', but looking up I realised that the near miss was a direct hit on the OP. Sam and George were both laying in unnatural contorted positions and had obviously been killed instantly right beside me. Blood was running from their mouths, ears, noses and eyes, and the field telephone was nowhere to be seen. I was badly shaken, not only because it could have happened to me, but two close friends had died right beside me. I remember thinking in the utter silence, 'What should I do next?' Staying there without the telephone was pointless so I staggered back through our forward company lines, where our own mortars were taking vigorous action against the attack. When I got to BHQ, I was taken to the field hospital suffering from concussion and loss of hearing. After three days I was assured the deafness was temporary and I was left to find my own way back to the battalion.

I Well Remember Normandy – Ron Dewsbury

I was with the 7th Battalion and I always remember the number of men we lost at Normandy. Before we even landed one aircraft was shot down with everyone on board killed. My platoon had forty men in at the beginning and we lost twenty-five killed by the time we left to go back home in August, and that didn't take into account the wounded and the trickle of replacements. There were never enough replacements. It was carnage on a vast scale, and not only for my battalion; all the battalions suffered the same, as did the Germans. The cream of each country died in these battles. It all looked great on paper, but on the day we jumped in we were scattered to hell and high heaven, and few if any of our heavy weapons arrived, having been lost in the drop. Yet we still rendezvoused with the men who'd taken Pegasus Bridge at Bénouville on the Orne Canal, and a nearby bridge over the River Orne, defending it against heavy German attack. Then we moved to Bréville and defended it. After that we went on to be used as normal infantry in battles that saw us fighting Tiger tanks, self-propelled guns, mortars, machine guns and fanatical Germans, often with little or no support. Time and again, we would have to hold positions that were mere dots on a map. I still recall the deep-seated fear each time I had to go on patrol, go into an attack, face a barrage, or see tanks and self-propelled guns coming toward us. And I clearly remember when we were told we were going home. It was as if the dark cloud that had been hanging over me for weeks suddenly lifted. I was alive when so many weren't; it was only when we got back to England and we were brought back up to strength that I realised how many we'd lost. But I knew I'd have to face it all over again, and the fear came back. I can still feel it to this day.

The Bugle Call – John Hamble

After I landed in Normandy and got together all my equipment, put it all on and cocked my Sten gun, I listened for the call of a bugle that was the rallying point for the battalion. And sure enough, over all the other sounds of weapons being fired, explosions, aircraft engines and hunting horns, there was the sound of the bugle being repeated time and again. Once I heard it, it wasn't difficult to head toward where it was. Some twenty or so minutes later and I was at the RV and trotted up to the CO to report in. Alongside him was the bugler, still blowing for all he was worth. As I passed through the circle of men that was the CO's protection party, I heard one of them say, 'If that prick plays that stupid tune one more fooking time I'm going to grab the bugle and stick it right up his arse, and if he can bend over and play it afterwards I'll admit defeat and fooking help him get it out!'

The Mouth-Watering Password – Don Crookshank

Suddenly the red light flickered on, followed by what seemed to be endless minutes of fidgeting and uncertainty. Just when

I thought it would never happen, the green light changed everything and our lives instantly altered forever. The 'stick' shuffled towards the aperture in the floor and we stooped beneath the low struts of the fuselage, our kitbags hooked to the front of our webbing. I felt the pent-up tension of the momentous occasion; I was now going to war on the fields of France some 500 feet below. Then someone in front of me stumbled and this ripple effect ran down the stick. By the time it got to me I was forced to dive out of the aperture into a night sky lit by anti-aircraft fire. I fell for an eternity while my last connection with England and safety, my static line, snatched, setting into motion the series of events that would pull the parachute clear. My harness finally grabbed me like a giant hand and the silken canopy breathed as it swallowed the rushing air. For a few seconds, I just hung there as I tried to get my bearings. All around me there seemed to be streams of anti-aircraft fire, long lines of aircraft and hundreds of grey, white and black parachutes in the night sky. I quickly unclipped the kitbag and paid out its attachment line through my gloved palm. With nothing to gauge my descent, with no horizon to fix my position, this kitbag dangling below me would be the only thing to tell me where the ground was. Automatically, I ran through the checklist and everything was where it should have been, then once again I strained for something I could recognise on the ground, a house, a tree, anything.

Suddenly the dangling line slackened. Instinctively, I braced for impact – bent my knees and hit the ground, doing an automatic side right. Months of training now kicked in and in next to no time I was wearing my webbing and radio, had my Sten gun ready, and was on one knee so as not to present a target. I made out a low wall and stands of trees; I also saw a series of farm buildings in among some trees some distance away on a hill. I could also see the furtive movements of men making for the buildings like ants making for their mound. As quietly and as low as possible, I moved toward them. I was about 20 yards short of the wall when a whispered voice said, 'Ham!'

I immediately stopped and for some unknown reason thought, 'What if I get the password wrong?' Anyway I said, 'Jam!'

The voice then continued with, 'Eggs, bacon, chips, sausages, onions, fried bread, mushrooms with tomato sauce, and a pint of best Newcastle Bitter.'

As I came to the owner of the voice, I whispered, 'It'll be a long bloody time before you get them again.'

'I know,' he said, then added gloomily, 'but every time I say "Ham" I think of it and it's bloody well killing me.'

Chewing Cud – Frank Butler

On D-Day and in darkness, most of my platoon landed on the very edge of the DZ. I landed in a tree that decided to make its home on a Bocage-type hedge on the eastern edge of the DZ, and even after I climbed down I still hadn't reached Mother Earth proper and was completely enclosed in foliage. Feeling a little like Blind Pew from *Treasure Island*, I gingerly let go of a branch I was tightly holding on to and dropped all of 12 inches to the ground and then had one hell of a problem getting out my Sten gun, which was threaded under the parachute harness. For the next ten minutes I slashed away at the rope holding my equipment before it fell at my feet, where I unpacked everything. I must have woken up every German within a 10-mile radius I made so much noise cursing and slashing away. Finally, with my trusty weapon in hand, I pulled the bushes of the hedgerow to one side to reach the open field when I was confronted with a large cow only a few feet away, staring intently at me chewing cud as if nothing was happening in the world. As a farm boy, and under any other circumstances, I would have probably patted its head, but not now. We had been briefed that there was a big herd of cows in the area but to find one chewing cud without a care in the world amused me no end.

Just then the shadowy figure of Harry Wiltshire materialised in front of me. I'd recognise him anywhere, even in the dark. God had built him in such a weird and wonderful way even a blind man would know him. After giving the password he greeted me with the immortal words, 'I'm certain I just passed a bloody German camouflaged to look like a cow, I swear it said Heil Hitler to me instead of Moo!' We both had a chuckle over that. A little further on we then caught up with Stan Ogden, who had jumped number three and was carrying the platoon radio. He too had encountered the cows we'd all been warned about, only he had to jump into a ditch to avoid the stampeding herd. All he could say about them was, 'Typical Frogs, ya come to 'elp 'em and all they wanna do is bloody run ya over!' For a moment I had to stop myself laughing out loud as I don't think you're supposed to do it in the middle of a battle. Harry had no such compunction and roared with laughter.

A Cup of Tea – Huw Pyrs Wheldon

I was in one of 250 gliders escorted by a cloud of fighters as we were coming in over France. But there was nothing, absolutely nothing about D-Day that was turning out as I'd expected. There was no German fighter opposition, no real heavy flak, and no masses of wrecked gliders in the fields below. In our glider, some of the 'Red Devils' about to penetrate the Atlantic Wall were sucking jujubes. Or they looked like jujubes. Looking again, I saw that they had taken the barley sugars from the special airborne rations which were supposed to last for three days. 'Put them away!' I said sharply, before they devoured the compound cakes and porridge as well. 'Do you want to live on grass?'

'But, Sor,' said one Irish rifleman, 'they're very good them sweets.'

We weren't gliding in the accepted sense of the word. As always, it was as if we were in a very old railway carriage being yanked across the sky. For weeks and months we had rehearsed for this, landing on fields and roads and hills. Once we'd even turned over in the air, and, sitting upside down, strapped into his seat, the platoon sergeant, famed for his ferocity, had recited the Lord's Prayer seven times without pause or punctuation. Now this, this was a very strange business. From the moment we crossed the French coastline, sweat began to run down the back of the glider pilot's neck. There were two little runs of it, like bacon fat. He was working overtime. 'We're casting off!' he said matter-of-factly, and I turned round to strap myself into my seat. At first I couldn't believe it, but Mullins, the company runner, was asleep. Mullins was a magnificent character, later to become an excellent sergeant. He had been very good company all the way, and had now apparently decided to have a quiet nap just before the towing plane discarded us. 'Come on, Mullins,' I said, 'we're invading Europe.' Groaning, he scratched at his eyes and, looking bored, he began to buckle up. Released by the towplane, the glider came down with all the grace of an empty can. We made a perfectly smooth landing in a soft field on a glorious summer's night. Other gliders, quite undamaged, did the same. France, we're here, but it was pretty difficult to believe it.

We had been warned and trained, trained and warned, that the dangerous time for us was the moment immediately after landing, when we would be disorganised and defenceless, relaxing in the relief of being down. Like everybody else, I had to leap out of this cardboard aeroplane, for at that point I became part of an organised cohesive unit round the Bren gun. Well, I leaped out and the grass smelled fine and sweet. All around there was action and machine guns were hiccupping, but nobody seemed to be firing at us. After two hours in the glider I wanted to relieve myself first, certain that the others would gather round the machine gun. When I looked round to make sure that they were in what we were pleased to call an all-round defence, I saw that all of them – all of them mind you – were following my example. Despite the rifles and the ammunition, despite the camouflaged smocks and parachute helmets, despite the blackened faces, they looked like small boys on a Sunday school treat. I think the absurdity of it dawned on all of us at once, and we were down behind the Bren gun as if our lives depended on it. Our next job was to leave this area, which was not all that healthy, and then rendezvous with the rest of C Company, 1st Battalion, Royal Ulster Rifles, in a wood. Thereafter, C Company as a whole would go to the battalion start line for the intended attack. When we reached this little wood, one of the riflemen from another glider was waiting for us at the edge. As we crouched to talk, I noticed that he was feeling like the rest of us. He had this dreamy, slightly mystified, let's-try-to-take-it-seriously look. 'Captain Wheldon, sor,' he whispered to me. 'It's a miracle. Not a casualty. Not a single Anglo-Saxon man. Every Anglo-Saxon man's arrived unharmed. The whole Anglo-Saxon company's here. It's an Anglo-Saxon miracle.'

While we were cowering there, Company Sergeant Major McCutcheon came out from the wood. He was the bravest man I ever knew, sometimes I think the best man I ever knew. 'Sir, come into HQ,' he said.

'Let's get on,' I said. 'We don't have to go into Company HQ, Sergeant Major – got to get on!'

'Sir,' he said, and there was determination in his voice, 'I would like you to come into Company HQ.' Through nettles and brambles, we plunged into the wood. Right in the centre of the wood there was a lean-to hut and a small fire. I had been fifteen minutes on the soil of France and the men in that hut had been ten minutes at the most.

Nodding like a chummy Naafi girl, Rifleman Rimmer handed me a steaming cup of delicious sweet tea, just the thing for a man at the beginning of a war. As he did so he said, 'I hope it isn't too sweet sor!'

Syntax and Parsing – Jeremy Spencer
I was a lieutenant with 11th Battalion and jumped in on 6 June. When we arrived at this house it was only the firing and the French being spoken that made me believe we were in France. It seemed incongruous to me, never having been abroad before. I felt somehow I would know there would be something different about the countryside that would tell me this was France. My French isn't as good as it was. The simplest words are forgotten, my syntax is pathetic and my parsing is lamentable, but somehow we get along. The people are amazingly cheerful considering what they have come though, and help us quite a lot, although quite naturally they'd go to ground when things get warm. As usual I'm sleepy. Then I decide after all that I'm not sleepy, but anyway sleep is a nice soothing inviting thought. The boys are in terrific fettle, still cracking jokes. I must hand it to them. I knew they were good, but they have outshone expectations and done more than they were asked to do. There's a piano here, and unlike my last

place, it's in tune and periodically a quiet waltz comes lilting through the hall. A little speckled terrier has adopted us. At least he keeps me warm. Usually he goes to investigate any strange noises, so when he comes back we know all is quiet again. Although I had some trepidation in advance, curiously enough, when it came to the time there was no emotion of fear, merely intense curiosity and eagerness to do one's job. When we were crossing the French coast and our plane was rocking, with flak exploding outside, it never occurred to me that those strange orange streams of fire, curving lazily up to us, might shoot us to bits. The plane was so stuffy and we were so loaded with equipment that we couldn't sit down. We emplaned about 2300 hours on 5 June and took off half an hour later. Each man had a kitbag that was stowed forward in order to allow the plane to take off. As soon as we were airborne we started passing the kitbags back, each one about 60 pounds weight, and we strapped them to our legs. Thereafter it was a case of all breathing at the same time, as the crush was pretty terrific, and we were glad to get out.

There was a little difficulty as one of the lads conked out, and the pilot had to run in three times before everyone had jumped. The landing was beautifully soft. I wonder how long I sat looking at the long grass, the anti-paratroop poles, the vicious tongues of light flak, and our planes roaring overhead. We must have presented a terrifying sight when we landed, because most of the Jerries in our area ran off in their pyjamas. I was completely lost, as I didn't land quite where I was supposed to. I was not very far off, however, and after tending a few casualties on route, rounding up the stragglers, and dealing with the odd surviving Bosch, I wandered into the village just as dawn was breaking. The welcome was astounding. French people were leaning out of the windows, shouting, laughing, singing, and giving little bunches of flowers to the lads. After that it was grim hard work for days where we took a lot of casualties. Death is the friend of nobody, he stalks the countryside day and night and takes people at will, and it was terrible to see a close friend who you'd been talking to a few minutes before, lying on the ground lifeless, their eyes often open but unable to see. I think we've been in most of the sticky places on the east flank.

Proceeding with some caution, my platoon and I followed the rest, thankfully finding that we had stopped to dig in, and we stayed there for two nights due to there being a German strongpoint still holding out. They put up one hell of a fight, refusing to give in. In the end we used a PIAT anti-tank gun to destroy the place and followed it up with grenades. Not one German survived. There is still small-arms fire going on all around us as the Germans have finally decided we're here to stay and they don't seem to like it. We did have one major alarm last night, but the infiltrating Germans turned out to be a herd of wandering cattle, much to the CSM's annoyance.

The Sniper – Barry Jones

Sometime after we broke out of Normandy, we were clearing a large wood. In two extended lines we advanced through the trees, waiting for machine guns to open up, but they didn't – the Germans had packed up and left. Well, most of them had; a sniper hadn't. Suddenly there was a load crack and my best mate Jack was thrown backwards; he'd been shot between the eyes by a sniper. He was the only one to get killed. Everyone scattered and threw themselves down behind trees. It was obvious he was up in a tree somewhere, and he must have been a fanatic, as he had no way of escaping with over fifty of us looking for him. He shot two other lads but they both survived, although they were seriously injured. Miraculously, Eddie Wilson saw the smoke from his rifle when he fired the third time and emptied a complete magazine from his Bren gun into the sod and literally blew him out of the tree in the process. He tumbled out of the branches on to the ground and lay there in a crumpled heap, riddled with rounds. That was the only time I really hated the Germans; before then they were soldiers like me, fighting for their country. But this was personal and I made a point of walking up to the body and giving it a good kick in what was left of his head to help him on his way to Hell. Nobody said a word, not even the major, because they knew what I felt.

Quick Promotion – Dave Louder

By the end of the fifth day the battalion had lost one hell of a lot of men – all the battalions had; some were down to less than half strength, ours wasn't far off that. The loss of NCOs and officers was so high that privates were now sergeants and sergeants were now lieutenants. In our company the adjutant had taken over as the OC, and the acting CSM had started as a platoon corporal when we jumped in. The adjutant had called an orders group in what was left of a barn. He looked around the scruffy unshaven bunch, many of whom weren't wearing rank as they simply didn't have time to sew it on. We might have been depleted in numbers but our fighting spirit was still high and everyone was raring to get on with the job we'd been sent to do. It was at this point the adjutant saw a 'new' sergeant, a man named Henry Phipps, and he said, 'My God – it's you, Phipps; someone actually made you a sergeant?'

'Yes Sir,' answered Henry in as cheeky a fashion as he could. 'We lost Sergeant Tucker and then the next two to get made up were wounded, so the lads voted me in as I was already an acting Corporal!'

The poor adjutant's mouth dropped before he said, 'Your men voted you in. Didn't the company commander have a say in the matter?'

'Oh yes, Sir,' answered Henry. 'He said that I might as well try it as he couldn't think of anyone else, so I got it.'

The adjutant responded with, 'But you've been paraded before the CO so many times you wore a trench to his desk!'

'I know Sir, but since I've made sergeant I've kept an eye on myself, and so far I've been good!' Even the Adjutant smiled at that one, and we got on with the orders group.

The Church Service – Malcolm Coombs

Whenever I attend a church service, especially a Remembrance service, I can't help but let my memory take me back to those days so long ago now when, as a private in the Parachute Regiment, I listened intently to the Padre conduct church services not far behind the line. Most of the time these services weren't held within the sanctity of a place of worship, or beneath soaring vaults surrounded by the icons of Roman Catholicism; they were, through circumstance and necessity, held behind the bomb-shattered and bullet-scarred walls of any building that would serve the purpose. At times, whenever possible and prudent, they were held in the open, in a ravine or valley out of sight of the malevolent eyes of the enemy artillery spotters who, we could be sure, would have soon unleashed their hate upon us. Wherever there was a service we all listened keenly to the sermon and our beloved Padre. We were closer to God than we'd ever been, unlike so many services held in England when other things were on our young minds. We sang the treasured hymns, among them the most treasured of all, 'Abide With Me'. Never had a hymn meant so much to us as it did in those unlikely places of worship. We sang with uncommon reverence, drawing on the power of those moving words to bring forth out of our inner selves whatever courage was there that we needed to ease the rising fear within our hearts knowing we were going into battle within hours.

We would need this courage in abundance to face the terrors we knew soon would come. On this one occasion that memory brings to mind, we stood, crowded upon each other, in the battered, draughty and dusty interior of what had once been a farmer's barn a mile or so from the front line, paying heed to what the Padre had to say. Only a couple of hours earlier we'd been put on notice that at first light the next morning the battalion would put in an attack on the strongly held enemy positions in and around the next village down the road. And then the service came to that part where we sang 'Abide With Me'. The expressions of faith that made up this beautiful hymn crossed my mind, and as we sang I found myself inserting my own feelings between the lines, feelings that harboured the fear that perhaps I might not be coming back at battle's end. Now, so many years removed from that worrisome moment, I can't remember exactly what those thoughts were that my mind inserted between each line of the first stanza, but I think they went something like this, or close to them: 'Abide with me; fast falls the eventide;' God – tomorrow we make our big attack. Take care of me, God, I'm afraid to die – 'When other helpers fail and comforts flee.' The sergeant says don't worry, everything will be okay, but I'm still afraid. – 'Help of the helpless, oh abide with me.' God, I don't want to die so young. And after we'd sung the next two stanzas I couldn't help but let my mind take me home, wondering how my mother and family would take it when the telegram came saying I'd been killed in action. At this point, in an unspoken prayer to God, I asked Him, 'Oh, God, if I should die today, give my mother the strength to accept my death with the same courage and strength she has shown me all the days of my life.'

The Nervous Germans – David McDowell

After we'd settled in at Normandy the Battalion received information from one of patrols that the German unit facing us was bringing in more men so the CO ordered a pre-emptive mortar 'stonk' on their positions. Taken completely by surprise, the Germans must've thought this was the beginning of a major night attack. Once the mortar rounds began landing on them, they returned fire, and his machine guns and rifles also opened up indiscriminately, spraying fire everywhere even though they couldn't see anything because we hadn't opened fire with our small arms. Their mortar fire was so indiscriminate that 70 per cent of it landed harmlessly to the flanks or behind our positions. It was a complete waste of ammunition on their part and it lasted over two hours, during which it allowed each of the companies to pinpoint numerous positions and call down accurate fire on them using the mortars – some 800 bombs were fired. Such a big reaction was suspected to be the result of the Germans having a large number of conscripted non-Germans in their ranks, as well as untried men who hadn't been under fire before. I was the company signaller and heard the CSM jokingly comment to the OC, 'I don't think Jerry knows exactly where we are Sir!'

The OC replied, 'I agree CSM. Have we moved since this morning?'

I could tell the CSM was smiling when he said, 'Not unless the lads have sneaked out for some fish and chips and came back without me knowing Sir!'

The OC carried on the humorous conversation with, 'I thought not!'

'Would you like me to check with the platoon commanders Sir?' asked the CSM, taking the conversation to absolutely ridiculous lengths.

The OC thought about it for a second then said, 'Yes, you do that CSM. Though I'm sure they'd know, wouldn't they?'

Le Plein – George Smith

As the battalion drew near to Le Plein, we came under heavy fire. The Boche immediately withdrew to prepared positions near a crossroads, and the leading company attacked and dislodged them, capturing two MG42 machine guns, killing fifteen of them, and took seven prisoners. They were from the 12th SS Panzer Division 'Hitlerjugend', one of the most fanatical units Hitler had ever produced; many were only sixteen years of age and only their officers and senior NCOs had seen combat before, but that didn't stop the division from getting a bad reputation for not taking anyone alive – they'd shot quite a few out of hand, grotesquely mutilated bodies, and in one case beheaded a major from the Canadian battalion. Most of the lads had stopped taking them prisoner and the ones we captured were extremely lucky to be alive and didn't get treated lightly either. I watched one of them spit in the face of a corporal. For his trouble, he got a rifle butt in his face that smashed it up really bad [sic]. It definitely took the wind out of his sails. He was lucky he didn't get killed on the spot. The Canadians had already stopped taking them prisoner. In fact, we heard they weren't taking any Boche prisoners, including wounded, such was the uncontrollable rage within the battalion because of these butchers shooting our men out of hand.

The buildings on the crossroads were seized and I went forward to see what was happening. The CO called to me to cross the road and as I did so as a hail of bullets chased me. It was almost as if the Boche had been waiting for me to expose myself. The position was a strong one, being a large building with sturdy, high stone walls. The Boche held a similar building about 80 yards opposite and a sniping battle commenced in earnest. Then a counter-attack suddenly developed on our left flank, but we saw it coming, held our fire until the enemy were 50 yards away, and then opened up with the Vickers machine guns and Bren guns. They left behind at least twenty dead bodies and fifteen–twenty wounded. We left them there as the Boche had a nasty habit of firing on parties who went to recover any wounded, even under a white flag. So these men lay there in agony as the battle raged around them, and I have to say I didn't have an ounce of compassion for them; fanatics like them didn't deserve any at all.

Twice more I had to cross the road to issue instructions for the CO as the radios were playing up. It was rather like being a moving Punch and Judy show, and 80 yards away Punch was ready to hit one with a big stick. One side of the road was a deep ditch that gave me cover, and the other side a high stone wall. One had to dash across the road, then along about 9 feet of wall with bullets splashing against it, and finally crab through an open door. CSM Miller tried the dash and was unlucky to receive a bullet. His wound, however, was not severe as it struck the fleshy portion of his shoulder. Mind you, the language he used when he was hit was extremely descriptive and straight to the point. After a while the CO instructed me to make a reconnaissance of the rear of our position, find a safe route and tell the second in command to bring the remainder of the battalion into position by it. I went alone and had to detour much further than I expected. Nearing the end, I jumped through a hole in a wall on to a road and a burst of Bren gun fire nearly got me. Once I got over the shock, I walked down to the main crossroad, where a sentry apologised for shooting at me. I informed him that next time he fired he better be a bit more accurate, even if it was one of his own side; ammunition was not to be wasted. I led the remaining companies into their new positions at the Château d'Amfreville. The main building in our position was a Boche army billet. All the personal belongings of the men were strewn about, even arms and ammunition. The larder was stocked with a magnificent supply of food, sides of beef, a barrel of butter, sacks of sugar, large stone jars of jam, a huge tub of pure cream. A number of shots came into our enclosure over a high wall, and it was obvious that they must come from a church overlooking us. One of the men spotted a loose slat that looked rather like a sniper's slit. Every time a shot came from it we sent back one in return and after nine shots it became quite quiet again.

On 8 June brigade HQ at Le Mesnil was hard-pressed by a Boche attack and Brigadier Hill sent a call for assistance. Lieutenant-Colonel Otway ordered me to proceed to the area with a small party to cover an improvised force from HQ and C Companies led by Lieutenant Christie. The CO decided to attack the rear of the Boche so he sent a party of twenty-two men round to the left flank to make the assault. I took two sergeants, each with a German MG42 machine gun and bandoliers of ammunition, and three private soldiers to form a covering party. We went down the strip of wood bordering the road on our right flank, but were unable to obtain a field of fire. I climbed a small tree to get a better view, but could see nothing but trees. Suddenly we were fired on – the Boche must have heard us and fired in our direction. We returned fire and bounded forward twenty yards. This we repeated three times while making headway to safety, for the Boche seemed to duck for cover and stopped firing while we were doing so. To my distress, both the Boche machine guns jammed, and I left the sergeants tugging at their guns while I went forward with the three privates. We fired our Sten guns instead of the Spandaus and dashed forward in the same manner, occasionally throwing a grenade as far as we could. We no doubt sounded quite a strong force. Anyway, about eighteen Boche fled from us, darting down a hedge, away from the wood and right towards our flanking party, who had no difficulty in shooting the lot. I did not know this at the time, and thought the firing on the left was nothing to do with me.

We came to a fence and across the road was a small cottage. The Boche might be in it, so I threw an anti-tank bomb at the wall and charged to the gap it made. There was a howl from inside, and I was just about to throw in another hand grenade when I saw it was a goat – I shot the poor thing. An officer from brigade, Captain Tony Wilkinson, the intelligence officer, joined us. I gave the direction of our next bound, up a ditch on the side of the road opposite the strip of wood. Moving off, the captain darted in front of me. I was a little annoyed for it rather hindered my ability to see ahead, but I admired his keenness. He'd been trying to take a Boche prisoner for intelligence purposes; unfortunately a sniper fatally wounded him shortly afterwards. I told him to keep still and that I would send the stretcher bearers directly we had finished. He spoke perfectly calmly, saying I need not do that for he was going to die, which he did almost immediately. What a waste of a good life, one of many the battalion would lose over the following days. Battles like this frittered away so many good people in the crucible of war and I often think, was it worth the cost? But right then his body blocked the ditch and we dare not go on or we might the same fate, so we went back about ten yards and dashed across the road into the same wood again where the Boche went. Here we found two Canadians sheltering in a ditch, wondering what it was all about. They had been adrift since the drop and were just finding their way back. I told them to join forces with me, and the chase continued in the same manner. Suddenly, one of them said the Boche were behind us, hoping we would pass. I threw a couple of grenades over and told them to surrender.

The grenades did the job for there was only one of the seven men left standing. He was a sergeant-major from Dresden. One badly wounded fellow begged to be shot, but someone jabbed him with morphine and told him to wait for the stretcher bearers. We collected two more Spandaus, for this was now our fire group, and they were 'red in the face' after having lost direction in the woods. The assault to help relieve brigade HQ had been a success. So we retired to the 9th Battalion's area where, during the night, the Boche in the Bois-de-Mont lobbed grenades and fired directionless shots. The Boche came near to our position on several occasions and called out in English. The objectives, I believe, were twofold; to keep us awake and to make us fire and disclose our automatic weapon positions. Our fire control was excellent and nothing was given away. Unfortunately, the battalion's 2IC, Major Charlton, was killed on 10 June while leading an attack against another infiltrating Boche patrol; yet one more wasted life. Every day we lost more and more good men; it was so random, just like some form of lottery where you bought a ticket to win some wonderful prize, yet still lost.

A Quick Smoke and a 'Death Sentence' – James Thurgood

One afternoon, infantry backed up by around six self-propelled guns, Sturmgeschütz IIIs I think, plus three or four Sd.Kfz. halftracks, attacked the battalion. As they advanced under a mortar barrage, the Sd.Kfzs moved with the infantry providing covering fire, but the assault guns stopped about 500 yards away and continued to fire over the heads of the advancing infantry. Even though they were partially hidden by a bank, they were a sitting target for our six-pounder anti-tank gun, as were the halftracks, but for some unknown reason the one we had in our position didn't open fire – I just couldn't believe it. Shortly after, a soldier crawled up to me on hands and knees and saluted! I couldn't believe that either – he was kneeling and he saluted. He said they were sorry about the six-pounder not firing but the breechblock had cracked. For the life of me I could not be angry with him as he was so apologetic, but the knowledge that there weren't any heavy weapons to defend us from the monsters was devastating, as well as frightening. One of the PIATs we had finally opened fire on a halftrack and stopped it, then it took out a second one, but against the SP guns it simply didn't have the range. Unfortunately, the guns and mortars were causing us a lot of casualties all along our front. The man on my right was dead, another was dying, and yet another with a massive chest wound died trying to say something as he crawled toward me. The Forward Observation Officer with us had been badly wounded as well, and his radio was destroyed. Meanwhile, the Boche infantry had spread out and were charging us and we didn't seem to be able to stop them. Then a miracle happened. Sergeant Waddingham had withheld the Vickers machine gun until the last minute. I was in the process of firing two red flares into the sky, a prearranged signal that we needed help from the mortars as we were just about to be overrun. I found out later they were already firing in support of C and B Companies for the very same reason, and they had every able body belonging to HQ Company, including the cooks, assisting them. It seems that the Boche were determined to break through somewhere and it looked like it would be us.

The Boche mortars and the SP guns suddenly ceased firing so their infantry could close with us. They now moved out from behind the half-tracks and spread out for the final assault. A second halftrack was hit by a PIAT and the battle slowly turned our way. It was at this point Sergeant Waddingham took control and ordered the company Vickers to fire, and from less than 100 yards the Boche were simply cut down like chaff in a cornfield. As old as it was, the Vickers with a good gun crew was a Godsend at times like this. It didn't have the high rate of fire that the Boche MG34s and 42s had, but it could fire all day long. In the end they simply took too many casualties. We'd lost two Bren gun crews and one gun, but now the Vickers was being used, along with the remaining Bren guns, and the Boche were in trouble. Without officers and senior NCOs, their leadership structure didn't function too well, which surprised me, as their corporals were damn good. Anyway, they began to withdraw, dragging as many wounded with them as they could. I know it seemed ridiculous, but silence reigned for a few moments and I was so dulled by exhaustion I did the most stupid thing a soldier could do, I stood up. How I wasn't shot I do not know. Thank God my orderly, Private Thomas, spotted a sniper crouching in among the hedgerow that ran along a bank some 150 yards to our right; it was extremely unusual for them to be so easily spotted as they were normally invisible until it was too late. Thomas quickly fired and actually killed him, which was a surprise as he was probably the worst shot in the company; he then dragged me down behind cover. I deserved the strong words he used to describe my actions; as a Liverpudlian he could be very descriptive when he wanted to be.

I still couldn't figure out why two of the self-propelled guns beyond the bank had quietened down and only one of them was now firing. We found out later that the one had lost a track and while the crew were trying to repair it, the second one was keeping our heads down. Mind you he was damn accurate and was picking his targets. They must have known that we had six-pounders as a day or so before we had knocked out two tanks that attacked us. But there they were, as bold as brass, firing at us. Then, to my utter amazement, I saw the hatch on the one not firing open, and a German officer, splendidly arrayed in polished jackboots, stiff cap and Sam Browne, leisurely climb down with a cigarette in his mouth. It was almost arrogant the way he did it. He must have thought he was completely out of sight and protected by the main body of the gun and the hedgerow. He probably got down to see how the work on the track was going. He was puffing merrily away when Wally Howison, our CQMS, crawled up to me and took aim at him with a sniper rifle. We could just see the top of his hat as he moved. Talking to nobody in particular, Wally adjusted his position and peered into the telescopic sight, then said in his usual accented tone, 'Yus can have two more puffs yar square headed bastard.' Some ten seconds later he fired and we watched as the officer's cap flew up in the air, as did one of his arms; he was certainly dead. Not long afterward our artillery came to our rescue and the field in front of us erupted in a mass of explosions; the CO had recognised our plight. The German wounded still out there didn't have a chance. When the firing ceased and the dust had settled we saw that one of the self propelled guns had been hit, almost certainly the one with the track problem; it was burning fiercely. The other one was nowhere to be seen. The attack had cost us dearly; about a third of my company was killed and wounded, something we would have to get used to in the future as we drove the Boche back inch by inch.

Impressions of a Medic – Walter Scot

I was an orderly room corporal in the RAMC and I landed in a glider on the second day. Once the advanced dressing station was set up, the casualties started to pour in. Unbelievably, the first one was a German sergeant-major, a right arrogant bastard he was too; he demanded a cigarette, and he got it, and I've never seen a man enjoy a cigarette like he did. Someone told me later it was because our cigarettes were 'real', whereas theirs weren't. Then another stretcher came in with a badly wounded Jerry on it. I didn't think he would make it he was so badly wounded; at least three rounds had hit him, probably from a machine gun. Suddenly, all hell broke loose as shells exploded all around us. The stretcher was dropped, the stretcher-bearers leaped into the trenches, and I dropped my helmet over Jerry's head. 'What the hell did you do that for?' was a mate's reaction. 'He's only a Jerry.' Which made me think later – it was not bravery but instinctive reaction. Bravery is going forward into battle, knowing somebody will be killed. I have always had quick reactions, but brave – not really; anyway, it's not our job to decide who should get medical attention. The German died not long afterward.

After that casualties were coming really fast and the MO decided to move the advanced dressing station (ADS) a short distance away, where it had better protection from the odd flying shells. Once it was up, we put a huge Red Cross flag on the top of the tents. As I recall the Germans never deliberately aimed at it, although I did hear a few tales about German atrocities, especially about the 12th SS Panzer Division, Hitlerjugend. It was a Waffen SS division and they were real fanatics who were mostly young men from the Hitler Youth movement. Evidently they didn't take kindly to getting beaten at Normandy and shot a lot of prisoners out of hand. After they heard about it, many of the lads were very reluctant to take them prisoner, and I mean 'reluctant', or should I say they didn't. In the beginning I just could not believe I was in France, and at war. Did the folk back home know where we were, I wondered. We were lucky as the French folk from a local farm gave us milk. They seemed relieved and pleased to see us, but not wildly excited. Anyway, we eventually moved to a new location some 500 yards to the rear that was protected by trees. Some of the lads had gone up the line and set up another advanced dressing station and we had our first 'friendly fire' casualty when a British tank came through a hedge and killed one of the doctors. I never knew him as he had just been posted to us.

A lot of my work had to do with urgent medical supplies such as the new 'wonder drug' penicillin, which saved a lot of men's lives by stopping infections. As the days wore on the shelling eased off a bit and the OC said we should work in shifts as too many had been working continuously and were falling asleep on their feet. It was like a giant lottery and I had survived where many others had died. Other days lay ahead, and on one of those shrapnel shredded our sleeping tent, fortunately when we were not in it. Curiously, one of the big things that stuck in my mind was seeing a line of about twenty dead outside the hospital tent and the local Catholic priest would only bless the three Catholics among them, refusing to pray for the rest. It was Christianity gone mad. I told our senior doctor, who stormed out, grabbed him and threatened to tear him apart unless he did all of them. He put the fear of God into the old priest, who then did as he was told, but I don't think his heart was in it. Our military padres didn't differentiate; they blessed everyone whatever religion. It was stuff like this that left a lasting impression on me even though I saw many other terrible things.

Stuck up a Tree – Bert Clements

Within a short space of time the Germans reacted to the landings at Normandy on 6 June 1944 and sent infantry and armoured vehicles against the hurriedly prepared defences. The airborne artillery component had landed in gliders. Several contained six-pounder anti-tank guns towed by jeeps, and four of these had been set up in and around the woods near the DZs. As the Germans approached, the crews were warned to expect them. I was in charge of one of the guns and took the decision to post a man high in a tree to give us better warning of the approaching Germans. When they appeared, there was infantry backed up by five armoured vehicles, which consisted of three Panther tanks and two 'Schwerer Panzerspähwagen' heavy armoured cars. If they keep coming, I thought, with luck I might be able to get two, but certainly not all of them. I was hoping the other six-pounder, which was nearby, would help in taking care of the rest of them. As the German infantry were crossing a path through the corn some 200 yards away, their officer called out and pointed towards the trees where the gun was hidden. It was an obvious vantage point as it was on much higher ground and would be ideal for the Germans if they could take it. The armour was now 175 yards away and closing fast. Miraculously, even though we weren't in contact with one another two guns fired simultaneously, hitting a different armoured car, causing both to burst into flames. Two other six-pounders now joined in and soon all the enemy vehicles bar one tank were ablaze, and it was limping away with smoke pouring from it. The attacking infantry quickly retreated under a storm of fire, leaving behind a lot of dead and wounded. It was at this point the poor Gunner up the tree yelled out above the noise, 'Sarg, I feel a little exposed up here, especially as someone is shooting at me. Can I come down?' In the excitement I'd forgotten all about him, so I quickly gave permission and he clambered down with all the speed of an excited monkey.

Slippery Slide – Montgomery Laylaw

When I jumped into Normandy, I was the PIAT man in the platoon, and was detailed to fly in an old Albemarle. It was dark as everyone boarded through the aperture at the back. With kitbags between our legs, each of us sat down one behind the other. There was only one man left to enter the aircraft and he was carrying the heavy base plate of a 3-inch mortar. He pushed his weighty kitbag ahead of him and then followed it, but as he clambered through the aperture, the aircraft's tricycle undercarriage reared up and several of the lads literally slid toward the aperture, and one fell on top of the mortar base plate man and both ended up in a heap hanging on to the edge of the aperture. There were hoots of laughter as well as a few well-chosen words in ancient Swahili. Because of this, we all got out so the aircraft could right itself. Once the thing was back on its feet, we got in a second time, but as the last man clambered aboard the same thing happened again, and several of the lads slid toward the aperture a second time. By now everyone was rolling around laughing uproariously, including our platoon commander. We all got out a second time and the pilot followed us and kicked one of the tyre struts, which was now bent. Then he shouted aggressively at the ancient Albemarle, 'Doris – 'ave you been bloody well been staying out late again wiv those bloody Yanks? Well this time you've gone too far, go to your bedroom and stay there!' He then abandoned the take-off and we were all squeezed on to other aircraft and flown in on the second wave.

Confusion at the Merville Battery – Alan Parry

The chief responsibility assigned to the company was to fly to Normandy in three Horsa gliders, and get inside the Merville Battery and attack the casemates with Sten guns, flamethrowers and explosives. I was to be one of the ten-man advanced party of the 9th Battalion who were to jump with the pathfinders at 0020 hours, half an hour before the main force. My task was to establish the battalion RV and signal its location by means of a red Aldis lamp. The glider assault was felt to be extremely risky, an almost suicidal venture that could result in severe casualties among those taking part. Nevertheless, the whole company volunteered to be a part of it, but I made a point of only selecting from among the volunteers as few married men as possible. Once over France, we couldn't get out fast enough. I eased my way towards the aperture and just fell out. Catching my kitbag on the port side of the aperture caused numerous twists in my rigging lines, a sight that made me extremely worried. Worse still, I couldn't reach sufficiently far down to release my kitbag. I was beginning to think I wouldn't succeed, when with a final effort, I released it. All this took time and I didn't once look down to see how I was doing. It was, therefore, with a considerable shock, that I literally hit the ground like a bag of concrete. Before landing, however, I was conscious of hearing bullets and made up my mind then and there that they were all destined for me. I felt a devil of a target sitting on the ground, ridding myself of my harness and emptying my kitbag. Unfortunately, quite a few men had been dropped off target and for some it was a lonely walk to find anyone. The 100 Lancaster and Halifax bombers of the RAF, which were to bombard the Merville Battery, put in an appearance; regrettably they missed the battery completely and managed to bomb the battalion's advance party instead. Many dropped in the field in which I found myself. I took cover in a ditch and, while hoping for the best, feared the worst. I was scared out of my wits. I bit the dust and prepared to meet my end. When they ceased to fall I breathed a huge sigh of relief and cursed the RAF.

By this time I was getting a little agitated at the passing of time and I still hadn't made the RV. I collected about a dozen other chaps and eventually saw a red light. For the third time, I breathed a sigh of relief and approached the red light that was held by the inevitable Lieutenant Joe Worth, the battalion's intelligence officer. Sergeant Easlea was there, waving his torch, also Major Eddie Charlton and Captain Hal Hudson, but precious few others. I eventually found the tree I was looking for, the designated RV, and was amazed to see my orderly was already there. His direction-finding at night was evidently better than mine. I congratulated him and he said, 'Good evening Sir. What kept you then?'

I replied, 'I had one or two little jobs to do on the DZ and here I am.' That didn't impress him either! All this time I had been lugging the heavy kitbag with which I had jumped. It contained an Aldis lamp that I was to flash to mark the RV for the battalion. I knelt to unpack the bag, pulled out the lamp and my haversack. To my surprise there was another haversack. Adsett, who was leaning over me, said, 'Thank you very much Sir, I believe that one is mine!'

I said to Private Adsett, 'Now you go up that tree and I will hand you the lamp, and when I give you the word you can start flashing.'

He was extremely indignant and said to me, 'Oh no, you're OC party, you go up the tree and I will hand YOU the lamp!' So up the tree I shinned and he handed me the lamp.

Despite waiting for several hours, only 150 men presented themselves at the RV, so Lieutenant-Colonel Otway made the decision to proceed and attack the Merville Battery with what men and equipment he had. I led the advance to the battery with some thirty men of A Company at my side. The CO decided that I must lead the assault in the absence of Ian Dyer, OC, C Company, and that what was there of A and C Companies would constitute the Assault Party. The signal for the assault to begin would be the blowing of the Bangalore torpedoes.

There was no time for anything more than cursory orders. I explained that there would be no communications, as we had no wireless, and that each party would work independently. I would blow my whistle and we would charge. We deployed along the line of the cattle fence that marked the perimeter of the minefield. I decided to split the men we had into four groups, one for each of the gun casemates. The battalion waited for the gliders to arrive before beginning the assault, but after one passed over unsuccessfully, and the others were nowhere to be seen, the attack could wait no longer so I blew my whistle to signal the assault. Everyone lay down to the ground and moments later the Bangalores blew a 20-foot gap in the wire. Lieutenant-Colonel Otway shouted, 'Get In, Get In!' And so I ran into the minefield with the Assault Party charging after me. I must admit I was expecting to do a tap dance on a mine but it didn't happen, thank God. More by luck than judgement I shot a German who materialised in front of me, then I was shot in the left thigh and my leg collapsed under me and I fell into a huge bomb crater. I saw my orderly, who was just alongside me, looking at me as if to say, 'Bad luck mate', and off he went. Regrettably, he was killed during the assault.

In the bottom of my rather personal bomb crater, I assessed my position. My left leg was numb and my trouser leg was soaked in blood. Having a minuscule knowledge of first aid, I removed my whistle lanyard and tied it to my leg as a tourniquet. My knowledge was evidently too limited, as I applied it to the wrong place. After a brief interval I realised my error, so I removed it, restoring some form of life to my leg, sufficient at any rate to enable me to clamber out of my hole and continue with my appointed mission. By this time the assault was drawing to a conclusion. I made my way to Number One casemate and noticed a lot of dead Germans as well as bodies belonging to our lads. There were a few prisoners too. As I entered the enormous casemate, there was only two or three of our own men; the rest were missing. I was told they were either dead or wounded. Somewhat weakened by the loss of blood, I passed through the casemate to the firing aperture at the far end, where, to my intense dismay, I saw not a 150mm gun, as was expected, but a tiny, old-fashioned piece mounted on a carriage with wooden wheels. I estimated it to be a 75mm and it was clearly a temporary expedient pending the arrival of the permanent armament. This was an awful anti-climax, and made me wonder if our efforts had really been worth the loss of men we had incurred, but of course it was, as we had no knowledge what was really in the casements did we? I sat on the sill at the bottom of the firing aperture, but moments later there was an explosion immediately outside and I felt something strike my wrist. My first reaction was that I'd lost my hand, but upon inspection I was considerably relieved to find that I had suffered only a small cut from a shell splinter so I proceeded to deal with the captured gun. We all carried sticks of plastic explosive, detonators and fuse wire and I instructed a sergeant to make up a suitable charge, which was placed in the breech of the gun. We re-entered the casemate, now full of acrid smoke, and upon inspecting the gun I was reasonably satisfied that sufficient damage had been inflicted upon it to prevent it playing a part in the seaborne assault, which was due in two and a half hours.

I now proceeded to check the damage inflicted upon the remaining guns. And as I moved toward them I came across more bodies belonging to our men. I visited number three gun after the party responsible for its destruction had withdrawn. Lieutenant Halliburton went to inspect the last gun and reported to me that he considered it had been successfully neutralised. While marshalling the prisoners prior to withdrawing, Lieutenant Slade came along and informed me that the position was due to be shelled in a very few minutes by HMS *Arethusa*. I ordered Lieutenant Halliburton to lead numbers one and two parties back to the battalion. At this stage I was feeling weak from a considerable loss of blood. Nevertheless, I felt the need to continue to carry out my duties, as decisive leadership at these times is important. The naval liaison party had not arrived so I ordered that yellow smoke candles were to be set off at intervals of no more than five minutes, half an hour after dawn. I hoped that a spotter aircraft might see the smoke and relay a signal down to the *Arethusa*. As it happened it did not fire its guns. The reasons for this have never been firmly established. I believe *Arethusa* was told that they should only open fire if confirmation was received that the Battery was still active and firing at the fleet.

What was left of our attack party then prepared to leave the Battery. There were quite a few soldiers still in there, as well as the dead, and, as best I could, I warned everyone to get out as quickly as possible. Slowly, and with some difficulty, I made my way to the point of exit, where I saw what could only be described as an urchin's soapbox on wheels. This seemed to me a godsend, and I decided to mount it and begin my withdrawal. By lying on my back, and propelling myself with the heel of my right foot, I was able to make very slow progress. It was, however, exhausting, and I considered my chances of reaching the rallying point remote. As I was reflecting upon my chances Sergeant Taylor of my company came into view, took off his toggle rope, attached it to my 'chariot' and proceeded to drag me along the dusty track to the rallying point. During this journey, shells were still landing nearby; I drank several mouthfuls of whisky from the flask attached to my belt, which I regarded as an important part of my battle accoutrements. Sergeant Taylor wheeled me to the rallying point, during which my unusual mode of transport was witnessed by Major Smith of HQ Company; he took a brandy flask from his pocket, gulped a mouthful and beamed, 'A jolly good battle, what?' The grim faces of the men around us burst into smiles, and the sullen group of prisoners looked on in bewildered amazement. I wanted to stay with the battalion, but the commanding officer ordered me to go to the Regimental Aid Post and reluctantly I obeyed him. The aid post was established at a farm called the Haras-de-Retz. I was one of twenty-two wounded who were left here as the battalion pushed on towards Le Plein. I lay on the floor next to Captain Hal Hudson, who had serious intestinal wounds. He was barely conscious and deadly white. The medical orderly, Private Watts, came in and dressed my leg, assisted, I believe, by Private Comley. The MO had to leave hurriedly to re-join the battalion, but left us in the charge of two German medical orderlies who were awfully good, and couldn't do enough for us.

Sniping in Normandy – Dennis Edwards

In the early hours we were roused and ordered to pack everything and be ready to move out. Because the 51st Highland Division had just moved into our area, some of the lads got the bright idea that we were being pulled out and taken home.

At around 0400 hours we were quietly ordered to get ready to move off. We advanced eastwards up the lane towards the higher ground of the Orne river valley. This was a very odd route to be taking if we were being pulled out! As we trudged up a track, we passed some of lads from the other battalions who were being pulled out. They had been badly mauled. Most had blood-soaked field dressings covering various parts of their bodies and they looked terribly shaken. It took about three hours to cover the mile or so to the top of the east bank of the Orne, arriving around 0700 hours. For the first time we saw the carnage of the night-time battle as we met up with the shattered remnants of those units that had been involved. All around was evidence of brutal warfare such as I had never seen before; it was horrific, a scene that will stay with me for the rest of my life.

Before long we encountered the lads of the Highland Division, and here was shellshock on a massive scale. The poor devils stood around in groups, staring at us through vacant and bewildered eyes. I had never seen the result of warfare so grimly demonstrated, with every ditch, gully, hedgerow, track and roadway strewn with dead and shattered bodies of both British and German soldiers of various units. We moved up the drive that led to the Château St Come, stepping around what the day before had been Sherman tanks and armoured troop carriers. Now they were simply twisted, smouldering and burnt-out wrecks. Beneath one burning tank were the shrivelled and blackened remains of two burnt bodies. The scene was horrifying but the smell was even worse. The air was heavy and sickly with the smell of burnt or burning flesh and clothing, wood, leaves, grass, petrol, oil and cordite. The rain had stopped soon after dawn and been replaced by warm sunshine, which was already having its effect upon human flesh. Near Bréville I saw more horrific sights, one of which was a weird tableau in which one of the Canadian lads had been run through the middle of his body by a German bayonet, pinning him to a tree. As it happened he had reached over the bent German and plunged his dagger into the middle of his opponent's chest. The two had died during the night, but in daylight they were as they had been when they died together, still propping each other up with a rifle in between them.

Wednesday the 14th began with the normal stand-to, followed by heavy and accurate shelling and mortaring from the enemy. Soon after breakfast I went out with an officer who led a small recce around the hedgerows to our front. He wanted to see the area and plot possible routes from which an attack might come, in particular the route along which tanks and self-propelled 88s might approach our positions. German snipers still infested the area and were taking a toll of men that we could ill afford to lose. To discourage their activities, we snipers were sent forward in small groups to find a secluded spot from where we could watch the taller trees in which we guessed enemy snipers would be located. When a sniper fired, a telltale wisp of smoke could be seen. His position would then be given a real pasting, but they seldom worked alone, so that when we hit one, another would fire at us, so it was a case of firing and quickly moving to another location. Sometimes it was a matter of hurling a smoke grenade or two to cover our move. Using smoke was often a problem, however, because it worried Jerry, who took it as a prelude to an attack, and he would usually retaliate by mortaring and shelling the whole area. We took turns in going out to the front on patrols and sniper hunts. One team decided upon an ingenious innovation – they took a PIAT with them. When a sniper was spotted, a PIAT bomb was fired at the top of his tree. We had no way of measuring the success of their effort other than from the fact that several of us thought that fewer snipers were bothering us after this incident!

On Monday 19 June the dawn stonk saw the CSM killed when a shell exploded near his trench and detonated his Gammon anti-tank bombs. These bloody awful things were standard issue for us all and we hated them. They consisted of a bomb that was sticky and had a handle resembling a large toffee apple. The bombs were highly sensitive and exploded with little encouragement. Standing orders were that these should be kept in every trench and if tanks overran us you reached up and stuck the bomb on the thin underside of the tank as it passed overhead. From fear of the sensitivity of these infernal things, born of past experience with them, most of us dug a shallow hole within arm's reach of the trench and placed the bombs there. If tanks came our way, we could grab a bomb before they arrived. The only occasions that we took them into the trench were when the officers came round on a tour of inspection. Since the CSM was a stickler for discipline and orders, he probably kept his bombs with him inside his trench, and when an enemy shell exploded nearby it set them off. There's discipline, and then there's common sense.

Before dawn on 7 July, three of us were sent on another trip. This time we aimed to reach a farmhouse at Longuemare. We wanted to be there early to see if the Germans occupied it during the night. If there was no sign of life, we hoped to enter the house or at least the outbuildings. On the way there we heard the sound of many people digging trenches on the far side of the crossroads. One at a time, and flitting from cover to cover, we reached the farm and after many stops to listen and observe, managed to get inside the place. From the upper floor we overlooked the road junction and saw a mass of Germans digging new trenches. While the other two stayed to observe I went back and reported what we saw to Major Howard. After getting the OK from regimental HQ, he organised and led a large and well-armed fighting patrol out to the farmhouse. After withdrawing the other snipers, we lined up along the edge of an adjoining orchard and on his signal let fly with rifles, automatics, machine guns and mortars. A few minutes later, having caused pandemonium, we stopped firing and quickly withdrew to our lines. It must have really annoyed the Germans as they mortared us for about three hours afterwards. But we'd expected that and for once we only had a few casualties.

When I went out sniping, I invariably took my captured German weaponry along with me: a Schmeisser, the P38 pistol, and the Helios wristwatch. Wally Parr and Paddy O'Donnell, my fellow snipers, joked that if I were to be captured, Jerry would execute me on the spot for carrying such an arsenal of German equipment, but I always reckoned it was worth the risk. In all the grime and mud that we had to contend with, crawling through ditches and so forth, the chances of having a weapon jam when it was most needed were pretty high, and I was of the opinion that it did no harm to have back-up defences. It was quite likely that when their stand-to ended, Jerry would be out of his trenches drying out after the rain of the previous day. This proved to be the case and we had no difficulty in spotting targets. All was peace and tranquillity until Wally let fly at an excellent target. By the time he hit the ground the rest dived for cover. It was a long time before they began to reappear, probably assuming that the man had been hit by a stray shot. I took careful aim at a hole in the hedgerow. It was well lit by the lighter background. Soon it filled as someone peered across the orchard towards us. I held my fire, hoping that it would encourage others to surface. After a short time the hole reappeared as the man moved away. Then it filled again. This time I gently squeezed the trigger and the target crashed backwards. Paddy should have been the next to fire, but as I was closing the bolt on a fresh cartridge which I had just loaded into my rifle, I saw a well-built German out in the open and exposed to my view from his head to his knees. I waited for a few seconds for Paddy to fire, but assumed that he could not see this target. I fired and almost certainly winged him as he let out a loud yell and disappeared from sight. Paddy was furious, and all the more so when I whispered, 'Blast – I think I only winged him!' It was several hours before they got over the shock of two kills and a wounding. We had to wait until getting towards lunchtime before, once again, they began moving around, probably on their way to the cookhouse, and at last Paddy was rewarded for his long vigil. Happy to have made a hit apiece, we reckoned that three 'kills' would mean that no further targets would appear, so we decided to call it a day and we returned to our lines.

To my surprise and delight, on Tuesday the 25th I was issued with a brand new sniper rifle straight out from Ordnance. It was covered with a thick layer of grease and wrapped in greaseproof paper. I spent much of the day taking it apart and cleaning it. Until this time, my rifle had been a completely standard-issue Lee Enfield .303 with no telescopic sights, and

1. Lines of paratroopers jumping from three aircraft.

2. & 3. The British airborne forces were formed after Churchill had seen the effectiveness of German airborne troops, the Fallschirmjäger, in the invasion of the Low Countries and also in Crete. These two photographs show Fallschirmjäger preparing for the attack on Crete.

4. A trainee paratrooper makes a practice jump from a tower.

5. Paratroopers with the Free Polish forces train using Bren guns.

6. Trainee paratroopers march past Whitley bombers prior to a training exercise.

7. Paratroopers jumping as part of a training exercise somewhere in England.

8. & 9. A visit by the king to airborne forces in training. He is seen inspecting some of the men and watching an exercise.

10. A flight of Hotspur gliders, used to train glider pilots and glider-borne infantry.

11. Trainee glider pilots in the cockpit of a glider with an instructor.

12. Glider-borne infantry climb aboard a glider for a training flight.

13. Part of the armada of transport ships carrying the troops for Operation Torch, the amphibious assault on North Africa, including the Airborne.

14. & 15. Paratroopers disembarking from their ships in North Africa.

16. British paratroopers involved in fighting at Medjez-el-Bab in Tunisia march along a road near the town.

17. German prisoners march through the streets of Medjez-el-Bab following the fighting.

18. A paratrooper unpacks a miniature motor scooter, known as a 'Welbike', from an air-dropped supply canister.

19. This paratrooper demonstrates a collapsible bicycle, also designed to be dropped in a supply canister during an assault.

20. Preparation for D-Day: a transport officer checks motorcycles as they are secured to the floor of a Horsa glider.

21. Preparation for D-Day: a paratrooper is about to jump through the cargo door of a transport aircraft.

22. Part of the vast armada of transport aircraft that carried the airborne portion of the D-Day invasion force.

23. Horsa gliders coming in to land in a field in Normandy on D-Day.

24. General Montgomery addresses recruits at a barracks in the UK.

25. Paratroopers moving from their drop zones towards Arnhem and the bridge over the Rhine.

26. Two sergeants from the Glider Pilot Regiment enter a school in Arnhem to check for snipers.

27. Paratroopers using a 6-pounder anti-tank gun against a German self-propelled gun during the battle for Arnhem.

28. Men of the 1st Airborne Division keeping watch from a shell hole during the fighting in Arnhem.

29. Some of the paratroopers who were successfully evacuated back across the Rhine following the failure of Operation Market Garden. Although this is an official photograph, their relief to be out of Arnhem must be genuine.

30. A long line of gliders and towing aircraft ready for take-off prior to the crossing of the Rhine.

31. One of the landing zones on the eastern bank of the Rhine. A glider is coming into land at the top of the picture, while an airborne soldier leads a prisoner away.

this new weapon was much more suitable for sniping, especially for when we would leave our trenches and get moving again. I discovered that no one from the forward units was out sniping, so I pestered the officers and eventually obtained permission to go out into no man's land. After finding a suitable spot in view of the German positions, and waiting for a little while, I saw a German in a small gap, took quick aim and fired. Judging by the way he fell backwards, I was satisfied that the weapon was correctly zeroed. Like a kid with a new toy, I spent most of that afternoon and evening looking for more targets. To my disappointment none appeared. Eventually, I returned to the company lines, where I found to my astonishment that the entire battalion had packed up and gone. I gathered my kit and went in search of them, and found that they had been moved even further back from the front line, still in the area of Le Mesnil but considerably further from the front line than we had been previously. Everyone was busy digging new trenches as I arrived, so there was nothing for me to do except dump my kit and join in everyone's favourite pastime – digging.

Early in the morning of 17 August, and not before time we all thought, the long-awaited advance began. After being cooped up in the trenches for so long, it was a wonderful feeling to be on the move again. Jerry said farewell with a really heavy barrage along the entire front. Eventually all went quiet. He was on the run, off towards the east... The advance began at 0930 hours but was hardly dramatic, more of an anticlimax after our high hopes for an easy advance. It was a tiring, stop-go process, a case of jump to your feet – advance a few hundred yards – stop – sit down at the roadside – up on your feet again for a few more yards – and so on, as the day wore on. The cause of the problem was that Jerry was using tough and determined rearguards to cover his withdrawal. It took an entire morning for us to advance no more than a few hundred yards. It was now D Company's turn to take the lead in the advance towards Varaville. As we neared the village, the leading section came under fire from a German MG34 machine gun. Lance Corporal 'Smacker' Drew was killed and Corporal 'Smoky' Howard and Private Dancy were both badly wounded. It was very easy to slip into complacency and this incident was a grim reminder that the war was far from finished. Two snipers, one of them being myself, were sent ahead to locate the machine gun and silence it.

We thought the gun was located in or near some far buildings a short way off, but the terrain thereabouts offered no chance of concealment for a direct approach and we were forced to make a wide detour around. We clambered through a hedge and worked our way around to the side of the buildings, with an officer and a section of men following in our wake, not far behind. Ready to shoot up anything we saw, we made a dash into the farmyard. As we did so, we heard a motorcycle engine roar into life. A motorbike with a crew of two men, complete with MG34 mounted on a sidecar, sped out of the farmyard and down the road. We fired wildly at the speeding machine, having no time to take a decent aim, but in an instant it was gone. We were a little bitter at having to let this successful enemy unit get away.

At 0300 hours a long night march began in pouring rain. It was an incredibly tiring and difficult march, all of us virtually asleep as we marched, but, despite our state of extreme fatigue, we could hear the sound of a furious battle up ahead of us. The Commando that we had met earlier at Varaville had overtaken us again at some point, and had gone ahead to Brucourt, where they had set up a splendid ambush against a large German force that was moving down a hillside track. Almost completely exhausted, at 0800 we arrived at Brucourt, where we witnessed the Commandos' handiwork. Attacking from both sides of the track, they had trapped and then wiped out the enemy force, causing massive casualties. The hillside was strewn with German dead, upturned carts and abandoned weapons and equipment. We pressed on until we arrived at a road junction just to the north of Heuland. One of our companies pushed ahead to try to make contact with the retreating Germans, while we settled in for the night, fraternising with the locals, handing around our cigarettes and chocolate, and even having a sing-song with them, until finally I got some much-needed sleep.

At first light on the 23rd we were on our way eastwards from the village. At 1000 hours we came to what I will always remember as 'Hellfire Hill'. Across the open hillside, we had to negotiate a steep uphill track, which led up and around to the north-western outskirts of St-Arnoult. This meant that we were completely exposed to the enemy mobile artillery and we were continuously shelled by Jerry 88s firing from another nearby wooded hilltop. Near the top of the hill, on the outskirts of St-Arnoult, we were still taking punishment from the German 88s. An old French woman came out of her cottage to offer us shelter, but tragically she too was killed by a shell-burst as she stood in her garden calling to us. A well-organised and determined group of really young German fanatics caused us plenty of trouble that afternoon. There were not many of them, but they held us up very successfully, and before we could advance we had to kill all but two of them. These last two finally surrendered, and it was pitiful. They looked as if they should have been at school rather than on a battlefield, dying for a lost cause. The two were well and truly indoctrinated by their Führer's regime and one made the dreadful mistake of spitting at one of the lads guarding him. For his efforts he got a thorough beating that even the officers didn't stop. We'd seen too many of our lads killed by these young animals, and their division had a reputation for shooting prisoners. When it was over, the other one looked genuinely shocked as if it was OK for them to react that way, but not us.

Not much further ahead was our next objective, the village of Manneville-la-Raoult, which was on higher ground and separated from us by a densely wooded valley. The company commander came to our lead position with the news that the village was occupied by a handful of demoralised troops who wouldn't put up much of a fight. The idea was to soften up the defenders by means of a barrage from our 25-pounder guns, after which we were supposed to stroll in and accept their surrender. It sounded too good to be true – and of course, it was. As soon as the bombardment ceased, we advanced, weapons at the ready, towards the village, and I was sent ahead to scout the approach, closely followed by the rest of our section. Suddenly, and to our rear, came a sound. I looked around, startled, with the hairs on the back of my neck telling me that I was in immediate danger. I was alarmed to see a Jerry soldier standing there, high above our heads, with just the upper part of his body showing above the hedge along the top of the bank that rose from the side of the lane we were in. However, to my relief, the man had his hands in the air, apparently as if to surrender, but he still held his Mauser rifle, horizontally above his head. He started to shout, 'Me good, me Russ, me good, Russ, Russ.'

I wondered why a White Russian was fighting here in Normandy as I shouted to him, 'Drop the weapon,' and then in pidgin German, 'Drappen ze Waffen.' I couldn't get to the man, as he was behind the thick hedge, and so I had no way of removing his weapon, nor did I seem able to communicate to him that he must throw down the wretched rifle. The scene was now commanding all our attention, with the result that we were no longer watching the street, from which direction there came the clattering sound of rapidly moving feet.

One lad swung around and shouted, 'Look out – Germans,' and at the same time from somewhere across the road an enemy machine gun opened fire with a long burst. The German up on the bank, still swaying in a drunken fashion, swung his rifle downwards with its business end pointing at me. A corporal standing next to me fired his Sten and simultaneously I fired my rifle from the hip. The German above the hedge fell backwards and at the same moment those further along the road dived for cover and began firing in our direction. We returned fire as we dived for cover below the low front garden wall. At this point, if an enemy grenade had come our way it would have accounted for quite a few of us and we desperately needed to take up more dispersed positions. We rushed out into the main road, firing from the hip and fanning out to right and to left so as to present the fewest targets to the enemy. As we hit the ground German artillery and mortars opened fire and bombarded the village, presumably on the assumption that the village was now in our hands. When, after a few minutes of heavy bombardment, the enemy guns ceased firing, we immediately set about clearing the row of cottages along our side of the road. The fronts of the houses were under direct fire from the enemy machine guns and snipers across the other side of the main road. Working our way along the back of the properties, we hurled hand grenades and fired as we entered each house, some of which had been set ablaze during the bombardment.

While we fired across the road, we were restricted by the fact that we were not too sure where our own lads were now located. I was watching a gap in the hedge at the side of a small orchard where I suspected a Jerry machine gun might be located. Eventually I saw the machine gunner and managed to hit him and so silence the gun, but no sooner had that one stopped firing than another opened up nearby and a stream of bullets came through the upper window through which I had fired. The Germans had certainly done a good job since they held us up for a day and most of the following night. The intelligence report had said that we would only find a handful of demoralised, poor-quality troops ready to surrender. It had been very wide of the mark, but I shall always wonder whether we would have been able to take the village without a fight if we had managed to take the White Russian prisoner and the rest had seen that he had come to no harm. As it happened, an unfortunate set of circumstances had arisen at the critical moment. This may have decided some of them to make a fight of it, even though not all of them would have realised that the Russian had been shot. It still concerns me, however, that I may have contributed to what might have been an unnecessary day-long battle that resulted in the loss of the lives of some brave comrades. Others, with whom I have discussed this incident, have all been of the opinion that what happened was unavoidable. It has always been an unpleasant memory for me, and has left me with a bad taste in my mouth.

The Elephant Gun and the 'Umbrella Man' – Thomas Black

One of the majors in the divisional reconnaissance regiment was rather eccentric. He flew into Normandy in a Tetrarch tank. Just like all other tank crews, he would have to be inside the tank for the whole flight as there was no room to clamber into the thing once it was inside the Hamilcar glider. On the side of his tank he'd strapped a huge elephant gun he'd acquired for African trips before the war. In his words, 'It was there in case any Boche got too close and needed seeing off!' He also had a large black umbrella that he liked to use in case of rain.

The umbrella fascinated one young trooper and he asked his troop sergeant, 'Why does he need that stupid umbrella, Sarg?'

The reply he got was: 'Don't ya know anything? He's ex-Guards and all the Officers carry 'em in case of a downpour of Artillery!'

The Standing Patrol – Les Hawkins

Every night we used to have a four-man 'standing patrol' hidden behind a bank about 250 yards ahead of the battalion. It was there to warn if any Jerries were trying to creep up on us. To say the least, it was a nightmarish job staying awake the whole time and trying to figure out if the noises in front of you were animal or human, and if the trees and bushes that were moving in the breeze were the Jerries or simply the wind blowing them back and forth. It was at times like these that your mind played terrible tricks on your vision if you weren't on your toes. Even though I had many frightening events during the war, I always remember one night when we caught a Jerry fighting patrol creeping towards our lines. There would have been about twenty of them and they were using the woods to screen their movement, but one of them stepped on a twig and when it snapped it sounded like thunder rolling in the night and it definitely wasn't normal. Animals tend to clump around like elephants; the bigger ones do anyway as they had nothing to be worried about if they were that big. It's amazing how sound travels in the dark and that night had been especially quiet, with only distant mortar and artillery fire and the occasional burst of small-arms, and this was definitely only 30 or so yards away.

I gave Charlie Pickering, our section corporal, a shove and he woke the other two up. Charlie spent his normal life dodging gamekeepers and it didn't take him long to spot the Jerry fighting patrol creeping toward us. Whoever was out on the standing patrol carried a Bren gun, a Thompson and two

Sten guns, so we had a lot of firepower, and that didn't include two grenades each of us had. We dare not use the telephone, as they were already too close, so Charlie carefully turned to face our lines and used the backup system. He slowly got out his torch that had red glass in it, and holding it well below the level of the bank began flicking it on and off. The red light it gave off would easily be picked up by one of the pickets and relayed to BHQ. Several flicks and he turned off the light and we got on with getting ready for them. I was on the Bren gun and distinctly remember lining up the slowly moving outlines and waiting for Charlie to say 'fire'. The way Charlie was going, they would be walking on top of us before we opened fire. In the end he let them get within 15 yards or so before he, Bert Hemings and Taffy Meredith threw hand grenades. I remember the distinct click as they released them and the safety clip flew off. Some 5 long seconds later, there were three enormous detonations and we were up and firing for all we were worth. I emptied a magazine into the darkness, where I could hear the screams of pain from the wounded. All of us changed magazines at least twice, firing in sweeping motions to cover all the ground in front of us. At that range it was impossible to miss. In three or four minutes it was all over and I don't remember them firing a shot.

Charlie, never one to take unnecessary risks, lobbed two more grenades, and then he and Bert sprayed the area one more time to make sure anyone lying doggo was taken care of. Once the sound died down, there was a deafening silence. Charlie rang through to BHQ and told them what had happened. He wasn't going out there in the dark so we lay there until first light and with me covering them, the others went out and checked the bodies. One them lay just the other side of the bank, well what was left of him anyway. The rest were scattered all over the place in all sorts of grotesque positions. The grenades had done a lot of damage, and all of them had multiple bullet wounds; some were totally unrecognisable. Charlie counted thirteen bodies and one blood trail going into the woods. I don't think he would have gone too far before dying a very painful death. They were SS so we lost no sleep over them.

Onward Christian Soldiers – Victor Ball

The flight over the Channel was uneventful, but everyone inside the Horsa glider had no illusions as to what was in store for us once we cleared the French coast. I sat next to the platoon commander, a very young second lieutenant. For someone so young he was still a good officer, and the lads would follow him into the jaws of Hell if necessary. We all knew straightaway we'd crossed the French coast as the anti-aircraft fire began pounding the sky. The Germans were as nervous as we were and they must have known the invasion was imminent. Everyone had been singing 'Onward Christian Soldiers' and outside the anti-aircraft firing became louder and louder. Suddenly there was a huge BANG! that shook the glider like a giant hand had grabbed it angrily. The singing instantly stopped and in the gloom everyone looked at one another expecting the worst, then the singing began again only with much more gusto and volume. The platoon commander turned to me and yelled in my ear: 'It's amazing how a bit of incentive from God improves the quality and vitality of the singing isn't it?' I just had to laugh.

Renaming 'Pegasus Bridge' – Billy Rowlands

There is an interesting story how the bridge over the Caen Canal got the name of Pegasus Bridge. The 51st (Highland) Division, upon arriving in the divisional area after the 6th Airborne had left, started to paint their divisional sign on anything and everything that stood upright and didn't move, and they even went as far as to put up a sign on the Bénouville bridge which said 'Highland Bridge'. This so incensed Major General Gale that he ordered its removal and one bearing the name 'Pegasus Bridge' was erected in its place. The Highlanders had enough common sense not to interfere with it.

Padre Power – Allan Brown

A Father Briscoe of the 5th Airborne Brigade was your typical Airborne 'Cadbury fruit and nut case' priest, only in his instance, once he'd qualified he became addicted to parachuting and he simply couldn't do enough of it. He seemed to be challenging God to see if his parachute would fail and God ignored him. He was eventually ordered by the brigadier not to jump because of the risk of injury. He disregarded the order and sneaked jumps in whenever he could. He even became involved with testing the new 'drop leg bags', and when he was caught by Lieutenant-Colonel Pine Coffin, held his finger up to his mouth and whispered, 'Not a word to the old man Sir!' He was but a long line of very 'special padres' the Airborne had. One long-serving divisional padre said that for thirty-two years he placed all his trust in God, but for the five seconds it took for his parachute to open he prayed that the RAF packers had done a good job, and they never let him down because God was obviously watching over them when they packed his parachute. At Normandy, another padre was captured when he landed. He had been presented with a shillelagh just before the operation and after getting annoyed with being poked with a bayonet, abused and made fun off, swore at the Germans and promptly set about them with the shillelagh, knocking two out and driving the rest off before escaping.

The SS Officer – Dales Winsely

My company landed in the south of France as part of Operation Dragoon and although we had no opposition we were dropped miles from the DZ so we had no option but to make for the brigade HQ, some 20 miles away. It turns out that only seventy-three of 125 aircraft dropped their troops accurately, with the remainder of us all over the countryside. As the company was moving inland, we came across a château. We were moving down a road that ran parallel with it when suddenly a machine gun opened fire from a window; this was followed up by rifle fire. Somehow nobody was hit and we all took cover behind a high stone wall and returned fire. If they had let us walk across the entrance to the place, they would have had an ideal target. As it was we were able to get behind them by using the wall that surrounded the place. Once we were in position, a PIAT fired three rounds into the building. No sooner had the third one hit than a white flag was shown from one of the windows. Not trusting the Germans inside, we rushed the place under cover of the Bren guns. Once we were up against the walls, the

2IC called for the Germans to come out the front door with their hands above their heads.

One by one they did, then an officer came out. He was the only one with SS badges on his collar. No sooner had he stepped into the sun than he reached behind his neck, pulled out a miniature pistol and shot Corporal Barry Davies dead. We were all going to shoot him there and then but the OC stopped us, as if we'd opened fire, some of our own men might have got killed. As it was, he was thrown to the ground and given a good kicking. The OC pulled him to his feet and the bastard was still grinning like an ape even though he was covered in blood. 'Lance Corporal Davies – Here – Now!' the OC yelled, and Dai Davies, the battalion heavyweight boxing champion, ran forward. Davies was huge, well over 6 feet tall and built like a bull. 'Corporal Davies, you will act as escort for this man. He is to be alive when we get to the brigade. Is that understood?'

'Yes Sir!' answered Dai, and proceeded to tie the German's hands behind his back. We buried poor Corporal Davies in the grounds of the château then set off, Dai and his prisoner at the rear, out of sight. Every ten minutes or so we'd hear a yell as the German 'fell over', then Dai would curse him for being so clumsy and would pick him up. Ten minutes later, he'd 'fall over' again. By the time we got to brigade HQ the German must have fallen over 100 times and when he was paraded before the brigadier his face looked like someone had hit him with a shovel. His nose was broken, both eyes were swollen into slits, he had about three teeth in his mouth, and his jaw looked to be broken as it sat at an awkward angle. He also had breathing problems because Dai had hit him in the ribs numerous times. All in all, he was in a sad state of affairs, and although it didn't make up for him killing Corporal Davies, it went a long way to evening up the score. The brigadier just looked at the man and said, 'Take him away,' and for some unknown reason he tripped over again.

7

Arnhem:
17 September 1944

To Arnhem by Accident – Ken Rose

On 17 September 1944 I was based at Ringway, the Parachute School, and I'd just been made up to sergeant in the RAF. We knew that something was happening as we'd heard a whisper about an operation called Market Garden but we didn't know what it was. We were fitting winches on an Albemarle aircraft used for towing Hotspur gliders used for training glider-borne troops when all hell let loose. Everyone was in a complete flap and we didn't know what was happening. We found out that one of the larger Stirling aircraft had an engine failure. It should have been towing two Horsa gliders. Because this meant the Horsas couldn't take off, the troops were redistributed into smaller Hotspur gliders. We hooked up to take them round the perimeter of the airfield, thinking it was a training exercise. We were fully suited up for high-altitude flying and the paratroopers were fully equipped but we were a bit slow and the penny hadn't dropped! In the end we found ourselves at the tail end of the Arnhem drop! Hotspurs had never been used in combat and the Albemarle had no defensive weapons whatsoever. When we came back, the aircraft looked like a lace curtain and the four of us were awarded a big evening meal. It took me five cups of coffee to calm down I was shaking so much! Thank God I wasn't a paratrooper!

18 September – David Austin

In the hectic days following the successful Normandy landings, no less than sixteen operations were planned for the 1st

The Netherlands, Belgium and Germany, showing the advance of 30 Corps towards Arnhem and 1st Airborne.

Division, all of which were cancelled for one reason or another. At the beginning of September, an audacious operation code-named Market was devised involving three airborne divisions, the object of which was to secure the Rhine bridges from Wesel to Arnhem ahead of the fast-advancing 30 Corps. The concept was to unroll an airborne carpet from Eindhoven all the way to Arnhem. With this bold stroke, Monty expected the airborne divisions of the 1st Allied Airborne Army to capture and hold the bridges over the five major water obstacles spanning the 100-mile route from the Dutch frontier to the Rhine. The first four 'lesser' crossings were the responsibility of the two American airborne divisions, the 82nd and 101st, while the most distant and difficult task, the capture of the bridge at Arnhem, was given to the 1st Airborne Division. As soon as all the crossings and connecting roads were in Allied hands, the British 2nd Army, led by 30 Corps, were to push forward to the Zuiderzce and effectively seal off the German forces in western Holland.

Once we had a look at the plan, many of us realised there was a great deal that could go wrong, not the least that the DZs were some distance from the bridge at Arnhem, which would give the Germans time to collect their wits and fight back, even if there weren't many of them there. The presumption that it would be an easy operation went against everything we'd learned about the Germans in North Africa, Italy, Sicily, and Normandy. Once cornered, they came off the ropes like a world-class heavyweight boxer fighting for the title when the odds were 10 to 1 against him winning. Personally, I had strong reservations about what we were expected to do, especially as well over a quarter of the men had never been in a battle before, and we only had seven days to prepare, when Normandy took months of training to get it right, and even then lots of things still went wrong. But then I was only a very small cog in a very big machine. Unfortunately, there were not enough aircraft to transport the three divisions in one lift. So we would need four days of perfect flying to put everyone on the ground at Arnhem. This meant that 50 per cent of the troops dropped in the first lift were required to hold the drop zones for those in the next drop, thereby halving the number of men able to push on to their objective – the bridge. However determined we were, it was still a huge ask for anyone to attempt, especially without the armoured and artillery support that we would need to hold it once we got it.

So we had the disadvantage of using DZs and LZs some 8 miles away from the bridge, due to the supposed presence of heavy flak batteries in the vicinity of Arnhem and Deelen. All of us, from the lowest private to the colonels, knew that airborne troops need to land on top of their intended targets and take the risk of losing men – it was the nature of the beast so to speak. In the end, those 8 miles proved to be the straw that broke the camel's back. Yet another problem was the fact that one of Germany's best generals was at Arnhem. Field Marshal Walter Model was taking lunch at the Tafelberg Hotel in Oosterbeek, right in the middle of the battle area, when we landed. He immediately took control and within the space of two hours a battle group from the crack 9th SS Panzer Division was on its way to attack the division as it formed up. On the 18th we arrived at the DZ five hours late because of bad weather and from the moment we appeared we came under heavy attack from around the DZs. With aircraft and gliders taking heavy fire, we still managed to get a large number of men on the ground, but we now had to fight our way off the DZ.

My platoon fought its way to the RV point, where those still standing collected. We were losing men all the time but we received the order to move off towards Arnhem while still under a heavy fire from the now reinforced 9th SS Panzer Grenadier Regiment. It was truly horrifying to see men getting mowed down and there was little we could do about it if we were to achieve our objective. On the 19th we'd only been on the ground for 12 hours, yet the battalion was already down to 70 per cent of its fighting strength. Valuable officers and men had been lost, and we had nothing tangible to show for it. How I was still alive I don't know, as several of my mates had died within arm's reach of me; it was like a lottery with death as the prize. By now the battalion was literally dead in the water as the Germans had effectively stopped our advance and there was no way around them.

I was involved in a number of attacks against self-propelled guns, Panzer III tanks and halftrack troop carriers. The self-propelled guns, whose shells were bursting at treetop level, inflicted terrible casualties and some of the halftracks had MG42s mounted up top, one of the best machine guns ever designed. My section accounted for one of these halftracks and another platoon managed to destroy a self-propelled gun. After five hours of desperate fighting in the woods, we realised that it was impossible to continue as we simply couldn't make headway against the dogged German defence. So late in the afternoon, the brigade commander, Brigadier Hackett, ordered us to disengage and withdraw to the south of the railway, where we would attempt to renew the advance along the Heelsum–Arnhem road. It was during this withdrawal that the battalion suffered a great number of casualties. We were fighting a battle on three sides and the Germans were starting to move in behind us. By now I had about thirty rounds and one grenade left. Most of the others were in the same boat. When the orders to withdraw were received, we definitely took the Germans by surprise, but it still didn't stop them butchering us as we moved out onto open ground because we simply couldn't go through the woods.

The Germans were dug into strong, commanding positions on the edge of the woods and the withdrawal coincided with the landing of the third glider lift with the Poles on board. As they landed, German infantry supported by tanks appeared on the edge of the wood and started firing into the gliders and us at the same time. We were like sitting ducks, as were the Poles. It was then that I saw a German half-track come out of the trees with a MG42 on it. It stopped about 30 yards from one of the gliders and fired straight at it, turning it into matchwood in next to no time, and then it turned its gun on another glider just landing. By doing so it showed up a weak point in its defence – it exposed the MG42 gunners and one of our Bren gunners killed the crew with a long burst and someone with a PIAT finished the halftrack off. It was about this time that one of our lieutenants, who was about 2 yards from me, took a burst from a machine gun that sent him tumbling forward as if he had been hit by a truck, and the same burst hit me in the shoulder, knocking me over. I think it saved my life as moments later the machine gun killed and wounded several of the lads as it swept the platoon. Luckily mine was only a minor wound and I was able to carry on. That withdrawal was a terrible time for the battalion, probably the worst time of the whole battle, as we lost more men on the first two days than in the remaining seven.

Head for the Bridge – Phillip Newman

It's dark, yet the sky beyond is illuminated by the red glow of distant fires. Lines of coloured tracer arc upwards into the heavens, white and red flares and the muzzle flashes from artillery pieces offer an eerie burst of light. We're on the outskirts of Arnhem and the heavily built-up areas ahead of us look badly shelled. Countless men scramble over the piles of masonry, following streets and scampering through buildings as we advance. I carefully follow the man in front of me – I don't know who he is as so many of them have fallen along the way to snipers and ambushes. 'Slugger', my best mate who I was behind, was killed two streets ago when he walked in front of a house on fire and was lit up by the flames. He provided a sniper with a perfect target and paid the price. It shocked the hell out of me as one minute he was clambering over the rubble, the next he was sprawled on the bricks. I knew he was dead the moment I looked at him, as there was a neat hole in his cheek and the other side of his face was missing. A day later other units made a somewhat hesitant progress through the same streets we were going down and it cost them dearly too. My battalion, the 11th, and the 2nd South Staffordshire Regiment made their way through the heavily built-up area between Saint Elizabeth's Hospital and the Arnhem town museum. We came across the dead bodies of the men from the reconnaissance regiment whose job it had been to rush ahead of everyone and hold the bridge. They had no chance as they were in jeeps and on motorcycles when they were ambushed, and they were slaughtered before they could put up a decent fight. Only a few got away. Nobody had moved them as the snipers shot several men who tried and we were warned to keep well clear of them. It seemed wrong to just leave them there, but I wasn't going to risk getting shot to cover them up.

Dawn is unusually quiet, apart from the occasional report of a rifle or small-arms fire. The sun arose over the town and a thick misty haze has settled all around. Saint Elizabeth's Hospital is a large hospital that stands in a cobbled stone square surrounded by old buildings and alleyways. From here we can see the River Rhine, the waterfront buildings, and the huge iron span of Arnhem Bridge in the distance. A couple of companies of the 2nd South Staffordshire Regiment had been sent earlier to reinforce the men already on the north end of the bridge. They return with tales of being trapped and ambushed by veteran SS troops backed up by armour, including Tiger tanks and self-propelled guns. This was not what we'd expected. As we advance deeper to Arnhem, the dead lay alongside the road where they'd been shot, the wounded and dying are being ferried on jeeps, on stretchers and over men's shoulders back to the nearest aid post. Around them several large groups of able-bodied men assemble and listen as serious-faced officers give out orders. These men had landed on the 17th and had made little progress. They look weary and drawn and have that grey pallor that men get when they are near breaking point but refuse to be beaten.

Suddenly, mortar fire starts to rain down on the surrounding area and multi-barrelled flak guns open up from German positions in the brickfields on the opposite bank of the Rhine. There are also heavy bursts of fire from MG34 and 42 machine guns. Nearby is a road running down towards the Rhine and it's littered with destroyed vehicles of all descriptions – German and British, taken out in the heavy fighting as both sides vie for supremacy. The Germans appear to be winning the battle even if they are taking heavy casualties doing so. They are like fire ants – once stirred up they are deadly. Having made their plans, the officers move out to their separate units and the column moves off and makes its way along the road towards the river, still heading for the bridge. I begin to see the occasional knocked-out German self-propelled gun and Panzer IV tanks; later on they would almost all be Tigers, huge monsters and just about unstoppable. I now realise what we're up against. These monsters weren't supposed to be here, neither were there supposed to be the elite SS units. With Saint Elizabeth's Hospital behind us and the museum to the north, the long column makes its way along the riverfront towards the huge bridge. Still more wrecked vehicles litter its length, and bodies from both sides are scattered like dolls on the roadway. It had been a bitter struggle here and it is difficult to see who won.

The Germans are everywhere. Leading up to the southern end of the bridge is a quarter-mile-wide stretch of exposed territory. Officers shout encouragement to their men and soon everyone at the front is breaking into a scattered run like the charge of the Light Brigade at Balaclava, all heading for the bridge. Excitement, fear, enthusiasm, a million emotions written on young eager faces, then a German shell whooshes through the air and explodes nearby, killing one officer and several men. Their bodies are ripped into a hundred parts and scattered everywhere. This is the signal for the Germans that have been lying in wait to open fire. From the far riverbank, from the bridge, from buildings around the southern end of the bridge, the Germans unleash a devastating barrage of fire – small arms, heavy machine guns, mortars, 88mm guns, 20mm anti-aircraft guns, self-propelled guns and tanks. It catches our men in the open and butchers them by the dozen. Nobody could possibly get through it. Men are scythed down like corn in a field, and we can't get to the wounded because the risks are too high – too many have already tried and died.

Yet the struggle to get to the bridge seems to be all-consuming for some and using smoke grenades and fire and movement, they encourage each other on despite the horrendous casualties. To watch it is awful as in minutes there are masses of dead in pools of blood and gore; incredibly, some still trying to drag themselves forward. In the initial attack most of the officers are dead or wounded, as are many of the NCOs, because they are all in the lead. Some of the remaining men take shelter in roadside buildings, where they are shelled. They can't reach the bridge because German fire is too intense. Everywhere men are struggling forwards, trying to find what's left of their units so they can join the 2nd Battalion at the north end of the bridge. Men from the 1st Battalion get within a few hundred yards of the objective before being driven back, taking losses disproportionate for what they are trying to achieve; it's sheer suicide to try, yet men are still pushing ahead and dying because of it. Meanwhile, at the rear of the column everything has ground to a halt. The confusion and carnage up ahead has brought them to their senses. We can see what is going on and it makes us sick because we finally realise that it is now impossible to get through.

I am forced to look away from it; instead, I look down to the water's edge where not 20 yards away a dead civilian in blue overalls is lying in a ditch by a water pipe, I don't know why but it really affects me, even among all this carnage. Water is lapping around the body and it gently spins in the flow. I can still see that man in my mind's eye to this day. He was an innocent caught up in a war he wanted no part of, and he paid the ultimate price. It was then that a black fog literally enveloped me. A mortar bomb had exploded almost alongside me and picked me up and threw me down the bank right next to the civilian. I can remember that I could barely breathe. I came to the conclusion in those first few dreadful minutes that I was dead, as I couldn't move a muscle. My legs seemed to be outstretched and my torso was twisted to the right. Some time later I come around and all around me is a slaughter house and everyone is gone, leaving me to fend for myself. I eventually get to my knees expecting to be shot, but I wasn't, and at first I crawl, then I stagger off following the scattered equipment and bodies left behind as our lads escaped.

Ambushed – James Lawrie

We had been advancing fairly quickly toward Arnhem when it occurred. We expected to get ambushed, but when it happened it was still a huge shock. The leading company came under heavy machine-gun fire from MG42s, which fire twice as fast as a Bren gun and have a very distinctive sound. They were deadly in the right hands to say the least. We automatically did what we had been trained to do when under fire – overcome the enemy as fast as possible – only we couldn't because we were taking huge casualties as the machine guns cut a swathe in the forward ranks. There were tracked vehicles there too – you could hear the high-pitched squeal of their tracks and engines as they churned up the ground when they manoeuvred. It was a frightening thing to face, especially if it was a self-propelled gun or tank, particularly the huge 60-ton Tigers. I could see what was going on up front with men falling everywhere, some screaming as they lay wounded, others chopped to bits and unrecognisable. The CO reacted quickly and ordered one of the other companies to outflank them, but the Germans were ready for that and forced them to retreat as they had set up mutually supporting machine guns. It was like watching skittles being bowled over, one after the other. Luckily the ground was easy to dig down into and we had to dig in very quickly so as to prevent getting overrun. One man was killed right next to me. He was running one minute, the next he was shot in the back of his head and his face exploded outwards into a thousand unrecognisable bits, blood and gore splattering the side of my face. His arms and legs just flopped like a toy puppet being dropped by a child, and he fell headlong on to the ground and partially rolled forward before being hit by more rounds and knocked over on to his back. Even though he had no face to speak of and was obviously dead, as he went down he still made a moaning sound as if he had been shocked by what had happened. It was the beginning of many horrifying and unforgettable experiences I would have over the next days.

The Killing of General Kussin – James Cleminson

The platoon had been selected to lead the 3rd Battalion's march into Arnhem, and for the first two hours we made good progress, scouting ahead of the main force. As we approached Battalion Krafft's blocking line east of Wolfheze, a German Citroën staff car suddenly appeared at a junction in between two of the platoons, prompting everyone to open fire with their rifles and Sten guns, killing those inside. So enthusiastic had been the firing that both the vehicle and passengers were literally riddled with bullets and it took my intervention to get the men to cease fire. This prize put the platoon on a high. Unfortunately, I did not discover until after the war that the men had killed General Friedrich Kussin, the German commander of the Arnhem area. He had been visiting Battalion Krafft when he unwisely decided to return to the town and his own headquarters by this route.

Pennies from Heaven – Vince Hargraves

I was the OC's orderly and had been since after the Normandy landings. The major was a good OC and well liked by everyone in HQ Company. I overheard him just before we left for Arnhem, talking to the company 2IC. Like many of the officers, he was uncomfortable with the planning and preparation for Arnhem – it was too hurried and underestimated the Germans, making out they wouldn't react quickly, and it had been his experience that the Germans normally reacted very quickly, especially when cornered. But the plan was set in concrete and there was absolutely nothing they could do to change it. Anyway, the day before we took off, for some unknown reason he said to me, 'Sew some pennies into your smock breast pockets – they may save your life.' It puzzled me as to why he would say it, as he didn't give a reason, and to be truthful initially it seemed stupid. In the end I thought 'What the hell' and went around and asked the lads if they had any pennies, half pennies and farthings they didn't want, and ended up with a pocket full. I took them down to the armourer and asked him to drill a hole in the top of each of them, after which I got my darning kit out and sewed then into the inside of both top pockets of my smock.

The lads took the mickey out of me no end as the smock looked ridiculous with the bulging pockets, and I did feel a little uncomfortable when I had a pack and webbing on. On the big day I followed the OC out the door, had a perfect exit, lowered my equipment bag and landed not 50 yards from the OC. Minutes later, along with the CSM, the pair of us were rounding up the lads and heading for the RV. Little did we know what was in store for us. It turns out that old Adolf was really peeved off with the landings and gave Arnhem top priority for reinforcements; no wonder they gave us a hiding to hell. He even sent specialist street-fighting and machine-gun battalions. Think of it, a battalion of machine-gunners, that's around 300 MG 34 and 42 machine guns; MG 42s can fire around 1,200 rounds a minute. Anyway, we were soon pinned down and taking heavy casualties. Initially it was only snipers, but those buggers can create havoc in a unit, especially when you can't see where they are. As we got closer to the built-up area in Arnhem, we began to face stronger opposition of around platoon strength, so they often became pitched battles. It was during one of these that I got shot in the chest. The round hit me so hard that I was literally knocked off my feet. It was like having a 20-pound sledgehammer hit you. I lay there for several minutes looking up at the sky, wondering what the hell had happened to me. Everyone around me thought I was dead so they left me alone, then I rolled over onto my stomach, and did it bloody hurt. After that I crawled into an open doorway. I couldn't believe it – the armour plating pennies had saved my life.

What Is A Bollock? – John Baxter

Between D-Day and 17 September we were briefed for no fewer than eighteen operations; each was cancelled at the last minute due to the rapid advance of the Allies through France and Belgium. Not unnaturally, this created a lot of tension and we were over the moon when it was finally decided that the Arnhem operation was on. At our briefing we were told that we were required to hold and defend the bridge for 48 hours, and that we would encounter only second-rate German troops made up mainly of old men and boys, so it was with great optimism that we took off from Barkston Heath near Grantham on Sunday morning, 17 September. I went in with the 1st Brigade, and we had the good fortune of being in the first wave, thereby having the element of surprise. The 2nd Brigade, who dropped on the following day, were not so lucky; they had a strongly opposed landing and took a lot of casualties. It was 1400 hours when we dropped. We flew over the bridge, which was our objective, our landing area being some 8 miles distant, a little bit optimistic I felt. After capturing and holding the bridge, it was planned that the 2nd Army would be with us within two days – what could possibly go wrong?

On the march from the DZ to the centre of Arnhem, we were met by civilians who were really happy to see us, and in some cases literally overjoyed. 'Thank you,' said one lady, 'we are free at last.' I thought a lot about her words later on, for their war was far from over. Our move into the town was delayed at one point by enemy machine-gun fire, but we soon sorted them out and continued on our way. By nightfall we had established our brigade headquarters, near to the bridge in a large four-storey house, still occupied by the civilian inhabitants, who kept us supplied with hot drinks. Come the morning the action became very heated as the enemy deployed Tiger tanks and self-propelled guns against us. They weren't supposed to be here according to our briefing back in England. We were also heavily shelled and mortared all day. When the upper floor of the house was destroyed, we moved to the next floor down and continued the battle from there, which involved fighting well-trained and aggressive formations of enemy troops as they attempted to move along the road that faced the headquarters building. These troops weren't second rate, they were SS units who it turned out had fought at Normandy and Russia. How could our intelligence bods miss that?

For a further two days we battled on, fighting from house to house, room to room in many cases. As we'd lose one house, we'd retreat to the next one and carry on fighting, all the time hounded by tanks, self-propelled guns, mortars, machine guns and an ever growing number of German infantrymen. On Wednesday afternoon I was handed a situation report that was to be sent to England by carrier pigeon. When I dropped on the Sunday, I had a container tied to my chest that contained a pigeon, together with a small bag of grain, its only ration until it got back to England. Anyway, I had to rewrite the message on to special thin rice paper and attach it within a

small cylinder fixed to the bird's leg, and in order to launch the
bird successfully I had to go to the upper floor of the house,
where the roof had been blown away, leaving just broken
rafters reaching for the sky. The report gave the situation as it
affected us, ending with an optimistic statement: 'Our morale is
high and we can hold out forever.' I thought then that the last
bit of the message was really stupid, typical officer rubbish. If
the last two days were anything to go by, we were already in
deep trouble without some form of support. When I launched
the bird, instead of flying off it settled on a broken rafter. This
attracted enemy machine-gun and rifle fire as they tried to
shoot it. Bullets were coming thick and fast, but I had to get
the bird on its way, so I picked up a section of copper aerial,
about five foot in length, and prodded the bird until it flew
off. It was with a feeling of envy that I watched it head safely
for England. There was an end to this episode, for when I
returned home after having been released from the prisoner of
war camp, my wife related to me a radio broadcast from the
BBC about our last-ditch stand at Arnhem. It was just about
word for word that which I had written. It felt good to know
that my pigeon had made it back even if the message was stupid
and wildly inaccurate.

For those of our mates who were wounded, it was becoming
desperate. The Germans had cut off electricity and water
supplies. The medical officer had the badly wounded in the
cellar, but without water or sufficient medical supplies he
could do little for his patients. His only option was for him
to surrender, so that the wounded could be cared for properly.
In order for him to do this, we had to evacuate the building
under cover of darkness. Our orders were to split up into small
groups and try to avoid capture and await the arrival of the 2nd
Army. We had finally been in radio communication with their
advance units, but they were unable to say when they would
be able to join up with us. They had major problems that we
knew nothing about. After quitting the headquarters building,
another soldier and myself began to look for somewhere we
could take cover from the heavy shellfire, some of which
was from the guns of the 2nd Army. Eventually we found an

opening to a cellar, which gave us some cover and a place to catch up on some much needed sleep, for I don't remember sleeping since we landed; we were later joined by an officer and a number of men. The next thing I remember was this officer saying, 'It's all over chaps, you'll have to come out with your hands up.' Before I obeyed this order I had enough time to activate a Gammon Bomb, which when disturbed would erupt in a violent explosion, my final defiant act.

We were led into a square and made to stand facing a wall, with three machine guns trained on us. I honestly thought that we were about to be shot, and I said to the fellow next to me, 'What a way to go and we can't do a bloody thing about it.'

He must have thought the same as I did; he didn't say anything, but he looked very pale. I just felt very angry that it had to end like this. Surprise, surprise, all they wanted to do was search our rear pockets for any weapons.

After the search was over, a group of us were standing together when an English-speaking German sergeant-major came up to us and said, 'If you would like to give me your number, rank and names I will make it my duty to see that this information reaches the Red Cross.' We then began asking him what his different medal ribbons were for. He told us of each campaign the medal was for and finally he said, 'And this is for the Russian Front.'

My Liverpool mate then said, 'You dropped a bollock there, didn't you?'

'A bollock!' he said, 'What is a bollock?'

Outside Oosterbeek – Jim Hodges

It seemed like ages since I had landed inside a glider, and this time the Germans were shooting at us. There were twenty of us trapped inside this thing with no way of defending ourselves As we came down towards the ground, it wasn't the crash landing that we were worried about – it was the rounds making dozens of holes in the glider. It looked like a giant colander by the time we came to a stop. 'Strip', one of my mates, was hit in the wrist; another one of the lads was shot in the back and died instantly. He didn't even make a noise; he just slumped forward with blood coming out of his mouth. A third was hit in the chest and died very slowly and in pain. Just as we slid to a halt, there was a huge explosion in the cockpit. There was smoke everywhere. The Germans had fired some form of heavy shell at us. The shell literally took out the front of the glider; there was nothing left of the pilots, just bits and pieces of body and a gaping hole where they were sitting. In some ways it wasn't the glider that we were worried about most of all, it was the mortar bombs we were carrying. If one of them had been hit we would have gone sky-high! Luckily we didn't have any more casualties and were able to get out, fan out and check for any Germans in the direct vicinity, but most of the firing was from elsewhere. Where they fired the heavy gun from, we never found out. But from the outside, the front of the glider looked like a giant guillotine had hacked it off. On occasions like this, fear is a great incentive and we unloaded everyone we could faster than we'd ever done it before.

Other than being shot at in the air, nearly everyone from our lift landed without any major problems, basically because there weren't that many Germans covering the DZ on the 17th, although those that were certainly made you think quickly. In next to no time we could see hundreds of men with jeeps, anti-tank and field guns moving in one direction, toward Arnhem. It gave us a great deal of confidence that this mission was going to be a success and that we would all return home victorious. It was when the aircraft came over and the sky filled with parachutes that I felt a real sense of anticipation, for in the distance we could also hear the German resistance building up and there was firing coming from the far end of the DZ. The planes were no more than 500 feet when everyone jumped. In fact, they were so close to the ground that some of us waved to the number one in the doors and lots of them waved back. The sky was then filled with hundreds of men gliding down to their drop site on the other side of the railway to us, which was an amazing sight to behold.

It was when everyone was collected together that we were deployed to different places. I went to a village called Helsam to guard the crossroads. It was obvious that the Germans would want to try and attack the landing site where all the supplies were held and so defending the crossroads would stop them getting any advance on the division. We dug in there for the night and rested up until what would be an eventful day. During darkness the fighting intensified and first light the next day finally showed me exactly where we were. The houses were small bungalows, much like the ones in Cornwall, with large hedges surrounding them. From my position in the trench I could see through a gap down the road to where the Germans were advancing. As I looked, I was the first to spot the movement that was coming our way. Soon we were swamped with Germans attacking us, determined to drive us from the crossroads. They pushed forward from two different directions and were supported by armoured cars. During this attack two of my mates were killed along with three others, and numerous men were wounded. This wasn't supposed to happen according to all the experts back in England.

It was after this that we made a night move to another position, where we met the Dutch Resistance. Looking back on it now, they should have made more use of them while they were there, just as the Americans did, but among our officers there was an opinion that we didn't need them, that we had all the information and fire power we wanted, and they would only get in our way, or could even be spies. In the long run this kind of superior arrogance cost the division dearly, it was sheer officer upper-class egotism that cost us a lot of lives and certainly changed the outcome of the battle. It was their home so they knew every inch of it and where the Germans were collecting. It was late when they appeared on the road where my platoon was. We'd placed mines there so that if the Germans drove along it they would set them off. The Dutch Resistance nearly drove over them but luckily the men in the ditches at the side of the road pulled on the ropes attached to each mine and moved them out of the way. Nobody knew if a motorbike would have made the mines go off, but luckily they got moved anyway.

The men, who wore orange armbands, gave us the locations of the Germans and their movements so that patrols could

avoid them. Late that night we got orders to move to the
last position while we were at Arnhem. It was a road outside
Oosterbeek, which is the other half of Arnhem on the west
side. When we first got there, we started to dig trenches, but
as we did so the Germans fired mortars at us. Mortar bombs
raining down all around you is a great incentive to dig faster,
and contrary to popular belief while we were digging in, except
for the mortars, there was very little fighting going on. One of
the main concerns was for food. Everyone had enough food
for two days but it soon ran out. Resupply came in the form
of containers dropped on the DZs, but by then the Germans
had captured them and so they got most of the food. There
were a lot of men killed trying to recover food from the DZs
in both daylight hours and darkness. The smell of the Germans
cooking a stew dinner recently recovered from one of the
containers used to drive men mad. The day after we dug in
at Oosterbeek, I broke into my emergency rations, which was
a very rich chocolate. I had the sudden thought later on that
maybe the Germans had chocolate as well. When there was
a lull in the fighting, I looked out into the field some twenty
yards in front of us, where six dead Germans lay, and my mate
and I crawled out to check their pockets for food. We found a
number of things including watches, but we only managed to
find two tasteless black biscuits! Searching through one of the
soldiers' pockets, I found something that changed my whole
perspective on the war. This soldier carried a picture of his wife
and two beautiful children; it was then I realised that the men
on the other side of the line were exactly the same as those on
ours. They had families they had left behind and somewhere
a mother and children would be weeping for this man lost in
battle. After that we left the bodies as we found them, taking
nothing from them but the food they had.

One container came down halfway between a wood and us,
where the Germans were hidden. Many of the lads thought it
was full of food. The Germans must have been hungry too as
they rushed out to retrieve it and lost two men as they did so.
The rest ran for cover before anyone could get a clear shot
at any of them, and so began a minor battle over this basket.

Eventually the Germans were pushed deeper into the wood and the container was recovered. It contained 25 gallons of petrol, but no food! The following day, when I was on lookout, I spotted some tanks in the distance. We knew that following the tanks would be infantry and so a general 'stand to' was given and everyone waited for the inevitable. It wasn't long before the tanks began taking potshots at us; one of the shells exploded near me and a lump of shrapnel knocked me flat on my back in the trench. I felt my arm go dead and for a few moments thought it had been shot off, but it wasn't, there was simply a bad gash in it. The medic, Danny Fowler, crawled over to my trench and bandaged it up.

All around us heavy fighting continued and I later found out that the shot had broken my arm in three places, and to this day I have not regained my full movement back in it. A French tank, a Renault – the Germans had captured lots of them during the Dunkirk debacle – decided to move around one of the houses we were defending. It was firing its machine gun as it did. There was a six-pounder anti-tank gun sited near there so I knew the tank could be knocked out. Regrettably, the corporal in charge of the gun was machine-gunned before he could fire. Luckily, someone else dived behind the shield and fired the gun at almost point-blank range and the tank blew up. One look at the burning tank and the others following it quickly retreated. Tanks never again tried to infiltrate the position because the road between the houses was too tight and they couldn't manoeuvre enough, so they stuck to trying to bombard the houses from a distance. The wounded, including Jim, were taken down to the cellar of the nearby house. For the next four days the Germans pounded the whole area with artillery, mortars, tank fire and self-propelled gunfire. Infantry attacks followed each barrage, but by some miracle the line held, but at what a cost: whole units were decimated. The cellar where I was soon filled with over forty wounded; there wasn't enough room to lie down. Next to me lay a badly wounded lad, Geordie Long, from Newcastle, who sadly didn't make it back to see his family again. We had no food supplies left, but luckily we found some pickled apples and every so often some potatoes would be brought down, having been dug up by those brave few who continued to fight on.

It was now ten days since my glider had first touched down and the decision was taken to try and get everyone who could walk to safety across the river. That night it poured with rain and by morning those of us in the cellar surrendered to the Germans, as we had no way of escaping. A wounded lieutenant put up the white flag and it wasn't long before a German came down the steps to see who was there. We were all given a cigarette. As we were led out, some walking, some on makeshift stretchers, I was shocked to see all the dead littered everywhere, both German and British. It was a disheartening sight to see and clearly showed that the cost to both sides had been enormous. The house we were in was no more than just a pile of bricks and tiles above cellar level, and the rest of Oosterbeek was unrecognisable; it was if a giant had swept every building away and simply left the outer shells of the houses. We'd thrown away well over 2,000 lives in Arnhem and hundreds more trying to get us out, and for what – a flawed plan that needed every part of it to be successful if we had any chance of succeeding – what a waste.

Heads in or Out – Stephen Kelly

I was a lieutenant at Arnhem. I remember my platoon sergeant and I standing with our heads out of the door, watching all the flak and tracer rounds rising up at us. The Germans were well entrenched around the DZ and were waiting for us. It is a terrible feeling knowing that you have to jump into something like that. The two of us were almost mesmerised by the black and white puffs of smoke the flak gave off. You could see it but you had no real idea what danger they represented. That was until one of them went off right next to the wing of our aircraft, and one big puff of black smoke suddenly enveloped the doorway and dozens of bits of shrapnel reverberated all along the outside of the fuselage like machine-gun rounds. A number of small bits actually came in the door, right between us. Some of the bigger bits must have penetrated the outer skin but none of it hit anyone, thank God. The aircraft shook like a horse shaking to get the flies off itself. Luckily none of the stuff hit us, but it gave us one hell of a shock and we leapt back inside as if the frame of the aircraft could really protect us. As we stood there looking at one another, I suddenly burst out laughing, then the both of us were laughing – it was insane, and it was the last time we would laugh for a long while.

Aircraft on Fire – Frank King

As we flew in over the DZ at Arnhem, the flak was heavy. The DC3 was leaping around like a bucking bronco at one of those rodeo events in America. I noticed the dispatcher leaning against the bulkhead on the other side of the door with his chin on his chest as if he was having a nap and I got angry and pushed him to wake him up. It was then I saw the blood pooling at his feet – he was already dead; shrapnel had come up through the floor and up between his legs and killed him. There he was with his legs slightly buckled, head on chest, one hand grasping the framework above the door, and he was dead! After I pushed him he simply folded over and fell onto the floor. I looked out of the door and immediately noticed the flames coming from the engine. The whole section of wing behind it was on fire and a thick black pall of smoke was flowing through the air behind us like a long tail; then I was drawn to the fact that we were much lower than the rest of the aircraft – in fact we couldn't have been more than 250 feet off the ground, and a parachute needs at least 98 feet to open. So I quickly turned and yelled to the CSM to check the cockpit. He opened the door and was literally hit by red flames and more black smoke. The pilot and co-pilot were dead – nobody could live through that inferno. He slammed it shut and looked at me as if to say 'What's next?' There was not time to waste; we had to jump, so I yelled, 'CSM, we're going now!' even though the red light was still on and it went against all our instincts to go.

I signalled to everyone we were jumping and a moment later I launched myself out the door; hopefully everyone in CHQ would follow in quick succession. I felt my parachute tug at my shoulders; I didn't worry about doing drills as it seemed superfluous – I just dropped my bag and suddenly I was on the ground. I could hear the sharp snapping sounds of the rounds from machine guns as they flew all around me. The air was alive with anti-aircraft and machine-gun fire, but I still stood up for a second or two and watched the aircraft go into a slow spiralling spin and smash into the trees just beyond the DZ. It seemed like an eternity, but obviously it wasn't. The next thing I knew the CSM came rushing up to me and yelled, 'We better bloody move Sir! Before Jerry finds our range!' I got out of my parachute harness, fumbled like a fool opening my bag, grabbed what I could from it and ran for my life. By a miracle we only lost two men in the aircraft. One fell at the door, another one left it too late to exit, and a third had his parachute shot to hell on the way down. One was also killed as he ran off the DZ. We were lucky as the majority of the Germans were concentrating on those in the air at that point and basically left us alone. Nevertheless, a few seconds more and none of us would have made it out of the door of the aircraft. And now we had to go to war – and what a war it turned out to be!

The Disaster – Len Pearce

After the butchery that is the DZ, in the woods what's left of the battalion gathers and does its best to form into ordered sections, platoons and companies, depleted but still functioning. Continuous red smoke drifts through the trees. In the distance we can hear the cough of mortars, chattering machine guns and the explosions caused by 88mm shells. Already the medics are overworked, tending to the wounded whose cries are mournful and desperate. My platoon commander walks through the woods followed by several of us – where the others are, I don't know. He is holding a walkie-talkie tightly to his face and trying unsuccessfully to contact someone, but none of the radio sets seemed to work. Through the trees comes another man, his face is covered in blood; he looked maniacal and already had that haunted look on his face that we'd all get very soon. Evidently, during the drop someone near him was torn to bits in the air and he was covered in the remains. At a briefing we were told that the 4th Brigade had been dropped farthest away from Arnhem. They had some 7 or 8 miles to go. The 11th Battalion had been ordered up to reinforce the 2nd Battalion, already in possession of the north end of the bridge.

We move out along a country road. In the distance a few houses are burnt and black with swirling smoke rising from the ruins. We all hear the explosions, artillery, sporadic mortar fire and the occasional crack of a rifle, but especially the heavy rattle of machine guns. Along the length of the road, members of the 4th Battalion are strung out in a long column; they have suffered horrendous casualties. Every so often a jeep towing a gun or trailer roars passed, parting the column like a boat's bow wave. I am lagging behind because I am hauling a load of PIAT bombs and I am in agony from a back injury. After a while the column ahead stops dead, causing a knock-on effect that slows the traffic up all the way to the tail. Breathing hard, I gratefully accept the rest, slumping down on the roadside bank. Some sporadic machine-gun fire goes off up ahead and then there's a distant whistle. Getting louder, it becomes a whoosh. Everyone takes cover by diving this way and that behind trees and into bushes, down banks, anywhere but get behind some form of cover. For a split second the noise stops and then BOOM! The mortar shell explodes nearby, followed by several more. Dirt and smoke are thrown up into the air, but as suddenly as it started, the firing ceases. Through the falling dirt and choking smoke, a lone soldier can be heard screaming like a child for help. I look up from my hiding place and see the man is covered in blood, screeching and yelling because he's in agony.

A couple of medics run to his aid. But the move cannot be stopped and slowly the rest of the column emerges and resume their places. It's as if nothing happened. A jeep then parts the way, heading back down the road from the head of the column. Sitting in the passenger seat is the platoon commander. He orders that all the PIATs and bombs be loaded into the jeep and sent up to the front as they're encountering German armour. This suits me fine and Bill and I load the PIAT bombs into the back of the vehicle. I learn later that the jeep full of PIATs and bombs was commandeered by a

Padre who wanted to attend the wounded; neither he nor the jeep was heard of again. It's assumed he was killed and the jeep destroyed, thus depriving the battalion of greatly needed anti-tank weapons. Not long afterwards, a couple of us were ordered to investigate a farmhouse nearby where a German mortar crew have been spotted. We cautiously approach the place, which seems deserted. Some chickens cluck and strut near the main building. It's a surreal scene, eerily quiet. We make our way towards the buildings, using whatever cover comes to hand, and are ready to offer covering fire should it be needed. I cautiously peer around a low wall into the farmyard. A mortar has been set up nearby, sandbagged and camouflaged.

It's quiet and discarded empty boxes that contained mortar shells lie everywhere. Moving to the farmhouse doorway, I push it open and peer inside. The inside of the farmhouse has been wrecked. I hesitate and then step inside, glass crunches underfoot. Furniture is broken, deliberately smashed. There's not a whole plate or bowl anywhere. Sat in the corner, on a wooden stool, is a Dutchman. He's middle-aged, balding, dirty and small. He looks up, face stained with tears, eyes red. He makes a gesture with one hand as if to ask 'Why?' and then puts his head into his hands in desperation. His whole life, all he's worked for, has been destroyed by the Germans for no other reason than they could. Three or four of the others check upstairs. Outside we hear some Sten gun fire. We charged out, expecting the worst, only to see that one of the 'new boys' on his first operation has emptied the magazine from his Sten gun into a tree and branches, twigs and leaves are floating down in all directions.

It was then that a German voice calls out timidly from within the tree: 'Kamerad!' The branches rustle as a pair of booted legs swing down. The heel of one of them has been shot off. A young bespectacled German no more than sixteen years of age drops down to the ground, face white with fear and his hands up in the air in a gesture of surrender. As he lands on the ground some of the lads start giggling and joking that Tony, the firer, couldn't hit a barn door. He just looks at his Sten gun in amazement. Suddenly, the young German starts laughing too and points to his boot, raising it to show that the heel is barely hanging on by a thread. We lead him away across the field towards the now moving column of men as they march up the road. At least someone is out of the slaughter.

Clearing The DZ – Day Two – Frank Kent

Men were landing all around me. It was absolute chaos as heavy machine-gun fire raked the area from concealed German positions in the woods. Men were being wounded, being torn to ribbons, and were screaming as they lay in the open, unable to move. Gunfire exploded nearby, ripping into the ground, throwing up puffs of dirt. The air was alive with flying lead. The wind caught my parachute and inflated it while I was trying to struggle up and release my harness and I was thrown off balance. I couldn't get to my heavy leg pack so I was being pulled in two directions at once as bullets tore through the canopy. My best mate Bill landed nearby in an awkward heap. I called for help but he had his own problems as he was trying to get out of his harness too. He was engulfed in his parachute like a ghost and his arms flapped around as the material was torn apart by stray bullets.

I was free at last and in desperation I ran over to him and hit the release buckle on his harness. This was the wrong way to do it, but who cares? From a nearby copse, the distinctive sound of a MG42 machine gun unloaded its deadly firepower at us. It was belt-fed and fired 1,200 rounds per minute, and it only had one weakness; the barrel overheated very quickly and needed to be changed often. It sounds like a madman rapidly twirling a children's ratchet at a football game. I dived onto the ground and crawled desperately to my leg bag, then stupidly sat up to open it just as the heather was torn up mere inches away. If I hadn't sat up I would have been dead. Miracles do happen! With added incentive I rolled over and desperately grabbed my leg bag and cut the rope with my fighting knife. Not a minute later the pair of us ran away, crouching over as we did, hauling the heavy equipment bags with us, as it was too risky trying to open them on the DZ. My back was killing me as I ran, but what choice did I have? It was either that or be killed. Smoke and flames billowed up all around us. As we ran mortar shells exploded nearby. It was a nightmare.

Having opened up our bags and retrieved our webbing, packs and weapons, the two of us scurried past the crashed fuselage of a Horsa glider that had hit the trees, crushing the front like crumpled paper. Several dead men lay in contorted positions in the heather alongside it, and one of the pilots hung out of the shattered cockpit window with blood and brains from his head running down the smashed nose of the glider. He, and probably the other pilot, had been killed when they collided with the trees; the others were probably killed when they tried to get out of the glider and were shot. Pausing for a moment to gather our breath, both of us instantly threw ourselves onto the ground when a burst of machine-gun fire took huge chunks out of the trees above our heads. 'The Devil's Cauldron', as the Germans eventually called Arnhem, was becoming worse by the minute.

Glider 161 – John Bradbury

After the war I found out that the estimated life expectancy for bomber crews over Europe during the war was approximately 1 hour 46 minutes. For fighter pilots it was 19 minutes, and for glider pilots it was 17 seconds. Luckily nobody had ever told us, as I would have transferred immediately out of the air-landing brigade and gone to the RASC bath unit. It was 18 September and as we flew across the edge of the Landing Zones at Arnhem on the second day, we came under fierce fire from German flak batteries sitting among the trees. There was a cry from the rear of the glider: 'The tail's coming off!' This message was relayed up to me. I was sitting just behind the cockpit. Sergeant Alan Watson and the platoon commander had not heard what was said, so I leaned over and yelled the message to Lieutenant-Colonel Place, the pilot, who sent Lieutenant Maltby, the co-pilot, to investigate. He returned from the tail end with a cheerful grin on his face and yelled to one and all that it was only flak and that no serious damage had been done. He had just returned to his seat when there was a massive explosion right next to the cockpit that shook the whole frame and he slumped sideways in his seat. The side where he sat was a complete shambles and couldn't possibly be used again. Both Sergeant Watson and I immediately rushed to help the lieutenant, despite the fact that Sergeant Watson had also been wounded in the head. Regrettably, he was dead before any of us could reach him; his face was an unrecognisable pulp, and his chest look like a huge claw had dug its way into him. Everyone, including me, realised what the outcome was, and a sudden fear gripped each of us.

All of us must have thought, 'What if Colonel Place should receive a fatal injury? Who would pilot the glider then?' Not that it made any difference, as by that time the glider would probably be in a deep dive and spinning like a corkscrew, which nobody would be able to get it out of, so the outcome was inevitable – we would all die. Soon we were turning over the LZ, nose down, diving almost vertical towards the ground to get away from the flak and machine guns. Rounds ripped through the fuselage and our Bren gunner was shot in the knee by one round that came up through the floor. His loud scream did not help anyone overcome their fears one little bit, especially as more rounds ripped through the side of the glider at the same time. At the last minute the nose lifted and the landing was fast and furious and we bounced around like a rubber ball before we came to rest jammed between two trees with the nose inside a wooded area – our prayers had been answered! All we had to do now was get out without being shot and fight a battle against an enemy who were waiting for us.

Out The Door – Henry Cross

Our eyes were on that red light above the door as if they were magnetised to it. Then there was an explosion right outside it. The platoon commander, Lieutenant Vickers, and I could see what was happening below us without straining or craning our necks like the others had to. The drop zone appeared to be on fire, literally. We shouldn't be meeting this kind of resistance. They had told us there were next to no Germans there and those that were, were only second rate: old men and boys, they said. The red light died and suddenly the green appeared. The dispatcher jettisoned the pneumatic trolley that would carry the PIAT and watched the parachute engage. Then he immediately turned bug-eyed to Lieutenant Vickers, shouting at him to 'Go! Go! Go!' The lieutenant moved into the doorway and inexplicably froze with his legs apart, hands either side of the doorframe. Between his legs I could see a C-47 in flames from tip to tail, crashing headlong towards the ground; men jumped from it, many on fire. They were even exiting as it ploughed into the woodland and exploded.

The dispatcher looked at Vickers angrily. He was holding everyone up. My trolley was now out of sight and I knew that I'd never see it again. The dispatcher shouted at the lieutenant to get out. Finally he hurled himself out through the door. I tried to take a step, but unexpectedly struggled with the huge pack strapped to my leg. Under pressure from the eager men behind me I eventually tumbled awkwardly out through the doorway. My mind was filled with fear as I prayed my parachute would open and I would reach the ground. I felt the tug as the canopy opened, then I was swinging below it, watching the tracer fly by me, feeling that I was the only target in the sky. I suddenly felt my rate of descent increase and looked up to see a huge hole in my canopy; luckily I was only about 100 feet above the ground. I hit the grass so fast I smashed my chin on my knee and felt the blood in my mouth where I had bitten my tongue.

I rolled onto my back and hit the quick release plate with my hand, turned it and felt the harness fall apart. My Sten gun fell onto the ground and I reached for it. Now I had to get to my kitbag as it lay some 15 feet away, and all the time spurts of earth exploded around me as some German machine-gunner targeted me. I wanted to curl up into a little ball but I knew it was a waste of time. I had to get off the DZ and I had to take my equipment with me or I'd be defenceless; and all around me men were being killed or wounded, some in the air, some on the ground. How I made it into the trees I don't know. The action between opening my kitbag and scrambling headlong off the DZ was like a Charlie Chaplin slow-motion picture. All I know was I got there and put a magazine on my Sten gun, then just looked in horror at the absolute carnage that was the DZ. It wasn't supposed to be like this.

Blindly Into Arnhem – Neville Ashley

We passed through Wolfhezen in the late afternoon and there was one hell of a lot of damage done by our bombers. What a pity this lovely country had to be wrecked by war. The Dutch people were genuinely glad to welcome us, greeting us with cheers and pointing the direction the retreating Germans had taken. Along the road were signs of a hasty Jerry retreat, equipment strewn all over the place. A German staff car lay wrecked on a crossroad, the four occupants inside dead; one sprawled grotesquely out of the door. This looked like strafing from our fighters – nice work! By this time we were approaching Arnhem and things were definitely warming up. Snipers were all over the place and we had to move warily as the town looked lively, with fires blazing everywhere. We halted, but after an hour we moved on into the town and spent the night very uncomfortably thanks to more snipers. One shot a young lad right in front of me. The round went into his chest and literally tore a huge chunk of his smock out the back. On the morning of the 19th we tried to get to the bridge, but things were not going to plan.

We should have known better as it was one of Montgomery's famous master plans, wasn't it? Anyway, the boys on the bridge had been cut off and all attempts to reach them were in vain and it was costing us a lot of dead and wounded just to stay where we were. We should have known better as Jerry hadn't hit us hard up until that point, but he made up for it when we had to move out into the open on the banks of the Rhine and he hit us with everything he had at his disposal and massacred the front of the column. From the other side of the river he used the dreaded 88mm anti-aircraft guns and rapid-firing 20mm anti-aircraft guns firing on a flat trajectory and pumped shells into the packed front ranks, cutting them to pieces. He also had MG34s and 42s everywhere, and with the 42 firing 1,200 rounds a minute you can imagine what it did to anyone it hit. I saw several of the lads literally chopped into bits by one;

they were unrecognisable. And all the time Jerry's mortars and artillery were plastering the area. He butchered us like cattle at a slaughterhouse and we had no option but to retreat, or as the officers put it, 'do a fighting withdrawal'. We couldn't even recover the wounded, the area was so engulfed with fire of one sort or another. Anyway, in the end it was literally every man for himself. I clambered on a jeep, one of a long column of vehicles pulling out in the direction of Oosterbeek.

I soon decided that riding was not good for my health after a sniper shot the driver, so I dropped off and nipped away behind a row of houses and had a breather. Meeting two or three of the lads on the way, I got as far as a railway station, where we stayed for a while owing to more attention from snipers. One by one we made a dash for it until we came to Oosterbeek. In a dugout on the bank of a stream in front of the village church, I met up with some of my company, well what was left of it anyway. I decided to muck in with them, as I couldn't see any sign of my platoon. Everybody was busy digging in, the deeper the better. We were a mixed lot – four or five of our signal platoon, two men from C Company, an orderly room clerk, and myself. An NCO from the signal platoon was in charge. Behind us was a battery of 75mm howitzers. I spent most of my time in that spot from the 19th to the 21st, and it was very lively at times. Everyone was amazed that the Germans were able to react so fast and with so many troops, especially as we'd been given to believe there were only supposed to be old men and boys defending the place.

I reckon I escaped by the skin of my teeth several times; my lucky star must have been with me. Much of that time we were pressing our brackets into Mother Earth as mortars plastered the area around us. In company with Lance-Corporal Chillingsworth, I was manning a Bren gun that was covering a crossroad. At about midnight on Saturday the 23rd it was quiet for a change. Jerry must have thought it was too quiet, so he started slinging mortars bombs at us again. We didn't take much notice until one dropped about 15 yards away; the next one landed right in our positions. Poor 'Willy' Williams was badly hurt. I was dazed, but after pulling myself together

I looked around for Chillingsworth. He was staggering about shouting, 'I've been hit – I've been hit!' I didn't even see him get out the trench. So while I quietened him down, Danny Pegg went and fetched a stretcher. We put Chillingsworth down on it and carried him to the RAP. The place was absolutely crammed with casualties, and outside the dead were stacked like cordwood, and a lot were dying inside, too far-gone to be helped, so they got a dose of morphine and were made as comfortable as possible. We took the stretcher straight to the medical officer's room.

I waited outside and after a while one of the orderlies came out and I asked him if there was any chance for Chillingsworth; he said he was in a bad way; he didn't give much hope for him. I asked if he had seen Corporal Pegg, he said, 'Yes he's over there,' pointing to a body covered in a bloodstained dirty sheet. This shook me, as he seemed OK when we carried the stretcher across. I went and had a look at him and saw he had been hit above his left eye. He seemed to be asleep so I left him. I was told afterwards that Chillingsworth died next day, but miraculously Corporal Pegg recovered. I shall never forget the cries for water, though, as there was a terrible shortage and the only water was from a well and Jerry had a sniper covering it. We lost several men trying to get water out of it. They managed to kill one sniper but Jerry simply replaced him with another one and continued shooting any of the lads that went near the well.

Next morning I joined up with number 1 medium machine gun platoon, which was at the church in defensive positions. There I met Ernie Young out of our platoon, and Jimmy Renwick, a Geordie boy, one of the best. All day Sunday we didn't have much respite from Jerry; what with his mortars, self-propelled guns, tanks and armoured cars, he gave us hell, and still there was no news of us getting relieved – it looked as if we had had it. There was a rumour going around that an evacuation was going to be tried across the river. Orders were given out stating that we would commence to move toward the river at 2345 hours on Monday night, the 25th. I spent Monday inside the church, which by now was practically in ruins, but the walls provided good cover. I was with Jimmy Renwick, but we lost sight of Ernie Young, who left the church – I never saw him again. I was told he was killed. In the early part of the evening men from the Dorset Regiment came into the church. They had come across the river to contact us; evidently they had taken a hammering from the Germans as they crossed – more unnecessary slaughter because of one man's egotistical, flawed dream. I always remembered thinking, do any of the senior officers really care about us, the poor man at the sharp end? If they did then why did they throw us into a situation like this?

We left the church for a slit trench while we waited for the order to move. It was here that we encountered 'Mucky' Hall – was he a sight for sore eyes. It was dark and raining and we dozed until the time came to go. It was an eerie procession that wound its way out of the village and set off across country for the river, which lay about 1½ miles on our left. It was a long column and of course we had to move cautiously. It seemed a long way, as we had to halt frequently on account of flares and machine-gun fire. After about two hours we reached the ferry, and there were only a couple of boats for evacuating about 800 men, each of which held about fourteen men. We were told to line up in an orderly manner, but they were beyond control and were dashing about and shouting. The officers were helpless; most simply wanted to get on the boats too. In the move up to the river, I lost contact with Jimmy Renwick. I could see it was fruitless as regards getting across, as by now it was 0300 hours and would soon be dawn. Yet the Canadian Engineers did a sterling job with what they had.

Many men tried to swim across but it was a fast-moving current and the majority of those who attempted to swim were drowned. Daylight came and with it I gave up hope of getting across; we were caught like rats in a trap, exposed to murderous machine-gun fire which came from left, right, and alas, behind us. The last boat across was riddled and I doubt if there were many alive when it reached the other side. Dozens were shot as they attempted to swim across, as they had to face a veritable hail of lead. I should imagine Jerry was enjoying himself immensely with the plight we were in. There was not a vestige of cover on the riverbank and tracers were weaving about in all directions; I saw plenty of the lads get hit, but there didn't seem to be one with my name on it, so I was fortunate. It would now be about 0600 and there seemed to be no escape; from somewhere a white flag went up. This did not, however, stop the machine-gun fire from Jerry, but there was such confusion, or maybe he thought it was a ruse on our part because I'm quite convinced that Jerry never anticipated taking such a bag of prisoners – there were over 500 of us.

Fighting for Our Lives – Edward Clements

Before us stretches a railway marshalling yard that runs alongside the River Rhine. A few hundred yards away stands the Arnhem Bridge, still being held by the 2nd Battalion. Burning vehicles litter its length, sending up plumes of black and dark grey smoke. From the houses on the escarpment opposite, the area is being raked by heavy machine-gun fire, mortars, artillery and 20mm flak guns. Dozens of dead men still lay sprawled in grotesque positions where they fell when we tried to get through to the bridge a few days before. None of them have been moved because it is simply too dangerous to collect their bodies. The scene is one of appalling devastation and bloodshed. Trapped on the tracks between several burning railway carriages, a small group of us are pinned down by exploding mortar shells. Down below us, two of our mates from the battalion stand in a trench on the edge of the cutting. They duck as they are fired upon, then pop up to see where they can go. They're silhouetted against the background and are trying to escape because they are always being targeted. One of them is Taffy Williams from my platoon.

I desperately want to help the pair of them so I shout to attract their attention then throw a smoke bomb down the bank. It rolls to a stop to their left and then spews out red smoke. Williams moves too soon, before the smoke is thick enough. He scrambles out of the trench while he can still be seen. He only gets two paces up the embankment before he is hit by machine-gun fire and is thrown forward on to the ground and slides back into the trench. The sight of the torn body landing at his feet sends the other man mad and he leaps out of the trench and runs the wrong way, down the bank, and is shot by a sniper – what a waste. Just then mortar bombs land not far away from us, showering us with rocks, dirt and the ever-present sand. It turns out that they're falling short of their real target, the museum, and it's soon adjusted – I don't know whether I am happy about it or sad. Some bombs hit the trees and woodchips become as dangerous as shrapnel. Several hundred yards away, in the garden of a house on the opposite escarpment, small puffs of smoke show a German mortar crew in action. Sandbagged, the crew, including a spotter, are firing with deadly monotony. More artillery shells fly overhead – we look at one another not knowing quite where the incoming shell will land. After a few moments, it explodes above us, sending a particularly large branch crashing down.

We foolishly risk all and take to our heels, running deeper into the surrounding woods like scared rabbits; our nerves are so wound up. These days we never seem to stop running. This time we meet another group who are as lost as we are and agree to stick together. They are in one hell of a state. Some are wounded and being supported by the able-bodied; they are headed anywhere as long as it gets them away from the German onslaught. They say the railway is crawling with Germans and that they are close behind them. We can hear the sound of German voices as they approach through the woods, then their crouching, bobbing silhouettes become clear in the moonlight. It is enough to send us scurrying off once again in all directions. Two of us, Bob and I, head off together. We have no idea where to go; as long as we are putting distance between us and Jerry, we're happy. Eventually we slither down a steep slope and coming to rest by an abandoned sandbagged emplacement facing the river and secured behind it, we take a breather. I am short of ammunition and there are .303 shell cases everywhere and there's a tipped-over Vickers tripod as well as an ammunition box lying on its side; inside the box there is a full bandoleer of .303 ammunition. Where the gun is I don't know; someone must have taken it in a hurry and left the tripod. So we start removing the ammunition from the bandoleer and stuffing it into our pouches and loading our magazines. We don't have any food left so we might as well top up on ammunition.

After a while Bob pops his head over the top of the sandbags just to take a shuftee around when suddenly there's a rifle shot and a round slammed into the top bag near where his head was. Bob quickly drops back down, swears, then leans on the sandbags and looks at me with that 'Jesus the bastard nearly got me' look. As he lay there another shot rips into the top sandbags and over the next couple of minutes there are several more, each one sending sand over on to us. Whoever it is seems determined to get us but he's not able to get the shot he requires because of the thickness and the shape of the sandbags, so he keeps firing into the bags in the hope one of the rounds might penetrate. We have to do something or at this rate he is eventually going to destroy the bags and get at us.

He must know that he has us trapped. In the end I've had enough and after yet another round hit the top bag I leap up and dive behind a large tree about 2 yards away. I was expecting to get shot at but he seems to have missed my movement to the new position. I lie behind the tree with my rifle aimed in the general direction where the shots came from when I see a coal scuttle helmet and head appear from inside a culvert about 80 yards away. Clearly he hasn't seen me move and he carefully aims and fires two more rounds into the sandbags. As he cocks his weapon a third time and takes aim, I have him in my sights and I fire. Much to my amazement I'd fired a tracer round, which I see pass straight through his neck, sending his head back, after which it bounces off the side of the culvert. The impact flings him backwards into the wall of the tunnel and slides downwards and rolls over, his rifle lands on the ground outside. I can only see his feet so to make sure I fire two more shots, one of which hits the sole of his left foot lifting it upward and it disappears from sight. His other foot is still visible but it's not moving. I got back to where Bob is and in the half-light the two of us finish loading our magazines and get ready to move once again. We don't even talk about the dead Jerry as we've got too many other things on our plate. Some twenty minutes or so later we pass the tunnel and I see him lying there, face down and half his head is missing.

Pure Luck – Colin Firth

After the Germans' first attempt to regain control of the bridge had failed badly, there was a period of relative quiet for about two hours before they began attacking the Van Limburg Stirum schoolhouse, a crucial position in the defence of the bridge; I was one of the defenders. They mortared and put down artillery fire on us and at one o'clock they fired on it for an hour, after which they sent in their infantry. It was during this battle that I had a miraculous escape when a flying round literally took away the sights of my Bren gun yet barely cut my cheek in the process. Tosh, my mate, who was next to me, looked at me swearing and yelled, 'Your bloody aim was useless when you 'ad sights, so what's gonna be different now?'

I was that angry I was using some extremely flowery language that my mother would certainly not appreciate when I spotted several Germans sneaking toward the building and I fired on them. I got three before they finally took to their heels and disappeared. I was so pleased with the result that I shouted back at him, 'Useless eh! There's three that won't bloody annoy us again, how about that then?'

He fired a couple more rounds and, without even looking at me, yelled over the din, 'Bloody beginners' luck!'

From the Chaos – George Beynon

After the slaughter on the riverbank everyone was retreating like a chaotic mob through the narrow streets, with the remaining officers, sergeants and corporals trying desperately to maintain some sort of control, only it was impossible, especially after what has just happened. Everywhere there is the echoing sound of German mortar, anti-aircraft gun, rifle and machine-gun fire, all too close, and all we wanted to do was get away from the carnage. On either side old buildings rise high into the sky, their plasterwork peppered with bullet holes and windows smashed beyond repair. Every so often we come across dead Germans, as well as our own men who have recently died. There are so many of them in grotesque positions with their unseeing eyes open as if searching for heaven or hell. Dutch civilians risk their lives to collect and cover the dead bodies in white sheets from their own beds. In places the corpses are stacked three and four high by the side of the road, as there is nowhere else to put them. Ken, my mate, and I move forward and crouch down at a street corner, looking into a small square where several alleyways meet. In one of the alleyways there is a 6-pounder anti-tank gun, set up but apparently abandoned with discarded shells littering the road. Not far away is a German halftrack that the 6-pounder had fired upon. Whips of smoke come from the smashed engine compartment and two Germans hang over the side where they died. Looking up a side road, I see a stationary German self-propelled gun about a hundred yards away, with some crew standing around it smoking while the engine is running, spewing out heavy black diesel fumes. One of them is in the cupola holding on to a heavy machine gun.

I want to take a shot then with the Bren gun, but I know there's too great a risk if I miss. There'd be only one chance before they turn the thing around and fire the main gun at us, or the German spins the machine gun and does the same thing. I look back and see the last of the fleeing men disappearing up a side street. Now there are only two of us, is it worth it? No! Keeping low, we both turn and scurry away like frightened rats, heading up the narrow side street in pursuit of the vanishing shadows. Behind us we hear the gun's roar and along with it the machine gun chattering – they've found a target. Next morning we are in Arnhem town square, looking down through an archway on to the cobbled square, which has an ornate fountain in the middle. Above us is a large bell and somewhere below a clock mechanism whirs and ticks with ancient precision. Some of our lads make their way cautiously around the edge of the square, taking cover where they can. Their progress is slow; to rush headlong is to risk almost certain death.

Suddenly the whole square shakes from an explosion that sends brickwork and masonry all over the place. Tearing through the smoke and dust, machine-gun bullets ricochet across the open space, catching a few of the lads before they can dive for cover. At the end of the street a King Tiger tank rolls and squeals into view. The ground literally shakes as it moves. It has an 88mm cannon and is a frightening sight to anyone who doesn't have the firepower to stop it, and we don't. It's over 70 tonnes of pure mechanical hell on tracks with armour plating the width of a man's hands. Everyone else who's seen it doesn't need to be told what to do. They all scurry for cover, this way and that. The tank advances down the narrow street, scraping along both sides, just able to squeeze through without destroying the buildings, not that the crew would worry about that. The machine gun on the front spits hot leaden death and several men who are still searching for cover are cut down.

The two of us have clambered down the stairs of the bell tower in record time, and both of us sprint towards a large building that is a bank that we've seen other men disappear into, but because of my injured leg I make slower progress, praying to God that the machine-gunner doesn't notice me – he doesn't. The Bren gun slips from my grasp as I scramble over some rubble. It clatters to the ground. Stupidly I think the noise of me dropping it will attract the tank's attention. I hesitate for a moment then decide there's not enough time and continue on without it. The tank turns into the far side of the square, stops, the turret rotates and flames belch from cannon. The carved fountain in the middle of the square disintegrates into 10,000 bits. Why would they want to destroy it? There's no point to it, except they can. The previous day's fighting has damaged the inside of the bank. The windows are all smashed and the huge, once proud oak doors hang loosely from their hinges. There are at least ten men inside the bank, twelve now that we enter the place, followed by a cloud of dust and debris that floats on the air like a ghostly mist. Outside the powerful sound of machine-gun fire can be heard. Sergeant Morgan's section killed some Germans earlier and he said they were from the battle-hardened 9th Hohenstaufen and 10th Frundsberg Panzer divisions. They're veteran SS troops who really know how to fight. Whatever happened to the old men and young boys we were told about?

One of the lads has a radio and calls for some support – a PIAT to take care of that tank – what a joke, a PIAT against a King Tiger tank? Hell, a 17-pounder anti-tank gun with the new sabot round maybe, but not a PIAT. All it would do is annoy the goliath and get us all killed. Through a door in one side of the room I can see a heavy steel vault. A direct hit from an earlier barrage appears to have damaged it, lifting the hinges on one side. I want to raid the vault and bury anything of value for later in the war but an officer in the room says he'll shoot any man that indulges in looting. The man's a bloody fool; if we don't do it now, the Germans will do it later. But I have no time to argue as we are ordered to leave the bank and run down a backstreet towards a large, ornately decorated building set in wide grounds. As we do, we come under sporadic machine-gun fire, forcing us to dive for cover. I lie behind the body of a young German soldier. He has some blood running from his mouth and looks peaceful. He's no older than me, maybe nineteen or twenty, and for a moment the sight of a dead man just a few inches away mesmerises me. By the time I look up the others are disappearing down the street. Only Ken has remained behind to help me; I pick up the dead German's rifle and set off – God is my leg hurting.

Nestling between a heavily built-up area and the river is a large museum building, set in its own grounds within a wooded area. It's already seen extensive shell and battle damage. Our side is making a stand here, but are under constant heavy bombardment from German positions near the southern end of the Arnhem bridge. Ken and I are separated from our lot in the chaos and have run this way and that, searching for a safe place to sit out the barrage. There are several loud explosions close by. They must be heavy shells of some kind; they're ear shattering and huge divots of earth are thrown up as each shell impacts on the ground. I automatically throw myself over a low stone wall and crawl along on my belly for cover. Showered with dirt, I come face to face with another man coming the other way. It's Sergeant Driscoll and he's breathing hard as if he's just run a marathon. The two of us grin weakly at each other. Driscoll tells me that there's a machine-gun emplacement back there, just behind an outhouse, and we'll have to take it out. I must admit I was not at all happy with the idea.

Around us the battle rages and close by we can hear intense small-arms fire and mortar shells exploding as the conflict intensifies. A small plume of smoke rises from behind a line of trees, above which the roof of the main museum buildings can be seen. In front of us is a large brick outhouse that before the war was probably used to store museum exhibits. Beyond that, a German machine-gun crew fire an MG42, spraying the whole area with a deadly barrage of 1,200 rounds per minute. Driscoll and I observe them from relative safety behind a thick brick wall and decide to wait until they have to change the air-cooled barrel, the one weakness the machine gun has. As if on cue, they are forced to stop firing. They change the smoking barrel over for a 'cooler' replacement and Driscoll seizes his chance and steps out with his Thompson sub-machine gun. It goes off with a very gangster-like rat-a-tat-a-tat. Smoking shells tinkle on the ground as he sprays the German position and the gunner is hit and screams comically 'Ow! Ow! Ow!' as he falls over. Following suit, I step out from my hiding place and fire the rifle I acquired. I miss, and the number two stands up holding a machine pistol and fires from just 30 feet away, spraying the area around Driscoll and me rather inaccurately, causing the bullets to ricochet off the wall. Looking surprised at this unexpected turn of events, Driscoll pulls a hand grenade from his tunic and hurls it at him. We both crouch down and seconds later the grenade explodes and we run out screaming and firing, but our rounds only impact on a pile of split sandbags. The German has already taken off towards the woods, running in a zigzagging pattern. I took aim and fire four shots from the standing position. All of them miss and he escaped, but at least we now have an MG42 and quite a lot of ammunition.

Ordering British Supplies – Ritter Fassbinder

I was a radio operator in General Bittrich's HQ and we had the English signal codes, their attack plan, and English radio sets, so it was quite easy to find out what frequency they were transmitting on. Once we heard that the General issued instructions that we were to order certain supplies and food to be dropped onto the captured landing zones we had under our complete control. Our men were also told to stand on the edge of the drop zones and whatever smoke bombs the British used, they were to throw the same colour to confuse the pilots, and it worked perfectly. We knew they would send resupply aircraft and although we would shoot many of them down, enough supplies would land for us to use. Some of our labour battalions, who were basically non-combatants, and who'd been thrown in on the first day, were still fighting with old French weapons, and soon we had enough brand new British ones with plenty of ammunition, care of the British aircraft. It seemed ironic that we would fight them with their own weapons, but we did. And the food – the luxuries, real coffee, chocolate and tins of meat we had never seen since the beginning of the war, as well as unheard of medical supplies and real cigarettes by the box load. If I remember rightly, they were called 'Woodbine' and 'Craven A'; I nearly choked to death when I first inhaled one. And best of all, there was nothing the English could do about it.

Oosterbeek Experience – David Hindley

The sound of exploding mortar shells, artillery fire and machine guns drifts all around us, carried on the wind. In less than seventy-two hours the building has been reduced to a shambles. It's now a desecrated and raw landscape. There's rubble and charred wood everywhere, slit trenches have been dug in the sandy ground and in the windows of abandoned buildings tattered curtains blow in the breeze through the shattered glass. Spent cartridges lie ankle deep in places like so much fool's gold. Roads are barricaded with burned out vehicles and war debris – jeeps, tanks, trucks, anti-tank gun and Bren gun carriers. Bodies of our soldiers lie stacked everywhere, along with the Germans who lay where they fell, all mixed in with the innocent civilians and members of the Resistance. In other places, where it is too dangerous to collect them, they lay like chaff bags scattered in the wind. Tom and I trudge wearily with a few others who have been separated from their units. Near the church in Lower Oosterbeek, in the deer park around the

Hartenstein Hotel, hollow-eyed, once young paratroopers man positions. All of them are now old, gaunt and grey, exhaustion and lack of sleep deeply etched in their faces.

We traipse into town with the other motley-looking collections of men and head towards the hotel, where German POWs are kept under guard in tennis courts surrounded by a chain-link fence. We eventually drop into a trench near some other men, who are brewing up and cooking food. Tom rummages through his smock, taking out scraps of paper on which he's written all kinds of observations and so-called intelligence, as if it will be of value to anyone. Who cares? We all know we're against the two SS divisions and their King Tiger tanks and assault guns. And their MG42 is probably the best machine gun in the world because of its mobility, a rate of fire of up to 1,200 rounds per minute, and a range of 1,500 metres; its only drawback, like the MG34, is the need to change barrels as they get hot very quickly – that's when you get them. Though I still have to say, a good Bren gun crew is hard to beat. Over the past few days the Germans have brought up more and more men, ones who are combat hardened. The first ones we met were basically railway workers thrown in to fill the gap, backed up with smaller SS units that did all the damage. None the less, they still did the job of slowing us down and then chopping off our head when we tried to get to the bridge. The latest batch knows exactly how to suppress a position with machine-gun fire while their infantry pepper pot forward under a hail of stick grenades. They also use their mortars to screen the infantry. So you end up firing through the thick dust the mortar bombs create as you rarely have a clear target. They often don't even need tanks they are so good at it. I look across to the next trench, where the smell of cooking food wafts across and makes my mouth water. Both of us start to climb out of our trench to see what's cooking when a mortar bomb goes off no more than fifteen yards away, violently throwing both of us back into the trench.

A huge black cloud goes up into the air, and dust and sand settle back down on us. The men who were cooking the meal have been killed outright and what's left of them is scattered everywhere in among their equipment and large pools of blood.

I'm in pain and my ears are ringing and I have a headache that feels like a tank has landed on me. Tom is lying in the bottom of the trench with his mouth wide open, chin on his chest and his eyes are closed. I thought he was dead, but then he moans. I feel my head; as illogical as it seems, I'm certain it's been blown off. Tom's eyes are now wide open, staring and glazed. He just sits there, head in hands, making no noise. I shake him, trying to get a response, but he's catatonic. I take off my helmet and I feel a wide imprint it's made along my forehead. The explosion has literally pushed it into the skin. I tentatively touch the top of my head, knowing it's still there, but I want to find out if there are any wounds; there aren't, thank God. A man scurries past, pausing to look down into the trench. He kneels and asks me how I am. I tell him and he gets up and moves on to the next one, or what's left of it. There is nothing he can do for those that were once in it so he stands up and walks away. Other men and medics start to appear and deal with the wounded. I haul Tom out of the trench and help him towards the hotel in search of medical assistance.

Some time later, a senior officer spoke to us both and, realising we were from the same battalion, arranged for us to go with a 17-pounder towed by a cut-down Morris C8 truck to join what I now know was a new unit called Lonsdale Force. This is a motley collection of men from units that literally no longer existed as a fighting force so they are lumped together under a 11th Battalion major by the name of Richard Lonsdale. As we drive there are snipers are everywhere and we wearily keep a low profile in the back of the truck. We cross a T junction and come face to face with the rear of a Tiger tank sitting some 150 yards away and the 17-pounder crew rush to unlimber the gun and take it on. We take cover while the crew load the gun. A German crewman suddenly stands up in the cupola of the tank's turret and sees us and disappears inside, then the turret begins to turn, and was still turning when the new armour-piercing sabot round smashes into its engine bay. Miraculously, they have managed to disable the king of all tanks. The gun is quickly hooked back onto the truck and we roar off before anyone can catch us. It was to be short lived as a sniper killed the driver a short while later and we crashed into a house. We managed to get a grenade into the gun's breech and then ducked for cover. The sniper fired two more rounds but never hit anyone. An hour or so later, after dodging Germans, who seemed to be everywhere, we ended up at Lonsdale Force where we battled on until the final withdrawal.

Destroying a Flamethrower Tank – Leonard Mossman

Two men carrying a PIAT scurried behind the wrecked building that was soot-blackened and still on fire. From around one side of the building comes the sound of machine guns, men shouting commands and unholy screams. The Germans are advancing behind a flamethrower tank and a heavy Panzerspähwagen. I watch the two PIAT men peering from out of a lower ground floor window of the smouldering house. Periodic clouds of white smoke floated over them as they watch the lumbering tank intently, waiting their chance to attack it. Even if they destroy the tank, how they will deal with the Panzerspähwagen behind it, I don't know. The tank lumbers down the middle of the road, appearing and disappearing through the smoke coming from many of the buildings. It flames as it passes a house, leaving it burning. Periodically it stops and the turret swings first to one side and then to the other, each time spaying flamethrower fuel, then lighting it with a burst of flame. It is an effective way of getting maximum burn. The fuel drenches whatever it is aimed at and the flame ignites it, creating a fireball that consumes everything. As I watch, bullets ricochet off the turret and metal bodywork and a couple of Gammon bombs land near it and explode, but they have no effect on the monster. It replies with machine-gun fire and a burst of bright red flame that engulfs the front of a house. High-pitched maniacal screams come from those inside as they are trapped before they can escape and die a horrible death.

The Panzerspähwagen spits out heavy machine-gun fire, trying to suppress the fire from another building. The German infantry are tightly bunched behind the tank's body, using its bulk to protect them as they advance. They'd throw grenades into buildings on either side as it clanks forward. Their job is twofold: to protect the tank, and to finish off any resistance after it has passed by. And they are good at it. The tank continues to spray everything within range with short bursts of fuel and flame like an evil carpenter cleaning the varnish off an ancient door. It is now in line with me but we've been told to let it pass and get the men following it. The two PIAT men have withdrawn into the house and wait in the middle of the room, hidden by the smoke. As the tank gets in line with them they fire and the bomb comes out through the window and hits it right where the turret joins the main body, one of the few weak points it has. There's an explosion and the monster grinds to a halt. They've disabled it and it's now time to attack the infantry following it. From several houses we all open fire. One member of the crew tries to scramble out of the tank's turret and is cut down. It's over in less than a minute and the infantry are either killed or wounded. As the last one crumples, a ragged cheer goes up from the surrounding buildings. We'd had a small victory in a battle that is getting more one-sided as the days pass. The Panzerspähwagen, now on its own, halts, then attempts to retreat, firing its machine gun as it goes. Its crew are oblivious to the fact that the PIAT crew have dashed out the back of the building they were in and have run down the back gardens and into another house, putting them alongside the armoured car.

We're all firing like mad at it when the PIAT shoots for the second time and hits it. There is a huge bang this time and the thing stops dead in its tracks, smoke pouring out from it. Two kills in less than 15 minutes. We know it's only a short respite, as the Germans will soon begin to advance once again, probably with Tiger tanks this time. First they'll plaster the street with a barrage of mortars and artillery, and then attack with tanks and infantry. We are so short of men, ammunition and PIAT bombs that we get the order to withdraw before they begin. We'll ambush them once again further back, but how far back can we go before there's no more room to manoeuvre?

A German at Arnhem – Matthäus Drechsler

Even though I had been a member of a light anti-aircraft company in all of the action up to that time, both on the

Russian front at Buczacz and in Normandy, I had never had
the opportunity to experience an 88 mm anti-aircraft gun in a
ground battle firing on open sights at such short range. Here in
Arnhem, that was now possible. We were situated next to the
prison and fired shot after shot into nearby buildings until they
almost burst apart. Somehow the English Fallschirmjäger got
around behind us and attacked us, killing most of the crew and
disabling the gun before being driven off. During this fighting I
had lost sight of my comrade Emil Paulig and found myself in
the plumbing shaft of house number 72. I stood on a borrowed
easy chair and from this place I was able to survey the entire
battlefield in front of me. In addition to a flowerbed straight
ahead, I was provided with natural camouflage. I had spread
out my arsenal of weapons and ammunition with the hand
grenades primed and ready for use.

In the early afternoon two or three Englishmen came out of
a bush in the front yard. Some of our people left their cover,
probably out of fear of being seen, I don't know why, and
suddenly indiscriminate firing raged along the whole street.
It was a deceptive manoeuvre by the Englanders that almost
worked. In a wild panic many of my comrades scattered and
many were wounded and some were killed. I stayed in my
hideout and just had to pull my head in a bit because of the
ricocheting bullets. It was terrible to hear the wounded crying
and calling out, especially as you knew that if you moved to
help them you would get shot too. When I was able to glance
through the flowers again, a number of badly wounded and
dead comrades lay in my range of vision on the street and in
some of the front yards. Several Englanders now rushed out
of house entrances across the street and moved forward in my
direction. No more shots were to be heard from our side so I
fired a full magazine at the Englishmen and I think I killed one
and wounded another.

It was then that my position became indefensible, because
diagonally across from me one of their machine guns was firing
downward into where I was, and into the house entrance next
to it. At that moment I was no longer in a position to shove
a new magazine into my machine pistol, so I threw a hand

grenade in the general direction of the machine gun. I threw more hand grenades, one after another, and still the machine gun was shooting into the ground around where I was, and into the wall behind me. Then I pulled the pin of my last hand grenade, counted off two seconds, stood up and threw it directly at where the machine gun was in the window of a house. A bull's-eye! The machine gun and the crew fell silent. The roadway and the front yards were covered with dead and seriously wounded from both sides. Maybe twenty-five to thirty men all told, and all of them had been hit within the last 30 minutes or so as each side battled for control of the street. Behind me, in the grounds between the houses, there were still Englanders. When I heard a battle going on, I immediately got out of where I was and ran toward it, hoping there were no snipers watching the street – luckily there weren't. As I went around a corner I bumped into my comrade Emil Paulig, once again a painful occurrence for him, for he lost his footing and hit his steel helmet against the pavement with a loud clatter. How he wasn't shot, he didn't know. Luckily the Englanders were down the street a little so we stormed back into a house at Hyennoordseweg and fired through the windows with our machine pistols. The English side returned fire with a machine gun and rifles and in a few minutes none of the windows or the tiles on the roof were left. Unfortunately, we simply didn't have the firepower they had; we were helpless against them.

We dashed out of the house via the front door and into the yard. Outside there was an SS sergeant looking for his men. Emil, who was running along on my left side, told me that I was leaving a trail of blood behind me. Flabbergasted, I looked at my left foot and found out that the back portion of my boot was missing and that I'd been shot through the heel. Forgetting about it, we ducked into a nearby house entrance and he helped me pull off the rest of my boot and I immediately applied a field dressing to what was left of my foot. This street was in our hands and filling up with men getting ready to attack the Englanders. Hopping on one leg and at the same time leaning against Emil, I went right away to the nearest dressing station, which had been set up in a doctor's office some three or four streets away. Inside, wounded Englishmen were also being attended to. They all looked exhausted and some of them looked at our SS uniforms with extreme anxiety. They were, however, treated very correctly and supplied with English cigarettes, a hot drink and some food. Then I was appointed to act as a transport leader for the prisoners and off we went to Apeldoorn in a captured British jeep, with several seriously wounded Englishmen. The further the vehicle got from the battle area, the more Dutch people were standing around motionless and quiet on the edge of the road. One of the wounded English soldiers, an older sergeant, knew some German and inquired how old I was and asked whether I had fought at the front? When I said I was nineteen and proudly announced that I had already fought with the SS Armoured Division 'Frundsberg' in Russia, and during that summer in Normandy, where I had won the Iron Cross 2nd Class, he said they were losing the battle because the Waffen-SS were involved, and it made me feel proud. As we went our separate ways in Apeldoorn, we 'enemies' wished one another all the best with a handshake.

A Medical Officer at Arnhem – Derrick Rendell

After we'd landed and divisional HQ moved away from the Landing Zone, I also moved, and later that day joined them in the new HQ set up in the Hartenstein Hotel. I set up my regimental aid post in a room in the basement, which had reasonably easy access, even though it was down a few steps. Fortunately I was able to board up the window and for a short time we had electric light, but very soon my precious Tilly lamp became invaluable. Soon after I set up the casualties started to come in. There were only a few at first, but it wasn't long before there was a steady stream, partly as the battle hotted up, and partly as the perimeter tightened and other medical aid became more limited. I had no orderly of my own but the Assistant Director of Medical Services loaned me a corporal, who proved invaluable. The casualties had injuries caused by anything from small arms to mortars and even buildings falling in on them. Treatment was basically primary care: morphine as necessary, the control of bleeding, and treatment of wounds by cleaning and application of shell dressings, with splintage as required. Where this was necessary, it was of the first aid variety, for I carried no custom-made splints. Above all we were able to give a little comfort and rest. Tea was plentiful and thankfully received. This and food, when available, was donated by various units.

Non-surgical casualties were virtually non-existent. One, I remember, was a soldier with convulsions, like epilepsy, which was attributed by his companion to some 'plastic explosive' that had fallen in his tea! Recovery was quick and complete. Within an hour or two he was back on the firing line and thoroughly enjoying himself, so I was told afterwards. I had no psychiatric casualties. Only later in the battle did we have a few cases of true 'battle exhaustion', all recovered when allowed 12 hours or more continuous sleep. They found no problem with this despite the noise. At first we were able to evacuate those casualties requiring operations or other treatment to the dressing station, now established at the Hotel Schoonhord. This was done by walking or by jeep, with the patients either sitting or lashed onto stretchers that were fixed on the top of a stripped jeep. It sounds pretty primitive but it really worked very well. The situation often appeared to be fluid and one day my corporal set out with some casualties when he was unexpectedly stopped by a very smart SS lieutenant and asked in excellent English where he was going. The corporal replied he was taking casualties to the dressing station and hoped that he would be allowed to proceed. The SS officer replied, 'If I do, I suppose you will give away my position?'

The corporal truthfully replied, 'Yes Sir.'

After a pause, the officer told him to 'carry on', which he did.

After a few days the Germans occupied the dressing station itself and evacuation of casualties became impossible, so I had to hold them wherever I could in the basement of the Hartenstein. By this time General Urquhart and his staff had to move to the basement, and as everywhere was filled with casualties work at HQ became very difficult! Though they were very tolerant, as the congestion increased it became even more important to find somewhere else. We managed to 'evacuate' them to various houses nearby, where they were looked after, first by my corporal, then the odd stretcher-bearer, but mostly by the magnificent local inhabitants. I visited them as and when I could get away from the RAP. The eventual loss of my corporal was serious; luckily I was ably assisted by various Padres, who worked wonderfully, and when one went off to look after a house of wounded he was replaced by another Padre.

Eventually these houses became overcrowded, and in many cases, untenable, as indeed by this time were most of the remaining medical stations. So on Sunday the 23rd, the chief medical officer negotiated with the Germans for some of the more serious casualties to be evacuated through the lines, mostly to the Saint Elizabeth Hospital. My original supplies of dressings and morphine were very soon exhausted but we kept going without serious shortage as every man in the division carried two shell dressings and two ampoules of morphine in his smock pockets. Thus the casualties often had their own dressings and morphine with them, and others were donated by various troops around us. It is interesting to think that, although there were up to 12,000 men, all carrying two ampoules of morphine, each ready for a needle for self-injection, I never heard of a single case of wrongful use. To start with, we had a supply of water for essential washing of hands and wounds, but very quickly this dried up and I relied on the extreme kindness of individuals from surrounding units who would bring in supplies of water, at first as filled jeep trailers. It later became heartbreaking to see these holed by shell or mortar fragments and the precious water, obtained at great risk, quickly drained away. Still the various troops around would voluntarily, usually without being asked, bring in supplies of water in any container they could find, large or small, and always at great risk to themselves.

To the very end we were able to maintain dressings, morphine and tea as required. Even the latter was voluntarily donated from any meagre supply that they had managed to salvage. As you know, extremely valiant attempts were made to resupply us, but due to poor intelligence caused by lack of radio communication, most of it fell outside the perimeter. All units made great efforts to retrieve whatever they could from the resupply, whenever it landed anywhere near. In this way a little medical equipment was obtained. On one occasion, when the dressing stations were no longer within the perimeter, some was still brought to me. It contained, in addition to the much needed dressings and morphine, a novelty called Penicillin. I had heard of such a substance before leaving the UK as it was not generally available, and indeed it seemed to be a little hush-hush. I had never seen any and knew nothing of its proper indications or uses. I vaguely thought of it as a rather superior sulphonamide. Though the packets told me how to mix it, there was nothing about its uses!

At that time evacuation of casualties from my post was not possible and I was holding many seriously wounded. These included two with severe abdominal wounds that really required immediate operations. There was no chance of this where we were and peritonitis was inevitable so I gave each of them one of my precious ampoules of penicillin. By chance both were later evacuated through the lines, had operations and, surprisingly, completely recovered. Many times since I have seen pictures of one of them and often wondered if my ampoule, of what in those days was a dirty brown solution, helped to hold the situation until operative aid was available. We were confidently expecting the arrival of the relieving force and though no armour appeared, we were delighted to hear the medium artillery, and later to welcome their Forward Observation Officers, who directed their fire. It seemed most helpful. Certainly it was good for our morale!

As the days went by the noise became greater and greater; it seemed almost continuous. Lack of rest and sleep was a problem and perhaps this accounts for why I, like many others, find the time sequence confused. From this dreamtime I have one rather silly memory. One afternoon, early in this chaotic activity, we wanted to get casualties away to the dressing station. No one was sure, at that time, whether the dressing station was in or out of our lines so, there being some let up in the 'stonk', I was to go in a Red Cross painted jeep to see what was happening. I was called to the command room, where General Urquhart's ADC emphasised to me how useful it would be if I could note the various enemy positions! I remember that I set off, jolly pleased to be able to get around a bit more. I certainly do not remember whether I was able to report anything of value, but I do have a silly memory of a pang of conscience as to whether it was quite correct to report any military information from a Red Cross jeep. So much for memories!

As the days went by, the noise and the activity seemed to increase, as did our confidence that the 30 Corps would eventually relieve us. Monday the 25th seemed much as usual till early evening, when a staff officer came to inform me of the decision to evacuate across the Rhine that night and, 'presenting the General's compliments', asked me to stay behind and look after the wounded. I accepted this as necessary. The last thing before leaving, he brought me a map showing the evacuation routes, so that I would be better able to find and deal with the casualties of the withdrawal. That night the regimental aid post was relatively empty for during the day we had evacuated many of our patients through the lines. The noise, however, gradually increased as 30 Corps artillery put down an extremely heavy barrage to accompany the more sporadic 'local' firing, with the appropriate German response. To me it seemed not only to be getting louder but also to be coming more on top of me. Eventually there was a lull in the casualty inflow, presumably because of the evacuation from the area around, so I took the opportunity to lie down on the floor. I must have been so tired that, although the noise was getting louder and nearer until I was expecting it to completely encompass me, I still fell fast asleep.

I awoke about dawn, I think because it was so quiet; in fact it seemed unreal. I checked the casualties in the regimental aid post and then went outside in the uncanny quiet. I first started my tour around the regimental aid post. There were a number of Germans around, including some stretcher-bearers. As I was widening my search I was somewhat surprised to see the Assistant Director of Medical Services drive up in a jeep. I never did ask him where he came from! He took over my maps of the evacuation routes, said that he would deal with these as he had the jeep, leaving me to spend the day collecting the local casualties and putting them into ambulances or trucks for evacuation. During the course of my searches, I had come across the Royal Artillery trailer with which I had originally left the UK, so when I had finally finished my collection of casualties, I went back to examine it. I found that although it was pretty badly damaged, quite miraculously the small pack of my personal things was still there, unharmed, so I collected it before the Germans got it and must have been one of the few POWs from Arnhem who had a clean shirt!

Mister Churchill Please! – Stephen Epsom

There wasn't much to laugh about at Arnhem, but occasionally something would happen that gave us a bit of a chuckle. One happened when a German Me 109 fighter aircraft flying in close support for their tanks and infantry swooped down low and machine-gunned several houses. The pilot concentrated so much on machine-gunning the lads he took his eye off where he was going and slammed in to one of the two steeples of Saint Walpurgis Roman Catholic church, demolishing it and his aircraft. The jeers and laughter from our lads could be heard over the noise of the battle and it really annoyed the Germans. On the ground floor of the building that I was in, and right in the middle of yet another mortar stonk, a private found a battered telephone hanging off the wall and grabbed the receiver. He put it to his ear and shouted, 'Give me Whitehall 1212 please.' He paused for effect then continued with, 'The Prime Minister please – Mister Churchill? We're having a bit of a problem here, there are some men outside deliberately annoying us!' For the next couple of minutes there were roars of laughter, including from the platoon commander.

I Am the Gingerbread Man – Len Stebbins

About 50 yards beyond where Donny and I lay, there was a 6-pounder, sandbagged and ready for action, partially concealed by camouflage netting. The crew lay around it dead, they have been machine-gunned at some point and the angles their bodies lay gave the impression they were puppets that have just been dropped by the puppeteer. The muzzle and front of the gun shield are almost invisible unless you knew where the gun was. From where we are, we can see inside the shield and there are ricochet marks and blood splatters where the crew has been shot. As I look around I have the shock of my life. Not far away, I spot the stationary form of a Tiger tank parked further up the leafy lane with its deep-throated engine idling over. The two of us look at one another and nod. A few seconds later we are dodging from tree to tree while we run crouched over toward the gun. When we get there we have a quick root around amongst all the empty six-pounder shell casings and ammo boxes. All the shells are spent.

I cautiously peer over the top of the shield and see that the turret hatch on the tank has suddenly opened. The tank is no more than 400 yards away. No one has appeared from inside the armoured gargantuan but they are clearly feeling safe. I don't know why, but I carefully open up the gun's breech and much to my surprise there is an unfired shell inside. The shock is almost too much. I closed the mechanism as quietly as I could lest the Germans hear us. Then I slowly traverse the gun's barrel so it is lined up with the centre of the tank, where the turret joins the main body. Donny is having second thoughts and wants to go, but when he sees the look in my eyes he reluctantly does as he's told while I juggle the elevation control. When I am satisfied it's right on target I press my eye against the eyepiece and reach for the firing mechanism. The gun crosshairs are in line where the turret joins with the chassis, dead centre. I fiddle with the elevation and traverse wheels to get everything right. I have never been so excited in all my life. For once I am hitting back at the biggest beast that the Germans have. I take out my last grenade, pull out the pin and hold it in my free hand.

Just then a Jerry officer clambers out of the tank and sits on the edge of the turret and smokes a cigarette. Both of us look at one another. Donny nods and I check the eyepiece once more to be sure. If this fails we are dead men for sure. I squeeze the trigger and the gun bucks, the barrel roars, spitting flames and smoke, and the shell casing ejects out the back. I quickly shove the grenade up the breech, close it and we both are off like scared rabbits. I must have got it fractionally wrong and as I turn I see that the shell has hit the turret and literally bounced off. The officer that was sitting on top of the tank has disappeared, probably knocked off the tank altogether, but the tank is still 'alive', although I'd hate to be any of the crew inside as they must have got one hell of a headache. Through the smoke another Jerry rises out of the open turret, sees us and aims his sub-machine gun at us. Five seconds is up and the grenade explodes and destroys the 6-pounder mechanism. The Jerry fires his sub-machine gun at us but we're too far away. Then the turret turns and its machine gun opens fire and rounds hit the metallic shield of the gun. We are well away from the gun by then. Zigzagging left and right, both of us run deeper into the woods as gunfire from the tank's main gun destroys the six-pounder. But we have the satisfaction of knowing that the tank crew has lost its officer and as we jog along through the wood, I can't help but hum, 'Run, run, as fast as you can, you can't catch me I'm the Gingerbread man!'

Raining Cabbages – Arnold Westfield

Deep down, we all knew that the battle was lost. Those of us still standing were desperately fighting a holding action until someone decided what to do. About a dozen Poles who'd crossed the river two nights ago had reinforced what was left of our company and as my mate Ted had been killed the previous day by a sniper, I'd got one in the trench with me. I hated the Jerries, but it was nothing compared to the hatred this Pole had for them. He told me in broken English that he was Jewish and they'd murdered his family. Luckily for him, when they were rounded up he'd been away at university. You could see the hatred etched in his face every time he shot a German, and since he'd been with me he'd taken to carving his score on the butt of his rifle. He'd already got seven notches on the butt. I warned him not to do it as the Germans wouldn't take kindly to that type of thing. He simply looked at me and said they'd never take him alive so it didn't matter, and I believed him too. He never wasted a round. He would pick a target and only fire when he was certain he could hit the bugger.

Jerry was putting in yet another attack after mortaring us for about thirty minutes. He was determined I'll say that for him. He'd got two halftracks and two older versions of the Panzer tank covering the infantry; I think they were Panzer IIIs. The infantry were tucked in behind them and they were trying to get as close as they could before rushing us while their mortars kept up a steady rate of fire to keep our heads down. As they got to within about 150 yards there was a sudden WHOOSH! CRACK! directly over the top of us that frightened the hell out of me and suddenly cabbages started to land all around us, some hitting us before falling into the trench. Whatever it was, it was like an express train and we felt the air pressure as it passed, then one of the tanks stopped dead and began billowing smoke everywhere. Not 20 seconds later there was another WHOOSH! CRACK! and a half-track burst into flames and another dozen cabbages bombed us. By now both of us had turned around to see what had caused it, and there was a six-pounder anti-tank gun tucked in alongside an old milking shed. This time we had a grandstand view as the third shell came over the cabbage field. The vacuum from the shell as it zoomed through the air literally sucked up a furrow of cabbages, and a second halftrack stopped dead in its tracks and was disabled.

Jerry didn't seem too happy about this new opposition he had, so the lone tank suddenly began backtracking before it too got hit, leaving the infantry desperately chasing it while the lads took great pleasure in cutting them down. We'd been laughing so much over getting showered with cabbages that we only fired about five rounds apiece before the Jerries disappeared into the tree line. I think the young Pole was angry with himself as the retreating Jerries presented a perfect target. Me, I considered myself lucky that I was still alive, and that's what counted, but we knew they'd be back; they always came back, and next time they would be in greater numbers and even more determined to overrun us. Sure enough, about an hour later, they started pounding our position with artillery and mortars. They kept it up for about 15 minutes then began dropping smoke everywhere to form a thick carpet they could advance through. Next we heard the sound of tanks and other armoured vehicles advancing. The shelling stopped and the sounds got closer and closer until the first of the tanks poked its nose through the smoke. Except for a few mortars and the anti-tank gun, we had nothing to stop them.

By the time the third tank had come through the smoke with infantry following it, they had destroyed the 6-pounder for the loss of one of their mobile guns; the rest kept on coming. Anticipating this, the platoon commander blew his whistle and we threw several smoke grenades of our own and withdrew to pre-prepared positions a few hundred yards back. By now there must have been a dozen tanks and mobile guns advancing toward us and at least 500 infantry. I took off like a scared rabbit and as I did I called out to the Pole to run. I never saw him after that – he must have stayed there, taking pot shots at the infantry. Once the platoon was in their new position, a Forward Observation Officer called in the artillery from 30 Corps on the other side of the Rhine, and they literally carpeted the area forward of our old position. When the firing stopped we walked forward again and took up our old position. The Jerries had lost a total of three tanks, two self propelled guns and two half-tracks along with around 150 infantry. I never found the young Pole; all I did find was a dirty big hole where my trench had been and the remains of a .303 rifle butt with seven notches on it.

Crossing the River – Don Ashton

Hundreds of us converged on the crossing point during the withdrawal from Arnhem; along the way, we found others stationed as guards to help protect us and show us the way. These guards stayed at their posts to the very end, some giving their lives as they did so. For the most they were anonymous figures in the shadows, making sure each group that stumbled forward was British and not Germans trying to infiltrate the long lines of exhausted troops, as they had done successfully on a number of occasions throughout the battle. Our group was lined up at the water's edge, waiting to board a boat, when a lad in front of me whispered to a sapper sergeant getting men into the boats, 'Hey mate where do we change for Liverpool Street Station?'

The whispered reply he got was, 'Get out of the boat and catch the 303 bus heading west!'

'That can't be right. If I do that I'll end up in Charing Cross!'

The indignant sergeant replied, 'Then why bloody well ask me? I come from Manchester!'

The Last Stand – William Gordon

While we were holed up in a house, two German self-propelled guns came down the street and stopped directly outside our front door! We saw the SS crews get out and make coffee from tins that they had taken from our captured ration baskets that had fallen into their hands. They also had chocolate and Woodbine cigarettes. They were as happy as Larry and chatting away to each other, totally unaware that we were only a few feet away. We just stayed still and did not make our presence known as there were just too many of them to take on. They moved off the next morning, much to our great relief! We were then ordered to throw smoke grenades to allow General Urquhart and his officers to escape, then we were to follow immediately, which we did, making our way into Arnhem West, near the civilian prison, where there was very heavy fighting going on as the Germans had formed a blocking line and cut us off, preventing us getting back into Oosterbeek. By this time we were very low on rations and ammo, therefore we had to hide during daylight. On the Wednesday night we moved down to the river, but were unable to find any means to cross it and had to return to shelter in a house near the Glass House Pavilion. Unfortunately, we had been spotted and a Tiger tank came down the road and stopped outside the house. The tank had a loud speaker fixed on it and a voice with an Oxford English accent announced, 'Gentlemen of the First Airborne Division, you have fought a brave and sustained battle with great courage against a vastly superior force, however the situation is now hopeless, think of your wives and sweethearts! Surrender and you will be treated as honourable prisoners of war.'

A lone voice answered, 'Mate, stop mucking around. You're surrounded, so you give up and we won't say any more about it!' It was typical never-give-in Airborne humour. Unfortunately, someone in the house next door fired off a burst from a Bren gun at the tank. A Bren gun – I ask you. The fool might as well have fired a pea-shooter! There was a long silence after he emptied the magazine. Then slowly the tank's turret whined into life and turned to point its main gun at the house, the barrel elevated and there was a loud BANG! They'd fired solid shot; the result I can only describe as being catastrophic. The round made a giant hole in the front wall and made even bigger ones as it went through the internal walls before exiting out the rear wall, which then made the whole house collapse; everyone in the building must have died. The gun then swung around and pointed at another house, almost daring some other fool to fire on the tank. We all knew this was it and we quickly threw our rifle bolts and fighting knives out the window, followed by our weapons. I think there were about ten in our house, and 10 minutes later there were about fifty of us standing in the street with our hands up. We were all very nervous about surrendering to the SS, having fought them in North Africa. As I walked out of the house with my hands above my head, one of them struck me in the face with his rifle butt saying, 'You English Swine!'

The Elastic Band Called Arnhem – Barry Ingham

Although we were quite a distance away by then, on the second day I saw a large Hamilcar glider covered in flames trying to land on the LZ. It didn't seem possible that it was still airworthy there was so much smoke and fire coming from it. Christ! They were still firing at it? I'd never seen a Hamilcar crashing in flames before. It's definitely going into the trees. Long before it get there, it simply splits in half in the sky and rolls over and a Bren gun Carrier drops from inside it and tumbles toward the ground; several bodies follow. Another one, trailing smoke, nosedives and turns on its back about 500 feet above the ground, and out the front comes what appears to be a 17-pounder anti-tank gun and a jeep as if someone had pushed it. More bodies fall after it, twisting and turning in the sky before disappearing from my sight. It's a sickening dream I want to switch off, only I can't. And the slaughter goes on as the Germans target the parachutists following the gliders. How anyone could possibly survive the amount of fire coming from the ground is a miracle. Where did all these Germans come from? It's like a shooting gallery and we are all the targets. It's just like grouse shooting on a huge scale, only the targets are human.

We could do absolutely nothing to prevent what was happening so the CO ordered the advance and a platoon from A Company moved out first, leading the battalion to its new positions somewhere around Arnhem. My company followed them but came under heavy machine-gun and rifle fire from an entrenched German platoon on our flank and we were forced to deal with it or take severe casualties. As it was we lost eight men and had several wounded before we overcame them. How we didn't lose a lot more was a miracle. We hadn't gone half a mile before the battalion came under a concerted infantry attack supported by armoured cars. C Company was forced to withdraw but counter-attacked and regained the initiative. Once again we took a great deal of casualties and we hadn't even got within a stone throw of our objective, the bridge. Where did all these Germans come from? We were given the impression that Arnhem was only defended by third-rate troops, mostly old men and boys. These were not third-rate troops. They were front-line troops and well led.

We dug in that night and tried to get some sleep, as we knew this wasn't the end of the attacks. B and D Companies were heavily mortared during the night. The next morning heavy shelling caused numerous casualties; an infantry and tank attack followed this up. Where did the tanks come from? They weren't supposed to be here. It was repulsed with the loss to the Germans of two tanks and quite a few infantry, but they had forced us off the high ground. Our company tried to regain it but were repulsed and we had to move to a house in

Hemelscheberg. Two platoons from HQ Company under the OC were sent stabilise the situation. They were never heard from again.

By the 22nd the battle was in full swing with attack after attack. The battalion area was the target of all types of mortar and shellfire, including from self-propelled guns. All the vehicles, less two jeeps and one motorcycle, were destroyed. Then at 0910 hours there was a direct hit on the ammunition dump that caused considerable damage, and the fire enabled accurate registration by the German mortars so that any movement from slit trenches was extremely risky. Even so, the accuracy of the mortaring still resulted in numerous casualties. We were being whittled away by the inch, hour after hour. At 1200 hours the acting battalion 2IC took a composite force of Border and South Staffordshire men to B Company position to clear the woods and hold the south-western approach to the divisional area. This force was known as 'Breeseforce'.

The Glider Pilot Regiment formed a second defence line from Breeseforce west of D Company position and linked in with C Company's southern flank. The battalion fought off numerous attacks during the day as by now the Germans were determined to annihilate us. Luckily, we now had the assistance of the Allied medium- and long-range artillery and were able to punish them as they attacked, but it certainly didn't stop them. On our flank, D Company reported they were almost surrounded and had only two officers and thirty-five other ranks capable of fighting. We were not much better. I am truly amazed that we have survived for so long. It is only because of dogged determination that we've been able to do so. I had fought with the division in North Africa, Tunisia, Sicily and Italy, but it was never like this. We were like an elastic band that was being stretched further and further. It has to break, it stands to reason, and it eventually did.

Into 'The Devil's Cauldron' – Ray Goldie
On 17 September I was floating down on a serene and sunny afternoon after an uneventful flight. I found myself heading helplessly toward the trees on the edge of the DZ and I braced

myself for the inevitable impact. I hit with an almighty thump that took the wind out of me even though I had done the right drills. I found myself suspended about 3 feet from the ground. My Airborne ego may have been bruised but I only suffered minor scratches. So I undid my harness and dropped gently to earth. Unbelievably, the monotonous drone of incoming planes, the sound of breaking tree branches, and the loud voices of NCOs and officers were the only noises I heard. It was a stark contrast to the memory of the fiercely opposed night-time descent to capture the Primosole bridge in Sicily, which had occupied my thoughts since take-off. It seemed to confirm the expectations that this operation was merely a formality: a quick advance over the 8 miles to the town of Arnhem, overcoming any slight resistance from demoralised groups of second-class enemy soldiers, after which we would secure the bridge over the river then just wait for 30 Corps to relieve us within forty-eight hours. My thoughts were suddenly disturbed by the sound of running footsteps and through the undergrowth burst a small Dutch boy carrying a silk parachute. He was bloody lucky, as I was ready to shoot him.

I eventually established contact with my section, part of HQ Company machine-gun platoon. When we were all together we waited for orders to move off. Screened from view by a canopy of trees, we munched chocolate, smoked cigarettes and debated the possibility of spending the next weekend at home. Eventually we became impatient for the order to move off. Suddenly the sound of machine guns and rifle fire in the distance intruded on our thoughts of elation. It must be one of the other battalions sorting out some Jerries. Finally, with the rifle companies leading the way, we started to advance in single file. Threading our way through discarded parachutes and past the civilians busy collecting souvenirs, we left the landing zone and emerged on to a narrow road, bordered on both sides by an avenue of trees. Suddenly, we heard the crack of a rifle somewhere ahead and, on the urgent command of our platoon commander, took cover. There were sounds of a brief exchange of gunfire and after a short period we resumed our progress, passing on the way the body of a dead German lying at the base of a tree. If this is all they can do to stop us we will be at the bridge within hours. But the sounds of battle, both near and far, grew more insistent as we moved forward in fits and starts, with no clear conception of what was happening ahead. We did know, however, that we needed to press ahead urgently to our objective, the bridge at Arnhem, and also that our forward platoons were clearly incurring casualties.

We'd been told to expect casualties; it was part and parcel of being an airborne unit that jumped in ahead of the advancing army. We didn't have heavy artillery or armour to support us, so when we came up against the Germans, we'd been trained to go straight for the jugular and we often did not wait for our mortars and heavy machine guns to come into action. It meant that we took casualties in the process, but weighed up against all the other factors it was an acceptable risk that up until now had been a successful strategy. As darkness descended, we left the road and took cover in the welcome refuge of a wooded area. By now there was a general feeling of disquiet; everything did not appear to be going according to plan as there seemed to be quite heavy fighting going on ahead of us. We should be advancing rapidly through the outskirts of the town, with the 2nd and 3rd Battalions on our right flank, on separate routes, but converging as we neared the objective. Instead, the Germans had somehow blunted our advance and we'd lost more men than we'd anticipated yet made little progress. Because of a shortage of aircraft, we'd been forced to improvise and leave the majority of the Airlanding Brigade back at the DZs, preparing defensive positions to protect the landing zones for the second airlift, which would arrive the following day. There had been a lot of discussion about this as it meant we didn't have the numbers on the ground advancing with us in case something went wrong and we needed a backup. But we'd been told it was a minor problem considering we'd have taken the Germans completely by surprise. I'd fought the Germans before and I remember thinking they were like their world heavyweight-boxing champion Max Schmeling; you could hit him as hard as you like, but he'd roll with the punches and come after you half a minute later.

Not only that, but we found ourselves effectively isolated from the other two battalions, who were somewhere out there on their separate routes. It was then that a whispered order was relayed quickly from man to man: 'Freeze!' We heard movement in the vicinity; a group was moving through the undergrowth on our left flank that had been identified as enemy. Our task was to arrive in force at our destination, so it was important that we did not engage in unnecessary combat, sacrificing precious time and possibly sustaining further casualties. The sound of the enemy approaching grew louder, so that we could hear them talking, and then gradually faded as they passed, unsuspecting, across our front. This wasn't a small group either. Sometime before dawn, jeeps arrived, which transported us to an area at the outskirts of Arnhem, on a major road where the battalion was assembling for a determined thrust towards the bridge. We learned that the 2nd Battalion had reached their objective and controlled the north bank of the bridge. Less welcome was the news that the rifle companies of our own battalion had suffered heavy losses during the night, shortly after the start of our advance. That must have been the firing we heard. Second-rate troops are not capable of inflicting that kind of damage on élite troops; whoever did it must have been well equipped and well trained to say the least, but where did they come from? Max Schmeling immediately came to mind. We eventually came to a residential area, a few houses with small front gardens. We halted and the residents emerged, waving and cheering, with offerings of fruit, drinks and flowers, obviously overjoyed that they were now liberated. The euphoria was short-lived, cut short by bursts of machine-gun fire from the wooded area a few hundred yards in front of us, on the opposite side of the road. An elderly lady, near to us, was hit in the back and was carried screaming into a house; meanwhile, we took cover in the front garden while forward elements of the battalion dealt with this threat to our progress. Some twenty minutes later they managed to destroy the machine gun and its crew. These were definitely not old men and young boys; they had to be hardened combat troops.

As the open countryside gave way to built-up areas, we progressed in fits and starts, coming increasingly under fire from groups of enemy snipers hidden among the buildings in the higher ground of our left flank and I remember a particularly long open gap where we ran singly, at intervals, under fire, to reach the comparative safety of the buildings at the other end; several men never made it, gunned down as they ran. We ended up firing valuable PIAT bombs into suspected houses in an effort to suppress the snipers. It didn't really work as they were too well hidden, well away from the windows, so we were only guessing where they were. Once again I thought that these couldn't be second-grade troops; sniping like this was a skill only selected men ever learn. What was worse, we couldn't get to the wounded without risking our own lives and it was terrible hearing them call out for help. One medical orderly rushed out and was shot for his efforts. I remember getting really angry thinking about the intelligence officers who told us that the opposition would be so soft we'd walk all over it. Well, we weren't walking all over it now were we? Progress became even slower as the forward companies encountered mounting resistance until darkness fell and we received orders to occupy the houses to our left. We now realised that we had lost the element of surprise; that any time wasted was to the enemy's advantage; and ominously, that before we could form a defensive cordon around the north end of the bridge, we faced a bloody battle through a built-up area against heavily defended positions.

That night, we settled down in a back room on the floor to get whatever rest we could before the next phase. We could hear movement in the houses above and at the rear of our position, which we assumed were the enemy, so we made as little noise as possible. The man next to me kept falling asleep and snoring loudly; I prodded him awake, lightly at first, but more and more forcibly as the night wore on. Having survived the night, rested and with our need for food satisfied, we emerged from our burrows in good spirits, ready to do whatever was necessary to cover the remaining 2 miles or so to our objective. With two hours of darkness left to cover our advance, our orders were to keep to the right-hand side of the road and proceed with all speed. The enemy commanded the heights on our left-hand side, so much of our progress was along the rear of buildings, which revealed an uninterrupted approach to the river. As the darkness gradually gave way to daylight, we found to our alarm that our position was totally dominated by an enemy strongpoint located in a large factory on the other side of the river. Armed with 20mm flak guns that could fire 450 rounds a minute, and MG42 machine guns that fired 1,200 rounds a minute, they raked our exposed flank with a concentrated barrage. As the light increased, this intense fire began to take a heavy toll. We had nowhere to hide and our machine-gun and mortar sections were deployed to counter this menace. It was like taking a fly swat to a rhinoceros. Positioned at the forefront of our advance, my gun crew were in an open position in full view of the enemy gunners. I was number three on the left-hand side of the gunner and he commenced firing across the river in the direction of the enemy force. Suddenly the number two, on his right-hand side, slumped sideways without a sound, and remained motionless on the ground, blood draining from his body. I pushed him aside, hoping that a random round had hit him rather than a targeted one, and took over his position. A shout from the rear signalled us to pull out and stopping only to collect the identity disk from my dead comrade, we grabbed the gun and beat a hasty retreat from our exposed position. We were but 1 mile from the bridge!

Rejoining the main body, we discovered a state of total confusion. Our line of advance was now blocked by armour, the battalion had, to all intents and purposes, ceased to exist, and we were to fall back to a more tenable position. Just up the road we came across Andy Milbourne, his hands shattered and his face covered in blood, being attended to by a medical orderly. He had been manning a machine gun left in position to cover our retreat and it had taken a direct hit. Nobody seemed to be in command as we retraced our steps back towards our starting point, not as a defined unit but as a mixed group from different units and battalions with no clear destination or purpose, bar to rejoin the main divisional troops, now reinforced by the second lift and located somewhere in our rear. It was at this point that an old friend, Jerry Curtis, overtook me. He'd been my section lance corporal way back in 1941, when we were designated 11 SAS and housed in civvy billets in Knutsford. We had become good friends and remained together until the North African campaign, when he had been promoted in the field to second lieutenant. Now a captain, he informed me that his runner had been killed and we agreed that I would take his place. We reached a road junction where everyone was halted and those officers that still survived were summoned to formulate a coherent plan. The conference was in the grounds of a large building on the corner of the road junction and Jerry instructed me to wait inside the building. Left to explore the various rooms in the building, I looked for and found a large kitchen with a stove, a fry pan, a supply of eggs and some butter.

Not one to pass up an opportunity, I threw four eggs into the fry pan and was soon rewarded with the characteristic sound and sight of eggs popping and crackling. I thought to myself how pleased Jerry would be when he rejoined me, but just as the yolks were firming and the outside turning white, I heard Jerry calling out to me from the front door. 'I'm just cooking some eggs for us,' I said.

'Never mind the eggs,' he replied. 'We have a job to do!' He explained that there were German tanks in the vicinity and the assembled troops were to evacuate the area as quickly as possible, making their way back to Oosterbeek, where a perimeter was to be defended and that he, me and a gunner from the anti-tank brigade were to remain behind for fifteen minutes to cover their rear. I was not altogether thrilled with this prospect and as the last of the column disappeared around the bend in the road, leaving us in isolation, we scanned the two approaches to our position and listened for any sound of approaching armour. I mentally counted each interminably long passing second until Jerry declared our mission completed and we set off to catch up with the main body.

We came to another road junction, a main open road on our right, sloping upwards and diagonally backwards to the horizon, and found the retreating column halted. After a brief fact-finding conference, Jerry returned and we took up a position among the buildings on this right hand road. Fifty yards or so ahead, on the opposite side of the road, were two gunners manning a solitary anti-tank gun. Without warning, a low flying Messerschmitt roared overhead, interrupting the now familiar sounds of battle. The sound of tanks approaching the crest of the hill in front of us was the signal for the anti-tank crew to prepare for action, and as a huge monster poked its snout over the top, they fired. The tank, mortally wounded, came to a halt sideways across the road and a second tank, following the first, although scoring a direct hit on the gun crew, killing all of them, was too late to stop them firing off another shell, which struck the tank and destroyed it too. As the fading light heralded the beginning of another night of doubt and confusion, we rounded a bend in the road to find a number of houses on each side; at last a defensible position that offered us a temporary advantage. We occupied the houses and dug slit trenches in the gardens at strategic points. During the long night of fitful sleep, we heard evidence of enemy troops in the vicinity and occasionally the rumble of distant heavy armour. As dawn approached, we dispersed among the houses and gardens, waiting for the inevitable onslaught, and listened in vain for some indication of the promised breakthrough by 30 Corps on the far side of the river. We sighted the only available Vickers on a low wall at the rear of the houses on the left-hand side, giving us an unobstructed view of the demolished railway bridge over the lower Rhine, about 1,000 yards to our left, then waited.

The attack, when it came, was heralded by the characteristic clunk of heavy armour. Round the bend came a tank. It stopped and began to systematically demolish the buildings that we occupied. The supporting infantry were engaged and they and the tank were driven off with casualties on both sides. In the meantime, we had observed a group of Germans approaching across the open land from the direction of the bridge. We opened fire with the machine gun, supported by riflemen, and the attack came to an abrupt halt with considerable casualties to the Germans. Twice more in the course of the morning, the tank attacked, each time destroying more houses and denying us vital cover. The enemy infantry had now infiltrated our defences and posted snipers, unseen, in commanding positions. The area was devastated, houses were burning and we were forced to take refuge inside the few houses still intact. We barricaded the windows with whatever furniture was available and prepared to make a last stand.

A load groan came from the front bedroom upstairs, followed by a heavy thud. It was the man posted at the window, obviously the victim of a sniper. Jerry ordered me to take his place. I thought 'Shit! – is he joking?' Creeping upstairs, I ran across the room to the wall by the window and tentatively pushed my rifle into position, careful not to expose myself, then I quickly moved behind the rifle with my hand on the trigger. To my immense relief, this did not draw the expected rifle fire and at least I had a theoretical advantage. From the other side of the road came a figure with a maroon beret. Halfway across, he just collapsed in the road, hit by enemy fire. He was followed by another one of ours, who stopped to help and was hit himself. Now there were two bodies lying in the road. I heard Jerry Curtis downstairs instruct everybody to stay in position, the front door opened and he was gone. Before he could reach the other two he was gunned down and died instantly. The house next door was on fire and death or captivity now seemed the only possible alternatives. The light was fading and we still survived. It was decided that we should attempt to escape via the back door. I was instructed to mount the Vickers in a position to cover the break out. There was no choice but to set it up in the middle of the narrow lane which ran along the back of the houses, facing the rear of the intended route. In the house we had occupied I had found a cigar and this seemed an appropriate time to savour its fragrance.

The survivors were quickly assembled and we moved off. One member of our mixed group, composed of remnants of the 1st, 3rd, and 11th Battalions and some South Staffs, was a Padre who, noting that I was still in possession of the machine gun, which seemed to grow heavier with every step, stopped to offer words of encouragement. I nearly told him where to go, but I was too tired even to speak. The noise of battle was evident, somewhere on our right flank, rifle fire, mortars and occasionally heavy artillery, but incredibly our progress was unimpeded. We reached the end of the track we were following, revealing a large expanse of grassy meadow. The leading elements of our group were part-way across, completely exposed, when a burst of machine-gun fire from the woods on our right cut them down. It was essential that we crossed this obstacle with the utmost speed, in order to join up with our main force at the far side. It was decided to cross individually, each man waiting until the guy in front was halfway across before commencing his run. Halfway across, running as fast as I could and hampered by the weight of the machine gun on my shoulder, and under fire, I stumbled and fell forward. The fellow behind me had fortunately commenced his run and I was able to get to my feet and reach the other side unharmed.

We had now got to the outer defences of the new defensive perimeter and I was ordered to surrender my machine gun in exchange for a rifle; not, however, before discovering that no one had thought to bring the ammunition! We were directed to the church, a small square structure, where we assembled and were addressed by Major 'Dicky' Lonsdale of the 11th Battalion. He informed us that we were now under his command and designated the 'Lonsdale Force'. We also learned that the 2nd Battalion at the bridge were still holding out, though seriously depleted, surrounded and isolated; also that the Guards Armoured Division had reached the Nijmegen area. Dawn on Thursday morning found us occupying a position on open ground, to the north of the Arnhem–Oosterbeek Road. Dug in behind a slight rise, we had a clear view of the road junction immediately in front of us. Before long we observed two self-propelled guns approaching the junction, supported by infantry. We opened fire, together with forward units on our left flank, causing the German attack to stumble and eventually halt; a few minutes later we were engaged by their heavy guns, firing on open sights. This attack was aborted and comparative peace reigned once more. A new sound intruded on the sound of battle, the throb of approaching aircraft, and then the sky was suddenly filled with Dakotas. They started dropping desperately needed supplies, but too far away from us.

We stood up, waved our yellow triangles, our arms, anything to attract their attention, but all to no avail. We watched, in horror, as planes were hit, caught fire and spiralled downwards to destruction. Then they were gone. Before long our position was being pounded with mortar shells from the dreaded Nebelwerfers, which were multiple barrelled. We withdrew to the tree-lined ditch at the rear of our position to wait for the barrage to cease. I was one of a close group of three, with a 1st Battalion sergeant in the middle. A salvo straddled our position, two live shells bursting, one to our front, the other to the rear, and another landing between the sergeant and the other man, which unbelievably failed to detonate. As night fell and the rain added to our discomfort, we moved to a position near a mortar group, with houses in the vicinity. The night passed with very little activity on the part of the enemy and we were able to snatch brief periods of sleep.

We now knew that the Germans had overrun the defences at the Arnhem Bridge and could concentrate all their available forces against us. As such, the perimeter was subject to intense mortar fire and snipers were inflicting heavy casualties. We remained in a defensive position during the morning, but with a lull in the intensity during the early afternoon a small detachment of us were sent out on a scouting mission. We searched a group of houses and noted the total devastation around us, with bodies and debris from previous battles lying everywhere. There were still a number of Dutch civilians occupying buildings, mostly living in the cellars. Without warning we were subjected to a barrage of shellfire. A soldier near to me dropped and although he was dead, there was no sign of an injury, so we presumed that he had been killed by the blast. Having established that the area at that time was clear of enemy, we returned to our lines to report. The Germans seemed to have a strange reluctance to fight during the hours of darkness, so as the light began to fade our hopes of surviving to see another day and maybe rescue by the British Army were rekindled.

We, a small detachment under the command of the sergeant, were, before first light, instructed to relieve another group, who were defending a house on a road overlooking a T-junction. The garden at the back of the house was separated from a similar house and garden by a hedge, which by now had been flattened. The other house was one of a cluster of houses, on a road running parallel to the road that we controlled. The force that we were relieving had been involved in a number of desperate enemy assaults by tanks, supported by infantry. Once we had taken up strategic positions in the various rooms, the sergeant instructed me to liaise with the forward airborne units and a group of pilots from the Glider Pilot Regiment, somewhere along the junction road facing the front of the house. Having accomplished this mission, I was then told to make our presence known to a group of South Staffs, located on our left flank, along the parallel road. I traversed the two gardens, noting with alarm the carnage and destruction, which signified the significance to both sides of the position we were holding. Emerging from the left side of the house, I found a lone soldier, the solitary occupant of the small front garden.

Vaulting over the low wire fence, I proceeded down the road, which was long and straight. A few yards further I found a stationary Tiger tank, obviously no longer serviceable: it had been hit in the rear, where it was vulnerable. Stopping to look inside, I saw the driver slumped forward with his head shattered. I went about 200 yards further on but there was no sign of any defence by our lot, so I shouted, 'Any South Staffs around?' No reply! Another 50 yards or so, then I heard the sound of digging on the opposite side of the road. Crossing the road, I located the source of the sound behind a low brick wall at the front of a house. Jumping over the wall, I said, 'Are you the..? Holy Shit! – Jerries!' It was a Jerry machine-gun crew. I kicked the MG42 machine gun into the trench, jumped back over the wall and starting running back, not straight but zigzagging. A hail of bullets escorted me down the road and reaching the wire fence, I literally dived over it. Running down the garden, I was passed by a figure, the man from the other garden! Describing my experience to the sergeant, he instructed the two of us to return to the forward garden and watch for any movement from the German position while he called for a salvo from our light artillery battery to shell the position they occupied. We saw a German standing in the road shouting. He sounded very angry. Then, a few minutes later, shells started exploding around the area. Returning to my original position,

I took up a position in the roof, taking advantage of one of the numerous holes in it. It was a good vantage point with a clear view in all directions. The sound of caterpillar tracks approaching down the road foretold a determined attack by a Tiger tank, supported by infantry. The troops forward of our position opened fire, supported by limited covering fire from us. After a skirmish with casualties on both sides, the Germans withdrew. Why they didn't press home their attack with the tank, I'll never know – it only fired its machine gun.

In the afternoon a line of Germans, presumably the unit I had found earlier, were observed approaching down the rear garden toward us. We opened fire and they quickly withdrew again, this time occupying the house in the rear. One of them had obviously been hit because we could hear him moaning. As the light deteriorated, it was obvious that we could not leave them occupying their present position, yet we also could not abandon our post without notifying headquarters. The sergeant left to report the situation and shortly after returned with an officer. We were to storm the position and eliminate the threat to our rear. As instructed, I left my rifle behind, replacing it with a Luger pistol I'd acquired. In the fading light, we moved in single file through the gardens adjacent to our position and, having reached the rear of our objective without detection, I was left in the rear to guard the closed back door while the rest moved to the side of the house. When in position, the officer shouted, in German, a command to surrender. There was no reply or sign of movement, so I fired my revolver through the panels of the back door. This brought an immediate response and the occupants came out and surrendered with no sign of opposition. We started to march them down the garden when the officer turned to me and said, 'Go back and make sure there are no enemy still in the house!'

'Not me again!' I thought, and reluctantly proceeded to obey his instruction. Moving through the various rooms with the speed of light, I was happy to report that the house was now unoccupied. We marched our captives to the enclosed tennis court, reserved specifically for enemy prisoners, and proceeded to search them prior to locking them away. I was about to search one of them when suddenly there was an explosion. I found myself on the floor and my immediate reaction was, 'Is this it? Am I about to die?' There was no pain and I found that I was the only one hit and in three places, my hand, arm and leg. My luck had run out. Bleeding profusely, I was taken to a temporary refuge in the cellar of a nearby house, where my wounds were bandaged with shell dressings. Later in the evening I was moved to the house of Mrs Kate ter Horst, a few yards removed from Oosterbeek church. The church was now an enemy target of prime importance. Its high tower, commanding an aerial view of the surrounding district, was being used as an OP to establish targets for the gun batteries of the Light Artillery Regiment and the distant heavy guns of 30 Corps, which were now within range. Defended by anti-tank guns and mortars, it was to be the scene of continual and intense enemy assault.

Oblivious of this, Mrs ter Horst and her children, confined to the cellar, moved among the wounded with words of comfort and compassion, helping with their dressings and, last thing at night, reading a passage from the Bible, moving from room to room. Throughout Saturday and Sunday, I lay on the floor, against the wall, in an upstairs room, with badly wounded men occupying every available space, listening to the sounds of immediate battle, which raged at the front and rear of the house. Twice during the two days, the house was shaken by tremendous explosions in the immediate vicinity, with broken glass and plaster falling around us. We wondered how all this was going to end. On the following Sunday night we were addressed by a medical orderly, sent from divisional headquarters, who informed us that the bridge at Arnhem was now in the hands of the British 2nd Army and that the Guards Armoured Division was expected to relieve us early the following morning. Throughout the night we heard spasmodic bursts of machine gun and rifle fire from near and further away. There was no longer the sound of battle in evidence, as daylight filtered through the shattered windows. We waited and wondered; it was then that Mrs ter Horst came in through the door. 'I'm afraid that I have news for you,' she said. 'Your comrades were evacuated across the river last night and the house is surrounded by Germans. An officer is waiting outside to speak to someone who is able to walk.' I volunteered and emerging from the front door, was confronted by this officer, who saluted and said in impeccable English, 'Your people have withdrawn back to their lines. I congratulate you on your efforts, but you are now our prisoners. Please distribute these gifts.' He gave me tins of cigarettes and bars of chocolate, obviously from the containers dropped outside our lines.

Relieving the Airborne – Albert Thompson

I learned later that by 17 September the German army was no longer on the run. Many of them had escaped the attempt to surround them and had crossed Belgium and gathered in the southern part of Holland. Some were even assisted by collaborators from among the civilian population. From among them, the German paratrooper General Kurt Student formed the 5th Parachute Army and it was these that would lead numerous attacks that slowed down 30 Corps' advance to Arnhem. The Guards Armoured Division had finally bridged the Albert Canal after a bloody battle that cost them a lot of men and tanks. Our B Squadron followed in their wake. After crossing the bridge we swung left to the village of Beverloo. However, our driver reported that there was no charge showing on the ammeter and he would have to investigate so he pulled into a field and attempted to rectify the fault, unsuccessfully. While he was trying, I watched the removal of the remains of a crew from a tank that had been hit by an 88mm gun. The shell had entered the turret and come out the opposite side. The far side of the turret was splayed out like the petals of a tulip. Ropes were being used to pull the remains out of what was left of the turret hatch; the bodies were bent, charred, angular and rigid, and were difficult to remove. The men who did this job must have had stomachs made of steel and I didn't envy them the job one little bit. I was reminded that my regiment had only one of its original tanks left since we landed at Normandy – the CO's tank. I'd been lucky so far and had got out of two that had received direct hits; the second time, I'd received a nasty shoulder wound and had only just come back from hospital and leave. Just about all of the original members of the regiment were either dead or so badly wounded they would never fight again. And almost every other regiment was in the same boat. The casualties were appalling. What could one expect when the German tanks mounted 88mm guns that could easily outrange us, and the 88mm anti-aircraft guns were used as tank killers too?

The mechanics were back at the canal, so we retraced our route and headed back. Their truck was parked next to a block of warehouses with a cobbled area in front. There was a nondescript platoon of armed civilians on parade in front of the warehouses; the commander was an attractive middle-aged woman in a tweed suit and high heels. I enquired from an onlooker who could speak English what it was all about. He replied that it was the Belgian Resistance Movement – the Maquis – parading for the first time after the liberation and the person in the tweed costume and sensible shoes was a man and used to be a major in the Army. He was now in command of the unit and he'd assumed the disguise of a woman and outwitted the enemy during the occupation. The mechanics soon got cracking to tackle the problem, watched by members of the Maquis. With them was a German paratrooper they had found in a nearby wood; he was very bedraggled and engaged in eating an equally dirty piece of bread, obviously in a state of near starvation. He had been hiding in the woods for some time.

The mechanics working on the battery in the turret traversed the gun for access and, unknown to the mechanic, it pointed at the paratrooper's head. This was thought to be a great jest by the Maquis; the poor German, still tearing at the bread, received a kick on the backside to draw his attention to it. He lunged at his tormentors, who led him away. It wouldn't surprise me if they shot him after the way the Germans treated them during the war. The paratrooper could have been a survivor of an attack on our A.1 Echelon – the supply lorries – that was staged by a force of about fifty enemy paratroopers. They set about fifty lorries on fire using machine guns that fired incendiary rounds. Among the casualties, the squadron sergeant major – the 'Rat'

– was captured. When the lads heard about this berets were thrown in the air with a mighty cheer, as he was universally disliked. We had instructions to join the troop at Oostham, but were told to make a detour across country and not to go directly down the road as Germans using a flamethrower were guarding it. We met up with the troop on the left flank of the village. We were leading and as we passed a large barn on our left, part of a group of farm buildings, there was a loud bang as an armour-piercing shell whizzed inches past the turret.

A frantic order to bail out was given by our commander, a second lieutenant, but Ken, our corporal, countermanded it. The driver reversed the tank back but within a few yards was stopped by thick trees. We waited with the engine switched off for the source of the shell to appear from behind the farm buildings, but in vain. The troop sergeant's Sherman Firefly tank was parked next to a roadside chapel with the troop leader's tank further back. The troop leader, with considerable courage, ran over from his tank to assess the situation himself and gave orders to get out of it. As he was getting down from our turret, there was an explosion from the vicinity of the chapel and smoke and flames came from the troop sergeant's tank. With great haste we accelerated out of the copse in which we were trapped and raced back past the chapel. The driver was lying next to the tracks of his tank, waving frantically for us to get the hell out of it. We didn't wait as whoever it was clearly had the area covered and was well camouflaged.

The troop sergeant had courageously dismounted to make a reconnaissance and was capturing eight German parachutists when he himself was surrounded and captured. Stan, the gunner in the troop sergeant's tank, was keeping watch from the turret when a parachutist climbed on to the tank from the rear and shot him in the head and threw a grenade into the turret. Tom Bevan bailed out slightly wounded and as he lay on the ground by the tank he could hear the screams of John, the operator, dying in the turret. Tom had seen the enemy in the nearby copse with Panzerfaust bazookas and so with selfless courage waved us away from danger. If we had infantry with us, they would have spotted what was going on and taken appropriate action.

As it was, we were without infantry – why? Senior officers higher up the chain of command didn't seem to think it was appropriate as tanks could move faster than men. Sometimes one has to wonder how they ever got to the top. The Germans worked in close co-operation with infantry. A self-propelled gun with a detachment of infantry generally worked together, assisting each other, the infantry observing for the armoured vehicle, which then gave any covering fire required.

The German infantry used 'Panzerfausts', a hand-held, one-shot bazooka that could penetrate 200 mm of armour at 30 metres. To counteract the effect of this weapon, chain link on steel framing was attached to the side of the Shermans in the hope that the bazooka would glance off. This 'do it yourself' was additional ironmongery to the track plates welded on the front and the turret to give additional protection. During an offensive, we were following another tank skirting the edge of a copse when the gunner spotted a German with a Panzerfaust ready to fire. The gunner, in his haste, fired the main 75mm gun instead of the machine gun. After the action we went to the copse and found the German – a massive man – decapitated by the shot. The route of the attack was to be the width of the road only – even we troopers at the bottom of the ladder could see that was a pretty stupid idea. We were to follow the poor Guards Armoured Division, who led the assault. The problem, of course, attacking on such a narrow front with a long tailback, was the possibility of flank attacks by the Germans, cutting off the supply route and reinforcements; which they did, as they weren't stupid by any means. As we motored north, alerts became frequent and it was necessary to stop and take up positions behind trees lining the road. Every minute of advance meant 2 miles of exposed flanks. The American airborne had successfully taken the bridge at Graves, so we pushed on to Nijmegen, which we reached without any difficulty. All along the route there were burning tanks that the Germans had shot up. They'd hit the lead tank and the next one that pushed it off the road, and in some instances got a third one as well. By then the RAF close support aircraft would come in at treetop level and fire rockets into the area where the Germans were, but they had done their job, and that was to slow the column down. It was at times like this that I wondered if the generals really cared how many men we lost. Once the German blocking party was taken care of, the column would rumble off again, only to be stopped by another lot of Germans just down the road. Nobody thought about having infantry to protect the tanks. I was later told that we lost eighty-eight tanks before we finally got to our objective on the Rhine.

Signal Procedure – Laurie Poole

A Tiger tank sat outside Lonsdale Force's position and bit by bit began destroying one of the houses. It just fired its main gun time after time, starting at the top floor and working its way down. Up until then, Bren gunners had created havoc with the attacking German infantry, and unbeknown to them one flight down was also one of the Forward Observation Officers' positions for calling in the guns. Gunner 'Willie' Speedie was the radio operator inside the building on the ground floor. Everyone else had beetled out the back door in a hurry, but never one to panic in any situation, he quietly sat there and in his broad Scots accent closed down his radio station and passed on his duties to another outstation. What he did was straight out of the all-arms training manual, right down to the last word. Once that was done, he too beetled out the door. Meanwhile the tank continued to blow the place apart.

Like Flotsam from the Sky – Stanley Derbyshire

As the second parachute drop on the DZs took place, the drop zone took on a three-dimensional picture for those on the ground. We had to get out of our parachutes and sort out our equipment, check where our RVs were, and at the same time keep an eye out for German fire, flotsam from aircraft that had been hit, falling bodies from burning gliders, and equipment that had been jettisoned from them as they split open in the sky. It all came down and could have hit any one of us. On top of this, there were the dead and wounded still in their parachutes. But for me it was the falling bodies that were the worst. One, a lad whose canopy had been shot to ribbons, screamed all the way down before he hit the ground, where he was literally turned into human jelly. He lay there in a broken heap with the remnants of his parachute across him like a shroud. Even though it was risking life and limb to stand upright and present the Germans with a target, I'm almost certain that everyone who saw it wanted to go and see if he was OK, but deep down we knew he wasn't. It seemed like a madman's dream, only I knew it was real, and it was a terrible feeling knowing that his young life, along with dozens of others, had been snuffed out before it began. So we tried to forget it and got on with getting off the DZ and not getting shot. How most of us succeeded is a miracle in itself. The smoke from a burning Hamilcar drifting over the DZ gave me the precious cover I needed. As I ran past it, I spotted several bodies, all lying around the burning fuselage, where they'd been shot before they had a chance to fight back. A jeep and trailer full of ammunition had smashed through the side of the fuselage after breaking loose from their moorings; boxes of ammunition lay everywhere, ammunition that we'd desperately need in a few days time. And hanging out of the shattered cockpit window were the two glider pilots.

Escape from Hell – Ken Parker

I watch the Panzer as it belches flames into the farm building and machine-guns it; we could be next. Yet it is still drawing fire from those trapped inside; they can't possibly be hurting it, it's suicidal, but they refuse to give in. It manoeuvres and starts to move away. It turns and smashes its way through a low hedge as if it wasn't there, churning up the ground and spewing a shaft of dripping fire across an area of trenches about 100 yards away. Men are clambering out and are running for their lives, but here again some of them stay and fight it. They are soon caught in its liquid flame and there are screams from those it engulfs, and then there's a terrible silence as they literally turn to ash. The clinking, squeaking wheels drive the tank onwards towards a couple of half-buried Hawkins anti-tank mines. The tank eventually rolls over one that explodes, blowing off a large section of the caterpillar track. It grounds to a halt, trapped, and is under intense fire from everywhere. Away to the left, some German infantry have seen the predicament it's in and are running down a lane toward the thing. They are partially shielded by a hedge. They're trying to help the metal leviathan that is stuck out in the open.

I grab the Bren gunner's shoulder and point. He is bloody slow to react and fires off a burst of tracer rounds at the last German as he dodges behind a hedge. The stupid bugger has missed. Next, a German machine-gunner attempts to run up the same path. The Bren gunner, in his eagerness to readjust his weapon and take aim, drops it on the floor. I could have hit the stupid bloody fool. The German gets closer, sees the pair of us and deliberately drops his MG34 and ducks behind a large tree, pulling out a stick grenade as he does, unscrewing the base as a prelude to throwing it. 'Shoot the fucking bastard!' I scream at the Bren gunner in desperation. He is still fumbling so I grab the gun myself. The German draws back his arm and goes to throw. I plant the gun on the wall we're behind and fire, and his arm is literally torn off. He screams and the grenade drops to the ground and goes off, killing him. Just then two men carrying a PIAT scurry behind the blackened and burning barn some 100 yards from the farmhouse and 60 yards from the tank. Men are scrambling out of the building the tank has just flamed, as it is no longer considered a safe haven. Peering around the corner of the barn, the PIAT team can see the tank through the gap it's made in the hedgerow; its rear is towards them because it has spun on its single track as it tried to escape. It is the one real weak spot almost every tank has for a PIAT. It may be stopped, but the flame-thrower is still doing its work, flaming anything within range. Bullets ricochet off the turret and metal bodywork like ants attacking an armadillo; useless, but when you have nothing else you use what you have. The turret turns once again and replies with machine-gun fire and the flamethrower belches out more flames. One of the PIAT team kneels and places the PIAT on his shoulder and gets ready.

He has his back to us and as we watch he swings around the corner of the barn, takes aim and fires. When the tank went through the bank it left a huge gap to fire through. The bomb flies true and explodes against the engine compartment, rupturing the fuel tank and causing an enormous explosion, turning the evil monster into an inferno. Slowly the sound of small-arms fire recedes, fading away to the occasional rifle crack. The German infantry, cheated of their goal, retreat, leaving us to count our dead and wounded. It's late, dark and raining hard. For once there are no flares illuminating the sky and there's no sound of gunfire close at hand. We move to the battered farm. Rain hammers down on what's left of the roof and a few bedraggled lads stand on guard while water collects in large muddy pools around them. Outside are the piled bodies of those who have been killed, stacked like wood ready for the fire; as someone dies he will be added to the stack. With the flames now out, the large cellar under the farmhouse has been converted into a HQ, hospital and storeroom. The wounded and dying lie all around while the dead lie in the rain, impervious to the cold. There's hardly any room to move. The few officers left in charge try to make each other heard while a dirty radio operator sits hunched over a radio transmitter. Everyone quietens down. The order has been given that they're to move out in something called Operation Berlin. A few think it's a code word for an Allied push, a counter-attack, but then they realise it's the code name for retreat, and suddenly a murmur of disquiet and confusion goes through the room; all the death and destruction has been for nothing, a stupid waste ordered by a man who sacrifices whole divisions like pawns on a chessboard.

A skeleton crew will keep up radio transmissions and some level of fire while the main force retreats to the Rhine. Hopefully, by the time the Germans know what's happened, it'll be too late. Wounded men unable to travel will stay behind to man the positions, as will doctors and orderlies. They are told that when they leave no man is to fire unless fired upon; secrecy is vital. Their guides will mainly be glider pilots following paths that are already in place. They should be able to get everyone down to the river, where the Beach Masters will load everyone into assault boats that have been brought over by some Canadian engineers. I rest like a punch-drunk boxer slumped on a stool, staring into space while holding a mug of tea; I am out on my feet. Someone approaches and taps me on the shoulder. It's a young private who looks old beyond his years. He asks if I am coming with them. I just stare blankly into space. He explains that they're moving out tonight and advises me to pair up with someone wounded and offer to help them escape – unattached able-bodied men will be asked to stay behind. I follow him across the room, stepping over the dead and dying. I quickly find myself a wounded man who needs help to walk. In driving wind and rain, columns of men start to leave in a long, snaking line. Men are holding onto the one in front using the parachute smock tail flap or parachute cord. Visibility is down to just 4 feet. Artillery fire goes on in the distance. Red tracers can be seen in the sky to the south. White tape on the trees and rubble shows us where to go.

It's a slow and sombre retreat, made all the more eerie by the strange silence. No one utters a word unless necessary. A column of about forty or fifty men, each with the fit helping the wounded, is marching slowly into the night away from the farmhouse. It's pouring with rain. We have old socks and material wrapped around our boots in an attempt to keep the noise down. Those that have them wear waterproof smocks. The badly wounded are left manning radio and machine-gun posts, resigned to their fate, a terrible thing to have to happen to any man that has fought so hard and now had to watch their comrades go. Two bandaged men with grey, gaunt faces occupy a Bren gun position under a tarpaulin, sheltering from the rain. They try and smile, waving the column goodbye as if they are going on holiday. My mate and I are at the rear of their column and pass by. Soon they're out of sight. Rain continues to drive down. Very soon the first hurdle presents itself, a near solid 5-foot hedge that I have to push my wounded, groaning colleague over. He rolls onto the top and falls over the other side into the mud, groaning as he hits his wounds. I climb over the top and falls awkwardly onto him, causing more pain. I help him to his feet but it's hard to tell who's in a worse way. Hurrying on, we catch up with the rest of the column. In the darkness, off the path, someone calls out. By the sound of his voice it's a young paratrooper, badly wounded by the sound of it. He's in great pain, lonely, weeping in fear and panic.

His continuous pitiful cries make the marching column uneasy, but most men just put their head down and try to ignore it, as there is nobody capable of helping him anyway. When I pass by the cries, I go to break off from the column and want to help. I can just make out his prone shape lying in a ditch, reaching out, when a hand lands upon my shoulder. It belongs to a sergeant, a hard-looking soldier who hasn't shaved or washed in days. Reluctantly, I do as I'm told and rejoin the column; the rain soon blots out the pitiful cries of the young lonely man as we leave him. I honestly hope that someone comes along and helps him, as nobody should be left like that, yet I know I am incapable of assisting him; none of us are – we don't even have morphine to kill the pain he is in. It continues to pour down and the column has come to a halt. The two of us are still at the back, soaked to the skin and shivering. Up ahead, at the front of the column, we can hear the sounds of noisy arguing. A torch goes on and off, and it soon becomes clear that whoever is map reading isn't making a very good job of it. Up front the sergeant and several others gather around a map, trying to shield it from the rain and any Germans that might see it while using a torch to illuminate it. The hushed and muffled arguments suddenly get louder, more boisterous. The sergeant seems to be talking mainly to a private; neither of them seems to realise the need to be quiet. The arguments cease and the column starts moving again off into the night. It's finally stopped raining.

Two wounded privates nestle in their covered Bren gun position on the perimeter of the farmhouse. They would have clearly been soaking wet, cold and feeling sorry for themselves, as nobody likes to be left behind to a certain future in a prisoner of war camp. Half asleep, they would have occasionally scanned the surrounding area while in the distance two Bofors guns fire into the night sky so that the trajectories of the tracer rounds crisscross high above everyone. They see movement. Rashly, one of them cocks the Bren gun and lets off a short burst before being restrained, while one shouts for the shapes to identify themselves. We have all thrown ourselves onto the ground or taken cover behind anything we can. The sergeant crawls up towards the Bren gun and swears at them. We've been led in a circle back to our own perimeter. Some of the others gather round, including me. Bug-eyed with rage, the sergeant snatches the map and torch off the line leader and strides away. The column sets off again into the night. The Bofors guns are still firing tracer rounds into the night sky, telling us where to go; why do we need a map when as plain as day, there are the markers in the sky? The rain is still coming down once again. The sergeant is now leading; he pauses and signals for everyone to hold up. My mate and I have moved up the column and are now near the front. The sergeant turns on his torch to study the map; his face is clearly illuminated. Dear God, he's making all the mistakes under the sun shining a torch like that. He's either a complete fool or so exhausted he doesn't realise what he is doing.

Nearby there comes the distinct sound of a machine gun being cocked and a German voice calls out. The torch is quickly turned off and everyone either scatters or crouches down to hide behind something. Everyone talks in whispers. I make a whispered suggestion that we throw five or six grenades and make a run for it. We all know where the river is and we need to make as much ground as we can tonight before the mortars start up in the morning. The sergeant thinks about it for a moment. He seems unsure of what to do. Then, he agrees. Word goes down the line and people pass up grenades. We all look at each other, nod and pull the pins at the same time. Then, with a quick lob, grenades are hurled in the direction of the German voice. Everyone takes cover. Seconds later they explode and the dark figures are up and running. I take good hold of my wounded colleague and supporting him, we slip and slide along the muddy path. We pass a sandbagged German machine gun post, now burning, with a corpse draped over the top and another lying inside it. Off in the woods, German voices can now be heard, rising in intensity. Small-arms fire breaks the air and bullets whizz by. A couple of men are hit, fall down and scream out. Minutes later and it's stopped raining again, although water drip, drip, drips down from leaves and branches.

The moon peers out through a small break in the clouds, silhouetting the hedges, lanes and trees all around. All that remains of the group are twelve men, including the sergeant, my wounded friend and I. We huddle for shelter under some trees, looking pretty despondent. Those Bofors guns are still firing tracer rounds. I stare intently at them. The sergeant is examining the map and is looking worried. He's losing it. He turns the map around in his hands, not sure which way up it should be. I say that those two Bofors guns have been firing tracers, the trajectories of which are crossing high up in the night sky, so why not head for them as it's pretty clear they're doing it for a reason as there aren't any German aircraft overhead. The sergeant dismisses this idea as stupid. I say that's the way I'm going. The sergeant orders everyone to stay together. I say I'm going that way, and that's that. Once again the sergeant orders everyone to stay together and tries to stop me, so I pull my pistol and say, 'Listen you useless bastard, I've just about had enough of you, I'm going to walk towards those guns and if you try and stop me I'll fucking shoot you right now. I think I'm right and even if none of you care for the idea I'm going on my own.' The sergeant glances at the rest of the men, who are looking for leadership. A couple of them step forwards to follow me. Pretty soon the sergeant is isolated and he looks defeated. With me leading the way, the small column march silently down a narrow lane in single file; only their boots make any kind of noise in the mud.

The moon appears through the clouds and glints on something stretched across the road just beside my foot. I automatically raise an arm – Stop! A trip-wire stretches across our path. The column halts immediately and taking a closer look, I can see a metal trip wire extending six inches above the ground into the hedge either side of the road. Carefully, I step either side of it with the wire running between my legs and point downwards, showing the rest where it is. Everyone clears it and we carry on marching down the road before it starts to lead away from the tracer fire. I signal to the column to halt. I open a field gate and the men walk into it. Distantly they can hear mortar and machine-gun fire. Halfway across, some parachute flares are launched into the sky and start to drift down, illuminating the whole area. Everyone hits the ground and lies still until the flares die and fade. The men then get up and trudge on their weary way again. Approaching a hedge, a British soldier steps out of the shadows holding a Sten gun, looks us up and down, and using his thumb indicates which way to go, then melts back into the gloom. We walk on, out of the field and on to another small lane, towards the Bofors guns, which are still firing at regular intervals.

A few hundred feet further on, the same thing happens and another disembodied voice stops us and checks us out. Our pace quickens. The mortar and machine-gun fire we heard earlier is getting louder. We trudge on to the end of the lane and through a gate into a wide field. German mortar fire whooshes overhead, either exploding in the field or dropping into the River Rhine. There are men everywhere, some on guard, others marshalling the queues waiting to leave; it's a mini Dunkirk all over again. The lines stretch off into the distance, snaking all over the place, eventually ending up at the river, where boats are ferrying them across; there are literally hundreds of men. Germans attempt to fire on the area but generally the incoming mortar and artillery rounds are inaccurate. We're hopeful more than anything else. As we appear on the scene, a tired looking officer strides over. He tells us to make our way down to the bank and start a new line. When we arrive at the water's edge boats are heading for the shore. The ferrying takes place under mortar and machine-gun fire from German positions, which is becoming increasingly accurate. One large wooden launch is hit by a mortar shell in midstream and explodes like matchwood before sinking with everyone on board.

Men wait in lines for the boats to return from the far bank; they're large wooden boats powered by motors or oars, manned by big Canadian engineers who look like lumberjacks. In the dark many decide to swim for it. Most will never make it and will drown, others get shot, and all the while the enemy fire is intensifying. Flares almost permanently illuminate the night sky. My group stand in line patiently, some crouching down to keep warm, and present a small target to any opportunist German. Mortar shells continue to scream overhead, splashing into the water, which is filled with increasing numbers of men, still attempting to swim to freedom. As soon as the boats unload on the far bank they set off back to pick up more men. Each time they're overloaded with the wounded and men desperate to escape. The Canadian engineers rowing the boats are incredible. At last it looks as if a boat is going to pick us up. The rowers have shipped oars vertically but the boat has lost its momentum just a few yards from the shore. Soaked to the skin anyway, and without hesitation, I jump into the water and stride out into the river up to my neck. Choking on a mouthful of water, I grab the gunwale on the boat and start to pull it back towards shore; my wound kills me but I am determined not to let go. The river bottom has shelved quite deeply and I struggle to make progress but eventually the boat meets the steep riverbank. I try to scramble up the bank and a pair of hands reaches down from the boat and pulls me on board.

A big Canadian engineer puts a blanket around me while others help men aboard while I sit at the back of the boat, shivering like a small child. From my position I can see the lines of troops waiting to be rescued, the lost, lonely, cold faces, some terrified, some resigned. Machine-gun fire continues to rake the water. A dead body bumps against the boat and is grabbed by the water and quickly disappears; he's one of many I see carried on the current. I have nothing but admiration for those Canadian engineers as they ferried us across. Soon they are rowing the big crammed boat across the river and I start to relax. For the first time in days, I felt relatively safe. On the other bank its organised chaos, for as soon as the boats land, teams of men help everyone disembark. They're herded away by medics, men with blankets, and officers who are trying to make sense of the whole scene. Shivering against the cold night air, a blanket around my shoulders, I go with the flow and soon find that the sound of mortar and machine-gun fire is receding.

Over an earthen bank, down on to a road and towards the nearby village of Driel, columns of tired weary men make their way to safety. An eerie silence hangs over the tiny village of Driel, a few miles from the Rhine. Armoured vehicles stand idle with nowhere to go – the advance has halted for no apparent reason. Smoke rises on the horizon. Those who have been rescued are everywhere, sitting and resting, or marching on to some new place. Only the crunch of our booted feet on the gravel breaks the quiet. Nobody says anything; we're all too tired. I break away from the stumbling column and approach several mud-caked men sharing a cigarette by the roadside. I've only seen one wearing the shoulder patches of my battalion. As I looked around I saw tired faces everywhere, grimy, proud, undefeated faces, and I wanted to cry. I don't recognise anybody and had no idea how many others had made it. There are very few officers among them; surely they haven't all been sacrificed on the anvil of war simply because of the privileges of rank? All of these men have been through so much together yet they remain defiant. Everywhere I looked I see the eyes of men who had seen too much and given too much. Everywhere I see a hero. But for every man that had escaped many more have died, been wounded or captured, and they have no one to tell their story too. My experiences in those terrible eight days would remain with me for the rest of my life – they could fill a book, a book about the real 'Dante's Inferno' they call Arnhem.

Close Up and Personal – Benjamin Howfield

On 19 September we were ordered to withdraw; the Germans were simply too strong and by early afternoon it was obvious we were losing too many men and not gaining anything by staying where we were. If we'd have kept going they could have cut us off and butchered us at will. We didn't have the tanks, mortars, self-propelled guns or the artillery they had, nor did we have a never-ending supply of men. So we made a fighting withdrawal, one lot covering another while the Germans chased us like a cat chasing a helpless field mouse. Then the next lift of gliders arrived and the Germans had a field day. First it was anti-aircraft guns as they flew over and were released, and then it was anti-aircraft guns, mortars, machine guns and everything else they could throw at them as the gliders landed. We were desperately trying to defend the LZ as best we could, but it was impossible – it was sheer murder. It was here that I killed my first man with a bayonet, well he wasn't a man he was a boy really. Mind you, he carried an MP40 and would certainly have used it on me if I hadn't got in first.

We ran into his SS platoon as they were moving up to the LZ. A long black pall of smoke from a couple of burning gliders blocked our view and as we moved through it we were forced to step over a couple of dead bodies that had been thrown clear of the wreckage. They were so mangled it was difficult to recognise whether they were human or lumps of meat. Whichever way you turned, there was firing going on. Suddenly, out of the billowing smoke, both sides met. There was no time to think. The lieutenant who was leading us shouted and took off, firing his Sten gun, and we charged after him screaming like possessed lunatics. Although they outnumbered us, it took them completely by surprise. The sudden burst of fire from the lieutenant cut down their leader and the rest of us broke through the smoke and were among them, shooting, clubbing and bayoneting them in no time at all. There is something truly animalistic about screaming at the top of your voice: you have no fear, it's like being a cornered rat fighting to escape, and your body seems to have this unlimited amount of energy. I shot one German straight in the face, hit out at another with my rifle butt, missed him; he fell over, I tried to cock my rifle but for some reason I couldn't, then he aimed his machine pistol at me, but he waited too long to pull the trigger. The look of fear in his face was palpable, especially when he saw my bayonet. I simply didn't think about it, it was pure reaction; I just stuck it into him and a look of shock appeared across his face and he grabbed the barrel of my rifle as if he wanted to pull the bayonet out. I just pulled it out; he was just another dead German. It was then the remainder just broke and ran. We'd killed or wounded about ten to fifteen of them. By now the lieutenant was calling everyone to halt. I think we had two wounded, but nothing serious. I tried to eject the round still in the breech of my rifle but couldn't so I swapped it with the dead man's machine pistol along with about eight full magazines for it. He didn't need it, did he? It was then I realised that the German I'd bayoneted couldn't have been any older than sixteen or seventeen. After that, we headed to the railway cutting near Oosterbeek with the Germans right on our tails. One good thing that happened while we were being pursuit was seeing two German Me 109s strafe one of the units chasing us. I bet they got in the shit when they got back to base. There was a God after all. Once we stopped running we became part of 'Lonsdale Force' and fought on until the final withdrawal.

Metallic Sounds – Bob Hargraves
I was in one of the Hamilcar gliders that flew into Arnhem. Among other stuff we carried, we had a jeep and a trailer full of ammunition in the back with us. As we flew into the LZ I heard a series of metallic clunking sounds under the jeep and immediately thought the chains holding it were coming loose. We were just turning to begin our descent so I quickly got on my knees to check the chains to see if I could fix it, only to find a series of holes in the belly of the fuselage. As I lay there, another series of holes suddenly appeared alongside me. The metallic noises were machine-gun bullets coming through the floor. That was it; I made the quickest leap back to my seat I'd ever done. When I yelled what the noises were to the others, for some inexplicable reason we all took off our helmets and sat on them.

The Parachuting Priest – Roger Payne
When Padre Bernard Egan was asked if Padres were bulletproof, he answered, 'Only if the bullets are going the other way, my son!' And on another occasion at Arnhem he said to a group of Catholic privates who he was giving pastoral care to: 'The next time we meet I will talk about the sin of lying.' He paused momentarily, then asked, 'How many of you have read Mark Chapter 17?' Almost every hand went up. With a wicked smile on his face he said, 'Mark only has fifteen chapters. But I've also committed a cardinal sin as I deliberately tricked you!' After a particularly heavy bombardment on the defenders of the bridge, a private who had just had been wounded during a mortar attack yelled, 'Who the bloody 'ell looks after us Paras, Father?'

The good father answered, 'The patron saint of mental illness and spiritual disorders is Saint Dymphna, my son.'

'I've never 'erd of 'im Father!'

Father Egan paused for effect, then answered, 'Actually, the "him" is a "her"!'

The reply even made Father Egan smile, 'Jesus! All we need right now is a bloody woman poking 'er nose in!'

The Ceasefire in Hell – Arnold Brotherton

The streets had been swept by fire for over three days solid. Time and again both the Germans and us had taken houses and lost them, with neither side getting an overall advantage on the other. In one street alone two of their tanks, one a Tiger, and a self-propelled gun had fallen prey to one of our 17-pounder anti-tank guns and a couple of PIATs. They had repaid the debt by killing the crew of 17-pounder with snipers then bringing up a Panzerfaust and destroying it when a second crew had tried to man it. Now they had a 88mm gun at the far end of the street and were systematically destroying each house, one after the other, although our snipers and a Bren gunner had already killed four of its original crew, and three others of a new crew; we were definitely making that gun pay a high price for sitting out in the open, but no sooner had we shot the crew than another one dashed over to it under a hail of machine-gun fire. They needed to flatten the houses as we had the whole street, both sides, dug out like a rabbit warren. Almost every house had holes in the walls so we could retreat from one house to another. It cost the Germans a high price to dominate the other side of the street. Every house had to be paid for in blood, but in the end they forced us out. And every man we lost, we couldn't replace, whereas they could.

They would throw a grenade into a room then follow it up by charging in firing their machine pistols. We'd be in the next room, standing next to the hole in the wall; no sooner did they force their way in through the door, firing, than we would throw in a grenade. When it went off, we'd fire a full magazine from a Sten or Tommy gun into the room, then go in with our sharpened shovels, pick handles, picks and bayonets used like knives. In a confined space they would do terrific damage to the human body, as you simply didn't have time to change magazines on a weapon. Once we'd taken one room then we'd throw another grenade, then empty a full magazine from a Sten gun into the next one, then go in with the shovels again. It was pure backstreet fighting, no holds barred, but it worked. If we won we kept on going; if we didn't, we'd bolt through the hole in the wall into the next house, dash upstairs into the upper rooms of the house we'd just lost and throw grenades down the stairs. If they were upstairs we'd fire into the ceiling. Not that they weren't aware what we were capable of; on occasions they would turn the tables on us. But they were always wary when they entered houses as we would also booby-trap doors, windows and floors with grenades. Mind you, we had to be alert too as sometimes we'd retake a house and in the excitement forget which room we had booby-trapped and we'd lose one or two men until we learned to hang something above the door which told us immediately that a room was booby-trapped. In the end the Germans realised what it meant as well, but then we'd fool them by not booby-trapping a room but simply hang something above a door.

The street outside was littered with bodies from both sides, but you couldn't go out day or night, as it was a death trap. You just never knew where the next shot would come from. There were still wounded men lying there moaning, pitifully calling out to be taken care of, theirs and ours. Sometimes you just wanted to shoot them and put them out of their misery, but you just couldn't. Then, on the third night, one of our medics waved a white flag tied to a broomstick out of a door and waved it about for about five minutes. Once he'd finished he stepped out into the street and just stood there, waiting to be shot. When he wasn't, he turned and said something, and another medic carrying a stretcher stepped out after him, bold as brass. Now everyone had stopped shooting for the first time in three days, they both walked over to the first moaning figure, who just happened to be German. They knelt down next to him, rolled him onto his back and straightened his legs out, then one of them looked up the street and pointed to him, and they got up and walked over to one of our lads, who was also in a bad way. They rolled him over, put a wound dressing on him, stuck morphine into him, put him on the stretcher and carried him into the house. Five minutes later, they were back out checking on the next victim. By now three Germans had come out, only they had a door for a stretcher. They tended to their wounded while our men tended to ours. Four or five from either side were taken away, and still not a shot had been fired. The final gesture of this incredible ceasefire was seeing five men, three German and two British, standing in the middle of the road and the Germans handing over a couple of packets of Wills Woodbine cigarettes they'd taken from one of our containers on the DZ they controlled, then all of them disappeared back into the houses on their side of the road and the battle started again.

The 'Ruse de Guerre' Incident – Herbert Eastwood

After days of bitter fighting, much of it house to house, the company was involved in a controversial incident on Wednesday 20th. We were all exhausted and the Germans had been in the habit of calling upon us to surrender, and although I cannot be certain, it does appear that some of the men deliberately lured them into a 'ruse de guerre' (ruse of war). After a period of mortaring and machine-gunning, a German shouted out, 'Surrender Englanders!' Technically, one could have said that it was not clear whether they intended to surrender to us, or were calling upon us to surrender, although I was never in doubt that they wanted us to surrender. One of our corporals was a German Jew, so using him, one of the sergeants called upon them to come out into the open before any surrender could take place. Initially there was some hesitation, then about thirty Germans moved cautiously from their positions and started to come forward; all remained heavily armed and none displayed the slightest sign of submission. There was a mixture of Luftwaffe, Kriegsmarine and Wehrmacht among them; a Wehrmacht officer led them. They certainly weren't attacking us and I was unsure about this and said so to Rodley, the corporal. 'Tell them to lay down their arms,' and that is what he did, but they didn't. Then I said, 'Tell them we'll give them a minute.' But they simply stopped and began looking hesitant as if there was some kind of misunderstanding as to what was happening. Suddenly the glider pilots on our left flank opened up with their Brens, and the platoon quickly added their weight to the slaughter. None of the Germans escaped. Almost as soon as the firing started, I called out 'Cease Fire! Cease Fire!' and was shocked by the carnage, as to me it did appear that the Germans were coming across to accept our surrender, and although a 'ruse de guerre' is a totally acceptable, if unchivalrous, ploy of war, under any other circumstance this would have been classed as murder. But what could I do? It couldn't be undone.

My Time at Arnhem – Donald Arthur Wann

I consider myself lucky in being with the first wave to land near Arnhem, at about 1330 hours, because the Germans appeared to have been taken completely by surprise. There was no 'reception' in the form of the anti-aircraft fire that greeted the gliders, which happened to the rest of the lads the next day. Our RV was a hotel and we set off down the road, but as we got near there we were told by a member of the Dutch underground movement that the hotel was occupied by around 200 elite SS troops, so naturally we changed our mind and found somewhere else to go. None of us fancied taking on 200 SS at that point in time; anyway, how come there were SS troops in the place? We were definitely told that Arnhem was held by second-rate troops, mostly old men and boys. A day later, all hell had let loose and no matter where you went the Germans were liable to appear. What a difference twenty-four hours can make. The following day, an officer and myself were out hunting two tanks that had been reported in the area. Armed with a PIAT, we discovered them. One was a flamethrower type; the other one was a Panther. We crept up on the flamethrower, fired, and knocked it out, but we didn't get the larger one as the infantry moving with it turned and saw us and opened fire. A machine gun of some sort, probably one of those Schmeissers, hit the officer in the chest. His facial expression was almost comical as he looked down at the wounds. Then he let the PIAT go as the last of the rounds hit him and staggered backwards and fell on his back with both arms out to the side.

I couldn't believe it. One second he's taking aim with the PIAT, the next thing he was on his back, dead. There was no doubt he was dead, especially with the amount of blood that was coming out of his chest. With rounds flying all over the place I just took to my heels like a scared rabbit, as there was nothing I could do for him. The next morning I found two rounds from the machine pistol in my pouches. Both had been stopped by a couple of rifle magazines I had in there – talk about luck. But then, luck played a big part in our lives when the Germans were flinging everything at us. All of us carried food for two days and there was no resupply, as we couldn't get at it because they had all the DZs and were plundering our resupplies, so we had to spread our rations out carefully unless you got some of the larger ration packs, but they were being reserved for the wounded. Two of us did rescue two tins of soup from a container that landed near us. We had to wait until it was dark to get it as the Germans shot at anything that moved. I never crawled so close to the ground as I did that night. To make matters worse, they had snipers covering a well about 500 yards away and it was one of the only places we could get water after a couple of days. But night or day, this sod had it covered. He killed quite a few lads who took the risk of going there to collect water. Anyway, in the end we spotted him.

When a sniper was discovered and could not be hit by rifle fire, a message was run back to the artillery about 2 miles away. The artillery then fired on the tree in which he was, and took the tree and several others out in the process, but we got the bastard in the end. They soon replaced him, though, but they had to be very cagey after that. The glider pilots were a special breed. They not only flew the gliders, but when they got together in groups of ten or twelve they fought like tigers. They were perfectly entitled to make their way back to our own lines if they wanted, yet I know of none that did. When we finally pulled out, initially everyone stuck by the rules and kept quiet. There was no pushing or yelling at the river. Everyone waited in a queue, like queuing for the pictures, and all went well for about three hours in pouring rain and bitter cold. Mind you, near the end, when the Germans were firing indiscriminately, I heard that some of the lads went a little mad and started yelling and fighting to get on the boats, but on the whole they were pretty well disciplined considering what they had been through.

On the other side we were all given a large tot of rum, a tetanus injection and a cigarette, then driven to a large barracks some way behind the lines. All I wanted to do was sleep for a week.

Later on we were flown home. One thing that sticks in my mind about the time I was in Arnhem, besides the battle to survive, was the way the Germans treated our wounded. To quote an example, a party of Germans SS captured the small hospital where our wounded were, but after looking round they left without touching anyone or anything. And when the Germans wanted to fetch their wounded from in front of our lines, they just waved a white flag with a red cross on it, came over in an ambulance, collected them, and drove back without being fired upon. We did the same thing without the ambulance. Mind you, when the tank shells were hitting a building that had wounded in it, one of the padres went out under a white flag and walked straight up to the nearest tank, climbed on to the turret and banged on the lid; when it opened, he had a 'strong word' with a tank commander and he stopped the tanks firing. It was amazing that we could fight a war and kill one another in the most brutal way, yet we still had rules that protected the wounded.

Trapped Like Cornered Rats – Chester Clarke

The battle for Arnhem was lost and what was left of each unit was desperately trying to get to Lonsdale force that was already was making a nuisance of itself annoying the Germans. More and more tanks were smashing their way through the streets of Arnhem and Oosterbeek hunting down anyone who held out. Behind them were the infantry who methodically threw grenades into almost every house they passed by, and if necessary stormed the building afterwards. By now a lot of these were elite SS who'd fought in Russia and Normandy and weren't afraid to fight it out toe to toe with us. But it still didn't stop us holding out like cornered rats in a sewer. Four of us were in the upstairs bedroom of one house and we waited until the tank had gone by. It had already poked its barrel into one house and literally blowing out the back wall, and along with it killed three of the lads who we knew were inside. All it did was make us even more determined to get the infantry who were bunched up right behind it.

The ground shook as the growling Tiger tank rumbled passed. It was an evil frightening gargantuan that even a PIAT couldn't hurt. A 17-pounder maybe, even a 16-pounder if it got it in the right place; but they were all scrap metal by now. Devo held two grenades in his hands, Billy and I had Sten guns, and Phil still had a Bren gun. All of us crouch below the two windowsills. We dare not move as we were crouching on broken glass even if the noise of the tanks engine drowned the noise out. Devo watched the tank's aerial go by and silently counted to ten. We all looked at his lips, and the moment he said ten we stood up. He just dropped the grenades; there was no reason to throw them, as the Germans were right below us. The rest of us just emptied our magazines into them, and then we ran for the hole in that wall that took us into the next house. We heard the grenades go off above the noise of the tanks engines. By then we were down the corridor, through another hole in the wall in to the next house, down the stairs and out the back. We were at least 50 yards down the alley heading for another house when the back wall of the house we'd been in exploded outwards. Too slow, you square-headed bastards.

Desperate and Exhausted – Harry Wescott

A small group of us sat in the woods out of sight of the road, unwashed, unshaven, our uniforms torn and covered in a mixture of mud from the ditches, dust from the rubble of the town, and the blood from our comrades. We were hungry, thirsty, and tired beyond belief, yet too afraid to sleep. We had come from the outskirts of Arnhem the previous night, nights and days we'd lost count of. We had literally lost count of everything that was important in our lives; we were just mindless automatons wandering around in a hell made by man and his war machines. We had been fighting street by street, house by house, room by room through the town towards the bridge, only to be slaughtered and pushed back by a well-equipped enemy determined to destroy us, and the final onslaught had left us broken and shattered beyond belief. What was left of the 3rd Battalion was probably scattered in small groups like us, wondering what to do next. And although our bodies cried out for rest and sleep, we knew we couldn't stay still as the hunter was looking everywhere for us, and when he found us he would unhesitatingly exterminate us.

We wandered aimlessly, hoping to meet up with other groups from the battalion. Instead, we met a lieutenant from a glider pilot regiment with the three remaining men of his squadron. He confirmed that the bridge had finally fallen, so there was no point now in trying to head into the town; we had effectively lost it. He was on his way to Oosterbeck, which he said was still tenuously in the division's hands, and where there would be a stand made until 30 Corps arrived. It didn't take much convincing for the lads to agree to throw in our lot with him. At least he had somewhere to go; we had absolutely nowhere. He also had a map and seemed to know where he was heading. We were a ragtag lot, ten haggard men with only six of us capable of firing a weapon. We were like will-o'-the wisps, dodging from tree to tree, hedgerow to hedgerow, ditch to ditch, avoiding open country and desperately trying to keep out of sight while following the road to Oosterbeck; and lying low as German armoured scout cars, which appeared to be patrolling in twos and threes, passed by. It was sickening to see the destruction and the dead; they were everywhere, scattered like children's toys; many were comrades from previous times, men who lived and breathed a victory at the bridge only to end up like this. At one road junction, two German patrols met up. The leading cars pulled up side by side in the middle of the junction to have a chat. They were behind the hedge a few yards away. Everyone looked at each other knowingly; we probably could have ambushed them but dared not risk it as we simply weren't capable of travelling fast enough to get away if anyone else was nearby; the walking wounded certainly wouldn't have made it as they were on their last legs. Thank God the lieutenant held up a restraining hand; he was right of course, we weren't looking for a fight, we just wanted to survive and get to Oosterbeck, so we waited for them to move off before continuing on our way.

The closer we got to the built-up area, the more we saw evidence of the many battles that had taken place. Here there were bodies lying everywhere from both sides, as well as young Dutch resistance fighters. At one crossroads, a horse and cart carrying supplies for us had been ambushed. The cart had taken a direct hit from a mortar bomb or shell. The Dutch driver had been blown across to the other side of the road and lay at the bottom a tree in a mangled mass, and the bodies of the escorting soldiers were lying around as if a hurricane had picked them up and thrown them about. We noticed that the horse, although badly injured, was still alive. God knows how long it had been there, suffering. We all looked at one another and silently nodded, so the lieutenant took out his revolver to shoot it, but realised the shot might bring enemy patrols down on us, so one of the lads cut its throat. We eventually stumbled on the outer defences of Oosterbeck just before last light and managed not to get shot as we put our hands up and walked slowly toward the Bren gun being aimed at us. The men in the trench told us we were damn lucky as there was a German sniper in the area, and there'd been a heavy attack a few hours earlier. At that point the officer and the three men left us, but we reported to the church and became part of Lonsdale Force, which was a mixture of everyone who was left under Major Richard Lonsdale. Small groups were coming in all the time, making their way out of Arnhem, and from the surrounding countryside. There was a nice feeling of security being in a fixed position with an inner and outer perimeter.

Once the wounded were taken care of, the three of us still capable of fighting were then put to work digging trenches in gardens as part of the inner perimeter. Things were very well organised and with a full water bottle hanging from our hips, a rifle and a bandoleer of rifle ammunition each, we felt better; but there was no sign of food – now that was a worry. While we were digging, we were constantly being shelled, but we still managed to grab a few hours' sleep. I think it's called 'the sleep of the dead' because that's how we felt. Most of the shelling was coming from self-propelled guns that drove to certain positions within range and then fired off a couple of shells before withdrawing. They had to be quick because we had

75-millimetre artillery within our perimeter and they could fire 9,000 yards and had already taken a toll on German tanks and self-propelled guns. Some success had been achieved by parties with PIATs going out and waiting in ambush and knocking a few out, but the Germans were becoming crafty and were laying ambushes for the PIAT parties. There was one gun that shelled us each morning at daybreak; its position on the bend of the road outside Oosterbeck had been pinpointed. I was detailed to be one of the next PIAT groups that went hunting it. It was like being in Africa hunting a lion, only this lion was much more dangerous as it probably had its pride out there to protect it.

The patrol set off in the early hours, well before first light. It was really dark as we crept past the outer defences, each of us silently praying we'd come back. As we got nearer to the bend, we carefully searched the houses on either side, not wanting to be surprised by an enemy patrol. As I moved quietly through one house, I thought I heard a noise from behind a cupboard door. I opened it carefully and found a flight of stairs leading to the cellar. There was a dim light at the bottom of the stairs, just round a bend. I decided to shoulder my rifle and go down with my finger through the ring of a hand grenade; that way you can drop the grenade and have four seconds to get back upstairs. Many men have been killed while trying to reload their rifle in such circumstances. As I reached the bottom, I found myself in a fairly large room, lit by two candles. There was a Dutchman in the middle of the room dressed in his shirt and trousers. I took a quick look round. There were two double beds made up on the floor side by side. In one bed were two girls, aged about twelve and fourteen. In the other bed was a woman, obviously their mother, with large frightened eyes. The man said, 'Hello,' in good English. I slowly unwound and removed my finger from the ring of the grenade and put it back in my pocket; automatically bringing my rifle back across the front of me.

'I just wondered who was down here,' I said.

The man seemed very nervous. 'My family,' he explained. 'We have been down here from last Tuesday.'

Then the younger girl said, 'We don't like the English!' and then repeated it in case I hadn't heard. The older girl whispered hurriedly in her ear and the younger girl quickly corrected herself: 'We do like the English.'

I looked at the man and smiled and he relaxed. 'Would you like an apple?' he suddenly asked, pointing to a heap of apples in the corner. He crossed over and selected one with care, wiping it on his shirtsleeve before handing it to me. I sat down on a wooden chest with my rifle across my knees to eat the apple. The man asked me what part of England I came from and was impressed when he was told London. A lot of small talk followed. The two girls had crawled to the bottom of their bed. The girls took great interest in the questions and answers. I thought they could understand quite a bit.

The man was more at ease now. 'Are you married?' he asked.

'I'm getting married in a couple of weeks,' I replied. As I spoke, I realised how bizarre that sounded, how totally unreal. The man quietly told his wife, and the girls looked at me with renewed interest. I didn't allow myself to dwell on home and loved ones in the middle of a battle; this was just a conversation, nothing more.

The Dutchman asked, 'When will the armies get here?'

'Tomorrow,' I automatically repeated without any confidence at all. Finishing the apple, I stood up and said, 'I must be going, I've got a lot of work to do.'

This made the man laugh and he repeated it in Dutch to his family. They laughed politely as I went up the stairs.

I joined the rest of the patrol at the bend in the road where we set the PIAT up and settled down to wait. Just at first light, we clearly heard the sound of a large tracked vehicle and got ready. Round the corner came not the self-propelled gun, but a huge Tiger tank. Across to our right we could see another, with troops of infantry bunched up behind.

'Their bloody Tiger tanks,' the lieutenant leading the patrol gasped. 'Each man for himself, get back and warn the others!'

We all broke and ran. As if that was a signal, the tanks suddenly started firing their heavy guns. Shells went screaming overhead into buildings on the outskirts of Oosterbeck. I ran like I'd never run before; the tanks were firing their machine guns, strafing everything they could range on. A house loomed up in my vision; heavy shells had hit it but there was a Vickers gun firing from what was left of an upstairs window. Anywhere for shelter; I just ran in and upstairs to see if I could help with the Vickers. The chap on the gun said, 'It's no good, I'm all used up,' and he kicked the gun over in exasperation.

The view from the window was frightening. As far as the eye could see, there were armoured vehicles stretched across the horizon, and there were hundreds of troops bunched up behind them and more armoured vehicles following them up. We both looked at each other and then made a run for the stairs. I got to the front door first and stopped my tracks. Outside I could feel the ground shaking as the Tiger tank came down the street, and there in the middle of the street stood a huge German soldier with his machine pistol pointing right at me. I put up my hands and let my rifle drop to the floor. The German jerked his head towards the side of the house, where two soldiers grabbed me and went through my pockets, taking anything they thought of value, including my last grenade. They missed the cigarette lighter Dad had given me, but they found my fighting knife in my leg pocket.

Several wounded men came out of the house after me. I went to help them, but was pushed away by a German soldier and taken with another man to where a German officer was lying on a door that had been torn from a house. He looked badly wounded, but was bandaged up, and conscious. They indicated that the two of us should pick up one end of the door and two German soldiers took the other end and led the way. Across the road I saw the little Dutch family I had seen earlier in the cellar, coming out of the ruins of their house, accompanied by a German soldier. I was really glad they had survived the bombardment. The man was carrying a carrier bag, probably all that remained of their possessions. At that point I clearly remember looking down at the German officer on the blood covered door, watching as his life drained out of him. The German soldiers in front didn't know he was dead. Then I looked at the tanks and infantry going by and realised Oosterbeck would have to be overrun. Nothing could stop them. But what I didn't know until after the war was they didn't overrun Lonsdale Force. They were after the 75mm guns that had caused them so much trouble, and threw everything into the fray. But by now the artillery from 30 Corps was punishing them severely, although they did get close enough to warrant a bayonet charge made up of walking wounded, cooks, bottle washers, mechanics, drivers, signalmen, glider pilots and senior officers that finally forced their infantry back with big losses, but the cost to our side was enormous as well.

But for me it was the end, it was over: the days of fighting and killing and the dead and wounded. It was the blood, the fear, the fatigue, the terrible thirst, and the hunger that gnawed at your stomach, and the sights that made you think you could never eat again. No sleep, no rest, driving oneself on and on, as days and nights became one, in the tangled hell that was Arnhem. And now it was over, and we had finally lost. The 1st Parachute Division that had achieved so much in its short life was now being snuffed out as it made its last stand at Oosterbeek. The 'Red Devils' will be remembered for many victories, feats of endurance and courage, from the stony hills of North Africa to the olive groves and vineyards of Sicily and Italy. But there is no glory in defeat, no glory in seeing the dead and dying all around you and knowing it was a wretched, futile waste. The Dutch people will remember us descending from the sky one lovely, peaceful, sunny Sunday afternoon, giving them hope as they turned out to greet us. They supplied us with drinks from buckets of water at the roadside, to help us on our way. And then hope faded, seeing their homes destroyed; their young men, women and children who came forward to help were either killed or maimed – as were their families hiding in cellars or under beds. Then there was their beautiful town and the bombs and bullets from both sides destroyed it indiscriminately.

All normal life for these people had ceased and they were forced to eke out an existence like troglodytes in the cellars of their homes with no electricity, no water and no food. The streets and the countryside were littered with stinking bodies. Thousands were made homeless, their possessions lost or destroyed, their community and way of life gone forever. And all for nothing! I thought then that the people of Arnhem will never forgive us; and if Oosterbeck is ever rebuilt, the survivors and their descendants will probably hate us for generations to come. And as I was walking into captivity, carrying a dead German officer on a door, behind me the remnants of the brigade were still fighting, but just a short time away from defeat. I could hear the tanks firing as they battered their way into the town centre. Up ahead a German soldier was hustling along the Dutch family over the rubble. Was it too late to say sorry? Was anything gained from it all? I did get an apple!

An Unpleasant Incident – Bob Hilton

Shortly after being captured by the SS, I was taken to a mixed-bag group of captured Airborne types in a wood clearing. The group consisted of about thirty other ranks and three officers, of which I was one. The other two were a captain from the Glider Pilot Regiment named Muir, and an engineer lieutenant named Skinner. With the three of us at the head, we were marched down the road toward a German HQ. After we had gone a couple of miles everyone was exhausted, as we hadn't eaten a decent meal in days. We were also very thirsty, so I asked the officer in charge, an SS type, if we could fall out and get the chaps something to drink. He agreed to do this at the first opportunity, which he did. No sooner had we halted than a German with a Schmeisser machine pistol jumped from one of the slit trenches lining the road and opened fire. Captain Muir and Lieutenant Skinner got riddled, and a number of chaps behind us were also killed or wounded. Miraculously, although I was next to Muir and Skinner, I was not touched!

My first instinct was to scream at the SS officer and demand to know what the hell was going on, and he thereupon snatched a rifle from a nearby guard and shot the German with the Schmeisser stone dead. He then apologised to me, and said the reason was that all the troops were terrified of anyone with a red beret and would panic at the sight of us. He then asked me to give instructions to those remaining alive to remove their berets, which we did. Captain Muir was still alive, but in a pretty bad way, and pointed to his airborne smock pocket. I took out his wallet and he pointed to a picture of a person I took to be his wife and he endeavoured to make me understand to let her know what had happened. Just at that moment two rather fat German officers arrived in a staff car. One jumped out and gave me a kick in the ribs, knocking me over, then snatched the wallet from me just as Captain Muir died in my arms. When I got up I attended as quickly as possible to any others that were wounded. Fortunately, a German First Aid unit arrived and did what they could. After that we were marched away, leaving the dead and wounded to be taken care of by the Germans.

The Last Stand – Emrys Morgan

In those last days there were no battalions left; there were no cohesive units, almost no battalion officers, sergeants, and only a few corporals. Most of them were killed, wounded, or captured. There was no infantry as such; in its place were groups of engineers, signallers, glider pilots, cooks, drivers, mechanics and service corps, with a smattering of infantrymen, all fighting together and doing a good job of it too. While we bled to death an inch at a time, the Germans were always getting stronger. We hadn't met the old men and young boys we'd been told about; instead, we came up against an aggressive German soldier who was prepared to stand his ground and whittle us down, then melt away like quicksilver and appear somewhere else, always slowing us down, like a starving fox attacking a horse. By now we'd become cornered rats, sneaking from cellar to cellar, house to house, in small groups rarely strong enough to do serious damage, but strong to make them hunt us in packs. In some ways we were doing a better job of killing them than when we were in battalion size. We'd learned house fighting 'on the job' and the Germans had to winkle us out of each building. We had a warren of houses with large holes in the walls that ran the length of a row of houses so we could scamper from one place to another. They were always wary when they chased us as wires were often stretched across doorways and at the bottom of stairs, each attached to grenades, so they'd have to stop and check for the wires, which exposed them to being shot when they finally had the courage to step though. Their answer was to blow the houses down using tanks and self-propelled guns, or even worse, a flame-throwing tank.

We could hear a tank clanking along the cobbled surface of the road; it was probably a Panzer flamethrower as they had been using them more frequently these last few days, although it could be a Tiger. It didn't make a difference; tanks in built-up areas were vulnerable and needed infantry for protection, and they would follow it, ready to throw grenades into buildings and then spray machine pistol fire afterward. They didn't like going into houses, as they didn't have an advantage – they know it would be bloody. Some of us carried sharpened shovels that are an excellent close-quarter weapon; you can easily decapitate someone with it. Others used bayonets like fighting knives. In an all-out fight in a room, you simply don't have time to reload weapons. 'Wee Jock' had earned a new nickname, 'The Butcher', as he went feral when we were fighting inside houses. He swung his shovel like a madman, and the last time we took the Germans on he nearly sliced Tommy Wilson's arm off as he swung at a German's head. When it was all over and Jock had calmed down, Tom showed him the torn material in his smock and the neat cut where the shovel had sliced through it. Jock just smiled through the congealed blood that covered him from head to toe, blood that had come from the Germans he'd 'butchered'. Grinding its way around the corner came the Panzer; it was a flamethrower, and it was shooting fuel into the houses then sending a flame after it. By using this method, the fuel would run everywhere and then the flame would ignite it and engulf everything. Behind it came the protecting infantry, at least a platoon of them, and with them were two halftracks with MG42 machine guns mounted on them, then more infantry. We could hear the lads from two houses up charging through the holes in the wall toward us, as they didn't have an answer for a flamethrower. They jumped through each hole as the tripwires were almost invisible and most were placed at shin height, sometimes higher, and they didn't differentiate between the Germans and us.

The tank rumbled along the street and flamed several houses. Luckily there was nobody in them. The lads inside had taken off. The group that was on our side of the street ran through the hole into our room, out the next hole and disappeared down the stairs next door. Down there, in the room facing the road, there was a PIAT crew; they had two bombs left so they would wait until the last moment to fire each one off. We couldn't communicate with them so we prayed they would take on the tank, and if their luck held, the halftrack. The floor shook as the tank lumbered by. As luck would have it, it turned to flame the house on the opposite side of the street and there was a dull roar as it reached out and filled the house with fire. From not more than 20 feet away the PIAT crew fired into the side of the thing. There was an explosion as the bomb slammed into the side of the thing and the monster stopped dead. No sooner did we hear the bang than we were up and firing down onto the Germans from the two windows. A Bren gun, three Sten guns and a rifle can do a lot of damage in a small area like a street, especially if you throw a grenade as well. I remember looking straight into the face of one surprised German, then firing. His face literally popped like an apple being pulped, then I emptied the rest of my magazine into three or four others. We must have killed and wounded at least ten of them before they knew what was happening. The rest scattered.

The halftrack began firing at the windows but we had already bolted. We charged down the stairs next door and heard grenades going off in the room we'd just left. Cocking a PIAT is a sod of a job; it's like loading an ancient crossbow. But these two lads had got it to a fine art and as we ran past the door to the room where they were, there was another loud explosion; they'd got the first halftrack as well. Not long after we left the house by the back door they followed us. They didn't need the PIAT anymore, as they had no more rockets. It was dark when the Germans withdrew; they didn't like fighting in the night – they preferred to mortar us, or fire 88s, trying to force us out into the open. Stopping the Germans was like trying to stop a flood of water with only sandbags. Sooner or later the water found a way through the gaps and began its inexorable onward flow. A day later that flow had taken its toll; first Jock, then Tom, then Wally. How I was still standing I don't know.

A Drab Occasion – Clive Palmer

At Arnhem two batteries of 17-pounder anti-tank guns, plus an extra gun, went in with the 2nd Battalion to defend the now famous bridge. They eventually destroyed nearly fourteen armoured vehicles, including one Tiger tank, before running out of ammunition, after which the guns were spiked and what was left of the crews fought as infantry until the surrender. In the infantry role they gave a good account of themselves, proving that all the training that everyone got in both their own roles and that of the infantry worked. At one point a couple of gunners were fighting as part of my section and during a lull in the fighting one of the lads said jokingly to one gunner, 'See mate, now you know what it's like to fight at the sharp end!'

Over the sound of warfare, and even though all of us were exhausted from days of fighting, the reply from another gunner made all of us laugh: 'Yeah mate, but you gotta admit, having the Royal Artillery along adds a touch of extra colour to a battle that would otherwise be a monotonously dull, slash and bash event!'

The Polish Scapegoat, General Sosabowski – Jerzy Dyrda

General Sosabowski watched the unfolding horror from a point near the Driel dyke. It was clear his men were caught in a deathtrap and although some boats were managing to cross, too many troops were being killed to make the operation viable. He raced down to the riverbank and ordered his men to retire. Despite fearsome losses, and two attempts, around 250 Poles eventually made it to the Oosterbeek pocket to help in the final retreat out of Arnhem. One area where they were able to make a particular impression was at the crossroads of Utrechtse Weg–Station Weg. Here, the street fighting was exceptionally vicious even by the standards the 1st Airborne had shown at Arnhem, because they wouldn't give up an inch until they were literally exterminated like vermin. Only they weren't vermin, they were Poles fighting for Poland and all the terrible things the Nazis had done to their country, so no quarter given or expected. Following the bitter frustrations of the night before, the general was pleasantly surprised by the arrival of Lieutenant-

General Horrocks on the morning of 24 September. Both men discussed the tenuous situation of the 1st Airborne, with General Sosabowski suggesting that the 43rd Wessex Division and the Poles attempt to cross the Rhine several miles downriver from Driel, where enemy opposition wouldn't be expecting it and therefore it would be less strident. Later that day, he met Horrocks for a second time at a conference near Valburg, 5 miles south of Driel. Other generals present included Major-General Thomas, the commander of the 43rd Wessex Division, and General 'Boy' Browning, the commander of all airborne forces, who had arrived near Nijmegen on 21 September, transporting his HQ in thirty-eight gliders that would have been far better suited to bringing in a fighting unit or supplies for the beleaguered division, but that was conveniently ignored.

Entering a large tent, the British generals sat on one side of a conference table and motioned General Sosabowski to sit opposite like a criminal under investigation. No chair was made available for me, the general's English interpreter. The general was immediately informed that one of his battalions was to be seconded to General Thomas's command and would follow the 4th Dorset Battalion in another attempt to cross at the same site where the Poles had already lost so many men. Justifiably, General Sosabowski was far from happy that one of his battalions had been removed from his command without prior discussion. However, he set this point aside and tried to emphasise just how dangerous the plan was, that the Germans overlooking this point in the river had complete command of it and could pour a devastating amount of fire down on any attempt to cross. Once again he proposed an effort be made to cross the Rhine further downriver. In response, Major-General Thomas simply reiterated the initial orders and that was that, it had already been decided. Obviously they had concluded that his input was not needed. The general rose to his feet and, speaking in English, tried one last time to emphasise the futility of the campaign if no efforts were made to seek a sounder course of action. 'For eight days and nights not only Polish soldiers but also the best sons of England are dying there in vain, for no effect,' he added. The British generals remained stony-faced, deliberately ignoring his appeal. No sooner had he finished than General Horrocks called the meeting to a close with a curt, 'The conference is over. The orders given by General Thomas will be carried out.' I realised that the British generals had intentionally angered my commander. This strange conference was only intended to provoke him. They could then argue that his well-known independence and unyielding attitude made it impossible to organise efficient help for the airborne forces on the northern bank of the Rhine. They were prepared to sacrifice British and Polish soldiers simply to make a point.

Browning had stayed sombrely quiet at Valburg. He, Horrocks and Thomas already knew that the 1st Airborne was to be evacuated anyway. The decision to send over the Dorsets and us was simply a case of 'going through the motions' to avoid being blamed, regardless of the cost to those two battalions. As a sop to a guilty conscience, Browning invited General Sosabowski for lunch at his HQ in Nijmegen, leaving me at the junior officers' mess. The general returned an hour later in an excited state. Still seething from the 'conference', he was shocked when Browning admitted the operation that night would probably fail; he admitted in so many words that they were quite prepared to write off two battalions to create the impression they were doing all they could. The Englishman also confessed that the additional boats needed to cross the Rhine were struggling to get through the heavy traffic on the road leading through Nijmegen. For General Sosabowski it was the final straw and he'd voiced his opinion on the matter in the frankest of terms. 'I fear that my forthrightness hurt Browning's feelings, for he quickly indicated the end of our conversation.' One shred of good fortune for the general when he returned to Driel was the arrival of those Polish troops affected by the recall order on 19 September. They had landed at Grave a few days later and managed to hitch lifts all the way to Driel, making Browning's assertion about totally gridlocked roads extremely suspect. Comparatively fresh, my general decided the new arrivals would follow the British over the river.

Later that night, the Dorsets, along with our men, made their attempt to cross. Unsurprisingly, the effort rapidly turned into a nightmarish bloodbath and the operation was quickly called to a halt. It was now decided to initiate the evacuation of the Oosterbeek pocket – code-named Operation Berlin. In charge of transportation were newly arrived Canadian engineers, equipped with boats powered by outboard motors. A heavy downpour began on the evening of 25 September, making the movement of British and Polish troops heading to the north bank of the river for evacuation less susceptible to being detected. The Canadians worked bravely under fire until the first light of dawn and it was largely due to their sterling efforts that Operation Berlin was a success. The cost of Arnhem had been enormous. We Poles had also suffered, with 400 men listed as casualties – 23 per cent of our officers and 22 per cent of our other ranks. With failure came recrimination, and several British generals falsely tarred us, and the general, as a source of defeat. In a letter dated 17 October, Montgomery wrote to the Chief of the General Staff, Sir Alan Brooke, criticising our performance and demanding the general be replaced. But how could he have formed this opinion, given that he was nowhere near Driel during the campaign? The basis appears to be from talks he had with the others that were at the meeting with General Sosabowski, all of whom desperately wanted to cover up their own ineptitude by tarring him.

General Browning's attempt to smear the general's name was nothing short of libellous. In a letter dated 20 November to the deputy Chief of the General Staff, Lieutenant-General Sir Ronald Weeks, he declared the general unfit for command, and also raised doubts over the capability of the Polish brigade's fighting ability. In one sentence he added, 'This officer proved himself to be quite incapable of appreciating the urgent nature of the operation, and continually showed himself to be argumentative and loath to play his full part.' These are words from a man who had disregarded key intelligence, underestimated his enemy and went along with a plan he knew to be flawed, a man who had never been near to Driel during the fighting, and had failed, utterly, to push Horrocks into speeding up 30 Corps' effort to reach, and then cross, the Rhine and relieve the 1st Airborne. Like Montgomery, Browning requested that General

Sosabowski be replaced. Desperate to maintain haemorrhaging British support, the Polish government-in-exile acquiesced. The general was relieved of his command just after Christmas 1944. For the men of the Polish brigade it was an earth-shattering blow. We, and our general, were tainted because 30 Corps had failed badly in the planning and execution of Operation Berlin and wanted to cover up their leadership ineptitude. 'Colonel Blimp' was alive and well in the British Army.

Montgomery's Phantoms at Arnhem – Peter James Parfitt

It always shocked me that our radios couldn't do the job they were intended for at Arnhem. How could we have got it so wrong when we'd had the opportunity to get it right well before the landing? The 1st Brigade could not only have better co-ordinated its advance into Arnhem on Sunday 17 and 18 September, but it could have requested an early dispatch of reinforcements when they realised the difficulties they were in. Instead they had to wait until those back on the drop zone grew concerned over the lack of news and sent reinforcements in piecemeal formation in the general direction of the battle. Meanwhile, the 1st Brigade had to grope its way forward literally blindfolded. At one point, during a co-ordinated attack in the Arnhem area, the 1st and 3rd Battalions passed within several hundred yards of each other and did not realise it. The early stages of the battle are littered with accounts of small pockets of men fighting their own private actions without really knowing where they were or who was around them. With the gravity of the situation unclear, the 4th Brigade committed itself to an advance on 19 September, too late to force a way through to the bridge. Had the communications been working, they would most likely have abandoned it as a futile effort. It was not until units gathered in firm, static defensive positions, either at Arnhem Bridge or in the Oosterbeek Perimeter, that the division could put an end to this wasteful sacrifice of its infantry.

It was critical that the division could contact 30 Corps from the moment it landed, but it couldn't during the early stages of the battle. Nobody was able to contact 30 Corps Headquarters at Nijmegen, and many days passed before the outside world began to appreciate just how serious the situation was. As a result of this silence, the second lift could not be warned that all was not going well, nor could 30 Corps be urged to press on with all speed. It was not until Thursday 21 September that the division was able to establish its only reliable link with the ground forces on the other side of the river, via the gunners of the 64th Medium Regiment. Perhaps the most tragic loss was that of air support. The British fighter-bombers of the 2nd Tactical Air Force could have brought down decisive fire upon German troops and armour, yet they could not be contacted. Efforts were made to retune the radio sets, but very soon all were put out of action by mortar fire. The fighters circling overhead could not seek and destroy enemy targets on their own initiative as they were under strict orders to await requests from observers on the ground. The flaw in this system was exposed at Arnhem, and so it was that the crucial air superiority of the Allies, which had been gained after years of struggle and thousands of lives, was wasted.

Yet there was a signals unit embedded with Urquhart's HQ that had the capability to send and receive messages throughout the battle. It was a secret unit called 'Phantoms', highly skilled signallers who only took orders from Montgomery and nobody else. They were under strict instructions not to reveal what they did because they were there to spy on the division, as they had spied on other divisions since Montgomery took over in the desert campaign. They used the same 22 sets that the rest of the Army used. Their secret was the aerials on these sets, which again were the same as the rest of the Army, only they had found a way to reconfigure them. This could be done in next to no time; anyone could have done it if they had known, but the Phantoms never showed anyone how to do it. This alone could have changed the outcome of the battle. But even then there was another flaw. Someone in the Phantoms who gave out their transmission frequencies used the same one as the British Broadcasting Corporation frequency, so whenever they tried to send signals it was blocked by the BBC overseas service.

8

Over the Rhine and Walking to the Baltic

The Mad Artillery Major – Clive Parsons

On the first day all the airborne division's objectives had been taken on the far side of the Rhine. Anti-aircraft and small-arms fire had taken a toll on the gliders and parachutists alike, and many gliders missed their intended LZs because of smoke from over the river, intended to cover the river crossing by ground-based troops. The artillery units, in the absence of any major threat, settled into their positions and awaited orders. Only one episode disturbed the comparative peace of the first night. In the small hours a mixed force of about 100 Germans stumbled over our RHQ, purely by accident. They were fleeing the battlefield in disarray. Glider pilots, who were providing all-round defence, had challenged them and they had immediately withdrawn into the woods and initially tried to hide while they sorted themselves out. On hearing the disturbance, one of the regiment's fearless majors calmly walked out into the darkness, brandishing his Webley pistol and swagger cane, and found the heavily armed Germans crowded together, trying to decide which way to go around RHQ without having a fight. The glider pilots were astonished to hear his voice in the darkness say, 'I know where you are so unless you want me to get angry, you chaps ought to surrender. If you don't I will be forced to shoot.' There was a long period of silence then the major said, 'Drop your weapons, put your hands up and follow me, and no silly tricks!' Five minutes later he led the Germans into RHQ area and arranged for an armed guard to be put on them. Thereafter, everyone agreed that he was definitely insane.

Parking Space – Martin Reynolds

The Allied airlift over the Rhine consisted of 541 transport aircraft containing parachutists and a further 1,050 troop carriers towing 1,350 gliders. The American 17th Airborne Division consisted of 9,387 personnel, who were transported in 836 C-47 Skytrain transports, 72 C-46 Commando transports, and more than 900 Waco CG-4A gliders. The British 6th Airborne Division consisted of 7,220 personnel transported by 42 Douglas C-54 and 752 C-47 Dakota transport aircraft, as well as 420 Airspeed Horsa and General Aircraft Hamilcar gliders. This vast armada stretched more than 200 miles in the sky and took 2 hours and 37 minutes to pass any given point. It was protected by some 2,153 Allied fighters from the US 9th Air Force and the RAF. The combination of the two divisions in one lift made this the largest airborne drop in history in a single day. At 1000 hours, the parachute drop began. I was a staff sergeant pilot of a Hamilcar glider and my co-pilot was from the RAF, Flying Officer Terry Blackwood. As we flew in formation toward the Rhine, we could see the first of the anti-aircraft fire we would have to fly through. It was really amazing as the Germans had already been bombed, rocketed, shelled and machine-gunned not an hour previously. We crossed the river and prepared to cast off when Terry casually turned to me and asked, 'Have you booked us a parking space or will it be the usual all-out fight for a spot?'

I casually answered as he released us from the towing aircraft, 'I tried to book but was told to bugger off, first in first served!'

He replied, 'I hate that. Some idiots just don't care where they park. I think they should introduce fines for getting it wrong!'

As some flak exploded right next to us, shaking the hell out of the glider, I remember saying, 'A bloody fat chance of that; especially as the worst offenders are the bloody RAF!'

When we landed, we had no sooner stopped than another glider took the tip off our port wing. We were both badly shaken by it as it could easily have crashed into us. But Terry had the last word when he said, 'The bugger would have to have been an Army driver!'

The Rhine Landings – Stanley Holloway

Our next big battle happened when we flew over the Rhine in broad daylight, something a lot of us weren't too happy about as the Germans could use us like a ducks on a shooting gallery. I was standing at the door and christened the river by throwing an orange down on it. The next thing I noticed was the American dispatcher putting on his flak suit, which was slightly worrying! Then I didn't see any more of him. As we got to the drop zone I could see where we were going. The thing that struck me most at the time was the amount of flak that was surrounding the aircraft – the Germans really were pumping a lot of it into the Dakotas and Whitleys, and no doubt they'd have a field day with the gliders, but that didn't deter me; I simply had to conquer my fear once again. The red light came on, then the green, and my batman, Private Henry Gospel, was right behind me shouting, 'I'm right behind you, Sir!' and out we went! Although I felt the loud zip of machine-gun bullets coming right by me it didn't seem very long before I was on the ground and out of my harness. I threw away my helmet, put on my red beret and grabbed my Sten gun. The commanding officer had told us to put on our red berets as soon as we had landed in order to 'put the fear of God into the Germans'. As I moved off, I found myself with a platoon of Americans who had dropped on the wrong DZ and they now joined my company as we started to move off the drop zone towards the farm, which was our objective. The most amazing thing was watching the whole battalion in the air in one go – in fact, the whole brigade. The entire division, including the gliders, was on the ground within forty-five minutes in what we would call a saturation drop. But I have to say there were a lot of casualties in the air in both aircraft and men.

Once we were on the ground, we were immediately faced with the enemy. One of my platoons to my left captured a machine-gun position after a savage firefight and we started taking prisoners – the Germans were suddenly giving themselves up all over the place. There was a lot of firing going on – even 88mm and 20mm guns were firing on a level trajectory at ground targets. Yet one seemed to be oblivious to what was happening because once you had landed, it was into action straight away and your mind focused on what needed to be done rather than worrying about getting shot. There was the objective and that is what we went for – in many cases wearing our red berets and shouting our heads off. Like the commanding officer and all the company commanders in the battalion, I had a hunting horn. We each had our different calls to muster our men. I blew mine, calling my company as we went for specific objectives. My batman was still with me, saying, 'Right behind you, Sir!' as we took a farm with no problems. We then secured the place and it was all over pretty quickly. While we were at the farm the CO, Lieutenant-Colonel Peter Luard, and the divisional commander joined us. We invited them for breakfast and my batman cooked us all bacon and eggs.

The ground was covered in mist and haze, created by the bombardment from our guns and the smoke generators from the other side of the river, and it was very difficult to see. This caused a lot of problems for our gliders. I think that the saddest thing I saw was when we were moving towards our battalion objective, in the direction of Hamminkeln. There were glider pilots still sitting in their cockpits, having been roasted alive after their gliders had caught fire. They were melted into unrecognisable pieces of flesh and bone. A lot of people were lost like that; although we parachutists had lost quite a lot of casualties in the air, it was nowhere near what those poor devils in the gliders had. One of the major problems, as far as we were concerned, was that the 3rd Brigade was the first to go in and they had been dropped about ten minutes too early. Consequently, the artillery bombardment had to be lifted so that by the time that 5th Brigade and the rest arrived, the enemy were able to recover and organise themselves. That's why there was such a godawful lot of flak on my aircraft. However, there was nothing that could be done about it; it was then a question of rooting the enemy out of all the buildings. They put up some stiff resistance for the first few hours, but once they could see it was the 'Red Devils', as they called us, they started to give up pretty quickly.

The Flying Brick – Billy Griffin

We were packed in the back of the Horsa like sardines in a tin, and as usual the armchair experts who had told us it would be basically an unopposed landing couldn't have got it more wrong. Jerry may have been bombed, rocketed and shelled, but he was far from finished and he was throwing everything at us bar the kitchen sink. The glider was shaking as the flak exploded nearby and bits of shrapnel cut through the outer skin like a knife through butter. The moment we cast off, the pilot dropped the nose down so much I thought we were going to roll on to our back. And he held it there until the very last moment, when he applied the huge wing flaps, lifted the nose, and we hit the ground with an almighty bang and skidded along, bouncing and spinning out of control. Except for the flaps, once you're on the ground where you go is pure luck. We hit something big and spun around and there was a great tearing sound as part of the port wing got ripped off. I thought this is it, we're done for, when suddenly we came to an instant jarring halt and the whole fuselage lifted up to a forty-five-degree angle before smashing down onto the ground. Bodies went everywhere and there was pandemonium as the lads picked each other up, swore and cursed the pilot, and pulled mates from under the scattered debris. The platoon commander took charge and we all scrambled around for our weapons and kit, slashed open the sides of the Horsa and jumped out.

Miraculously, there were no serious injuries, just shock, cuts, severe bruising and a couple of the lads with broken arms. Everyone thought the crew must have been killed, but they too walked away with only minor cuts and bruising. A miracle had happened right there in the middle of a battlefield. We were lucky as the Jerries weren't bothered with us as they had enough targets to keep them happy already. As we got ready to move off, the senior pilot, an RAF flying officer with the typical handlebar moustache, shouted out in plum-like tones, 'I say chaps that that was jolly good fun, wasn't it. Anyone want to try it again when all this vulgar violence business is over with?'

Guarding Prisoners – Edward Shank

I was a platoon commander when my battalion landed on the far side of the Rhine. The platoon had been given the job of sweeping the LZs and clearing any German opposition still there. In front of us was a large farmhouse and I instructed everyone to be careful, as it would be a good place for the Germans to ambush us. With one section ready to give covering fire, the rest of us came at it from two sides. We cautiously entered it and found an artillery OP in the upstairs rooms, directing heavy artillery fire from over the other side of the Rhine. As I stood there talking to one of the artillery officers, my sergeant came up to me and said I should look at something. He took me out to a huge barn behind the house. It was full to overflowing with German prisoners, and guarding them was a private sitting on a chair with one leg all bandaged up and a Bren gun across his knee. The two of us walked over to him and he apologised for not getting up and saluting. I said that it wasn't a problem, and then I added, 'Aren't you a little bit worried about being on your own guarding so many prisoners?'

He replied, 'Nay a problem at all Sor, they're like sheep! Mind yew, if they knew that I dinna have a firing pin in the gun it could be a wee bit different!' and he smiled.

Free Trip – Freddy Hogan

A miracle happened when we landed on the far side of the Rhine. We had just got out of the Horsa when another one came hurtling straight toward us. Naturally, we all dived on to the ground but young Harry was a bit slow; we put it down to him being a big strapping farm boy. Anyway, he just stood there even though we all shouted for him to get down. The other glider was slightly tilted, so one wing was near the ground and it struck ours on the side and broke off the left wing of our glider, then it spun around in a big circle. As it did, its other wing literally picked up Harry by the back of his legs like a rag doll and we all watched him disappear. We thought he must be dead; nobody could possibly survive that kind of thing. Anyway, our officer, Lieutenant Henderson, got the rest of us together and we emptied the glider and were just going to move off when Harry appeared. We could tell he wasn't a happy man, but he was alive, limping badly, probably had a few cracked ribs, and bad bruising. It turns out that the other glider careered on for a further 50 yards or so and then stopped suddenly, flinging Harry on to the ground. The men inside scrambled out and began to unload the thing when Harry was noticed. The platoon commander saw him wandering around in a bit of a daze; well you couldn't miss him, as he was 6 foot 2 inches tall and built like a brick toilet. So he stopped Harry and evidently said, 'You're not one of my lads, does your platoon commander know you want to join our platoon?'

A Letter to My Father – Huw Pyrs Wheldon
Father – The flight was itself highly unpleasant, my glider pilot being a poor hand at the job, and was having difficulties, immeasurably increased by a sky full of slipstreams and air disturbances from aircraft ahead. The whole firmament was spotted and crossed with aircraft. We swung about, and long before we reached the Rhine apprehension was crawling into every man's brain. As we approached the Rhine, a pall of smoke from Montgomery's screen became evident. The Rhine could be seen through it, a silver ribbon shining through the uniform grey. Ahead, the other aircraft were still going on, and by now we could see bombers who had released their paratrooper loads and gliders dropping downward on our flanks. The smoke underneath grew thicker, and I could see very little. Ahead we suddenly saw the silent flak explosions. Knowing we had another four minutes to go, and hating the thought like hell, I got into my seat and strapped myself in. A moment later the pilot cast off from the tug.

I knew quite well he'd cast off too early, but I welcomed the snapping-sound as the tow-rope swung loose. Cowardly, as ever, I was only too pleased to be coming down. For me, strapped in, the descent was blind. We bumped a bit, and I recognised this as flak. After some little time I saw the ground through the little window and knew we were within 50 feet of our landing. Simultaneously, there was a methodical, impersonal crackle, and machine-gun bullets tore little holes in the fabric overhead, missing everyone. Then we landed in a splintering crash and then sudden quiet. No more wind was passing through the fuselage. The machine gun fired more briskly and everyone unstrapped like mad and made for the exits. The crash had buckled my seat, and my equipment had got stuck between the seat and the side. I was consequently trapped. At the time it seemed ludicrous, and I grinned at my musical comedy situation, the bullets zipping by my head doing absolutely nothing to disturb my thoughts, which were indescribable, almost insane.

In the end I grasped my smock and pulled it off and in this way extricated myself. Diving out the door, I found all the boys all unhurt in a ditch alongside the smashed glider; many of them gave that kind of look that said 'Where the Hell have you been?', and I don't blame them as in situations like this leadership from the front is essential. Beyond the glider, hidden to us, was a farmhouse, some 70 yards away, and in this farm was the machine gun. I decided to leave it to someone else, and led off in dead ground to a little wood. The sky was still full of aircraft in astonishing numbers, and on the ground all over the place were gliders and parachutes; my own chaps, paratroopers, chaps feverishly unloading guns, hundreds of American, miles from their objective, and far away, above the pendant smoke, the quiet sun. I found out where we were, and two hours later, after a rum journey, I found the Battalion, all objectives taken, our ebullient Glyn, the regimental medical officer, considering he was my brother-in-law, was still with us thank God, but many have not made it, including my CSM, old McCutcheon, the loyallest and most devoted soldier I ever saw, and a very great personal loss. There were hundreds and hundreds of prisoners, all digging away like mad on our positions, while our chaps stood happily by smoking cigars like the Lords of Creation.

On my way in to the position, moving along the edge of a wood, I suddenly stumbled on three Boche, not 5 yards away. I was unarmed, the magazine having dropped out of my pistol some time before, and all I had in my hand was a ration pack taken from a discarded haversack to make up for my own that was left in the glider. I was naturally petrified with horror. As soon as they saw me, the three Boche dropped to their knees and begged me not to shoot. With superb magnanimity I showed mercy, forbearing to throw my ration pack at them, and wheeled them in, now grist to the mill. My own company did magnificently, storming a position, killing many Boche in the process and taking over a hundred prisoners. I was away at the time and did not share this action; possibly fortunately, as under me it might have been a more academic advance and far less deadly. No casualties there thank the Lord, but then he'd already helped cut a big swath through our ranks already.

Hamminkeln – Over the Rhine – Ken Giles

Inside the Horsa there was absolute chaos. We had come through the intense anti-aircraft barrage and the machine-gun fire, only to hit the ground like an out-of-control roller coaster. We'd rebounded off one crashed glider, hit another and taken off a wing, finally coming to rest against a bank. Inside there were several dead and injured. Five minutes later, those on their feet were running, shouting, cursing and shooting. Guns, jeeps and trailers were being hauled out of other gliders and parts of gliders were scattered about the landscape at crazy, impossible angles. From all directions, more gliders kept coming in to land. Our faithful transport, home for the past few hours, was now abandoned, skewed across the field with one wing snapped off and its back broken, its job done and our relatively safe arrival a testimony to the skill and cool bravery of the pilots. I certainly thought of them as one of the larger, jeep-carrying gliders, ablaze from about half way along its fuselage, flew low over our heads like a flaming torch before hitting the ground and skidding along on its belly to come to rest in a blazing pyre of broken wings and fuselage. Nobody got out of it, but not far away other gliders that had flown through the blaze of anti-aircraft fire successfully disgorged their human and material cargo even though they were battered and tattered.

Through it all, a haze of thick smoke and mist was pierced by the sun, still shining as if the world was completely normal and not a holocaust of death and fire. For an eternity nobody seemed to know what to do, where to go, at least from where I was lying. Eventually someone, it could have been our platoon commander, took charge, ordering us to run like hell for some nearby cover, where we joined up with more of our scattered company. From there we took stock while the lieutenant decided where we were in relation to where we should have been. We could see that there had been five casualties from our platoon; four were still in the glider dead, and one was lying 100 yards away, between the broken glider and us. From the unnatural position of his body, and by its stillness, I was sure he was dead too, but while I was rehearsing in my mind the many reasons why I couldn't go and check that this was true, someone else had rushed out to him and came back with his rifle, which they then used. Only then did I realise how scared I was. I'd been chewing gum since the last stages of the flight and it had literally turned to powder in my mouth, a phenomenon that I would not have believed possible had I not experienced it.

The apparent chaos evolved into some semblance of order and the company moved off to help take our first objective, the town of Hamminkeln, about a mile or so down the road. Not too far, unless you are being sniped at for most of the way. But we eventually got there and proceeded to move through the town, house by house. I was ordered to the upstairs room of one house to keep an eye on a church, which was the source of some of the sniping. I was supposed to stand by an open window and watch for the flash of gunfire and return fire, keeping the German's head down while part of the company advanced to the next objective and cleared the church from the ground up. It occurred to me that if I can see a German's rifle flash then the German can also see mine. Sure enough there were Germans there. So I let off a few shots in their general direction, ducked down until they returned fire, then bobbed up very briefly for a quick shot to keep them quiet. I didn't know about their heads but I kept mine down most of the time. I yelled out that there were definitely Germans in the church tower, two windows down from the top, and the lads fired a PIAT rocket into it not long afterwards and I was able to come down.

As we slowly advanced the Germans were forced back, but they put up a good fight. When we got to the outskirts, there was yet another building reportedly holding more snipers and three of us were ordered to flush out its occupants. There was no cover anywhere so we rushed the place and made it to the front door. I threw in a grenade and we followed it. There was a lot of smoke coming from the top floor, where one of the others had lobbed two more grenades, and then two of us raked the ceiling with Sten gun fire. There was a dull thud as if someone had fallen over and then silence. The other lad rushed upstairs, firing his Sten gun as he went. He came back down and told us there were five dead Germans up there; all of them were Volkssturm, old men in odd bits of uniform – they weren't even proper fighting soldiers. As far as we were concerned, the town of Hamminkeln was now ours.

Was the Cost Really Worth It? – John 'Snowy' Wiley

We were now down to 450 feet and underneath the trajectory of the 88mm guns, although the machine guns and multiple 20mm cannon were still having a field day. I was looking out of the cockpit window, over the shoulder of one of the pilots, when I saw a Hamilcar glider ahead of us bracketed by 20mm cannon fire break in two as it was hit. The tail slowly came off, as did one wing, and then it gently turned on to its back and spiralled earthward; black smoke followed it downwards. Below and slightly in front of us was a small village, which must be Hamminkeln, our objective. The pilot suddenly shouted 'Stand By!' and we all interlocked arms and lifted our feet, bracing ourselves for the crash-landing, for that's exactly what it was, like all landings; once you hit the ground, the only thing the pilots could do was use the huge wing flaps to slow the glider down. There was a loud, harsh noise as we collided with the ground and the landing gear came up through the floor. We literally bounced into the air three times, and finally slithered along the ground towards the houses ahead. It seemed we would never stop before colliding with them. As it was, two

houses took off our wings and a large shed in between acted
as our final brake. It smashed the nose of the glider to a pulp
and killed both pilots, but by a miracle, although it threw us
around, it stopped short of seriously injuring any of us.

There was no time to worry about the pilots so the platoon
commander was up and screaming 'Go! Go! Go!' and was the
first out the door, followed by Corporal Trubshaw. I was next.
Both of them never made it – they were knocked back into me
by a machine gun that opened fire from about 200 yards away.
Behind me there was a mad rush and I was pushed forward and
by sheer luck escaped getting shot as the two bodies absorbed
the impact of the rounds and then just fell to the ground. I just
scrambled over the bodies and threw myself on to the ground.
The machine gun killed another couple of the lads as they
emerged. In all, we lost five men getting out of the glider and
had six wounded. Those of us that got out poured fire into the
building where the machine gun was and it stopped firing. But
now we had another problem. German artillery and mortars
had now begun to pound the LZ and surrounding fields. In
one way we were lucky as we were actually on the outskirts
of Hamminkeln and the guns weren't registered on the village.

Before I moved I was totally mesmerised as I watched two
Horsa gliders attempt to land nearby. One tipped up on its
nose and fell over on to its back; the other hit the ground with
its starboard wing and cartwheeled before becoming upright. I
saw a couple of men scrambling out of the second one; nobody
got out of the other one. I also watched a Dakota trailing flames
with men still trying to get out of it; it crashed just beyond the
village. Meanwhile, one of our heavily laden Hamilcar gliders
came in very low over the LZ. You could see the tracer rounds
hitting it, some going right through. I prayed that they would
make it, but it smashed into a railway signalbox and broke
up like a child's glider when it nose-dived into the ground. By
now, all around us there was organised chaos as units pushed
forward to their objectives regardless of their casualties. As
we entered Hamminkeln there was a church tower that cost
us a few men as it had snipers in it that were picking off easy
targets. As I was a sniper myself, I tried to fire on them, but I

was so close to the church all I could see was the very top of their helmets. The CO organised a 6-pound anti-tank gun to sort the problem out. It blew the tower to pieces, and we were in no mood to take one of them who survived as a prisoner when he came out of the church door with half a grin on his face. The Germans had also fortified a number of houses and we had to use PIATs on them before we rushed them. At one point we were getting fired upon from somewhere down the end of a street. The CSM yelled at me to sort the problem out before we lost any more men so I carefully looked at where he could possibly be firing from through my telescopic sight. The obvious place was a large house and a slight movement in the back of a darkened room caught my eye. Once I looked closer, I saw it was a boy of no more than sixteen or seventeen years of age. He was resting his rifle on a couple of sandbags set on a table in the middle of the room, typical of someone trained as a sniper. I didn't hesitate. I shot him in the head and clearly saw the impact of the round knock his head back and send him backwards. I never felt any emotion as I had seen too many of my mates killed the same way. Some time later, two of us went to confirm the kill and sure enough he was there, dead. He was no more than seventeen years of age, one of Herr Hitler's SS Hitlerjugend judging by his collar tags.

The battalion took about 120 prisoners, mostly older men and some Hitler Youth. Unlike the one I shot, these weren't fanatics. They were not exactly the cream of the SS that we'd expected, but they were fighting for their Fatherland and had put up stern resistance. Once captured, they seemed relieved that their war was over, while we had another six weeks of fighting before we met up with the Russians in the Baltic and called it a day. But for me, at least, the battle of the Rhine was over and, amazingly, it had only taken just over two hours since we landed, so I suppose the generals would be claiming it a resounding success, but the cost – was it worth it in the end? By the time we got to the Baltic, we'd lost another 150 odd men and had some 200 wounded. I couldn't help but wonder why the two airborne divisions didn't land as dawn was breaking. But after the debacle of Arnhem I had a strong suspicion that Monty didn't particularly worry how many men got killed as we'd won the war by then; it was simply a mopping-up operation. The public relations team that followed him everywhere would call it a great victory, Monty would be hailed a hero once again, and the general public would be happy, except those that lost their sons, brothers, or fathers. I remember reading many years later a newspaper story about the Rhine operation. Apparently, Monty took over a large chateau overlooking the Rhine and invited the Prime Minister and a heap of American generals. Unknown to Monty and Churchill at the time, the American General George Patton, Montgomery's worst enemy, had already crossed the Rhine on the night of 22 March and established a 6-mile-deep bridgehead after capturing 19,000 German troops. Patton, who was actually told not to do it, ignored the order and did so without an artillery barrage or bombing. The Americans did not tell Churchill and Montgomery until the night of 23 March; we jumped in at 10 a.m. on the morning of the 24th and Montgomery was furious, as up until then he simply detested Patton – afterwards he hated him. Anyway, they all sat down to enjoy a sumptuous breakfast under the chandeliers. And as 10 a.m. approached, they went out on the balcony to witness this great armada of planes flying over their heads. I hope they were suitably impressed as my mates and I would gladly have exchanged places with any one of them.

A Medic at the Rhine – John Cooper

After circling the airfield to get into formation, we set off for Germany. We'd been warned that the weather was poor and to expect a bumpy ride. The 195th Field Ambulance occupied thirteen gliders out of the total armada of 1,300. The flight was uneventful until we neared the Rhine, where a smokescreen set up by our land troops covered the countryside. This made it extremely difficult for the pilots to determine where our LZ was. The LZ comprised a circle approximately 20 miles in diameter with the nearest point to the Rhine some 10 miles east of the river. We would occupy half while the Yanks occupied the other half. Not only was there flak, it was accurate and targeted specific gliders and aircraft. Creating further problems, our own fighter escort weaved in and out of the gliders and dived to attack specific flak guns. Although, as promised, there was little heavy artillery fire, it has to be remembered that the gliders were made out of plywood and therefore were very susceptible to light AA or anti-aircraft fire, and even to small-arms fire.

We were cast off at 3,000 feet and came down to ground level in three swoops, and below 2,000 feet machine guns targeted us. Despite the warnings received at the briefing, the undercarriage of our glider did catch the power lines, and we nose-dived into a ploughed field. The skid, in addition to the tricycle wheels, was forced through the floor of our glider, later leading to difficulties in getting the jeep out. All of us inside thought it was the end when we crashed so heavily into the ground, so half hanging in and half hanging out of our seat straps, we clumsily released ourselves. My instructions were that I was to be first out of the rear section. I would then receive the packs of the remaining occupants. This I did. My first sight on disembarking was an 88mm self-propelled gun. Fortunately, it was pointing away from us. While fortunate for us, it was not fortunate for a Hamilcar glider. Larger than our Horsa, the Hamilcar landed and proceeded to unload its cargo of two armoured cars laden with ammunition. The first of these had just reached the foot of the ramp when the 88mm gun scored a direct hit, sending the whole assembly into the air in a terrible explosion. I don't think anyone on the Hamilcar could have survived. I prayed they wouldn't look in our direction, but they had plenty of targets to choose from. There was nothing left for it but to get on with my job and when I'd finally put all our packs on the ground, I noticed a hole some 24 inches in diameter through the tail of the glider. It wasn't far from the place that I had just recently been occupying. It sent a cold chill down my spine. In Normandy, fighting had taken place over a period of two or three weeks over the landing zone, and a great deal of damage had occurred to the gliders.

At the briefing before our most recent departure, however, we had been told to be careful not to cause unnecessary damage to the gliders, that it might be wise to recover them for further use. Did these people who came out with these stupid ideas even have an indication of what it is like on an LZ when you're under fire? Anyhow, we set about disconnecting the glider's tail section and according to the drill that we had performed on many occasions this was accomplished by unscrewing eight quick-release bolts. We had to take care to release the last two simultaneously, at which point the tail would fall away from the fuselage. This was done most meticulously, but nothing happened. In an effort to dislodge the tail, we swung on it. It was all to no avail, because all that happened was that the glider rocked on to its belly! It seemed ridiculous that in the middle of a battle we were swinging on a glider's tail like a bunch of naughty children. Then someone realised the pilots weren't anywhere to be seen. So off we went to look for them. They were trapped in the smashed cockpit and couldn't get out. So in the end we said 'Bugger it' and we decided that the only course of action was to chop away the glider's nose. This we did, and the pilots were eventually released.

We now had a nose-less glider with the hole large enough for the jeep to be driven out. The driver started up the engine and released the clutch. However, due to the damage to the floor the jeep's wheels were resting on the ploughed earth and simply spun around. A solution was quickly found as German machine guns were firing in every direction. Bits of the glider were pushed under the wheels. Consequently, when the driver engaged the clutch again, the jeep shot out like a champagne cork from a bottle. It travelled 100 yards before he could stop and return to us. He was still shaken when he did as a sniper took a shot at him and hit the steering wheel. I've never seen a jeep reverse so fast. We loaded the equipment on to the jeep, but after a discussion to determine the direction of the assembly point, machine-gun fire persuaded us to take refuge in a nearby farmhouse. We found a glider party of eight from brigade headquarters had already occupied the house. Not a minute before we arrived, two of them that had been outside behind a wall had got shot. Four of our party dashed out and brought them in and tended to them. Unfortunately, one died a minute or so later; the other one had a serious wound through his shoulder. Luckily we had the medical ability and stores to help him and we took him with us when we left.

The officer in charge, seeing that I had a revolver, detailed me to guard one side of the house. So there I was at an open window, protected only by a mattress, armed with a pistol with which I doubted I could hit a barn door at six paces. Fortunately, I was not called upon to prove it. At approximately 15.00, we saw the brigade major, a very tall Scot wearing a kilt, stroll across the landing zone as if he was out for a leisurely walk in Hyde Park. How he was never killed I don't know as he stood out like a red lamp post in the middle of Dartmoor. We were advised that our route to the main dressing station was clear, and so with the wounded man on the jeep we headed in its direction. When we got there we were immediately put to work. The initial casualties had been fairly heavy. A first count revealed a loss of 40 per cent of the brigade. A number had been taken prisoner, only to be released after a brief period, and were therefore able to rejoin their units.

Of the thirteen gliders carrying 195th Field Ambulance personnel, one came down in Holland. Another, with fifteen personnel, was captured as it landed, although the Americans released them a few hours later. A third, carrying twenty-five personnel, was also captured, and they remained prisoners of war till the end of the hostilities. Because of the number of casualties, I was put on stretcher duties. At midnight, half the unit was stood down and I was able to get some sleep till 06.00, at which time I had to complete a report for divisional headquarters. Finally, we ate some breakfast. It was the first meal we'd had since leaving England over twenty-four hours earlier, although we'd been sustained during that time by cigarettes. During the afternoon the 15th Scottish Division, spearheading the land troops, reached us after crossing the river. Some of them seemed to have a problem with distinguishing our men from the Germans and there were a few angry confrontations because of it. The Field Ambulance moved on 26 March. Travelling some 30–40 miles a day, on the way we passed numerous unarmed and unguarded Germans soldiers, twenty to thirty in number. Some were Fallschirmjäger, and if they were giving up then the war was near its end, thank God.

Walking to the Baltic – Eddie Horrell

As we formed up, it was a perfect morning with cloudless blue skies. We crossed the Channel, an unforgettable sight as we passed the coast of Belgium and flew over Brussels, with tug-planes and gliders going gently up and down behind them as far as the eye could see. The American 17th Airborne used Waco gliders, much smaller than our Horsas, so one of their tug-planes towed two Wacos. They weren't as well built as our gliders and the lads didn't like them. The Rhine soon came into view and we passed over it and on to our target, the village of Hamminkeln, which was an important road and rail junction. Our job was to capture and hold it until the land forces crossing the Rhine could join us. It was all jokes and songs up until that point, but once we crossed the river conversation dropped off and everyone became strangely quiet. The inside of a glider is dark, with only a few small windows. Looking out we could see thick walls of smoke from the smokescreens the army had been using to hide their movements from the Germans. It had drifted across our LZ and it was extremely difficult to see the ground. I remember thinking, 'I hope the bloody pilots can see where they're going.' Then there was complete silence apart from the swish of the wind as our tug cast us off. This was it: no going back or opening up the throttle for another circuit! If things don't look good, you just sit there and hope the pilots will do a good job, with a bit of help from the Almighty if he's in a good mood.

I was sitting at the back, right in the tail of the glider, and as we went into a steep dive I remember being fascinated by little patches of white light appearing in the fuselage; it took me several seconds to realise these were made by pieces of shrapnel coming through the fabric. We seemed to be diving for a hell of a long time, so much so that it didn't seem possible that the pilots could lift the nose up we were at such an angle. Suddenly, the huge wing flaps went down and the nose lifted and we hit the ground with a terrific crash. I don't think we rolled more than 10 yards; the pilots had put us down right on the button. But at what cost, as both of them were dead, together with the first six men behind them, and there were several injured. I was slightly hurt, as well as Nick, my best mate, but we scrambled out of the glider to do our job of blowing off its tail. The rest took up a defensive position, ready to get all the equipment out. No sooner were we outside than we were coming under heavy machine-gun fire. We managed to place our demolition charge while the others gave us covering fire. Just as we were getting ready to blow it, Nick gasped and collapsed, blood going all over me. As I caught him I saw he had two bullet holes through the neck, which had killed him instantly. He was another of our original crowd, we'd been together since 1940; it was like losing a brother. Our officer told everyone to take cover in a nearby ditch, sort ourselves out and proceed to wipe out that damned machine gun, which we did. Everyone opened fire on it, including the two Bren gunners. I saw one of the crew throw up his arms and fall sideways and the gunner's helmet literally lift off his head as rounds hit it, and the gun stopped firing.

The scene around us was beggaring description, with dozens of Horsas landing, some in flames, Waco and Hamilcar gliders coming in and paratroopers dodging in between them. One glider landed and collided with a group of men dodging their way across the LZ. It was like knocking down skittles. It seems the dense smoke had confused the pilots, and in some cases had blotted out the landing areas completely. I saw a Hamilcar glider hit in mid-air about 500 feet up. The 20mm anti-aircraft shells seemed to lazily arc upwards then tore into the front of the glider, smashing into the nose. What was left swung open like an over door and a 17-pounder gun with its tractor and crew spilled out in mid-air, spinning over and over as they fell. Moments later there was an almighty explosion as something inside detonated and what was left of the Hamilcar crashed into the ground in a hundred burning bits. I saw the gliders of Beethoven Company, whose job it was to knock out an 88mm anti-aircraft battery, landing smack on top of it, the gun barrels ended up poking right through the wings and fuselage of the aircraft. Miraculously, some men actually survived the landing and jumped out right on top of the shocked gunners, and by the sound of it a terrific fight went on. I have no idea who won, but the battery didn't fire any more as the gliders had effectively trapped the guns.

About an hour later, when things got a bit quieter, I made my way to the centre of Hamminkeln to RV with the rest of my platoon, and the first man I saw was my old pal Joe Marks. He was covered in blood, thankfully not his own. It's difficult to describe my feelings when I saw him safe and all in one piece, as he had also been flying in one of the Beethoven Company gliders and had experienced a hair-raising landing. After Arnhem we had lost so many trained glider pilots that for the Rhine crossing they had drafted in a number of RAF bomber pilots, one to each experienced glider pilot man. The RAF man in Joe's glider panicked as the dive began, left the cockpit and ran back through the plane and stayed in the tail until it landed. The glider pilot brought them in alright, but it was a nervous moment. The RAF man didn't like the idea of a plane without an engine! What a time to realise that. Anyway, by this time the fighting was easing off; Bill Pratt turned up slightly wounded, Wally Briggs and Ron Tarr also. Now we were beginning to find out what had happened to the glider carrying our platoon and all our stores; it turned out that it had been hit in mid-air by cannon fire and then machine-gunned and caught fire, though they managed to get down and scramble out. Babe Cox, our Canadian officer, emerged only to be knocked down by another glider; Bill Tagg was killed in the aircraft and burned with all our stores, jeeps, trailers and my brand-new motor bike – all gone. We had left England that morning with seventeen men and at the end of the day only six answered the roll call, including our officer and me. That evening we settled down in the cellar of a house, hopefully to grab some rations and a little kip, and I remember removing my helmet only to find there in the chinstrap two neat holes made by the bullets that hit poor Nick as he stood beside me.

We had 110 killed and wounded that day, with over 50 per cent of our transport destroyed. At an O Group called that evening by our CO, which I attended because of the death of my officer from a sniper, we were told that our battalion would lead the breakout over the River Issel, which was to become the most remarkable pursuit of the war's last stage. We marched without proper transport some 300 miles across

Germany to arrive on the Baltic ahead of the tanks and armour and the Russians. Having no vehicles at the outset, we simply seized from the Germans anything we could get hold of, bakers' vans and butchers' vans, post office trucks and some German Army trucks; they even used a German six-wheeled armoured car. They grabbed a tracked armoured car until one of the tracks came off. Nobody bothered to repaint them. One man was seen driving a steamroller – anything to get forward. I commandeered the village fire engine, a beautiful, almost brand-new Mercedes, painted white. I was quite pleased with my capture until the CO said, 'You can't possibly use that. They'll see you coming from Berlin.' So reluctantly I had to let it go, though we used anything else we could get our hands on.

We were eventually joined by troops that had succeeded in crossing the Rhine and soon we were on our way across north Germany, sometimes meeting only light resistance but more often than not having to fight a battle and take many casualties: our RSM, two company commanders, many junior officers and many, many other ranks were killed and wounded. This was very distressing as we knew the end of the war was only days away. On over the Dortmund canal and on to Osnabrück, village after village, without rest or respite, including a bitter battle with SS at their training school, absolute fanatics that had to be wiped out despite our own tragic casualties. And all the while streams of people were coming the other way, and long lines of German troops who'd thrown down their arms and were heading home. Towards the end of April we were moving up towards the Elbe. We had taken a village in the morning and lost a couple more of the lads in process and I was helping to blow up some captured German ammunition when airbursts began nearby, too close for comfort. I suddenly felt a thump in my back, good old me who was always going to be all right! I slipped a hand inside my back pocket, and it came out covered in blood. After a rough ride in a jeep to a field dressing station and several shots of morphine, I was taken back to the general hospital in Celle and a fortnight later back to Brussels for a further three weeks in hospital. My war was over, thank God.

The Day After – Sean Dickson

I walked around the platoon with a smile on my face and joked with them. It was expected of me, a game we all play, and they wouldn't have it any other way. It's been like this since we were at Normandy: we all laugh in the face of adversity. Although they appeared happy I noticed the gaps in the ranks where once some of them had been. You learned to live with it, as it is a fact of life in war, but as I looked back on the landing yesterday I remembered how indiscriminate death is. One moment someone is there, the next he is down, dead, never to see the light of day again. If he is lucky he is wounded, although some wounds are so bad maybe it would have been better if they were killed. I remember Private Tanner, the platoon comedian. He had a head wound so bad I expected him to die, but by some miracle he didn't, but he'll never have a normal life – he'll forever sit in a chair with a vacant look on his face, unable to think or speak. Having said that, all of us will be scarred by what we have seen and done – the horror never leaves you. Some cover it up, others can't. Yesterday we must have lost about a quarter of the platoon, either wounded or killed in those first few hours. The Germans put up a stout, spirited fight. I would too if it had been the other way around. I stop for a moment and daydream and I am brought back to life by the platoon sergeant. Under his beret his head is heavily bandaged where a piece of shrapnel tried to scalp him. Anyone else would have gone to hospital – not him. The platoon calls him 'Lucky Lowes' behind his back. At Normandy he charged a machine-gun position over open ground and killed the crew. How he survived without a scratch, God knows. How many has it been since Normandy? I could count on one hand how many are left since those first days. Sergeant Lowes tells me that the OC is having an orders group. I finish off walking around and congratulate Private Arnold on the birth of his daughter. It's the talk of the platoon; they all want to call her 'Pegasus', although I don't think Arnold's wife will agree. I have a large mug of 'compo' tea and a hard biscuit in my hand given to me by my batman, Sykes; he fusses over me like an old washerwoman. He seems to have the knack of knowing what

I need and presenting it to me before I can ask. I shall miss him when I leave the regiment and this wretched war is over.

A Pistol Without Ammunition – Henry Bagley

As we flew in over the drop zone the platoon commander kept looking out of the door. Even we could see the amount of flak that was curving up toward us and it was obvious to a blind man that we definitely hadn't surprised old Fritz. Then we had another shock in store for us. Our lot who were waiting to cross the river after we had secured Fritz's side were putting out an enormous smokescreen to cover their crossing. It was doing its job all right; it had partially covered our landing zones, making it extremely difficult for pilots to see exactly where to drop us. The Whitley shook as the flak bracketed us for about a minute, trying hard to shoot us down. It was the last shell that caused us no end of grief. It exploded right alongside us and literally threw the 30-ton monster to one side as if it were a child's doll. We were all watching the red light; the next moment we were all thrown on to the floor of the Whitley. By the time we got up the pilot had to do a wide turn and run in a second time, something I am sure he wasn't too happy about; for that matter, neither were we as the shrapnel from the shell had ripped huge holes in the fuselage.

When I dived out of the aperture the sky was a veritable mass of tracer and explosions. I felt sure I would never get through it all. Well I did, but I had drifted over a large wood and looked like I was going to come down in it. I crossed my hands in front of my face and prepared to hit the trees. With over 50 pounds of equipment in my leg bag, I literally crashed from the top branches through to the lower ones, but luckily, except for a few minor scratches, I was unhurt. Unfortunately, when I stopped I ended up hanging about 4 feet off the ground with the plate in the centre of my harness pushed up in my face. I was just about to cut it with my fighting knife when above the sounds of battle I heard German voices. My Sten gun was fixed inside my harness, but I did have a Colt pistol that I had won in a card game with some Yanks, and it was tucked inside my smock. So I at least had something to defend myself with.

I fumbled with the smock and after what seemed like hours I got it out and pointed it toward where the voices were coming from. Not a minute later two Fritzs moved into my vision. They were both crouched down as they moved, clearly trying to find where we had landed. How they missed me I don't know, but I dare not let them get out of my line of sight as if I did they could easily kill me.

In the end I shouted 'Hands Hock' in rudimentary German, and pointed the pistol at them. Shocked, they both turned and looked up at me, and then they slowly dropped their machine pistols and stood up. Some ten minutes later they had helped me down to the ground and I had relieved them of their stick grenades and was now holding my Sten gun while they stood with their hands up. My leg bag had been kindly unpacked by one of them and they seemed relieved they were prisoners. It was at this point I found out that my pistol didn't have a magazine in it, nor did it have one up the spout, and I was so glad the Germans didn't think it important enough to recognise the characteristics of our weapons, whereas we had to learn the characteristics of all theirs.

Into the Rhine by Glider – Alan Spicer

After being called up and bashed about in recruit training, we were all given a weekend leave pass and told if we weren't back on time we would do fifty-six days in the cells. That was incentive enough to arrive back early, even with the crowded trains. Standing at the end of my bed with all my gear packed and ready to go, the platoon sergeant marched in and began telling us which units we were to report to. I assumed it would be to a basic training unit to learn the skills each of us would need. Well it was and it wasn't in my case when along with five others I found myself posted as part of the 6th Airborne Division. I was about to learn about gliders, but first was expected to march with full equipment until I thought I'd worn my feet off below my knees, on top of which I clambered around an obstacle course until I was certain I'd become a monkey. And the weapon training – we had to strip and assemble every platoon weapon blindfolded. Near the end of this, we were introduced to gliders and I have to tell you the exciting prospect of actually going up in a glider – my first flight. It was not till after our first training flight that we could have refused to go up and thus been considered for a transfer to a more down to earth unit. But since nobody had refused, not altogether surprising since nobody was aware of the option (although I wouldn't have refused a chance to fly even if they'd charged a fare!), we were deemed tacitly to have accepted the posting as glider-borne infantry, a sort of retroactive volunteering, and we were paid an extra 6*d* a day for the privilege. Still, I was now qualified for the glamorous and famous combination of red beret and Pegasus flying horse shoulder flashes and as long as no-one was shooting at me it felt good to be part of the 6th Airborne. And one of my ambitions had, up to a point, been realised: I was involved with flying – although, with thirty odd men to a glider, it was not unlike travelling by tube, but with a better view. And you did get a seat.

Take-off. The roar of the Dakota's engines as it slowly moves off, the jerk of the towrope's slack being taken up, and we are away and gathering speed. First, the Dakota slowly lifting while we still race along the runway as if unconnected, then we feel the ground suddenly drop away as we climb into the sky behind the towrope bending up into the distance, our umbilical cord. Gradually our towing plane levels off, and now our suddenly fragile-seeming glider is in level flight, now rising, now, alarmingly, falling, every now and again buffeted against the force of the slipstream on our way up or down. Then, as we approach our dropping zone, the towrope is released, the umbilical cord cut. We are free, no longer dependent on that lumbering Dakota, suddenly and miraculously still sailing along without power, a new sensation of smooth, effortless movement through the air, the thin whistle of the wind over the wings the only sound apart from the idle chatter of the few too insensitive, or nervous, to appreciate the beauty of silent flight even though we always take a steep dive for several hundred feet, practising to get below the German flak and machine guns that can bring down a wooden glider with ease.

I really enjoyed the sensation of flying; then came the day when we had to put into practice all that glider training. In the early hours of 24 March 1945, a lovely, warm spring day, we were transported to an airfield in Hampshire crammed with gliders and their towing Lancasters and Stirlings. We made our way to our big, black, rather beautiful glider, past jeeps and trailers and other gliders and aircraft, and everywhere miles of tow ropes; and full of the bravado we needed to demonstrate to each other, we sang a stirring and comforting ditty to the tune of the Volga Boatman, the first, second and fourth lines of which went, 'The fucking rope broke.' We climbed aboard our Horsa and sat in our two rows, making jokes and laughing a little too heartily, trying to pretend we weren't worried about what was ahead as we waited for our turn to move off. Between us, at awkward intervals, were our trailers laden with assorted ammunition and weaponry. Ahead of us was the biggest airborne crossing of the war, over the Rhine and into Germany, while on the ground the Rhine would be crossed by thousands of other poor sods, on foot. Then we were off, part of this awe-inspiring armada of aircraft towing their gliders, stretching as far as the eye could see.

Our company was supposed to be dropped at Hamminkeln, on the far side of the Rhine, not far, someone said, from the town of Hamelin of Pied Piper fame. We didn't need to be told when we were near our Dropping Zone. Those innocent-looking little black and white puffs were familiar enough from all the war films I'd seen – what wasn't so entertaining was the crump, crump of their explosions above the hissing of the glider as we were released from our rope to start our long descent, and now we could also hear the very realistic sound effects of rifles, machine guns, bigger guns, and see those puffs getting bigger, and closer – and the realisation came to me that this was not just a bit dangerous, it could be suicidal, especially as some of those machine-gun rounds came straight through the side of the glider and wounded four of the lads and killed one of them. But it was all happening too fast to have time to worry properly, and seemed quite unreal. Then, as we could see the flaming and broken gliders on the ground below and other gliders milling around, apparently aimlessly, I had the not very comforting thought that the only way out of this thing was to land on that hostile ground and then begin to fight our way to our first objective, whatever that was to be.

While I was telling myself that one problem at a time was plenty, our pilot was more usefully engaged in wrestling with his rather limited controls, and losing height far too quickly and too steeply I thought, quite prepared now to risk the landing, as long as it was a landing. They say fear is relative, well I'd got enough for ten men going around in my stomach. Then, in what seemed one continuous manoeuvre, we suddenly flattened out of our dive and seconds later there was an almighty thump, and a lot more bumping and grating than I thought you should get in the air, until I realised that we were juddering along on the ground. We had landed. Knowing that the longer we remained in our Horsa, a prime target, the greater the danger of being trapped, we set about leaving it with the minimum possible delay, dragging the wounded with us. Get out first and worry about what's outside once we're there – that was our immediate philosophy. And then I found I had one less cause for concern. Along with more pressing problems, the prospect of the 8-foot drop to the ground with all my battle gear and among unfriendly people had been exercising my mind on and off since take-off. But fortunately our undercarriage had smashed off on landing, not to mention half a wing, and the exit was now at ground level. All I had to do was step out and run for it, but where to?

I recall a scene of utter confusion like nothing we had done in training. Figures were running, shouting, running, shooting; jeeps were revving and skittering off on urgent missions; guns and trailers were being hauled out of gliders and parts of gliders scattered about the landscape at crazy, impossible angles with dead men hanging from them. And more gliders were coming in to land, or crash, from all directions. And our faithful transport, our home for the past three or four hours, was now abandoned and skewed across the field with one wing snapped off and its back broken, its job done, our safe arrival a testimony to the skill and cool bravery of our pilots, for the moment unappreciated, unthought of. I certainly thought of them and their passive charges as one of the larger, jeep-carrying, gliders, ablaze from about halfway along its fuselage, hissed by low over our heads like a flaming torch before hitting the ground and skidding along on its belly to come to rest in a blazing pyre of broken wings and fuselage. There was no sign of life as it blazed from one end to the other like a Viking ship set ablaze for a funeral pyre. There but for the grace of God... And, through it all, a haze of writhing smoke and mist pierced by the sun, still shining as if the world was still normal.

The apparent chaos evolved into some semblance of order and we moved off to take our first objective, the town of Hamminkeln, about a mile or so down the road. Not too far, unless you are being sniped at for most of the way, but we eventually got there and proceeded to move through the town, virtually house by house. Every house is a potential nest of Germans. Some fight to the bitter end, others give up after a short fight. Our casualties are building one at a time. By the time we get to the last houses, we clear them with grenades. Each room gets one as we are fed up with Germans popping up from nowhere. Two of us stand either side of the door, in goes the grenade, when it detonates we follow it in, firing our Sten guns. If there is anyone in here they know what they can expect. We do the same upstairs. At the top of the stairs I throw the first grenade down the landing corridor. After it detonates, I hear the words 'Kamerad, Kamerad'. I signal the lads following me and we cautiously work our way down the short corridor at the top of the landing, checking each room as we go, ready to fire at anything that moves. We find an old dead German in one of them, one of Hitler's last-ditch, makeshift army made up of boys and old men, the Volkssturm. They are everywhere in the town. All they have as a uniform is a coal scuttle helmet and an armband. But they all have weapons of one sort or another, so they are extremely dangerous and can expect no mercy if they fire on us. Then I hear the word 'Kamerad' again and it's coming from the room at the end of the corridor. We edge our way toward it and I kick the door open and wait to throw the grenade while the others cover me.

There are four bodies in there, all dead, all in contorted positions. Two of them couldn't have been more than fifteen years of age. The other two are old men at least sixty years of age. They have an assortment of weapons including an MG34 and stick grenades. Half the outer wall has been blown away and bricks and cement dust lie on top of them. It looks like a PIAT was used against them. And there in the far corner was the origin of the moaning. An old man with a chest wound. He was lucky in some ways as he'd been away from the main blast. We walk over to him and he looks up at us as if he expects us to shoot him. Instead we tend to his wound, give him water, inject him with morphine and I wait with him until the overworked medical orderlies come and pick him up. I even share a block of chocolate with him and a cigarette while we wait. We now have Hamminkeln firmly in our hands. The rest of those first days are a series of disjointed scenes, a sort of screen montage.

The Crossing – John Stephenson

I saw the anti-aircraft barrage, and it was like Guy Fawkes Night, only in the daytime. It didn't seem possible that so many aircraft could get through it. It didn't seem possible that there was so much flak and ground fire considering the bombing and artillery barrage that had taken place just before we arrived either. The sky around us was full of aircraft and puffs of smoke that signalled the flak, and lines of tracer fired from the MG34 and 42 machine guns. The parachutists dropped and not long afterward the gliders went in to land, right in the east side of the battle. The sky seemed to be just bright red with flames coming from aircraft that had been hit, or grey and black with smoke from the other side of the river, making it difficult to see the ground, except that the unfinished autobahn was clearly visible. For a split second it seemed as if every glider had been wrecked on landing. As we touched down and halted, D Company HQ was soon out of the glider. We flung ourselves on to the ground, but not too close in case it got targeted. Major Tillett finally figured out where we were and after a dash across the road to a house, we secured it, then we were on our way to Hamminkeln railway station. I gave

Lieutenant Fox the company rum bottle – it saved me carrying it – I think it was a gallon. Eventually, we moved to take over positions near C Company, close to a rail bridge that carried the railway over the Issel River.

Our D Company had a platoon over the other side, in a house close to the autobahn and Ringenburg, and I was placed in command. Not many men were left, about twelve I think. The others were lying wounded or dead downstairs. Upstairs, I had men firing at the continuous German attacks. I could see the infantry, but only hear the tanks. We managed to break them up but the place was a shambles so I decided to move to another house. We got the wounded out first then we followed; as we withdrew from the house a tank demolished it. My next task was to take a platoon forward. I had about twelve men and three of them were wounded. Anyway, we had to try to capture a farm, but just as we were about to attack, we were stopped. Captain Scott, the company second in command, ordered the raid to be cancelled. It was just as well as we would have had to move over open ground to get to it. As the CSM, I was sent all over the place to visit different platoons. For a while, at midday, all was quiet for a few minutes. At one point Bernie Walsh, the CQMS, and I manned a PIAT to stop any tanks that were approaching. We didn't get any tanks but we did get a halftrack with a mounted 20mm cannon on that was creating a bit of havoc.

There were 103 killed and over 350 wounded in the battalion up to early on 26 March. The medical orderlies and doctors were pushed to keep up with operating on the wounded. There was little help to be had until the main army relieved us in the early hours of the 26th. Unfortunately, it was not a quiet relief as they made one hell of a noise as they advanced. We tended to be very quiet, so as to catch and kill the Germans before they realised we were there. On that first day I saw many of our dead hanging in trees by their parachutes where they'd been shot before they could release themselves, yet another problem with parachuting in during daylight hours that you never had at night. Throughout the battle we did not wear our steel helmets – we threw them away in case our own troops thought we were Germans. They simply didn't seem to be able to recognise us and tended to shoot first and ask question later. As for ammunition on that first day, every effort was made to get it and any weapons out of the gliders not totally destroyed. At the time it was pitiful to hear men trapped and being burnt alive, but there was absolutely nothing we could do about it in many cases as you left yourself exposed to machine-gun fire if you went near any of the gliders. An anti-tank gun platoon from C Company disappeared on the night of the 24th/25th. A German patrol must have taken them in the darkness – perhaps their sentries had been knifed. Personally, I kept awake for the first two nights, as did all of D Company. We had been issued with Benzedrine tablets to keep us awake, but in the end it took its toll and after they wore off it was one hell of a job to keep going. How the bomber pilots did it night after night I don't know.

On the morning of the 26th the battle of the landing area was over and the big surprise was to come. The division was told that as we were fresh troops, we would lead the advance and did so in a big way. Day after day, and without the help of the tanks, we took a lot of ground, mostly on foot. I well remember fighting over the Dortmund–Ems Canal as we suffered one hell of a lot of shelling after crossing it, then on towards Osnabrück on the River Weser. An assault was made over the Weser during which the 52nd Airlanding Division lost a lot of men to 20mm and 88mm flak guns firing on low trajectory. After an attack on Frillerbank and Heinrichsteich, we discovered the enemy had flown – he just didn't want to stay and make a go of it. On 8 April we started on a long march towards Winzlar, on foot of course as we always did. We moved on transport from Winzlar to Heitlingen and at this stage we were in the Corps Reserve. The 15th Scottish Division was up in front. About 14 April, we motored through Celle and then spent a night in the woods near there. I left my pipe and tobacco there and did I feel peeved about that. Jet planes bombed the column, Arado Ar 234s I think, near Kahlstorf. There were some self-propelled guns and troops nearby who stood their ground. A Company undertook a set piece attack;

there was much use of artillery and mortars and Kahlstorf was set on fire. The 52nd Airlanding Division was subjected to bomb attacks by these jets but because of their speed they were inaccurate. But the shelling was a different thing. It was pretty awful and I can still see poor Sergeant Howard running along for a few yards minus his head.

I can still see the huge numbers of Germans on the sides of the road near Hamminkeln, in their thousands, all awaiting movement to POW camps. I remember the awful fighting over the Dortmund–Ems Canal and the capture of the German guns. Most of the time we were all stupefied from lack of sleep and the first real rest was at Ebstorf, for almost a week. It had all happened so quickly since the advance started on 26 March. Russian and Polish prisoners were wild and ill disciplined. The staff of liberated camps were standing inside the wire, guarded by their former prisoners. Liberated slave workers or POWs were walking along, fainting and not getting up again. As part of 6th Airborne Division we went on to Bad Kleinen to help secure the line Wismar–Schweriner See, and to meet the Russian Army. On 7 May the 6th Airborne was selected to provide a Guard of Honour at Wismar for the meeting between Field Marshal Montgomery and Marshal Rokossovski of the Russian Northern Group of Armies. I was the CSM and stood on the right – you could say I was the first man of the 6th to look at a Russian marshal that day. It was a first-class parade and the lads did us proud. I doubt if the Guards could have done better.

Thousands and thousands of Germans arrived at Bad Kleinen to surrender and the regiment was kept busy. At the end of hostilities, Major Styles got so excited he fired his pistol at the ceiling of the officers' mess. While at Bad Kleinen there were several visits to the Russian Army. I went with Major Tillett to a house to meet some Russian officers and it was quite an experience. Their vehicles looked very impressive with large radio sets; their soldiers on the whole looked quite murderous, wild and very Asiatic. Their officers seemed to have dozens of medals, all of which appeared to be made out of lemonade bottle tops, and their uniforms were either boiler suits or blue denim with leather jackboots. Anyway, halfway through our get-together, a perfectly good tablecloth and glasses were gathered up and thrown through the window by the Russian waiter – our interpreter said he was a POW and expected to be repatriated to Russia and shot, or sent to Siberia because he was captured and didn't die for the Motherland. The table was then covered in newspapers and we had vodka, raw eggs and jam. I had some vodka and water – but not much, as a cupful of the stuff could have run one of our tanks for a week. As we left, all the Russians were on the floor quite drunk and snoring. We were glad to leave, as they are an excitable lot when they get drunk. It wasn't unusual for one of them to fire one of their Tokarev pistols into the ceiling for a bit of fun. I am told our soldiers really enjoyed their visits to the Russian units and took part in horse riding. We caught some Russian soldiers who ran out of vodka trying to steal the fuel from our tanks, which by now were on a train waiting to go back to Holland. They were armed and pretty peeved off when our lads told them where to go. It was in Bad Kleinen that I met a 'civilian' who winked and grinned at me. It was Private Roach of D Company, who had acquired a suit from a clothing factory in Hagen, near Osnabrück, and carried it until Bad Kleinen. I was seriously thinking of shooting at him when he disclosed his identity, then I nearly threw him in jail. He had been out to break the non-fraternisation ban, but I had second thoughts as he was one of the originals in the battalion and there weren't many of them left.

Go Away Please – Angus McCloud

Considering the Locust light tank was built by the Americans, it says a lot about the tank that they refused to use them. Yet here I was driving one as part of the divisional reconnaissance regiment that landed with the 6th Airlanding Brigade in landing zone 'P', east of the Diersfordter Wald and west of Hamminkeln. We flew inside big Hamilcar gliders, having had what appeared to be every German anti-aircraft gun try and shoot the lumbering giant out of the sky. They turned on one of the others and succeeded; the Locust that was inside it fell over 500 feet to the ground with the crew still inside it. Three more gliders, having been damaged by anti-aircraft fire, crashed on landing; one tank survived with a damaged machine gun; another crashed through a farmhouse when the glider it was in ran into the building – incredibly, the crash only knocked out its main gun and damaged its wireless set; and the third broke loose as the glider landed and smashed its way through the side of the glider and was flipped over onto its turret, rendering it useless.

The remaining Hamilcars landed safely, although a number of Locusts had significant damage and couldn't move. Two of these would never reach the RV. One undamaged tank emerged from the front of a Hamilcar, straight into a battle with a Tiger tank; predictably the Tiger came off best. A second tank broke down as it attempted to tow a jeep out of a crashed glider, although the crew did remain with the tank and provided fire support for one of the battalions. Of the six that eventually reached the RV, only four were undamaged and fit for action – mine was one of these. We were immediately deployed to the high ground east of the Diersfordter Wald, while being covered by the two damaged tanks. When we got there we stood out like sore thumbs and were immediately engaged by German troops and required support from an infantry company. Soon every German heavy gun, anti-tank gun and Panzerfaust within range wanted to blow us to kingdom come as four British tanks were prime battlefield targets. We had a lot of near misses, but the infantry company was copping a hell of a bashing, although between us we did a bit of damage to the Germans too. In the end their OC calmly walked up to us and politely asked us to go away as we were attracting too much attention, so we did.

The Russians Versus the Paras – Harry Logan

When the rush to take Kiel was over and the Allies had won, the Russian Army was forced to sit right outside Kiel. Its soldiers could still wander through the city, and they did, stealing anything they could get their hands on and raping any females they came across, and there wasn't much the Allies could do about it as the Russian authorities didn't seem to care. All of our lads were warned not to get into fights with the Russians as they had a nasty habit of pulling a knife or shooting you without blinking an eye. One day, about twenty drunken Russians came wandering up to Kiel hospital. Besides being drunk, they were clearly looking for trouble. They pushed past the guard on the gate and walked up to a second guard on the main entrance. He was made of sterner stuff and cocked his Bren gun and aimed it straight at them. One look at his face told them he meant business, and by now he was backed up by the gate guard, who stood next to him with a Sten gun, so the belligerent Russians wandered back to the gate and walked around the side of the hospital and stood there calling for all the females inside to be handed over or else they would come in and get them. Out the window on the second floor, a Tommy looked down, saw who it was, and yelled out in no uncertain terms, 'Fuck off Russkies – the females are ours!' The Russians may not have understood the exact words but they certainly understood the meaning and they were somewhat miffed. With that, one of them took out a pistol and fired it at the private, narrowly missing him. Naturally he ducked inside, but a moment later popped back out with a Sten gun in his hands and emptied a magazine into the crowd below, killing seven and wounding several others. The remainder took to their heels, leaving their mates where they were. The Russians demanded the Tommy be brought to justice. The British very diplomatically told them to bugger off as he was doing his job by protecting the wounded.

Pretend to Be a Battalion – Phillip Saunders

The original plan for the division called for two of the airborne battalions to march through Oslo in Norway on 10 May 1945, but a delay meant that only a few of us had arrived by this date. Instead, two platoons from our battalion, the 2nd South Staffs, and four military policemen on motorcycles accompanied General Urquhart, who rode in a commandeered German staff car. We were somewhat worried given the small size of our group even though the Norwegian population were ecstatic, as there were still 400,000 Germans in Norway. As we marched through the city centre, I said to my mate Charlie, 'Charlie, what happens if any Jerries open fire on us?'

Without moving his head he said, 'Not a problem mate. We'll tell 'em they can't do that as the war's over!'

THE END